Maps:

• Europe, ca 1792   recto/verso, immediately before p. 1 (Prologue).

- Colonial St. Domingue and the West Indies, Late 18th Cen.   - p. 22 (facing Ch. 1)

- France, ca 1789
  Paris, ca. 1789   p. 88 (facing Ch. 7)

     p. 158 (facing Ch. 14)

• Northern Italy, ca 1796

• Napoleon's Egyptian Expedition, 1798   p. 222

• Italy, ca. 1799   p. 265

THE BLACK COUNT

"In the early 1800s, General Alex Dumas was purposefully disappeared by his enemies. And though his son sought to make him live through his classic novels, for too long his story has remained silenced. *The Black Count* vividly vindicates the great general, restoring him to his rightful place at the center of the Age of Revolution. **Carrying us from the plantations of the Caribbean to Paris, the Alps, and Egypt, Reiss tells an engrossing tale of a life of social struggle, adventure, and courage—and of the frustrations and joys of a researcher on the trail of a forgotten truth.**"

—Laurent Dubois, author of *Haiti: The Aftershocks of History*

"**The real-life history of General Alex Dumas is as poignant and swashbuckling a tale as any his novelist son could have dreamed.** Tom Reiss has the dramatist's sense of setting and scene, the reporter's persistence, and the historian's eye for truth. **Would that the imprisoned Count of Monte Cristo had a copy of this book!**"

—Darrin M. McMahon, author of *Enemies of the Enlightenment* and *Happiness: A History*

"**Tom Reiss can do it all: gather startling research and write inspired prose; find life's great stories and then tell them with real brilliance.** In *The Black Count,* the master journalist-storyteller opens the door to the truth behind one of literature's most exciting stories and opens it wide enough to show the delicate beauty of the lives within."

—Darin Strauss, National Book Critics Circle Award–winning author of *Half a Life* and *Chang and Eng*

"*The Black Count* **is a complex work of political and social history gallantly masquerading as a fantastic adventure story.** As he did in *The Orientalist,* Tom Reiss has traveled far to stalk a forgotten legend, and has recovered for us **a vivid, dramatic tale that delights, moves, and inspires.**"

—Gideon Lewis-Kraus, author of *A Sense of Direction*

"*The Black Count* is totally thrilling—a fascinating, beautifully written, and deeply researched biography that brings to life one of history's great forgotten characters: the swashbuckling, flamboyant, and romantic mulatto count whose true life belongs in a Hollywood movie or Alexandre Dumas story."

—Simon Sebag Montefiore, author of *Jerusalem: The Biography* and *Young Stalin*

"Tom Reiss tells this amazing story, largely unknown today, with verve, style, and a nonpareil command of detail."

–Luc Sante, author of *Low Life*, *Evidence*, and *The Factory of Facts*

"We believe we know the glories of the French Revolution and the Napoleonic Wars. We believe we understand the horror of slavery and the oppression of Africans. But what is the relationship between the grand goal of liberation and the deep tragedy of racism? As Reiss shows us, answers can be found in the extraordinary life of a forgotten French hero of the great revolutionary campaigns—a hero who was black."

—Timothy Snyder, author of *Bloodlands* and *The Red Prince*

"Tom Reiss tells the incredible story of Alex Dumas with the same excitement about uncovering history that he brought to *The Orientalist*."

–Nina Burleigh, *New York Times* bestselling author of *Mirage: Napoleon's Scientists and the Unveiling of Egypt*

"Reiss combines the talent of a thorough English detective with the literary flair of a French novelist to produce a story that is as fresh as today's headlines but as old as the Greek classics."

—Jack Weatherford, *New York Times* bestselling author of *Genghis Khan and the Making of the Modern World*

"Colorful and utterly captivating . . . This is history that is vibrant, gripping, and tragic."

—William Dietrich, Pulitzer Prize–winning journalist and *New York Times* bestselling author of *Napoleon's Pyramids* and *The Emerald Storm*

THE
BLACK
COUNT

THE
BLACK
COUNT

GLORY, REVOLUTION, BETRAYAL,

and the REAL COUNT *of* MONTE CRISTO

TOM REISS

CROWN PUBLISHERS
NEW YORK

Published in the United States by Crown Publishers, an imprint

of the Crown Publishing Group, a division of Random House, Inc., New York.

www.crownpublishing.com

CROWN and the Crown colophon are registered trademarks

of Random House, Inc.

Library of Congress Cataloging-in-Publication Data

Reiss, Tom.

The Black Count : glory, revolution, betrayal, and the real

Count of Monte Cristo / Tom Reiss.

p.   cm.

Includes bibliographical references and index.

1. Dumas, Thomas Alexandre, 1762–1806.   2. Generals—France—

Biography.   3. France—Biography.   4. France—History, Military—

1789–1815.   5. Dumas, Alexandre, 1802–1870—Family.   I. Title.

DC146.D83R46 2012

944.04092—dc23

[B]   2012017633

ISBN 978-0-307-38246-7

eISBN 978-0-307-95295-0

Printed in the United States of America

Maps by David Lindroth Inc.

Jacket design by Eric White

Jacket illustration by Sam Weber

10   9   8   7   6   5   4   3   2   1

First Edition

For Diana and Lucy,
who know what it means to wait and hope,
and Melanie,
who knows why they blew up the bridge.

✦ CONTENTS ✦

BOOK TWO

BOOK THREE

THE
BLACK
COUNT

EUROPE, CIRCA 1792

MILES
0   400

KM
0   400

RUSSIA

PRUSSIA

POLAND

SMALL GERMAN STATES

Berlin

AUSTRIAN
EMPIRE

Vienna

A L P S

Venice

Rome

Naples

KINGDOM
OF NAPLES
AND SICILY

OTTOMAN
EMPIRE

SEA

FEBRUARY 26, 1806

IT was nearly midnight on the night of February 26, 1806, and Alexandre Dumas, the future author of *The Count of Monte Cristo* and *The Three Musketeers*, was asleep at his uncle's house. He was not yet four years old. He was staying there because his father was gravely ill and his mother thought it best for him not to be at home. As the clock struck, he was awakened by a loud knock. By the light of a lamp that burned by the bedside, he saw his cousin sit up, visibly frightened. Alexandre got out of bed. He recalled in his memoirs, forty-some years later:

> *My cousin called to me, "Where are you going?"*
>
> *"You'll see," I replied quietly. "I'm going to open the door for Daddy, who's coming to say goodbye."*
>
> *The poor girl jumped out of bed, greatly alarmed, grabbed me as I put my hand on the doorknob, and forced me back to bed.*
>
> *I struggled in her arms, shouting with all my strength:*
>
> *"Goodbye, Daddy! Goodbye, Daddy!"*

The next morning the adults came to wake the children, and one of them told Alexandre the news that his father had died during the night.

> *"My daddy is dead," I said. "What does that mean?"*
>
> *"It means that you won't see him again."*
>
> *"What do you mean I won't see Daddy again? . . . why won't I see him?"*

"Because God has taken him back from you."

"Forever?"

"Forever."

"And you say that I'll never see him again? . . . never at all?"

"Never at all."

"And where does God live?"

"He lives in heaven."

I thought hard about this for a minute. Even as a young child, even deprived of reason, I understood that something irreversible had happened in my life. Then, taking advantage of the first moment when they stopped paying attention to me, I got away from my uncle's and ran straight to my mother's house.

All the doors were open, all the faces were frightened; one felt that Death was there.

I went in without anyone's noticing or seeing me. I found a little room where the weapons were kept; I shouldered a gun that belonged to my father, and which he had often promised to give to me when I got older.

Then, armed with this gun, I climbed the stairs.

On the second floor, I met my mother on the landing.

She had just left the death chamber. . . . her face was wet with tears.

"Where are you going?" she asked me, surprised to see me there, when she thought I was at my uncle's.

"I'm going to heaven!" I replied.

"What do you mean, you're going to heaven?"

"Let me pass."

"And what will you do in heaven, my poor child?"

"I'm going there to kill God, who killed Daddy."

My mother seized me in her arms, squeezing me so tight I thought I would suffocate.

Alexandre Dumas wrote those lines when he had just turned forty-five and had decided it was time to reflect on his life. He never got past chronicling his thirty-first year—which was well before he had published a word as a novelist—yet he spent more than the first two hundred pages on a story that is as fantastic as any of his novels: the life of his father, General Alexandre—

Alex—Dumas, a black man from the colonies who narrowly survived the French Revolution and rose to command fifty thousand men. The chapters about General Dumas are drawn from reminiscences of his mother and his father's friends, and from official documents and letters he obtained from his mother and the French Ministry of War. It is a raw and poignant attempt at biography, full of gaps, omissions, and re-creations of scenes and dialogue. But it is sincere. The story of his father ends with this scene of his death, the point at which the novelist begins his own life story.

For anyone skeptical that a boy so young could recall such details, Dumas responded through the lips of the character Haydée, a white slave, in *The Count of Monte Cristo*. Haydée's father died when she was four, betrayed and murdered by one of the main villains in the novel. After speaking movingly of her father, she tells the Count: "I was four years old, but as the events held a supreme importance for me, not one detail has left my mind, not one feature has escaped from my memory."

To remember a person is the most important thing in the novels of Alexandre Dumas. The worst sin anyone can commit is to forget. The villains of *The Count of Monte Cristo* do not murder the hero, Edmond Dantès—they have him thrown into a dungeon where he is forgotten by the world. The heroes of Dumas never forget anything or anyone: Dantès has a perfect memory for the details of every field of human knowledge, for the history of the world and for everyone he has encountered in his life. When he confronts them one by one, he finds that the assassins of his identity have forgotten the very fact that he existed, and thus the fact of their crime.

I undertook the project of reconstructing the life of the forgotten hero General Alexandre Dumas because of that passage in his son's memoirs, which I read when I was a boy and have always remembered.

JANUARY 25, 2007

"I AM afraid the situation is most delicate," the deputy mayor was saying to me. "And most unfortunate."

Fabrice Dufour, the deputy mayor of the cobblestoned town of Villers-Cotterêts, wore a pained expression. He was in charge of the town's cultural heritage, which, notwithstanding its modest appearance, was considerable. It included a brief moment at the center of power in *Ancien Régime* France, when, upon the death of Louis XIV in 1715, his nephew Philippe, the Duke d'Orléans and regent to the five-year-old Louis XV, decided the court should spend as much time here as possible. This gray little town fifty miles north of Paris acquired an outsized reputation for royal scandal, misbehavior, and debauchery, which in eighteenth-century France was saying something. The early Renaissance château looming over the office where I sat had been the scene of nude dinner parties and large-scale orgies involving bondage, the comingling of royals and townsfolk, and the help of professionals both male and female. These festivities were referred to as "Adam and Eve nights," and one courtier recalled that, "after the champagne, the lights were turned out and the unclothed company proceeded to indulge in mutual flagellation, seeking their partners as the fortune of the dark dictated and with a thoroughness which diverted His Highness immensely."

Years later, Louis XVI, the shy and awkward husband of Marie-Antoinette, was said to blush if he so much as heard the town's name—which he wouldn't have often after 1723, when the regent died and the focus of court life moved back to Versailles. The town would really only be heard from again because of the man I had come here to learn about, who had lived and died here around the time of the French Revolution. The very backwater chill of the place, distinct on this raw January day, gave me hope that certain documents I believed existed might still be found here. Behind his desk the deputy mayor was an imposing man. He had a lazy eye that squinted involuntarily and an equally involuntary tendency to smile, slightly, as he spoke.

"Most delicate," he repeated firmly.

He then said nothing for perhaps thirty seconds, during which he cast meaningful looks at me, the window, and the objects on his desk. I noticed a motorcycle magazine on a side table, next to a pile of brochures about the château. I couldn't be sure, but it seemed to me the deputy mayor was wearing mascara. His large brown eyes seemed a little too well defined.

He shook his head, smiled, and made a tsk-tsking sound. "Sir, I know you have come all the way from America to see her, but I'm afraid it will be impossible to arrange."

I began mentally preparing the appropriate speech of protest in French. More than any other culture on earth, the French respect protest, which is why they regularly tie up their crucial industries and institutions in nationwide strikes—but one must protest properly. The deputy mayor spoke again, though, before I could say a word.

"It will be impossible to arrange, sir, because the lady you have come to see is dead."

I thought perhaps I had misheard. The lady who had agreed to see me, from a local museum—her name was Elaine—had not sounded old. I hadn't felt I needed to learn her last name, as she was the only person who worked there except a security guard.

"It was very sudden," said the deputy mayor. I thought he added something about an illness, perhaps cancer, but I wasn't sure. The shock of the information seemed to bring my French down two levels.

"She didn't mention anything to me about being sick," I said, apologetically.

"We are all very shocked and saddened," the deputy mayor said.

I tried to gather my wits and, after mumbling condolences, to explain about the importance of seeing the papers she'd been keeping: most of them had not seen the light of day for two hundred years, except for the odd

moments when they had been sold by one collector of obscure French historical memorabilia to another, eventually ending up here, in the tiny museum
that had a modest endowment for their purchase. I asked if anyone had assumed Elaine's duties; the deputy mayor shook his head. Had anyone inventoried her office? looked through the papers? could I be allowed to look?

"That's just it, none of the documents are in her office," the deputy mayor
said. "Elaine was worried about security, and she put everything in a safe.
A very big safe, very secure, but when she died she took the combination
with her. She told no one. She liked to handle everything herself. We have
searched everywhere but have had no luck finding the combination. . . . Sir,
I am afraid there is nothing to be done. A few weeks ago, it would have been
no problem, but now I am afraid, well, it is most delicate." He squinted at me.
"It is tragic."

Though uttered with complete bureaucratic equanimity, the word was
well chosen. This bland government office, tucked inside a courtyard next to
the notorious old château, was just up the street from the little municipal museum where Elaine had liked to handle everything herself. It was called the
Musée Alexandre Dumas. But it was doubtful if more than a handful of visitors to the town realized that the famous author of so many beloved novels,
who was born here, had himself been the son of a great man—the original
Alexandre Dumas.

━━

THE original Alexandre Dumas was born in 1762, the son of "Antoine
Alexandre de l'Isle," in the French sugar colony of Saint-Domingue. Antoine was a nobleman in hiding from his family and from the law, and he
fathered the boy with a black slave. Later Antoine would discard his alias
and reclaim his real name and title—Alexandre Antoine Davy, the Marquis
de la Pailleterie—and bring his black son across the ocean to live in pomp
and luxury near Paris. But the boy would reject his father's name, along with
his noble title. He would enlist in the French army at the lowest rank, taking
the surname "Dumas" from his mother for his enlistment papers. Once he'd
risen by his merits to higher rank he would not even sign his name "Alexandre," preferring the blunt and simple form "Alex Dumas."

Alex Dumas was a consummate warrior and a man of great conviction and moral courage. He was renowned for his strength, his swordsmanship, his bravery, and his knack for pulling victory out of the toughest situations. But he was known, too, for his profane back talk and his problems with authority. He was a soldier's general, feared by the enemy and loved by his men, a hero in a world that did not use the term lightly.

But then, by the wiles of conspiracy, he found himself imprisoned in a fortress and poisoned by unknown enemies, without hope of appeal and forgotten by the world. It was no accident that his fate sounds like that of a young sailor named Edmond Dantès, about to embark on a promising career and marry the woman he loves, who finds himself a pawn in a plot he never imagined, locked away without witnesses or trial in the dungeon of an island fortress called the Château d'If. But unlike the hero of his son's novel *The Count of Monte Cristo*, Alex Dumas met no benefactor in the dungeon to lead him to escape or to a hidden treasure. He never learned the reason for his trials, for his abrupt descent from glory to suffering. I had come to Villers-Cotterêts to find the truth of what befell this most passionate defender of "liberty, equality, and fraternity."

In his own lifetime General Dumas was a legendary figure. Official histories of the period often pause to relate some colorful anecdote about him. David Johnson, in his book *The French Cavalry, 1792–1815*, writes of the general's early career, "In addition to being a first-class soldier, Dumas was possibly the strongest man in the French army. . . . In the riding school he liked to stand up in the stirrups, take hold of an overhead beam, and lift himself and his horse bodily off the ground." A more plausible story that appears in multiple histories relates that he once fought three duels in one day, winning all three despite being gashed in the head—almost certainly the basis for one of the best-known and most comic scenes in *The Three Musketeers*, in which d'Artagnan challenges Porthos, Athos, and Aramis to duels on the same afternoon (the scene ends happily—"All for one and one for all!"—as a real enemy appears).

Alex Dumas first came to the army's attention when, still a lowly corporal, he single-handedly captured twelve enemy soldiers and marched them back to his camp. Not long afterward, he led four horsemen in an attack on an enemy post manned by over fifty men—Dumas alone killed six and took sixteen prisoner. As a Parisian society journalist in the early nineteenth century summed up, "Such brilliant conduct, on top of a manly physiognomy and extraordinary strength and stature, secured his quick promotion; it wasn't long before his talents proved he deserved it."

As his star rose, Alex Dumas was not one to give orders and then hang back in safety while his subordinates did the dangerous work: he led his troops by going out ahead of them. One of his commanding officers once remarked to him, "My dear Dumas, you make me tremble every time I see you mount a horse and gallop off at the head of your dragoons. I always say to myself, 'It's impossible for him to return in one piece if he keeps going at this pace.' What would become of me if you let yourself get killed?"

Even when Dumas became a general, commanding thousands of troops, he always preferred to lead small units on special operations where he could use his wits and outsized physical skills to prevail. As general-in-chief of the Army of the Alps, roughly the equivalent of a four-star general today, Dumas put on spiked boots and led his men up seemingly impregnable ice cliffs at night to surprise an Austrian battery that seemed as unassailable as the guns of Navarone. He captured the enemy's matériel and turned their own guns against them, forcing immediate surrender. He took not only 1,700 prisoners and over forty artillery pieces but Mont Cenis, the key to the Alps.

When they were still both generals in the French Revolution, Napoleon celebrated Alex Dumas's deeds in the classical terms favored at the time, proclaiming him the incarnation of Horatius Cocles, the ancient hero who saved the Roman Republic by keeping invading barbarians from crossing the Tiber. (French revolutionaries, like American ones, lived in a world of classical allusions—everyone referred to George Washington as Cincinnatus.)

When Napoleon launched the French invasion of Egypt, Dumas went as his cavalry commander, but it was there that the two very different soldiers came to loathe each other. The clash was ideological—Dumas saw himself as a fighter for world liberation, not world domination—but it was also personal.

"Among the Muslims, men from every class who were able to catch sight of General Bonaparte were struck by how short and skinny he was," wrote the chief medical officer of the expedition. "The one, among our generals, whose appearance struck them more was . . . the General-in-Chief of the cavalry, Dumas. Man of color, and by his figure looking like a centaur, when they saw him ride his horse over the trenches, going to ransom prisoners, all of them believed that he was the leader of the expedition."

—◂—

AT over six feet, with an athletic physique, Alex Dumas cut a dashing figure among the French elite. But how was it that he could enter the elite—and indeed be celebrated as a national hero—at a time when the basis of French wealth was black slavery in the colonies?

The life of General Alex Dumas is so extraordinary on so many levels that it's easy to forget the most extraordinary fact about it: that it was led by a black man, in a world of whites, at the end of the eighteenth century. His mother, Marie Cessette Dumas, was a slave, and he himself was sold into bondage briefly by his own father, an aristocratic fugitive who needed to pay his passage back to France. But by the time he was twenty, Alex had also made it to France and been educated in the classics, philosophy, fine manners, riding, dancing, and dueling. A life of Parisian parties, theaters, and boudoirs ended after a falling-out with his father, and he enlisted as a horseman in the service of the queen. This was in 1786, on the eve of the French Revolution, and when that storm came Dumas seized his chance and began a meteoric ascent through the ranks of the new revolutionary army. He rose to command entire divisions and armies. It would be 150 years before another black officer in the West would rise so high.

The explanations for how such a life had even been possible lie in another forgotten story—that of the world's first civil rights movement. In the 1750s, during the reign of Louis XV, a generation of crusading lawyers went up against one of the most powerful interests in France—the colonial sugar lobby—and won shockingly broad rights for people of color. Slaves taken to France from the colonies brought lawsuits against their masters and won their freedom. (Compare this with the infamous Dred Scott ruling of the U.S. Supreme Court, which—in the 1850s—would find that blacks were "so far inferior that they had no rights which the white man was bound to respect." The ruling actually contains language mocking the French freedom trials of the previous century.) The French lawsuits were decades earlier than the Somerset case, which launched abolitionism in England.

With the Revolution in 1789, the dream of equality in France suddenly seemed almost limitless. Dumas was not the only black or mixed-race Frenchman to rise up; he rode into battle with the Chevalier de Saint-Georges, the acknowledged master swordsman of Europe (and an acclaimed composer and musician). Like Dumas, the chevalier was of mixed race: his mother had been a freed slave. When the Revolution broke out, the chevalier formed a corps of mounted cavalry known as the Légion Noire, the Black Legion, and recruited Dumas to be his second in command.

By the time he was thirty-one, Dumas had been promoted to general, having earned almost universal admiration from every officer and soldier who fought beside him. A Prussian-raised French officer who openly proclaimed a "horror of negroes" (not to mention an "invincible antipathy for Jews") nevertheless wrote that General Dumas "might be called the best soldier in the world."

The story of General Dumas brilliantly illuminates the first true age of emancipation: a single decade during which the French Revolution not only sought to end slavery and discrimination based on skin color but also broke down the ghetto walls and offered Jews full civil and political rights, ending a near-universal discrimination that had persisted since ancient times. General Alexandre Dumas, wrote a French historian at the end of the nineteenth century, "was a living emblem of the new equality."

Much has been made of the beginnings of abolitionism in the British world and the question of equality during the American Revolution, but the life of Alex Dumas shows that it was the French Revolution that was the first unbridled age of emancipation, and its complex web of dreams and disappointments would underlie the history of freedom and prejudice for the next two centuries. This revolutionary age of racial emancipation introduced much of the world to modern ideas of human freedom—the idea that all men, regardless of religion or race, deserve equal rights, opportunities, respect—but it also spurred the backlash of modern racism and modern anti-Semitism, which fused older prejudices with the new political and scientific idealogies.

During the days of the Terror, Dumas showed a restraint and humanity that could have cost him his command, or even his life. At a time when the most radical defenders of liberty, equality, and fraternity committed atrocities in the name of these ideals, he never shrank from protecting any victim, no matter what his or her background or ideological complexion. Sent to suppress the royalist uprising in the west of France, the Vendée—the darkest hour of the French Revolution—General Dumas risked his career to oppose the bloodshed he saw all around him. Later, a pro-royalist writer would write, of this "generous republican," that Dumas was one of those rare generals who were "always ready bravely to sell their lives on the battleground, but resolved to break their swords rather than consent to the role of executioners."

Dumas—the son of a marquis and of a slave—had the unique perspective of being from the highest and lowest ranks of society at once. A true idealist, he did not cease to espouse his views once they'd fallen from favor. His capture and imprisonment in an enemy fortress where he languished for two years—until he was released into an even more agonizing labyrinth of betrayal in his own country, by his own side— foretold what would become of the ideals of equality and fraternity, especially for France's men and women of color. And Dumas's birthplace, Saint-Domingue, would have a violent revolution and reemerge as Haiti, to be ostracized by the white nations and moved from the center of the world economy to its desperate margins.

▶—◀

THE dizzying rise and downfall of General Dumas haunt his son's memoir. "I worshipped my father," the novelist writes. "I love him still with as tender and as deep and as true a love as if he had watched over my youth and I'd had the blessing to go from child to man leaning on his powerful arm."

His father had a fairy-tale romance with his mother, Marie-Louise Labouret, a white woman from a respectable bourgeois family; they fell in love when he rode in to protect her town from violence during the first months of the Revolution. This was how the Dumas family came to be based in Villers-Cotterêts; Marie-Louise's father, Claude Labouret, an innkeeper, had grown prosperous from the increased tourist trade the swinging House of Orléans had attracted to the town. Marie-Louise's father's only condition for his daughter's marriage was that Dumas, then still a private in the Queen's Dragoons, receive his first promotion and attain the rank of sergeant. When Dumas returned for his fiancée's hand, he was four ranks higher. He and Marie-Louise would go on to have three children, of which Alexandre, the writer, would be the last and their only son.

In fiction, his father most directly inspired Dumas's novel *Georges*, where a young man of mixed race from a French sugar colony makes his way to

Paris, becomes a great swordsman, and returns to the island to avenge a long-ago racial insult (itself an almost exact retelling of a searing incident from his father's youth).

By the end of the novel, Georges has married the woman of his dreams, proven himself superior to the whites in courage and skill, fought duels, rescued damsels, and led a failed slave uprising, which sends him to the scaffold, although he is saved at the last minute by his brother, a mulatto slave-ship captain. Georges has many aspects of Edmond Dantès, the Count of Monte Cristo, who would follow him into print a few months later. Georges remembers everything with an encyclopedic obsession. When he returns to confront the white people who have wronged his family, he profits at every turn by the fact that they live only in the present. The past is not alive to them the way it is to Georges; they do not remember—and thus do not see the reality of things. That reality is the dream Georges has come to embody: that a black man can become a nobleman and be better educated and more talented and powerful than the white plantation owners.

The author of *The Count of Monte Cristo* provided the standard account of the novel's origin. (Notably absent from it: the fact that Alex Dumas's disreputable uncle Charles, on his father's side, once used a Caribbean island called "Monte Cristo" to smuggle sugar and slaves). The novel's main plotline, Dumas once wrote in an essay, was based on a gruesome true crime story taken from the police archives of Paris, about a man who suffered false political imprisonment after being betrayed by a group of jealous friends. After serving seven years behind bars, the man was released when the government changed hands and proceeded to hunt down his old friends and murder them in cold blood. There are many details from this account that Dumas used, but the main character could not be farther from the deadly but ultimately humane count.

The essay ends with the novelist signaling that his various explanations might be mere talk and obfuscation: "And now, everyone is free to find another source for *The Count of Monte Cristo* than the one I give here," he wrote, "but only a very clever man will find it." It's impossible to know what the novelist hoped to inspire when he challenged his clever reader to "find another source for *The Count of Monte Cristo*," but it seems likely he hoped someone might one day guess another origin for his wronged hero. He had already transformed his father's character into the avenging mulatto justice-crusader "Georges," but the true-crime story he'd fastened on next offered the chance to universalize his father's struggles. By applying something of Alex Dumas's character to Edmond Dantès, he transformed a criminal—the equivalent of a modern serial killer—into a representative of the universal drive for justice.

In *The Count of Monte Cristo*, Dumas would give his betrayed protagonist not only the fate of his father's final years but also a fictional taste of a dark sort of triumph. In the novel's hero you can see the premise of every modern thriller from Batman comics to *The Bourne Identity*. No other adventure novel of the nineteenth century carries its resonance. After escaping the dungeon and securing the treasure of Monte Cristo, Dantès builds a luxurious subterranean hideout in the caves of the island. He becomes a master of all styles of combat, though he mainly uses his mind to defeat his enemies, bending the law and other institutions to his superhuman will. Knowing that the world is violent and corrupt, the Count becomes a master of violence and corruption—all with the goal of helping the weakest and most victimized people of all. The Count is the first fictional hero to announce himself as a "superman," anticipating Nietzsche—not to mention the birth of comics—by many years.*

The writer Dumas grew up in a very different world from that of his father—a world of rising, rather than diminishing, racism. His fellow novelist Balzac referred to him as "that negro." After the success of *The Three Musketeers* and *The Count of Monte Cristo*, critics launched an endless, damaging public attack on Dumas, mocking his African heritage. He was a black-skinned tropical weed in the literary soil of France, one declared: "Scratch Monsieur Dumas's hide and you will find the savage . . . a Negro!"

Newspaper artists in the 1850s depicted the novelist with a succession of racist clichés, mocking his literary efforts. One well-known caricature shows Dumas leaning over a hot stove on which he is boiling his white characters alive: his popping eyes glare demonically at a musketeer he is lifting to his impossibly huge lips, apparently about to sample the European's flesh. The

---

* The Italian Marxist Antonio Gramsci, writing at the height of the Nietzschean vogue in the early twentieth century, went so far as to declare that "many self-proclaimed Nietzscheans are nothing other than . . . Dumasians who, after dabbling in Nietzsche, 'justified' the mood generated by the reading of *The Count of Monte-Cristo.*"

writer was only one-quarter black, while his father had been half, but attitudes had dramatically sunk since the late eighteenth century, when his father's African heritage had been an object of admiration.

The novelist tried to make light of the racist insults, but they must have stung. The greatest sin of all, however, was that his father, General Alex Dumas, was forgotten. The son never managed to discover the full truth about his father, or to restore his place in the history books. But he avenged his father in another way, by creating fictional worlds where no wrongdoer goes unpunished and the good people are watched over and protected by fearless, almost superhuman heroes—heroes, that is, a lot like Alex Dumas.

━━

I read thousands of letters about and by General Dumas in the Château de Vincennes, the Bastille-like fortress that is now home to France's military archives. After passing life-size portraits of Napoleon and a chandelier made from hundreds of blunderbuss pistols, I sat surrounded by old veterans researching their regiments, shuffling onionskin pages and reading typed twentieth-century reports, as I read through stacks of elaborately handwritten documents on heavy parchment paper that told the story of the French Revolution as a spectacle of never-ending combat.

The exquisite handwriting that I would come to know as Alex Dumas's often spoke in surprisingly blunt language about his hopes for the future, about his frustrations with the army, and about his faith in the ideals for which he was fighting. The noble-heartedness and fierce physical courage that had made him one of his era's finest soldiers is evident even in piles of bureaucratic daily military reports. Dumas's mocking of army procedure, blistering warnings to those who abused civilians, and trash-talking takedowns of cowardly desk generals often made me laugh out loud. His goodwill toward his fellow soldiers and his willingness to sacrifice everything for the cause of the rights of man and the citizen, no matter who or what stood in his way, sometimes brought me nearly to tears.

Although I found his service records, his dispatches from the field, and the anecdotes about him in nineteenth-century military histories, I could find out little about General Alex Dumas the man—no love letters, no memoir, not even a will. It was as though he had been effaced by the celebrity of his son and grandson, who had both borne his name. Even the term "Dumas *père*" ("Dumas the father"), as the novelist is known in France, erases the existence of General Dumas: it distinguishes the novelist only from "Dumas *fils*" ("Dumas the son"), a playwright who wrote the drama on which Verdi based *La Traviata*. Indeed, I discovered that the Alexandre Dumas Museum in Villers-Cotterêts, though "dedicated to the life and works of the Three Dumas," was mainly a collection honoring the novelist, with a medium-sized room dedicated to the playwright and a small room dedicated to the general. The small room contained a few portraits, some letters about his battlefield exploits, and a lock of his curly black hair.* My great hope for understanding General Dumas was that the museum safe would contain personal letters, the deathbed papers, the documents that were really important to him, which his widow, Marie-Louise, would have passed on to his son.

The museum sold a booklet describing its founding, written with the sort of zeal for bureaucratic detail North Americans find hard to fathom. As I read about more than a decade of jockeying between the town, the region, and the central government over the status of the Dumas family artifacts, I despaired of my own situation: it could take the town's bureaucracy months, if not years, to agree on a protocol for opening the safe. They were in no hurry. The artifacts had accumulated over the decades in the museum's second-floor offices, and the only person who had known or cared about them was now gone.

As February turned to March, Deputy Mayor Dufour told me whenever I called that he was looking into the matter and seeing what the town intended to do about the safe. He told me he would know in two days. Then another two days. Then ten days. Then I had trouble reaching him on the phone. I came and went from Villers to Paris, then back to New York and back to Paris.

With my growing number of visits, I found out that there were still some partisans of General Dumas around. They called themselves the Association of the Three Dumas, or simply the Dumasians. It was not a big group— mainly a core of a dozen old-timers who considered themselves devotees of

---

* I later visited a Parisian shop in the shadow of the Luxembourg Palace, where I learned much about the oddly brisk market in revolutionary and Napoleonic hair clippings.

courage, camaraderie, and the Dumas spirit. They gathered at Le Kiosque, a little restaurant combined with a used book shop. The establishment was run by a Monsieur Goldie, whose gunmetal French growl was laced with Portuguese-Scottish, and whose grandfathers, both from families based in British India, had somehow landed here after many adventures. I attended the Dumasians' annual convention, where I met an Iranian lady from Maryland who was translating the Dumas oeuvre into Farsi. The association's newly elected president was a dapper international executive who had gotten sucked into the whole thing because he happened to buy a little castle, on the outskirts of town, that General Dumas had rented in 1804; he currently lived in Almaty, Khazakstan, but made sure to return to Villers-Cotterêts to preside over the convention.

The real head, and heart, of the association, though, was a former wine salesman who had just stepped down after founding and leading it for many years. His name was François Angot, and his family were the official huntsmen of the town, keeping alive the tradition that had for centuries made the nearby Retz Forest the destination of royals. Like the new head of the association, Angot had also become involved with the three Dumas via a real-estate transaction—in his case just after World War II, when his father happened to buy the house where General Dumas died. (When Angot's father was forced to sell the house, in the early 1960s, he tried to convince the town to buy it, but there had not been enough interest, and then the new owner, a dentist, put up a locked gate and a sign telling curiosity-seekers not to stop. It was then that Angot had decided the three Dumas needed an association to support their memory in the town.)

Angot had to walk everywhere on crutches because of a car accident. He moved much faster than I did because when he wanted to make some distance, he swung his body furiously forward, then planted the crutches far ahead of him, then swung forward, then planted far ahead. It was like a wild pendulum, an athletic event. And he never tired of showing me Dumasian details in every corner of the town—even the ordinary bars and taverns, with neon and sports and pinup posters on the walls, displayed a stock portrait of the novelist Alexandre Dumas.

Angot quoted lines from *The Three Musketeers* as if it were Shakespeare, and I saw anew the power of the stories to inspire someone to carry on jauntily, no matter how broken down his horse. He announced his politics as *legitimiste*—supporting not just monarchy but Bourbon monarchy, the most far-gone cause—yet he never had an unkind word to say about anyone. His romanticizing of the *Ancien Régime*, complete with fleur-de-lis ascots and letter openers, was balanced by his unbridled love for the ultra-republican, democratic General Dumas, whom he esteemed as the greatest man in the greatest family.

We discussed countless times how I might solve "the problem of the safe." Consulting a safe expert, I had been told there would be few alternatives to somehow blowing it open. This would require a specialist—a sapper, a locksmith, or even a safe-cracker, not to mention permission. But how was this to be accomplished without the cooperation of the town?

Angot was undaunted on my behalf. "What's an adventure without a little danger?" he said with a gleam in his eye.

I came to suspect that Deputy Mayor Dufour wasn't exactly unsympathetic to the problem, either—he just wasn't a convert to the cause. Someone told me that before he was named deputy mayor in charge of culture, his main cultural interest had been cars and motorcycles. It was not clear whether he had ever read a novel by his town's favorite son. So Dufour needed to become a Dumas fan in the broadest sense. After consulting with the Dumasians, I invited him to a lavish lunch at Le Kiosque, where, over several courses with different wines and Cognac, which in French style he commented on extensively, I explained more fully why examining the papers inside the safe was so important to the town's heritage, and even to France itself. The safe might reveal the truth behind some of literature's most beloved stories, Villers-Cotterêts's contribution to world culture, and the fact that his nation had broken down race barriers years ahead of its time.

Gradually the deputy mayor became animated, even excited: "One for all, Monsieur Reiss!" he said, raising a glass. "We must open that safe!" He shook my hand warmly when he excused himself to rush back to his deputy-mayoral business. I had a new ally, at least until the buzz wore off.

I took it as an invitation to crack the safe—for history, for destiny, for whatever the hell was inside it—and wasted no time. I found a locksmith in the regional capital who said he had experience in such things, and arranged a rendezvous when the museum was closed. I confirmed the plan with the deputy mayor, who brought up the matter of a donation—2,000 euros, in cash, *s'il vous plaît*—to a General Alexandre Dumas Memorial Safe Fund.

The next day, the locksmith showed up at the museum with cases full of drills and other equipment. The deputy mayor arranged for two policemen to be posted in the museum's courtyard, along with the security guard. The safe was in a corner of an upstairs storage room, strewn with cardboard boxes, old clothes, bits of imitation classical pottery, and an assortment of semi-intact department-store mannequins that made me think of revolutionary decapitation. Immediately beside the safe was a bisected mannequin—its upper half sported a tricolor bandolier, of the kind French officials wear at state occasions; its lower half, perched next to it, was clad in a pair of men's white briefs.

The locksmith took off his leather jacket and neatly laid out his drills. He examined the safe and carefully positioned an electronic instrument. "It's all about the spot," he said. "You just have to know where to make the hole."

Then things proceeded the way they do in the movies—finding the place with a stethoscope, drilling, drilling again, click-click, listen, tap, drill, listen . . . He had found the spot! The final sparks flew as he pressed his weight into the drill, and I held my breath.

The door swung open and revealed stack upon stack of paper—seven or eight feet of battered folders, boxes, parchments, and onionskin documents collected over the years by Elaine. All of it related to Alexandre Dumas—father, son, or grandson—but I needed to tear through it looking only at what related to the original: General Dumas. According to my agreement with the deputy mayor, I had just two hours to photograph whatever I could; then the policemen standing guard outside would take possession of the safe's contents and remove it to who knew where, for who knew how long. I took out a camera with a big lens and got to work.

BOOK

ONE

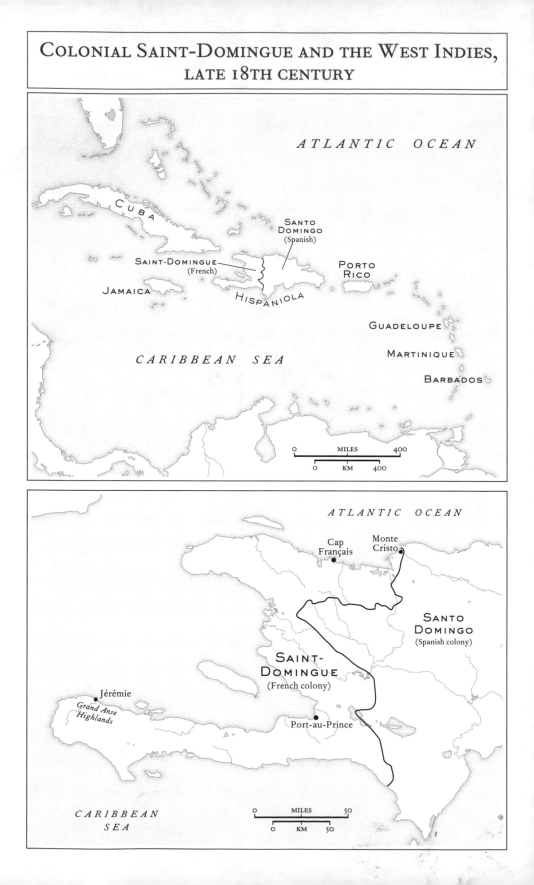

Colonial Saint-Domingue and the West Indies, Late 18th Century

ATLANTIC OCEAN

CUBA

SANTO DOMINGO (Spanish)

SAINT-DOMINGUE (French)

PORTO RICO

JAMAICA

HISPANIOLA

GUADELOUPE

MARTINIQUE

BARBADOS

CARIBBEAN SEA

0 MILES 400

0 KM 400

ATLANTIC OCEAN

Cap Français

Monte Cristo

SANTO DOMINGO (Spanish colony)

SAINT-DOMINGUE (French colony)

Jérémie

Grand Anse Highlands

Port-au-Prince

CARIBBEAN SEA

0 MILES 50

0 KM 50

THE SUGAR FACTORY

ALEXANDRE Antoine Davy de la Pailleterie—father of the future Alex Dumas—was born on February 26, 1714, in the Norman province of Caux, a region of rolling dairy farms that hung above great chalk cliffs on the northwest coast of France. A scrawled scrap of paper from the time states that he was baptized "without ceremony, at home, because of the peril of death," suggesting he was too sickly to risk bringing in to the local church. He was the firstborn son of an old family that possessed a castle, a scarcity of cash, and an abundance of conniving members, though Antoine would one day outdo them all.

The boy survived, but the following year his sovereign, King Louis XIV, the Sun King, died after seventy-two years on the throne. As he lay dying, the old king counseled his heir, his five-year-old great-grandson: "I loved war too much, do not imitate me in this, nor in my excessive spending habits." The five-year-old presumably nodded earnestly. His reign, as Louis XV, would be marked by a cycle of spending and wars so extravagantly wasteful and unproductive that they would bring shame not only on his person but on the institution of the French monarchy itself.

But the profligate, war-driven habits of its kings could not hold France back. In fact the "Great Nation" was about to unleash the age of the philo-sophes, the Enlightenment, and all that would follow from it. Frenchmen were about to shake the world into the modern age. Before they could do that, however, they would need money. Big money.

Big money was not to be found in Normandy, and certainly not around the Pailleterie château. The family's coat of arms—three golden eagles hold-ing a golden ring on an azure background—looked impressive but meant little. The Davy de la Pailleteries were provincial aristocrats from a region more abounding in old glories than in current accounts. Their fortune was not enough to sustain grandeur without work—or not for more than one generation.

Still, a title was a title, and as the oldest son, Antoine would eventually claim the title of "marquis" and the ancestral estate of Bielleville that went with it. Next in succession after Antoine were his two younger brothers—Charles Anne Edouard (Charles), born in 1716, and Louis François Thérèse (Louis), born in 1718.

Faced with their limited prospects in Normandy, all three Pailleterie brothers sought their fortunes in the army, which then accepted nobles as young as twelve into its commissioned ranks. Antoine received a commission in the Corps Royal de l'Artillerie, an up-and-coming branch of the service, as a second lieutenant at sixteen. His brothers soon followed him as teenage junior officers. The Pailleterie brothers were kept busy by His Majesty's plunge, in 1734, into the War of the Polish Succession, one of a series of dynastic conflicts that regularly provided excuses for the gory quaintness of eighteenth-century European combat. The big-power rivals behind this little war were the traditional competitors for European land domination, the Bourbons and the Hapsburgs, France and Austria. (England would soon play a bigger role, especially on the high seas and in the New World, but that was still one or two wars in the future.)

In addition to his commission in the artillery, Antoine served at the front as a gentleman in the entourage of the Prince de Conti, the king's dashing, fabulously rich cousin. Antoine saw his main action at the Siege of Philipsburg, in 1734—later written into the military annals by Karl von Clausewitz, in *On War*, as the "perfect example of how not to site a fortress. Its location was that of an idiot standing with his nose against the wall."* Voltaire was also there, fleeing a royal arrest warrant, and working as a kind of one-man eighteenth-century USO show during the siege, offering bons mots and brandy between bouts of battle and composing odes to the military men.

The most notable event in Antoine's service at Philipsburg, however, was

---

* Clausewitz meant that if you can't site a fortress directly on a river, you should site it far from one. Placing the Philipsburg fortress merely near the river had exposed it to every possible means of attack.

that he served as a witness to a duel that took place on the night of the Prince de Conti's birthday party at the front: it was between the Prince de Lixen and the Duke de Richelieu. The duke took offense when the prince mocked the Richelieu pedigree. The duke's great-great uncle had been Cardinal Richelieu (later immortalized as the mustache-twirling nemesis of the Three Muske-teers), an adviser to Louis XIII who had managed royal financial and building projects to great advantage—both for himself and for France. But such accomplishments did not measure up to the high standards of snobbery practiced by Lixen, who regarded the Richelieu clan as parvenus. To make matters worse, the duke had recently offended the prince by marrying one of his cousins.

At midnight, the illustrious in-laws met on the field of honor between the dining tents and the trenches. They began lunging at one another there in the dark, their lackeys lighting the swordfight with flickering lanterns. The prince took the advantage first, wounding Richelieu in the thigh. The lackeys switched from lanterns to bare torches, and the combatants chased each other in and out of the trenches, their blades reflecting fire. The prince stabbed the duke in the shoulder. At this point an enemy barrage lit the field of honor. One of the lackeys was hit and killed.

Richelieu counterattacked, and with Antoine watching, the duke sank his blade into the chest of his unfortunate in-law. Contemporaries considered it a sort of poetic justice, since Lixen himself had recently dispatched one of his own relations, his wife's uncle, the Marquis de Ligneville, for a similarly trifling offense. Such were the friendly-fire deaths of the eighteenth-century battlefield.*

In 1738, when the war ended, Antoine took the chance to get out of the army and Europe altogether. While he was stationed at Philipsburg, his younger brother Charles had joined a colonial regiment that went to the French sugar colony of Saint-Domingue, on the West Indian island of His-paniola. It was a fortunate posting.

>—◄

---

* The novelist Alexandre Dumas would dine out on the story throughout his life. He re-counts it in his memoirs, writing that the name Richelieu "appears so often in . . . my novels that it seems almost my duty to explain to the public how I came to have such a predilection for it."

SUGAR planting was the oil business of the eighteenth century, and Saint-Domingue was the *Ancien Régime*'s Wild West frontier, where sons of impoverished noble families could strike it rich. Barely sixteen when he arrived in the colony as a soldier, by twenty-two Charles Davy de la Pailleterie had met and wooed a young woman, Marie-Anne Tuffé, whose family owned a sizable sugar plantation on the colony's wealthy northeast coast. Antoine decided to join him.

Today, the world is so awash in sugar—it is such a staple of the modern diet, associated with all that is cheap and unhealthy—that it's hard to believe things were once exactly the opposite. The West Indies were colonized in a world where sugar was seen as a scarce, luxurious, and profoundly health-giving substance. Eighteenth-century doctors prescribed sugar pills for nearly everything: heart problems, headache, consumption, labor pains, insanity, old age, and blindness.* Hence, the French expression "like an apothecary without sugar" meant someone in an utterly hopeless situation. Saint-Domingue was the world's biggest pharmaceutical factory, producing the Enlightenment wonder drug.

Columbus brought sugarcane to Hispaniola, the first European settlement in the New World, on his second voyage, in 1493. The Spanish and the Portuguese had been the first to cultivate sugar in Europe, and when they began their age of discovery, among the first places they "discovered" were islands off the coast of North Africa just perfect for sugar cultivation. As the Iberian explorers made their way down the African coast—the Portuguese going around the Horn to East Asia, the Spaniards cutting west to the Americas—both powers had two main goals in mind: finding precious metals and planting sugarcane. (Oh, and spreading the word of God.)

The Spanish established a colony on the eastern side of Hispaniola and named it Santo Domingo; eventually, the colony would extend over the eastern two-thirds of the island, roughly corresponding to the modern-day Dominican Republic. (The native inhabitants called the entire island by another

---

* See Dr. Frederick Slare's 1715 "A Vindication of Sugars Against the Charge of Dr. Willis, Other Physicians, and Common Prejudices: Dedicated to the Ladies," which prescribed as a treatment for ocular illness "two drams of fine sugar-candy, one-half dram pearl, one grain of leaf gold; make into a very fine and impalpable powder, and when dry, blow a convenient quantity into the eye."

name: *Hayti*.) The Spanish brought artisans from the Canary Islands, off the coast of West Africa, to build the elaborate on-site technology needed for sugar production—presses, boilers, mills—and then brought the most essential ingredient of all: African slaves.

Slavery, of course, had existed since antiquity. The Greek city-states had created democracy among a small elite by enslaving almost everybody else, in some cases up to a third of the population. Aristotle believed democracy could exist only because of slavery, which gave citizens the leisure for higher pursuits. (Modern versions of this argument held that American democracy was born of the slave society of rural Virginia, because slavery gave men like Washington and Jefferson the free time to better themselves and to participate in representative government.) In Greece and Rome, slavery was the fate of prisoners of war and barbarians, anyone not lucky enough to have been born Greek or Roman. When ancient slaves managed to buy their freedom or that of their children, they would assimilate into the free population, with no permanent mark on their descendants. Though ubiquitous in the ancient world, slavery was not based on any sense of "race."

Until the mid-1400s, nearly all slaves imported into Europe were ethnic Slavs. The very word "slave" derives from this connection. "Slav markets" were found across Europe, from Dublin to Marseille, where the people being bought and sold were as fair-skinned as those buying and selling them. By the 1400s, white slaves were being used in the Mediterranean to harvest cane as part of the late-medieval sugar industry.

The rise of Islam had led to a vast expansion of slavery, as conquering Arab armies pulled any and every group of "unbelievers" into bondage. Arab slave traders captured whites from the north via sea raids on European shipping, and they acquired blacks from the sub-Saharan kingdoms. Over time, the Muslim slave trade focused increasingly on black Africans. Yet there was still no fixed biological marker for bondage. When Ottomans captured Constantinople, they diverted Europe's supply of white slaves to the Middle East instead.

Europeans began looking to Africa for slaves when Portugal created a new sugar empire on African coastal islands. Thousands of blacks were bought and sold to harvest sugar, and age-old negative stereotypes about them began to coalesce into a virulent new strain of racism. In European eyes, blacks now came to be considered uniquely destined for slavery, created by their white master's God for a life of permanent chattel servitude.

The Portuguese had first taken blacks to Madeira to cut sugarcane because the island was off the coast of North Africa and the Muslim traders there happened to deal in African slaves. When they sailed down the Guinea Coast, the Portuguese found the black African kingdoms were willing to supply them with slaves directly: the Africans did not consider they were selling their racial brothers to the whites. They did not think in racial terms at all but only of different tribes and kingdoms. Before, they had sold their captives to other black Africans or to Arabs. Now they sold them to whites. (The African kingdoms and empires themselves kept millions of slaves.) As time went on, Africans would learn of the horrors awaiting black slaves in the American colonies, not to mention on the passage over, yet they continued to export ever greater quantities of *bois d'ébène*—"ebony wood," as the French called their cargo. There was no mercy or morality involved. It was strictly business.

Spain laid the foundations of this great wealth and evil in the Americas, then quickly became distracted and forgot about it. After introducing the plants, the technology, and the slaves into Santo Domingo, the Spanish dropped the sugar business in favor of hunting for gold and silver. They moved on to Mexico and South America in search of the precious metals, leaving the island to languish for nearly two centuries, until the French began to harness its true potential.

━━

BY the mid- to late eighteenth century, the Saint-Domingue colony, situated on the western end of Hispaniola, where Haiti is today, accounted for two-thirds of France's overseas trade. It was the world's largest sugar exporter and produced more of the valuable white powder than all the British West Indian colonies combined. Thousands of ships sailed in and out of Port-au-Prince and Cap Français, bound for Nantes, Bordeaux, and New York. When the British, after winning the Seven Years' War, chose to keep the great swath of France's North American colonies and instead return its two small sugar islands, Guadeloupe and Martinique, they unwittingly did their archrival a favor.

Saint-Domingue was the most valuable colony in the world. And its staggering wealth was supported by staggering brutality. The "pearl of the West Indies" was a vast infernal factory where slaves regularly worked from sunup to past sundown in conditions rivaling the concentration camps and gulags of the twentieth century. One-third of all French slaves died after only a few years on the plantation. Violence and terror maintained order. The punishment for working too slowly or stealing a piece of sugar or sip of rum, not to mention for trying to escape, was limited only by the overseer's imagination. Gothic sadism became commonplace in the atmosphere of tropical mechanization: overseers interrupted whippings to pour burning wax—or boiling sugar or hot ashes and salt—onto the arms and shoulders and heads of recalcitrant workers. The cheapness of slave life brushed against the exorbitant value of the crop they produced. Even as the armies of slaves were underfed and dying from hunger, some were forced to wear bizarre tin-plate masks, in hundred-degree heat, to keep them from gaining the slightest nourishment from chewing the cane.

The sugar planter counted on an average of ten to fifteen years' work from a slave before he was driven to death, to be replaced by another fresh off the boat. Along with malnutrition, bugs and diseases could also eventually do in someone working up to eighteen hours a day. The brutality of the American Cotton Kingdom a century later could not compare to that of Saint-Domingue in the 1700s. There would be no shortage of cruel overseers in the United States, but North American slavery was not based on a business model of systematically working slaves to death in order to replace them with newly bought captives. The French sugar plantations were a charnel house.

Because Versailles loved laws and orders, France was the first country to codify colonial slavery. In doing so, King Louis XIV passed a law, in 1685, that changed the history of both slavery and race relations.

Le Code Noir—the Black Code. Its very name left no doubt about who were to be the slaves. It elaborated, point by point, the many ways in which black Africans could be exploited by their white masters. The Code sanctioned the harshest punishments—the penalty for theft or attempted escape was death—and stated that slaves could not marry without their master's consent or pass on property to their kin.

But the very existence of a written legal code—a novelty of the French colonial empire—opened the way for unexpected developments. If there were laws governing slavery, then slave owners, at least in some instances, could be found in violation of them. By articulating the rules of white domination, the Code—theoretically, at least—limited it, and gave blacks various opportunities to escape from it. It created loopholes. One of these was on the issue of sexual relations between masters and slaves, and the offspring resulting from such relations.

＞－＜

CHARLES Davy de la Pailleterie became an established sugar planter on Saint-Domingue in fine aristocratic fashion—by marrying into money. His union with Marie-Anne Tuffé brought a half stake in a plantation near Cap Français, the colony's busiest port, on the rich northeastern plains where sugarcane grew best. His mother-in-law held on to the other half stake, waiting to see how Charles managed his new responsibilities.

In an age when most industry was confined to small-scale or home-based labor, a sugar plantation was a huge undertaking, costly and exacting: sugarcane takes anywhere from nine to eighteen months to ripen, depending on various factors, and must be harvested at precisely the right time or it will dry out. Cut cane must be taken straight to a mill, to be crushed, pressed, or pounded to extract its juice before it rots or ferments. Then, within twenty-four hours, the juice must be boiled to remove its impurities and boiled again. While cooling and crystallizing, the mixture becomes molasses. Further processing produces a less dark, more chemically pure sugar—a gold liquid, resembling honey. Still further processing makes the white granules most prized by Europeans. A planter might use one hundred slaves for the brute fieldwork, and dozens more with artisanal expertise for the equally grueling work of boiling and refining. The production line was kept going nonstop—cutting, grinding, boiling, potting.

Sugar planting was the preserve of the great French families—rich aristocrats and *grands bourgeois* who could afford to invest vast sums and hire professional managers. The largest sugar plantations on Saint-Domingue employed several hundred field slaves. In addition, the planter needed mills, boiling houses, curing houses, and distilleries, along with storehouses to hold the sugar for shipping.

Without his advantageous marriage, Charles would have had to content himself with growing tobacco or coffee or indigo, none of which held sugar's promise of wealth and power. These less labor-intensive crops were the basis of most of the colony's smaller plantations or farms, some of them owned by free people of color (mulattos) and even by freed blacks.

Charles and his young bride had been married only a few months before they were surprised by Charles's brother Antoine standing on their doorstep, after a six-week passage from Le Havre and a daylong coach ride up from Port-au-Prince. Antoine told them he meant to stay temporarily. He would live with them for the next decade.

French aristocrats got mixed messages about work in the eighteenth century. The old line was that profiting by any sort of commerce was beneath them; the new line encouraged French aristocrats to grow wealthier through business and trade, although, in contrast to their English colonial counterparts, performing any manual labor was still out of the question. The Saint-Domingue slave economy suited the highborn French entrepreneur perfectly, allowing him to exercise the principles of political economy and wealth accumulation without getting his hands dirty.

On the surface, Charles satisfied every contemporary notion of aristocratic self-improvement: he married money and seemed to increase it through careful management. And unlike Antoine, he was energetic as well as greedy. Charles drove his slaves hard and the plantation prospered, so much so that after a few years he bought out the Widow Tuffé's half stake. He grew rich to the point where his estates dwarfed the family holdings in Normandy and he was able to send money home to his parents, the marquis and marquise, to support their last years in high style. The old marquis swore before a notary that Charles would get all his money back from the estate at the time of their death.

Antoine was cut from a different kind of noble cloth, a more traditional one in that he preferred to avoid productive work altogether. Indolent and carefree, he appears to have gone to Saint-Domingue intending to sponge off the industry of his younger brother indefinitely.

➤─◄

"A stay in Saint-Domingue is not at all deadly; it is our vices, our devouring vexations that kill us," wrote a young Frenchman returning after an eleven-year stay there. Everywhere in the sugar colony he had witnessed dangerous "excesses of pleasure," and confessed himself lucky to have survived. The climate and the constant search for profit, he observed, led to "violent and irascible" behavior among both old and new arrivals. "Burdened by troubles and work, the colonists surrender themselves to vice, and death strikes them down like the scythe mows down ears of corn."

The mother of one wealthy young Creole man* complained that her son was "given to amusement and a life of debauchery. He has fostered a harem of black women who control him and run the plantation." It was certainly common for white men in Saint-Domingue to take slave mistresses. In his *Voyage à Saint-Domingue*, the itinerant German Baron de Wimpffen describes interracial relationships as being visible everywhere, winked at by the most respectable members of the community. The baron even accuses a parish priest he encounters of "contributing to the population of the parsonage" by producing mixed-race children with his black mistress; the reason is not only lust, the priest explains, but the desire to increase his flock.

The French administration had tried to prevent this situation. One of the first laws in the colonial penal code, issued in 1664, forbade masters "to debauch negresses, on pain of twenty lashes of the whip, for the first offense, forty lashes for the second, and fifty lashes and the fleur-de-lis branded on the cheek for the third." But the rapid increase of the mulatto population over the next century spoke for itself.

Critics of interracial sex on Saint-Domingue mainly worried about its potential to break down respect for whites. Baron de Wimpffen bemoaned the "abuse of intimacy between master and slave," whose "great evil" lay in its altering "the first principle of subordination, the respect of the subordinated." Sex across color lines made maintaining strictly racist attitudes difficult: "The colonist who would be ashamed to work alongside the negress," wrote Wimpffen, "would not blush at living with her in the degree of intimacy that necessarily establishes relations of equality between them, which prejudice would challenge in vain."

---

* In the eighteenth century "Creole" had a different meaning than it does today, and signified white colonists who were born or at least significantly raised in the colony, rather than in Europe. To designate what we often mean by "Creoles" now, "people of mixed race"—part African and part European or Indian or Native American—the eighteenth-century French term was *gens de couleur*, literally "people of color."

It wasn't long before the Pailleterie brothers began to quarrel, sometimes violently. The diligent, pious Charles resented supporting his older brother, who took advantage of his hospitality, kept serial slave mistresses, and treated his plantation as the Saint-Domingue branch of the Pailleterie estates.

Antoine, for his part, must have despised his younger brother at least as much. Humiliation would have been unavoidable, with Charles accepting IOUs from their father, the marquis, while Antoine, as eldest son, had barely a thousand livres to his name.

One day in 1748, the brothers' quarreling took a dangerous turn. As a royal prosecutor later reported, Charles, "full of honor and feeling, . . . employed methods that were, truth be told, a little violent and . . . could have caused the demise of his older brother, if they had had their effect." (Since the prosecutor was moonlighting at the time as a private investigator hired by a member of Charles's family, we can assume that this conclusion was an understatement.)

Although Antoine was a soldier and could defend himself, on his own plantation Charles was absolute judge of life and death. Did he have his brother whipped, or subject him to one of the tortures used to put slaves in their place? Did Antoine's constant association with slaves finally make his brother decide to treat him like one?

Whatever occurred, it was severe enough to bring the brothers to a "rupture," as the investigating attorney wrote, which would end their relations forever. The night of the incident, Antoine fled Charles's plantation, taking three slaves with him—Rodrigue, Cupidon, and Catin, his latest mistress—and disappeared into the forest. He would not be heard from again for nearly thirty years.

THE BLACK CODE

CHARLES sent mounted slave hunters after his brother and the missing blacks. He himself rode with them and hired a ship to comb the coast. "Charles Edouard searched all the French possessions in the archipelago of America," a legal statement recorded. "It was in vain." As often happened in Saint-Domingue, once escaped slaves put some distance between themselves and the plantation, they were gone, vanished in the island's vast wilderness.

What was unusual in this case was that the slaves were in the company of a white man, a highborn one at that. The peculiar situation scandalized Saint-Domingue society: the ne'er-do-well brother of a respected planter had fled into the jungle with three slaves. One of the greatest concerns the authorities had about fugitive slaves was that they would join *marron* communities, encampments of runaways and their descendants who lived in the mountains and remote coves of Saint-Domingue, outside the influence of whites. (The word *marron* derived from the Spanish *cimarrón*—"wild, untamed"—first used to describe cattle that turned feral after getting away from Columbus's men shortly after they landed.) The densely wooded terrain sheltered the *marrons*—for Saint-Domingue was as thick with trees as modern Haiti is barren of them, another of history's surreal reversals—and made their capture nearly impossible. From their rugged camps, the *marrons* could prey on local towns and plantations, and the royal mounted police preferred to negotiate peace treaties with them rather than try to arrest them, which was too costly in men and arms, if it was even possible. Fugitive whites were also taken in.

Charles could only wonder if such was the case with his brother. If he were living in a town or on a plantation, wouldn't Charles's agents or those of the authorities have found him by now? Had Antoine boarded a ship to

Martinique or Guadeloupe—or perhaps to Jamaica, to hide out among the English? Antoine had left no trace.

In 1757, Charles and Antoine's mother died; in 1758, the old marquis, their father, followed her, on Christmas Day. A French tax official tried to investigate the whereabouts of the family's oldest son, the heir, but eventually threw up his hands, writing that "it is not known where he lives, what he does and if he is married or not. The rumor is that he is living abroad, but it is a mystery." In another report, the tax official wrote that some people said Antoine "had married a wealthy woman in Martinique." Yet others said that Antoine was dead.

▶◀

BUT Antoine was not dead and had not gone to Martinique or to live with the *marrons*, though he had been across their land. He and Rodrigue, Cupidon, and Catin had walked for weeks across the densely wooded mountains, more than seven thousand feet high, that separated central Saint-Domingue from the long southwest peninsula. They had arrived in the highlands region called Grand Anse ("Great Cove").

If Saint-Domingue was the Wild West, these were its badlands. Travel to the highlands was difficult, surrounded as they were by mountains, and communications usually went by sea rather than overland. The mountains gave ideal redoubts to fugitives of all kinds; two famous slave leaders led guerrilla wars from here against the French. Here the planters were often mulattos or freed blacks themselves. No one asked a lot of questions. It was an excellent place to hide.

The Great Cove highlands did not support big sugar farming, but the high mineral content of the red soil there was perfect for growing Saint-Domingue's second-most-lucrative crop: coffee. (As with sugar, by the late 1780s Saint-Domingue had become the world's largest coffee producer.) Coffee growers didn't get as rich as sugar planters did, but they also didn't need the same sort of capital to start up. Small hillside coffee plantations could be run with few slaves and at an entirely different pace of life. Here, carefully exploiting a few arpents of land—the French colonial unit of measurement, about 220 square feet—a man could sustain himself.

[handwritten marginal note:] A square 15' on a side, is 225 sq. ft.

Antoine settled in the parish of Jérémie, which at the time was sparsely inhabited, with a total population of 2,643 souls—2,147 slaves, 109 free "men of color" (black or mixed-race), and 387 whites. It was named after Jeremiah, the prophet of Lamentations. Nearby lay the village of Trou Bonbon, which had fifteen houses, including a billiard hall, and a private cemetery. Only one of the parish's settlements was large enough to classify as a city: its eponymous port town, which was officially founded in 1756 and would grow in importance as the parish rapidly expanded in the 1770s and '80s.

Highland planters lived off coffee, but they also grew a little of every other crop—sugar, cotton, indigo, cacao, lumber. The weather was mild, and though the rainy season lasted from April to October, the highlands were largely sheltered from the hurricanes that ravaged the rest of the island. Bananas, plantains, melons, and sweet potatoes were abundant, and scorpions, tarantulas, and poisonous insects were rare. Giant lizards, up to three and a half feet long, were plentiful but harmless, though the area was plagued by mosquitoes, flies, ants, aphids, and blistering "sticky worms." Not to mention the giant rats, though some people took these as pets. A kind of hybrid buffalo-cow roamed the hills, and the human inhabitants shared the land with all manner of feral beasts—wild pigs, cows, dogs, cats, monkeys; there were even reports, from around when Antoine arrived, of camels, imported by some colonist as souvenirs from North Africa, which spooked the horses.

The descendants of livestock and pets that had run away from the Spanish colonists had for a time provided a ready supply to the local buccaneers, who had roamed the highlands trading in untaxed meats.* When they joined pirate crews, the constant trouble they gave to the Spanish helped clear this part of the island for French settlement. The Spanish simply did not want to deal with it. The French authorities tried to eradicate them, but even in Antoine's time some buccaneers still survived in the highlands. When they weren't running meat—or rum—they worked as salt miners or piloted small boats along the coast. These highland Saint-Dominguans, along with more recent white immigrants, also from the middle and lower classes, were worlds

---

* The word "buccaneer" originated in a native people's term for smokehouse, which the French pronounced *boucan*. The original *boucaniers* didn't board ships and steal treasure; they were the jerky kings of the Western Hemisphere.

removed from the sugar kings, businessmen, and royal bureaucrats of the central plains, and they were Antoine's new neighbors, down the road from the coffee plantation he established at La Guinaudée in 1749.

━━◄

HIDING from his family and the world, he buried the name "Alexandre Antoine Davy de la Pailleterie." In his new life as a coffee and cocoa grower, he called himself "Antoine de l'Isle"—"Antoine of the Island."

Years later, the investigator hired by Charles's son-in-law in France would follow Antoine's trail and discover his false identity, though by then Antoine had long since cleared out. "The beginnings of Monsieur Delisle in this quarter were favorable enough," the detective reported,

> but having taken the farms, which served him poorly, and having done it in bad company, his good fortune was not long lasting: we do not know if he had any children from the negress Catin, but, finding her too old, he permitted her to live free, without having procured for her liberty according to the prescribed regulations. She still lives and resides with Sir Granfont, the former prosecutor, very aged now, and retired on the coast, three-quarters of a league from Jérémie.

The detective stated that Antoine had "of this one can be sure, four children who were mulattos and mulatresses." These were not from Catin but, rather, from another black or mulatto woman—colonial records contain both assertions—whom Antoine had acquired "for an exorbitant price."

Her name was Marie Cessette, and on March 25, 1762, she bore Antoine a son they named Thomas-Alexandre.

━━◄

"MY father's eyes opened in the most beautiful part of this magnificent island, queen of the gulf in which it lies, where the air is so pure that it is said no venomous reptiles can live there." Alexandre Dumas's rendering of his father's birthplace is romanticized, but incredible as it seems, given the colony's well-earned reputation for cruelty, the prospects for the half-white son of a slave born in 1762 were better in Saint-Domingue than almost anywhere else in the world. The French colonial empire's Code Noir could not effectively protect black slaves from mistreatment, but it could offer certain protections, as well as certain opportunities, to the children of mixed-race unions.

Article 9 of the Code began with the kind of draconian language we would expect:

> Free men who have one or more children from concubinage with their slaves, together with the masters who allow it, shall each be condemned to a fine of two thousand pounds of sugar; and if they are the masters of the slave with whom they have the said children, then beyond the fine, they shall be deprived of the slave and the children, who shall be confiscated to the profit of the hospital, without the possibility of being freed.

But then it provides an escape clause of sorts:

> The present article does not apply, however, if the owner, assuming he is unmarried at the time of the concubinage, undertakes to marry his slave under the laws of the Church; in this case, the slave shall thereby be freed, and the slave's children rendered free and legitimate.

Article 9 was drafted, at least in part, in response to widespread alarm over illegitimate unions in an environment that the colonists themselves frequently characterized as being awash in sensuality, temptation, and illicit alliances: "an empire based on libertinage." But the effects of this legitimization—and of the resulting class of free men and women of color it produced—were immense and unpredictable. It was not the creation of a free mixed-race class that made the situation unique, for such a class did exist in the Thirteen Colonies, though it was much smaller. It was the social mobility and rapidly increasing wealth of this group. In a world where slavery was legislated by race and practiced savagely, these people of color gained a remarkable set of rights: to receive fair treatment under the law, to petition government, to inherit property and pass it down.* The gains were especially stunning among the free women of color: they owned shops, businesses, and plantations; they went to the opera, dressed in Creole versions of the latest Paris fashions. Meanwhile, all around them, black and mixed-race slave women were losing their lives to backbreaking labor, often harder than that given to the men, because women could not apprentice themselves in the skilled artisanal trades. The Code made it possible for anyone's situation to change overnight, and, especially for women, the line between those in finery and those in bondage was surreally fluid.

Louis XIV issued the Code in 1685. By the time the Pailleterie brothers arrived on the island, it would not have been impossible for Charles to have married a rich mulatto woman to acquire his plantation. In the 1730s, there were many free women of color with significant savings and land; a generation later, free women of color on the island were, on average, more financially independent than white women. Colony officials noted, with alarm, that it was becoming increasingly common for new white immigrants, seeking their fortune, to marry well-off free women of color rather than Creole whites, who were both scarcer and often poorer.

Further laws against "concubinage with slaves" were passed to try to limit legal relations across the color line and the mixed-race children that would result from them. One ordinance from 1713 began with a preamble against masters who "instead of hiding their turpitude, glory in it . . . taking their concubines and the children they had had with them into their homes and exposing them to the eyes of all with as much assurance as if they were begotten of a legitimate marriage."

This, too, was a route to social mobility for people of color. But unlike official marriage, it also offered more chances for a common-law white husband to renege or choose to keep his "wife" enslaved in order to take advantage of her free labor, or to selectively free only some of his children. Such would be the case with Antoine and his favored son.

---

* Another paradox: Issued the same year that Louis XIV revoked the Edict of Nantes and banished Protestants from France, the Code Noir closely intertwined religious and racial regulations. It said all French slaves must be baptized Roman Catholic; it legislated anti-Semitic measures, ordering colonial officials to "expel all the Jews who have established residences from our isles," and it banned the public practice of any non-Catholic religion by either masters or slaves.

Like its detailed rules for the treatment of slaves, the Code Noir's provisions on marriage were unenforceable. The ultimate authority on Saint-Domingue was the master's will and, given the basic master-slave relationship, all sex was a form of rape. But masters were freeing their slave mistresses and mixed-race children at an increasing rate, now more often through unofficial, de facto manumission, producing a class of people called "*libre de fait*"—literally "freed by fact," or circumstance. A callous planter might adopt his lighter mixed-race children while keeping the rest in slavery, though he would often run into legal difficulties doing this. He might easily bring up a child as his own while continuing to own the mother to the day she died—since to free her legally required the paying of hefty manumission taxes.

Despite the claims of Antoine's grandson Alexandre Dumas, there is no evidence that Antoine and Marie Cessette were ever officially married. The chances that Antoine of the Island, a man doing everything possible to go undetected by the authorities, would have drawn attention to himself by a legal marriage to a former slave seem slight. No record of a marriage has ever been located and, unlike so much other material connected to this story, it is one document that would surely have been unearthed had it existed: the novelist Dumas later invested great sums in tracking down legal records of his own legitimacy.

━━

FOR his first twelve years, Thomas-Alexandre got his introduction to the world, with its extremes of injustice and progress, on the streets of the unofficial mulatto capital of the Western world: the port city of Jérémie.

Less than a decade older than he was, Jérémie was rough and unfinished, with taverns and billiard halls but neither a proper church nor a real government building. The colonial administrator, prosecutor, and local admiralty court all shared a residential townhouse. The Catholic parish also rented a private house for its services, and the rectory shared space with the royal gunpowder magazine.

Dueling was an essential part of manly comportment at the time, but Thomas-Alexandre's first exposure to violence was more likely to have been in the free-for-alls that daily spilled from the city's scores of billiard parlors, saloons, and "closed houses"—the brothels. Prostitution, cockfighting, alcohol, and opiates were all around, and no town authority could, or would dare to, regulate them. The town had no safe drinking water—a boon for tavern keepers—and drinking from any of the wells in the area was, as the great chronicler of island life Moreau de Saint-Méry observed, "a courageous act." A public fountain was promised for the upper town in the 1760s, but the pipes for it were still in transit from Port-au-Prince nearly thirty years later.

At least Jérémie did not need to worry about enemy attack. It was exceptionally well positioned for defense, perched on a hill overlooking the bay's natural amphitheater, which made land assault nearly impossible and left a steep climb for any attacker attempting to storm the town from the sea.

From the town's ramparts a boy could watch the sea's changing colors, its gray metallic waves turning blue green as the coffee schooners breached the horizon. Or he might idle in *la haute ville*, the upper town, which was planted with elm trees on three sides, with the fourth side, facing the sea, used as a public market where traders and small farmers, including slaves, could set up stands for their wares. The town bustled with carts drawn by mules, donkeys, and goats. The unpaved streets filled with dust in dry weather and became rivers of mud in the rainy season. Mounted gentlemen hopped from their horses and carried ladies out of coaches in their finery, while slaves waded knee-deep through mud. *La basse ville*, or the lower town, was one long street lined with small shops where free men of color worked alongside whites as tanners, distillers, potters, saddlers, wheelwrights, cabinetmakers, and smiths. The street also contained, among its other warehouses, "slave pens."

As one of the colony's least economically developed parishes, Jérémie had nowhere to go but up, and from the time Thomas-Alexandre was born that's what it did. By the early 1780s, its economy was expanding faster than that of any other area of Saint-Domingue, outpacing even the rich sugar plains in the north. The reason was a rise in global coffee prices (which should have allowed Antoine ever greater profits, if he had had an ounce of managerial skill). Ships lined the harbor to load the increasingly precious cargo for European markets. Sugar prices happened to be falling while coffee prices were rising, so the ranks of highland planters were swelled by ambitious newcomers both from France and from the rest of Saint-Domingue.

In addition to being unable managerially to take advantage of the coffee boom, Antoine could not have been pleased with the increase in police presence, as the local royal mounted-police force expanded its regional garrison to be headquartered in Jérémie—officially to combat *marrons* and buccaneers, but clearly also to bring government authority to this neglected outback. One fact about these new armed riders in their fancy white uniforms with gold brocade and fleurs-de-lis must have made an impression on young Thomas-Alexandre: they had faces as black as or blacker than his own.

The Jérémie mounted police were commanded by a white senior officer, but his deputy was a mulatto. And the corps itself was made up of four free black archers, as the policemen were called. Their bows or arrows now replaced by muskets and rifles, these men were trusted to go out among the white population armed with whatever they needed to maintain order and represent the state.*

More important still for the son of a slave and an aristocrat would have been Jérémie's increasing role as a mixed-race cultural mecca. While distancing themselves as much as possible from enslaved blacks and poor whites, free people of color learned to dance, ride, and fence like white colonists, whom they often surpassed in sophistication and snobbishness. As the coffee town boomed, the fashion-conscious *femmes de couleur* and *filles de couleur* copied the Paris styles—though the prevailing *mode* arrived a few months after the fact—and would change gowns multiple times during the course of an evening. On party nights, hostesses strove to outdo one another in imagination and spending. A fine lady of color would move from one ball to the next, each requiring a different style. At a first ball, reported Moreau de Saint-Méry, "One isn't admitted unless you are adorned in taffetas; in the second, unless you are dressed in muslin; in the third, unless you are in linen."

Births, weddings, and the birthdays of King Louis and Marie-Antoinette were all cause for lavish mixed-race balls. The hostesses wrapped their heads in sumptuous Indian silks and sported elaborate jewelry. Fashion wars broke

---

* Eventually, the increasing role free people of color played in the fight against fugitive slaves would cause a permanent poisoning of relations between mulattos and blacks; to this day, the port city of Jérémie remains remote and isolated from the rest of the country, not only because of its geography, but because of its strong mulatto and mixed-race heritage, which does not fit neatly into the identity and mythology of modern Haiti.

out between white and black hostesses to see who could throw more impressive balls. The *femmes de couleur* nearly always won, Moreau reported. They strove to acquire as much education as possible, and to appreciate the opera and the theater.

Largely as a result of this kind of aspirational mixed-race society, Saint-Domingue and the other French colonies became cultural capitals of the New World, excelling in the performing arts. Between 1764 and 1791 some three thousand theatrical productions were staged on Saint-Domingue. Along with opera, *commedia dell'arte* and Creole interpretations of Molière were popular. While performances in British North America took place in made-over courtrooms and warehouses, the French sugar colonies built lavish theaters and opera houses. At first, predominantly French, Italian, British, and Russian performers satisfied the demand, but as local blacks and mixed-race men and women trained in ballet, theater, and opera, they began to appear in major productions alongside whites. By the late 1700s, Saint-Domingue was home to the world's first black superstars, like the mulatto opera singers Minette and Lise, whose performances eclipsed those of visiting white divas from Paris and Naples.

The white colonists bristled, but the French colonial government encouraged such cultural pursuits among free blacks. An official colonial document promoting theater construction in 1780 argued for art's transformative power on people of African descent. Through exposure to French theater, it said, the free men of color had shed "the barbarity of their origin and, thus become civilized in their manners and customs."*

The colony so notorious for its treatment of black slaves was producing a mulatto cultural elite. Beyond the arts and entertainment, it also produced mixed-race businesspeople, plantation owners, lawyers, philosophers, and

---

*In the 1970s sociologists doing research in Haiti stumbled on a remnant of the eighteenth-century theater culture: though nearly two hundred years had passed, some local voodoo ceremonies showed unmistakable influences of the *commedia dell'arte* style. The sociologists noted this in the styles of improvisation, use of accents, costumes, and audience participation. When they looked at voodoo ceremonies from regions that had not had European theaters in the eighteenth century, as a control group, they found that these adhered strictly to traditional styles of voodoo still found in Africa. The sociologists wrote up their findings, dissecting the parallels between stock *commedia* characters and the local voodoo gods used in the ceremonies—Scaramouche and Ogu; prima donna and Ezili; Harlequin and Guède; Pantaloon and Papa Legba.

orators. In the 1780s, one of these men, Julien Raimond, moved to Paris and became a leading advocate for the rights of free blacks of the era, despite being the owner of hundreds of slaves.

But just as this new, racially complex society was flowering into being, the white colonists decided to fight back in a disturbingly modern way. While colonial racism against slaves was motivated by contempt and fear of rebellion, the backlash against Saint-Domingue's free people of color was spurred by a different motive: jealousy.

Since free people of color had come to dominate in fashion, culture, and commerce, racists tried to pass laws forcing them back to modesty, including the following ordinance (from 1779) about fashion: "We expressly forbid [the free people of color] to affect through their clothing, hairstyles, dress or apparel, a reprehensible assimilation of the way in which white men or women attire themselves. . . . Likewise we forbid them all objects of luxury on their exterior that are incompatible with the simplicity of their condition and origin, on pain of being stripped of them on the spot."

In 1773, the colonial court banned nonwhites from using "white" names. Thenceforward, people of mixed blood would have to take African names. The reason for the new law, according to the court, was that "the usurped name of a white race can place the status of persons in doubt, throw the order of successions into confusion, and ultimately destroy this insurmountable barrier between the whites and the people of color that public opinion has set up, and which the Government's wisdom maintains."

Along with this chilling white backlash and the use of mulatto police and soldiers against fugitive slaves, the increasing number of mulatto slaveholders was also driving a violent wedge between the black and the mixed-race communities. After a brief flowering, and despite the utopian predictions of those like Raimond, Saint-Domingue's multicultural society was producing glimpses of a far darker unraveling around the corner.

▸━◂

MEANWHILE, Thomas-Alexandre had spent his first decade of life on a farm on a tropical mountainside with his black slave mother, his mysterious Norman father, and three mixed-race siblings. He played in bamboo thickets

and creeper trees and chased feral animals like a buccaneer. One day, in another world, he would tell his own son about his life in the tropics and make it
sound like a wonderland, and so it must have seemed, in retrospect:

> I remember hearing my father recount that one day, returning home
> from town when he was ten years old, he saw to his great surprise a sort
> of tree trunk lying by the sea. He hadn't noticed it in passing the same
> place two hours before; so he amused himself by gathering pebbles and
> throwing them at the log; but all of a sudden, as the pebbles made con-
> tact, the log woke up. It was nothing less than a caiman [close cousin of
> an alligator] sleeping in the sun.
>
> Caimans, it seems, wake up in a foul mood; the one in question
> glimpsed my father and took it upon himself to run after him.
>
> My father, a true child of the colonies, a son of the beaches and
> savannas, ran well; but it would seem that the caiman ran or rather
> jumped even better than he did, and this adventure might well have left
> me in limbo forever if a negro, who was eating sweet potatoes astride
> a wall, had not seen what was happening and shouted to my father, al-
> ready out of breath:
>
> "Serpentine, little sir! Serpentine!"—a style of locomotion alto-
> gether contrary to the system of the caiman, which can only run straight
> ahead, or jump like a lizard.
>
> Thanks to this advice, my father arrived home safe and sound; but,
> he arrived, like the Greek from Marathon, panting and breathless, and
> nearly, like him, never to rise again.
>
> This race in which the beast was the hunter and the man the hunted,
> left a profound impression on my father's mind.

Island life no doubt honed Thomas-Alexandre's natural skills. A
nineteenth-century military biographer attributed his legendary horsemanship, which would allow him to fight on horseback on the steepest embank-
ments and the narrowest bridges, to the way he first learned to ride—"as one
learns in those new countries, where a man is called to tame the animal that he
will use, where vigor and agility replace the knowledge that is later acquired
in the riding school."

But apart from the land and the wild animals, Thomas-Alexandre had his father. Antoine was a rogue, but he was an educated one. Though no great scholar, he knew the literature and history of the Romans and Greeks, and his training as an artillery officer gave him more than a passing knowledge of science and mathematics. Perhaps he took his tall and handsome son to the theater and opera in nearby Jérémie; in just a few short years, Thomas-Alexandre would move easily in Paris society, admired for his grace and polished manners. The ex-soldier could certainly teach his son basic skills in riding and shooting and, most important of all to an eighteenth-century man, defending oneself with a blade.

Holding his old military saber, Antoine could tell tales of their Norman ancestors and of his own experiences in the wars, and of how the Duke de Richelieu stabbed the Prince de Lixen to death before his eyes. But what must the fair-skinned old man have felt, teaching his half-black son to duel like a young musketeer, darting in and out of the mangrove trees, glimpsing a talent for fighting that the family had not produced before, at least not in living memory? It was a talent that was about to become more significant than either of them could have imagined.

NORMAN CONQUEST

IN the early 1750s, just when his rapidly increasing wealth allowed him to buy his plantation outright, Charles Davy de la Pailleterie was beset by that scourge of eighteenth-century prosperity—gout. His doctors told him the Caribbean climate was worsening the condition and he would be better-off returning to France. So, leaving his plantation and its more than two hundred slaves in the care of administrators, Charles and his wife and teenage daughter, Marie-Anne, sailed for Normandy.

For a time they moved in with Charles's parents at the Pailleterie château in Bielleville. The marquis and marquise were gratified at the return of their successful son, who, after all, had been sending them money. There was nothing better, in eighteenth-century France, than having a *planter* in the family.

Charles's father told him about a recent money squabble over a strongbox full of coins that had been found in the château, hidden inside a straw mattress. The marquis's widowed sister claimed that she'd hidden the money and that it was hers. The marquis disputed her claim. A notary was brought in to resolve the matter, and when he asked Charles's aunt if she'd hidden the coins herself, she admitted she had not. But then the elderly lady suddenly threw herself bodily on top of the strongbox, crying and kicking and forcing the notary to struggle with her to regain control of it. As she did, it was recorded, the widow "hit and bit a witness." This was a vivid illustration of how things might go in the Pailleterie family when issues of inheritance arose.

After the deaths of the marquis and, a short time later, the marquise, though Antoine was next in line, Charles moved in to assert his claim to be the oldest living Pailleterie brother. As a court document later stated:

not knowing whether their older brother existed, in which country of the universe he could be if he did, and allowed by a silence of [so many] years to believe he was dead, [the two younger brothers] divided between them the revenues of the estate in accordance with the customs of the region. Charles Edouard then assumed all the advantages that the law accords to the eldest son.

As the new Marquis Davy de la Pailleterie, Charles settled into the ancestral château and all the property that came with it, while about a quarter of the rents and property went to the youngest brother, Louis. In short order Charles managed to get himself presented at Versailles and befriended powerful aristocrats such as the Marquis de Mirabeau (father of the revolutionary orator). He used his sugar plantation to secure loans and guarantees with which he began buying French real estate, and he borrowed ever larger sums to finance a lavish lifestyle.

But even as his fortunes rose, Charles knew that the plantation was doing badly. The outbreak of the Seven Years' War and its English embargo had wreaked havoc on colonial shipping; exports had slowed to the point where he lost tens of thousands of livres' worth of cane to spoilage. Large quantities of refined sugar were sitting around his storehouse, unable to be shipped. The business was in serious trouble. Yet with powerful new friends and his new title, Charles seems to have felt he was well equipped to fund a venture that promised to relieve his difficulties.

Whatever else they lacked, men in the Pailleterie—and, later, the Dumas—family never wanted for daring. War might have cut off official traffic between French and British colonies, but it hadn't reduced Europe's demand for sugar or the colonies' demand for slaves. Charles devised a scheme to smuggle "white sugar of the highest quality" out of his plantations in Saint-Domingue to New York. The ships would sail down the Atlantic coast flying British colors but enter Saint-Domingue waters with a set of blank passports from Versailles obtained through Charles's court connections. Charles formed a partnership with a French shipping magnate and a pair of Dutch brothers, based out of Amsterdam and New York.

Charles's smuggling scheme made use of a wharf located on a stretch of coastline just north of his Saint-Domingue plantations, which straddled the border of the French and Spanish colonies and was thus neutral territory. The place was called Monte Cristo.*

The plan went well at first, and Charles sent at least one load of pure white sugar from Monte Cristo to Amsterdam. But the waters were crawling with English ships, and the journey became fraught with risk. Eventually, the partners grew impatient and soured on the scheme, which had not made them as rich as fast as they had hoped and required them to trust one another with large sums of money over long distances.

In May 1760, Charles traveled to London—incognito, via Amsterdam, since France and England were still at war—to meet with a British banker from whom he was seeking capital to expand his smuggling business. But then someone suggested to Charles a new venture might bring greater profits than sugar smuggling: slave trading.

Charles asked his business manager to look into the costs and benefits of buying "pieces of India," as slaves were known (a term of barter), "from the Gold Coast or Angola" and selling them in Saint-Domingue. Evidently getting a good report, not long afterward Charles formed a partnership with a captain who had been working for the Foäche brothers, Stanislas and Martin, who were among the biggest shipowners in Normandy, having converted nineteen of their ninety-one ships into slavers. The Foäche brothers were the pinnacle of eighteenth-century slave-and-sugar wealth—at one point, they actually lent the king over one million livres for the administration of Saint-Domingue—and it was Charles's great aspiration to enter their league.

Charles bought a ship, and in a sign that he had no guilt whatsoever about his new enterprise, he rechristened it in honor of his daughter. The *Douce Marianne* sailed to British Sierra Leone, carrying, among other things, 225 bottles of champagne and 300 bottles of hard cider, and then picked up "300 captives at the Factory of Miles Barber from Lancaster."("Factories" were slave-wholesaling outposts, often on islands near the West African coast.)

Trading slaves could bring big profits fast but huge losses if something went wrong. And, as had happened to all of Charles's ventures since he'd

---

*Monte Cristo—sometimes spelled "Monte Christo"—included a small port city, a shoreline, a mountain, and a river. It still exists on maps of the area. The island of "Monte Cristo"—which Charles seems to have also used in his smuggling schemes—lay just off the coast, conveniently inside Spanish colonial waters.

begun life as a high aristocrat, something went very wrong. The ship's super-cargo, whom Charles had hired to travel to Sierra Leone to buy the slaves, turned out to be a volatile type; off the African coast, he got into a fight with the captain of the *Douce Marianne* and helped the crew to mutiny, locking the captain in his cabin. (After a few weeks, they transferred him to a small shed on deck, where they kept him locked up for three months.) Meanwhile the crew turned the ship into a debauched party, drinking and eating much of the supplies and abusing the slave women. They sailed to Martinique, against Charles's express orders, where they sold some of the slaves for their own profit. Records show that they ended up delivering less than half the original cargo to their destination in Saint-Domingue. Charles's first slaving venture was a bust.

One can only imagine the human suffering implied in the ship's fate. But to Charles it meant only that another business venture had increased his debt rather than his wealth. He tried again, but the second voyage of the *Douce Marianne*, though mutiny-free, was equally unprofitable. Charles's slaving operation was considered contemptible even by the low standards of the slaving business: Stanislas Foäche described him and his staff as "demanding, unjust, and ignorant of the business they're engaged in." And the magnate added, "His plantations could produce 600 metric tons of white sugar, [but] he's found the secret to making only 200. His workshops are in a terrible state." Foäche summed up the problem of working with Charles: "We will lose a lot of blacks."

In a perverse sense, it was appropriate that Charles named his slave ship after his daughter, for his most pressing need for cash was to pay back the ridiculous sums of money he had borrowed to cut a figure in society in the buildup to Marie-Anne's wedding. Her fiancé, a young count named Léon de Maulde, was from a nobler family than the Pailleteries, and he himself believed he was marrying new money that would help him pay off his family's debts.

Marie-Anne de la Pailleterie married Count Léon de Maulde in the chapel of Saint-Sulpice on May 4, 1764. As the notices in the *Gazette de France* make clear, her wedding was a major social affair, with the cream of French society in attendance. Her dowry included diamonds, sumptuous clothes, buildings, and hundreds of thousands in promised cash. The marriage contract was duly signed by the king and all the members of the royal family.

But Charles's debts overwhelmed his assets, and some of the great men at the wedding—notably his patron, Mirabeau—would soon become his angriest creditors. Charles returned to slaving in the hope of hitting it big. He staked his daughter's future—and his own—on the slave ship bearing her name.

"All your creditors are ready to attack," his son-in-law, the Count de Maulde, wrote from Paris in the spring of 1773. By that point Charles had moved back to Saint-Domingue, hoping to take his properties there in hand. But his plantation was in a dire state, with "houses, stables, and processing equipment" collapsing, one of Charles's managers wrote. "Forty-five of his negroes are sick and the others are pushed to the limit because they lack food and yet are forced to work. There are many dead for these two reasons."

As if ceding to fate, Charles himself collapsed—in a house he had bought in Le Cap to be close to his plantation—and, succumbing to complications of gout, died. Stanislas Foäche, for one, mourned his passing by noting: "M. de la Pailleterie just died, fortunately for his family, because he put his business in the greatest disorder."

Three months after Charles's death, Louis de la Pailleterie, still a soldier, was caught up in a scandal involving selling defective weapons to the French army. His reputation ruined, he spent fifteen days in a military prison and a month later, he, too, dropped dead.

The novelist Dumas would one day borrow features from both of his uncles, not to mention his grandfather, the acknowledged scoundrel, in fashioning the central villains of *The Count of Monte Cristo*. Reading court documents detailing the sordid unraveling of Charles's sham fortune, which would have devastating effects on his daughter and her unsuspecting husband, I couldn't help thinking that one of the interesting things about Dumas's villains is that, while greedy and unprincipled themselves, they produce children who can be innocent and decent. This was something that the writer understood very well from his own family.

With two Pailleterie brothers dead and Antoine missing and presumed dead, the title and property—along with the mountains of debt—passed to Marie-Anne and her husband. All the illustrious folk who'd been at their wedding now came to call as creditors, demanding that the estate pony up; the Marquis de Mirabeau claimed Charles had signed documents that meant he must be "first in line" among the Pailleteries' creditors. The Count de

Maulde estimated that his wife had inherited a quantity of debts that only the sale of her entire estate could match. He arranged for one of Charles's former agents in Saint-Domingue to assess the plantation, but received a dispiriting report: "[The] possessions are deteriorated, the slave houses fall into ruin, the cane fields are almost abandoned, the slaves are out of serviceable condition. It is a terrible picture."

Within two years, however, through careful long-distance management, Maulde had the plantation on its way back to a profitable crop. He had also settled with some of Charles's creditors and begun making plans for the sale of the Bielleville château to pay off the rest. The Pailleterie brothers had left destruction in their wake, but with that generation apparently out of the way, things seemed at last to be looking up for their more respectable heirs.

◆—◆

THE French military ship the *Trésorier* dropped anchor in Le Havre, Normandy, in the first week of December 1775. The vessel had sailed from Port-au-Prince, Saint-Domingue, and only one passenger disembarked. He was a rugged man of perhaps sixty, slender yet strapping, with the red-tinged tan of a Viking inured to the sun. He gave his name to the dockside customs official, who duly noted it in his book: "Antoine Delisle."

The keeper of the inn where Antoine Delisle stayed that night recalled that, for a stranger, he seemed to know the area remarkably well. Delisle wrote a number of letters from the inn, including one to the Abbé Bourgeois, the priest of the Bielleville estate. The following week he went to meet the Abbé and introduced himself: "I am Alexandre Antoine Davy de la Pailleterie, Father. I have returned from Saint-Domingue." For proof, he showed the priest his baptismal certificate, inscribed at the little church of Bielleville on February 26, 1714. "You will tell me what has happened and I will give you my instructions. I am the oldest son, the right is mine."

The Abbé thought he saw a strong resemblance to the Pailleterie brothers, but he wasn't sure. A resemblance wasn't proof, after all. This man could have stolen Alexandre Antoine's baptismal certificate or acquired it in some other way. But the stranger told him things about Alexandre Antoine's early life that the Abbé could not imagine anyone else knowing.

Now convinced the stranger was indeed the rightful heir, the Abbé wrote that night to the Count de Maulde, the man who would be most affected by the prodigal's return. He was at his family's estate, in the Champagne region. The Abbé suggested he come at once to Caux.

The Count de Maulde carefully noted the receipt of the Abbé's letter, as he did all events, in his family's account register:

December 11, 1775, letter from the priest of la Pailleterie, M. Bourgeois, who informs me of the return of M. de la Pailleterie, the eldest brother.

He crossed out the word "return" and inserted "appearance"—*apparition,* which in French, as in English, is also used for ghosts and supernatural visions. Maulde promptly replied: he was ready to recognize the return of the eldest Pailleterie brother once he'd met him and seen proof. In the meantime, he would not try to prevent Antoine's moving into the Bielleville château.

━━

ANTOINE moved out of the inn and installed himself in the family château in the second week of December 1775. The cold stone building, its many levels united by winding staircases and sloping roofs, must have been a shock after his years in the tropics. It was in poor repair but essentially the same as when he'd left; the primitive sailing boats he and Charles had carved in the stone of their bedroom wall, dreaming of adventures at sea, were still there. The staff was minimal, but the housekeeper, Mademoiselle Marie Retou, a spinster in her early thirties, seemed eager to please. She would take care of him during his first Christmas in France in more than thirty years.

Antoine's first official callers were Marie-Anne and Léon de Maulde. He did not treat them graciously. The Mauldes did everything they could to reason with "Uncle Antoine"—they'd sacrificed much to put his deceased brother's estate in order; they'd been promised a fortune under false pretenses and had since improved the condition of the inheritance—but the businesslike count soon saw the hopelessness of fighting the claims of the resurrected eldest son. He proposed that he and his wife give up all of their previous rights and claims against the estate in exchange for an annuity to help offset their costs. They drafted and signed an agreement with Antoine in March 1776.

To strengthen his case in any court battles, and perhaps also to satisfy his curiosity, the Count de Maulde decided to investigate Antoine's mysterious island interlude. Using the connections he'd made while inspecting Charles's Saint-Domingue properties, Maulde found a retired king's attorney living in Jérémie, a Monsieur de Chauvinault, to carry out an investigation.

Chauvinault reported that despite a promising start in the highlands, by the time he left, Antoine's property was worth little; in fact, the detective identified unpaid debts that Antoine owed on the island worth ten times the value of what he'd owned in Great Cove. Poor Maulde must have marveled at the similarities among the Pailleterie brothers and wondered anew how he could have had the luck to marry into a family of such thoroughgoing scoundrels.

Unlike his brother's affairs, however, Antoine's had not been primarily financial. So Chauvinault concentrated on uncovering and clarifying the prodigal's sexual relations and his possible offspring. He first reported on Antoine's relationship with Catin, the slave girl who'd fled with him from Charles's plantation; Antoine had ended it when he found her too old but, Chauvinault noted, had allowed her to live out her life as a free woman.

Chauvinault then reported on Antoine's purchase, in the late 1750s, of a beautiful black woman named Marie Cessette, for whom he'd paid that "exorbitant price," implying some unusual interest in her. From then onward, in fact, "he had always lived with her [and had with her] four mulatto children." Before Antoine's return to France, Chauvinault reported, he had sold three of his children, as well as Marie Cessette herself, to an M. Carron, of Nantes.*

The detective also brought the interesting news that Antoine's fourth child, a boy who was said to be his favorite, had *not* been sold along with the

---

* Future legal documents, notably Thomas-Alexandre's marriage certificate, contradict the investigator's conclusion about Marie Cessette. They state that she died "in La Guinodée, close to Jérémie," in 1772. No cause of death was given, but many died in the devastating hurricanes of 1772, which destroyed countless plantations in Saint-Domingue, Jamaica, and Cuba. The novelist Dumas, in his memoirs, only states that Antoine's "wife, to whom he had been warmly attached, had died in 1772; and as she managed the estate it deteriorated in value daily after her death." He implies that Marie Cessette's death was a cause of Antoine's decision to return to France. I have scoured every record and found no concrete evidence of her fate. Strikingly Thomas-Alexandre himself never mentioned his mother, at least in no document or letter I could find.

others. This boy was "a young mulatto who, it is said, was sold at Port au Prince," Chauvinault wrote, "conditionally, with the right of redemption, to Captain Langlois, for 800 livres, which served as the passage of Sir Delisle to France."

Arriving at the dock in Port-au-Prince, Antoine might simply have found he needed extra to pay his passage and sold his remaining son to buy it without a second thought. It would have been the final selfish gesture of a man who'd only ever looked out for his pleasures—as if, having sold off his lovers and children one by one, Antoine had kept his favorite mulatto son as one might keep a precious ring in one's shoe, to be sold in case of emergency. But such an interpretation is belied by the crucial detail in Chauvinault's description: The sale of the boy had been carried out *"conditionally, with the right of redemption."*

Antoine may have sold the rest of his family outright, but he had pawned his son Thomas-Alexandre. Restored to his title and property in France, he could now redeem the pledge.

—◆—

THOMAS-ALEXANDRE Dumas Davy de la Pailletrie, fourteen, stepped onto the dock in Le Havre on August 30, 1776. He was listed in the ship's manifest as "the slave Alexandre," belonging to a "Lieutenant Jacques-Louis Roussel." This was a necessary ruse, because a young mulatto could not simply walk off a boat into France by himself. Antoine had bought back his son's freedom from Captain Langlois and paid for his safe passage to Normandy in the company of an "owner."

Life in a Norman château must have been astonishing for a young man who had just been a slave in Port-au-Prince. And the new marquis's dark-skinned son must have equally been a surprise for the mostly blond, blue-eyed villagers of Bielleville. But the first mention I found of Thomas-Alexandre in France—in a badly torn letter from November 1776, from the Abbé Bourgeois to the Count de Maulde—referred to him offhandedly. The Abbé was more concerned with letting Maulde know of Antoine's apparent love affair with the housekeeper, Mademoiselle Retou, which threatened the estate with a marriage. "Monsieur and dear lord," the Abbé wrote:

I want to be the first to tell you that Monsieur your uncle envisages to augment the household with a live-in companion. He seemed to me uncompromising, declaring that he was free to do what he thought fit. Everything he [does] is in the worst possible taste. M. le Marquis seems determined to marry the girl and will not let anyone joke about it ([Another man] joked a little about that girl the other day—[the Marquis] de la Pailleterie didn't utter a word). . . . It is said that young Thomas has reached Le Havre, new inhabitant for Bielleville . . . (I write all this down for you only because you asked me to, but I hope you will only use it if the occasion requires it because I heard that he is mad at me.) Please burn this letter.

Having redeemed Thomas-Alexandre, Antoine decided to pawn the family estate.

He refused to honor the various commitments he had made to the Mauldes, and now the widow of Louis de la Pailleterie took all the parties to court to gain her piece of the pie before Antoine could consume it. Antoine's nephew-in-law and niece found themselves in the midst of a fierce legal battle with the previous generation.

Antoine, for his part, had come back from the jungle in a litigious mood. He seemed to relish every battle against the various members of his family. He won the right to call himself the Marquis de la Pailleterie, plus the right to the château and its land—while cleverly keeping most of the estate's debts at arm's length. In February 1777, Antoine flipped the main house of the estate, in a complicated deal, for a 10,000-livre annual annuity, to be paid to him by his now furious nephew-in-law, and he forked over the rest—lands, fief, seigneurie, farms, and château—to a Monsieur Bailleul, a neighboring landowner, for a cool 67,000 livres. (The young Count de Maulde lamented his plight to everyone, complaining in one letter, "Never has fortune persecuted anyone as cruelly as me.")

Meanwhile, Antoine bought himself and his son new outfits of silk, satin, and brocade and went house hunting. He also took Thomas-Alexandre to a baptism, where the young man signed the witness book—the first existing sample of his handwriting—as "Thomas Retoré, the natural son of Monsieur le Marquis de la Pailleterie who had been living in Saint-Domingue." It may have been a sign of his disorientation that he used the name "Retoré," which was perhaps picked up from a neighbor in Jérémie (where the name can be found on official records of the period).

In the fall of 1778, cash in hand, Antoine and his son moved to Saint-Germain-en-Laye, a small city on the western side of Paris. In some ways like an elegant suburb, Saint-Germain-en-Laye had been an aristocratic enclave in the time of the Sun King, not unlike a satellite Versailles, with its own royal palace. But in the mid-1700s, it had transformed into one of France's richest and fastest-growing small cities, thanks to an influx of industrious merchants and educated professionals, along with laborers and artisans to serve them. There could hardly have been a more pleasant place to live, with fresh country air, a reasonable coach ride to Paris, and magnificent strolling along the tiered steps of cliffside royal gardens.

With his son, Antoine brought along one other person from Normandy to his new life of luxury—the housekeeper, Mademoiselle Retou. The unlikely trio rented rooms in a townhouse on the rue de l'Aigle d'Or, "the Street of the Golden Eagle"—a fitting name, because of the golden eagles in the Davy de la Pailleterie coat of arms. The street was a winding, narrow passage of townhouses and shops close to Saint-Germain-en-Laye's palace and gardens.

It was also a short walk from the academy of the royal fencing teacher, Nicolas Texier de La Boëssière, where Antoine enrolled his son in his first formal lessons. Along with swordsmanship, the school instructed young men of quality in all facets of their intellectual, physical, and social development, providing the equivalent of a top secondary school education.

Antoine had legally recognized his son just before their move, so the boy now had the right to call himself Thomas-Alexandre Davy de la Pailleterie. Since Antoine was a marquis, "the slave Alexandre" was now a count.

Life in the French capital was complicated for a young mulatto aristocrat, and, as Thomas-Alexandre would shortly discover, he was alone neither in his unlikely fortune nor in the risks that increasingly accompanied it. Other mixed-race men were living in the land of the Bourbons. Some had wealth and noble titles; others had neither. Powers around the king had taken note of these persons—who, no matter how powdered or disguised, could not be taken as native Frenchmen—and they were not pleased.

‹ 4 ›

"NO ONE IS A SLAVE IN FRANCE"

UNTIL Antoine sold him to buy his passage, Thomas-Alexandre had rarely been away from his father. He was accustomed to Jérémie parish, where mixed-race businesspeople outnumbered whites and his father played the role of a modest, unassuming farmer. Now he found himself in the opposite situation. The man he'd known as a tough, cautious recluse was suddenly rich, titled, and carefree. There is no evidence that Antoine ever thought again about his other children, but he now seemed determined to give his remaining son every advantage, to turn him into a fashionable young count.

Thomas-Alexandre had missed crucial phases of an aristocrat's upbringing: early lessons with a governess followed by intensive tutoring and academy study, so as to be, by age ten or eleven, well versed in Latin, Greek, geography, history, grammar, philosophy, literature, and mathematics, along with dancing, a musical instrument, fencing, and riding. The idea was to give a nobleman, by the time he reached manhood at thirteen, all the skills he would ever want to shine both *à la ville et à la cour*—"in town and at court," as the expression went. Thomas-Alexandre was nearly sixteen when they moved to Saint-Germain-en-Laye, and he set about making up for lost time.

Mornings at La Boëssière's were dedicated to academics, followed by afternoons on horseback at the vast *salle du manège,* the riding hall in the Tuileries Gardens, and then fencing in the academy's *salle d'armes,* the "hall of arms" decorated with antique weapons and heraldic insignia. Thomas-Alexandre was an extraordinarily graceful athlete and excelled at all the physical arts. But he truly shone at the art for which the academy was best known. And it was here that he probably first met the mysterious swordsman, polymath, and fellow mixed-race aristocrat who would introduce him to the world of combat.

The Chevalier de Saint-Georges, a man of middling height and athletic build, was around thirty-five when Thomas-Alexandre came to La Boëssière's. Proudly elegant, he dressed in the finest clothing—silk breeches, cape, brocade vest—even when not at court. His skin was light, and made lighter by his habit of powdering it. He wore white wigs and rouged his lips in the high court style of Louis XV.

This mulatto gentleman could powder and dress as he liked, however, because he was acknowledged to be the greatest swordsman in Europe. Over the previous decade and a half, every white champion had stepped up to try to beat Saint-Georges; except for one Italian, who fought him under exceptional circumstances, they all failed.

Saint-Georges was born Joseph Boulogne on the small sugar island of Guadeloupe, in 1745, to a wealthy white father, likely a royal finance officer, and a free black mother named Nanon. Like Antoine, Joseph's father became a fugitive, in his case after he was accused of murder. He fled the island for France and was condemned to death in absentia. Less than two years later, however, he received a royal pardon, and he returned to Guadeloupe to collect his son. When Joseph was thirteen, his father enrolled him at La Boëssière's, where his fencing skill immediately announced a prodigy.

A crack shot and a great equestrian to boot, Saint-Georges had become an honorary member of the king's guard—allowed to take the title of "chevalier," essentially a knight—as a result of avenging a racist insult. A decade followed during which he became the heavyweight champion of the blade. But then the Chevalier de Saint-Georges changed course and decided to devote himself to music. Proclaimed almost as great a violin virtuoso as he was a fencer—he'd likely played since he was a boy in Guadeloupe—he turned to composing and conducting and received the patronage of Marie-Antoinette, fierce Austrian music snob that she was, who proclaimed him the only maestro in her adopted land worth listening to.

The chevalier's multiple talents were well summed up by John Adams, visiting Paris in 1779: The "mulatto man," wrote the future American president, "is the most accomplished man in Europe in riding, shooting, fencing, dancing, music. He will hit a button on the coat or waistcoat of the masters. He will hit a crown piece in the air with a pistoll [*sic*] ball." The chevalier eventually hit a racial ceiling. When he was nominated managing director of the new Royal Academy of Music and director of the Paris Opera, three of the Opera's divas submitted a letter to the queen protesting that their honor would never allow them to be directed by a mulatto.

By the late 1770s, the chevalier was devoting most of his time to his music and his love life, but he kept up with the blade by sparring with promising young fencers at La Boëssière's. One white student at the academy, whose diary otherwise reveals him as a thoroughgoing racist, wrote enviously of watching Saint-Georges duel with a "very rich young man, who was of the same race as he."

Thomas-Alexandre was going on seventeen, nearly four years older than Saint-Georges had been when he'd entered the academy, but his style was more muscular and aggressive, using his full height, speed, and power. He was a saber man. This would prove a fateful proclivity; while the shorter épée was polite society's favored dueling sword, the longer, heavier saber was the consummate blade for battle.

＞－＜

BUT how was it possible, when the French slave empire was at its height, for the sons of slaves, men of color, to be living as gentlemen in Paris—the capital of France, of Europe itself? The answer is that in France's courtrooms, no less than in its academies, an equally impressive and unexpected combat had been taking place.

French Enlightenment philosophers liked to use slavery as a symbol of human oppression, and particularly political oppression. "Man is born free but is everywhere in chains," wrote Jean-Jacques Rousseau in *The Social Contract* in 1762. A generation of crusading lawyers put Enlightenment principles into action by helping slaves sue for the right to be treated as ordinary French subjects. They took the issue of human bondage to the sovereign *parlement* courts of France—and won, in nearly every case, liberty for their black and mixed-race clients. The infuriated Louis XV found his hands tied. The phrase "absolute monarchy" is misleading: *Ancien Régime* France was a state of laws, of ancient precedents, where the spark of enlightened reason could and occasionally did ignite great things.

Royal France did not have a legislative body like the Parliament in England. The French *parlements* were judicial bodies. While the admiralty courts handled disputes arising from sea warfare and colonial commerce, most important matters went to the twelve regional *parlements*—and to the Parlement of Paris, also called the *Parlement par excellence*. The Parlement of Paris was a kind of superregional court, whose rulings were enforced in territories far beyond the capital's city limits, including almost one-third of the territory of France, and even the king at Versailles could find himself caught in the web of its jurisdiction. There disputes were subject to debate according to the ancient customs of France.*

Decades before the 1772 Somerset decision in London sparked the British abolitionist movement, French lawyers arguing before the *parlements* started, with their pens, a fight that Thomas-Alexandre and Saint-Georges would eventually take up with their swords.

It was all made possible by the concept, going back to the misty foundations of the nation, that France was the land of the free—that no one should be kept in unwilling servitude on its soil. The idea of applying this concept to the condition of slaves arriving in French ports began in the late sixteenth century. However, one instance at the end of the seventeenth century, just as the French Empire was taking off and black slave labor was exploding, set a kind of precedent and began the era of the judicially fought "freedom principle," which continued down to the Revolution. That case was resolved when Louis XIV, the Sun King, personally acknowledged a black slave's undeniable right to freedom once he landed on French soil.

It happened in 1691, when two slaves escaped their master in Martinique and stowed away on a ship to France. Once they reached port, the slaves were discovered and the situation was brought to the attention of the king. Louis XIV had only six years earlier promulgated the Code Noir for the French colonial empire. Slavery was one thing for the empire, however, and another thing entirely within France itself.

"The King has been informed that two negroes from Martinique crossed

---

* The Sun King's famous statement *"L'État, c'est moi"*—"I am the state"—was supposedly made during an argument he had with the Parlement of Paris. Indeed, Louis XIV managed largely to suppress the *parlements*. After his death in 1715, however, the noble law courts reasserted themselves, and most important government rules were made not on the king's whim but rather based on the extensive study of French "customary law." Unlike France's modern legal system, based on the Napoleonic Code, the *Ancien Régime* system relied heavily on precedent: France was governed through maxims distilled by lawyers examining hundreds of years' worth of paper. Absent a legislative body like England's Parliament, these French high courts not only interpreted the law, they wrote it. The power and independence of the *Ancien Régime* courts is all but forgotten today.

on the ship the *Oiseau*," reads the laconic record of the incident in the Royal Naval Ministry. "[His Majesty] has not judged it apropos to return them to the isles, their liberty being acquired by the laws of the kingdom concerning slaves, as soon as they touch the Soil." The slaves were free.

In a letter apologizing to the royal intendant of Martinique (a post that combined the roles of governor and police chief), the French secretary of state for colonial affairs wrote that he had tried to find a way to appeal the king's decision but had "not found any ordinance which permits colonists to keep their negro slaves in France when they want to take advantage of the liberty acquired by all who touch its soil."

Similar principles existed, theoretically, in other northern European countries, particularly in Great Britain. "England was too pure an air for slaves to breathe in," a popular expression went, and the song "Rule, Britannia!" featured the chorus "Rule, Britannia! Britannia, rule the waves: Britons never will be slaves." But the song did not apply to outlanders and certainly not to blacks from the islands. As an early-eighteenth-century British judge put it, "The law takes no notice of the Negro."*

In 1715, a young black girl traveling with her mistress in France was temporarily placed by her, for safekeeping, in a convent in the port city of Nantes. When she later returned to retrieve her property, the nuns refused to surrender the girl. The local admiralty court declared the girl to be free because the owner did not declare her as a slave when entering the country. The mayor of Nantes, France's main transit port for slaves and colonial products, appealed to Versailles to enact some sort of law to deal with such situations. The government responded by issuing the Edict of October 1716, intended to allow French subjects to bring their slaves into the country without risk of forfeiting them to lawsuits. But like the Code Noir in the colonies, the Edict of October 1716 provided opportunities for slaves by codifying their condition. It helped as well as harmed them. On the one hand, it acknowledged the legal institution of slavery and extended to owners protection from "freedom

---

* Until the Somerset decision, which was itself influenced by the many court cases in Paris, British courts passed only contradictory rulings on slavery and British lawmakers avoided passing laws on the subject. In the Thirteen Colonies, slaves actually had some luck petitioning for their freedom in various colonies, such as Massachusetts and even Virginia, but they found no consistent precedents defending the right to freedom, or courts that could decide the issue on more than a local or regional basis.

principle" lawsuits if they met certain conditions. The edict recognized two reasons for bringing slaves into the country: to teach them a trade or craft, or to provide them with religious education. If a master filled out the bureaucratic paperwork seeking permission from his colonial governor to travel with his slave and registered the slave upon arrival in France, the slave could not subsequently sue for his or her freedom. On the other hand: "If the masters fail to observe the formalities prescribed by the preceding articles, the blacks will be free, and will not be able to be reclaimed."

In the event, the Parlement of Paris, offended by the mere use of the word "slave" in a law governing actions within the kingdom, refused to register the law. A lawyer consulting for the high court used the occasion to produce an elaborate condemnation of the institution of slavery itself, on the grounds that it conflicted with, among other things, French legal tradition, French history, and Christianity. France had long been known as the first Christian country in Europe, the lawyer wrote, and "the God of the Christians is the God of liberty."

The next great leap for slaves' rights came two decades later, in June 1738, when the courts received a request from a slave petitioning for freedom. It came from a young man sitting in a prison cell in central Paris. His name was Jean Boucaux, and he had been the property of the governor of Saint-Domingue. But then the governor had died and a series of events ensued that led to Boucaux's arrest. His crime: getting married.

The trouble really started with another marriage—that of the governor's widow. Upon remarrying, in France, the widow, with her new husband, a low-ranking military man named Bernard Verdelin, had gone back to Saint-Domingue to settle her affairs. Among the inherited property they brought back to France with them was Jean. For the next decade Jean served as their cook. But then he fell in love with a Frenchwoman and secretly married her. The Edict of 1716 specified that a slave's marrying while in France was one of the conditions that voided his owner's rights over him. The edict also stated that slaves could marry only with their owner's permission. How the courts might decide the case was in doubt, but his owners had Jean arrested before he could bring suit.

Since getting married, Jean had been "the object of Verdelin's hatred. He suffered indisputably cruel treatment," wrote a well-known lawyer who took on Jean's case. A former royal prosecutor joined Jean's cause as well, and the illustrious legal team not only petitioned for his freedom and his right to rejoin his French wife; they sued Jean's masters for back pay for the years he had served as their cook. They got their client out of the cell and placed under royal protection pending trial.

Jean's trial would be a linchpin for defining blacks' rights in France during the fifty years before the Revolution, as his lawyers set out to prove, once and for all, that slavery was illegal, immoral, and, worst of all, anti-French.

In their opening statements, Jean's lawyers painted a panorama of slavery in ancient times, emphasizing that the institution had reached France with the Roman legions' enslaving of the Gauls, theoretically the ancestors of everyone in the courtroom except their client. From there, they argued that the Franks, who had founded the French nation and empire, had been fundamentally opposed to slavery. (The argument was etymological as well as historical, referring to the roots of the word "franc," which originally meant "free.") They quoted a passage from a book called *The Universal History of the World*, published in Paris in 1570, which stated: "The custom is such that not only the French, but foreigners arriving in French ports and crying 'France and liberty!' are beyond the power of those who possess them; [their owners] lose the price of the sale, and the service of the slave, if the slave refuses to serve them."*

Throughout the trial, Jean's lawyers portrayed their client's race as incidental to the greater issues at hand. In fact, they argued that he was "French, because he was born the subject of our monarch; our equal, as much by humanity as by the religion which he professes; and citizen, because he lives with us and among us." Nor was the race of the woman he married mentioned, though the miscegenation issue would have set an Anglo-American courtroom of the time ablaze.

Verdelin's attorney did not dispute the validity of the freedom principle,

---

* More than a century later, the American slave Dred Scott would try a version of this, claiming that his periodic residence in free territories should mean that he could not legally be kept in bondage. The United States Supreme Court ruled, in 1857, that Scott, as a person with African ancestry, was not a citizen, and therefore could not even bring suit, and that blacks, were "regarded as beings of an inferior order, and altogether unfit to associate with the white race, either in social or political relations." Justice Campbell, writing for the majority, attacked the decision in the Boucaux case.

but, he said, there was one small problem: *the principle had never been meant to apply to blacks*. The French rule that "whoever sets foot in this kingdom is free" was true for "any slave other than a negro slave." Slaves from Poland, Georgia, the Levant, or India would all be covered. American Indians would count. "If a foreigner or a French merchant arrives in this kingdom with some American savages that he claims as his slaves," the attorney said, this would be no problem: a clear violation of the law, set the men free. But blacks, Africans, were a different matter. To apply the freedom principle to blacks, he argued, would bring on a mass slave revolt in France's colonies: "the infinite riches that the King and the Nation take from these fertile regions would become the price of the disorder and of the revolt."

Jean won. The court ruled in his favor on all counts. His former master was ordered to give him 4,200 livres in back pay, plus court costs and damages for false imprisonment. The Verdelins appealed, but the king declared himself eager to "terminate this affair which, as you know, has already created too much uproar," and declined to reopen the case. However, in a sign of where he would stand, Louis XV banished Jean Boucaux from Paris and decreed that he must never return to his native Saint-Domingue, either.

In the trial's aftermath, the king proclaimed a new edict to address the problem of "the greater part of the negroes [contracting] a spirit of independence [in France] which may have troublesome results." It contained a toxic new provision: if owners failed to register their slaves or kept them in France longer than allowed or for an unauthorized purpose, the result would not be freedom for the slave—rather, he or she would be "confiscated for the profit of the King" and returned to the sugar colonies. The new law even prohibited owners from *voluntarily* freeing slaves on French soil (except in their last will and testament).

The freedom suits dried up, and as the 1740s brought Louis XV military victories and prestige he entered the brief period in his reign that gave rise to his overstated sobriquet "Louis the Well-Loved." But in the 1750s, as his reign was entering one of its more typical periods of failure and discord, a new flood of freedom suits hit the courts, and once again blacks began winning every case, either outright or on appeal. A generation of grandstanding trial attorneys took up the cause of "French freedom" as a fast route to notoriety and renown. These lawyers saw themselves as militant philosophes, a vision captured in a 1770 memoir by the civil rights crusader Henrion de Pansey: "Servitude, like a destructive volcano, desiccates, burns, engulfs everything it surrounds: liberty, on the contrary, always brings in its wake happiness, abundance, and the arts. . . . Everything is free in a Kingdom where liberty is seated at the foot of the throne, where the least subject finds in the heart of his king the feelings of a father. . . . No one is [a] slave in France."

The response to these idealistic antislavery crusaders was given by a former lawyer for the Parlement of Paris, Guillaume Poncet de la Grave, who had changed sides and gone over to work as a royal attorney to the Admiralty. This miserable precursor of so many villains of the nineteenth and twentieth centuries said that the courts' whole way of presenting the problem was wrong: The problem was not *slaves* in France. The problem was *blacks* in France.

"The introduction of too many blacks into France, whether as slaves or in any other guise, is dangerous. We will soon see the French nation disfigured," Poncet wrote, reacting to the case of a mulatto named Louis who had just been declared free and rewarded back wages. "The negroes are, in general, dangerous men. There is practically not one of those to whom one has given their liberty who has not abused it."

Poncet called for the compulsory registration of every black in France, slave or free, to manage the threat.

—◦—

WHILE Poncet was decrying a nation "disfigured" by mixed blood, Thomas-Alexandre's future mentor, then still known as Joseph Boulogne, was proving that skin color was no measure of a man. He had been admitted to La Boëssière's academy the same year Poncet joined the admiralty court. "No one has ever deployed more grace," the younger La Boëssière wrote of his friend. "Such dexterity must seem incredible to those who have not seen it with their own eyes." When another fencing master sneeringly referred to Joseph as "La Boëssière's mulatto," Joseph's white father encouraged him to stand up to the insult and actually promised him a new horse and carriage if he won the duel. Though young Joseph may have been thinking more about winning the carriage, the duel had great symbolism for civil rights partisans and race-law advocates alike. Many courtiers and other prominent people wagered on it. Hundreds packed the hall of arms and watched this elegant young man of color handily vanquish his more experienced opponent with "a perpetual series of hits" that were unsurprising to those who had seen him practice.

No matter what the king felt about men of color in France, he celebrated the victory by making Joseph a member of his elite honor guard, a *gen d'armes*—"man-at-arms"—attached to Versailles. This elite formation, sporting scarlet doublets with silver braid, stood beside the king on ceremonial occasions. Joseph had assumed the title of "chevalier" himself, and since a knight had to be "of" someplace, he called himself the Chevalier de Saint-Georges (some said it was after a plantation his father had owned in Guadeloupe). But even as Joseph Boulogne became a chevalier, Poncet de la Grave was promoted to king's prosecutor. And he expanded his demand that blacks be registered to include men of color—indeed, anyone with the slightest tinge of African blood residing in France—for the supposed safety of the public.

In the spring of 1762, an ordinance was published throughout Paris and its suburbs ordering anyone who had any black African blood to appear before the Parlement of Paris tribunal to register. All residents of Paris who kept blacks on their premises had to declare them as well. There was a one-month deadline.* Poncet would attend these registration courts personally.

On May 10, 1762, Joseph's mother, Nanon, whom Joseph's father had managed to bring over two years after he and his son made the journey, came before one of the first registration courts. The young fencing prodigy was scheduled to follow her two days later.

Instead, the record shows, on May 12 Poncet and his cronies received a visit from "Nicolas Benjamin Texier de La Boëssière, Esquire, master-at-arms at the academies of the King," who came "in order to satisfy the ordinance," since he "has entrusted to him as his boarding student a mulatto called Joseph,

---

* The widespread registration that the ordinance required left a detailed historical snapshot of the black population of Paris at the time: the majority who registered came from Saint-Domingue and other West Indian islands; 25 percent came from colonial outposts around the Indian Ocean (in Mozambique, Madagascar, India, etc.), while only 10 percent came from West Africa and about 6 percent from North America. Men outnumbered women three to one, and 27 percent of the registrants identified themselves as free.

aged approximately fifteen and a half." La Boëssière explained that his charge had come to France "in order that he may be instructed in the Catholic, apostolic and Roman religion, to be given all the education suitable to a young man, subsequently to return to the aforementioned islands of America as soon as the navigation shall become free."

Poncet must have been angry to have the fencing master appear in Joseph's place—he was probably looking forward to humiliating the famed young duelist. But now that Joseph was the Chevalier de Saint-Georges, permanent man-at-arms to the king, the prosecutor could hardly insist on his coming in person. The document registering Joseph Boulogne contains Poncet's signature alongside that of La Boëssière.

►◄

DURING the next two decades, while idealistic lawyers and philosophes planted the seeds of true abolitionism in France, Poncet de la Grave spent his time preaching racial pollution to whoever would listen in the halls of Versailles and Paris. He found his most powerful allies in the Ministry of Naval and Colonial Affairs, which issued a warning that a dangerous "mixed-blood" population in Paris and other cities "multiplies every day [as a result of sexual] communication that they have with whites." Those in charge of France's empire had every reason to embrace national racist paranoia, because of the very real international problem that beset France in 1763: the loss of France's entire North American empire—the price the British extracted for the peace treaty ending the Seven Years' War. "New France," which had extended from Newfoundland to Louisiana and the Gulf of Mexico, had taken nearly two hundred years of exploration and investment to build. (France was allowed to retain its colonial outposts in India on the condition that they not be armed, clearing the way for Britain's takeover of the subcontinent.) In exchange for all this, France had retained only Saint-Domingue and its other West Indian islands—islands seen as indispensable colonies compared to everything else. The French would simply need to double down on sugar and slavery.

In 1776, the year Thomas-Alexandre arrived in France, a new proposal was drafted to respond to the issue of blacks and mixed-race people. The problem, it said, was that lawyers and philosophers had turned slavery into a referendum on ancient French rights and current politics. It repeated Poncet's old diagnosis—the issue was not one of slavery but of race—and it proposed a new solution.

On August 9, 1777, King Louis XVI decreed the Police des Noirs, a comprehensive legal code whose chilling goal had been brazenly stated in an early draft: "In the end, the race of negroes will be extinguished in the kingdom."

The Police des Noirs established "depots"—prisons, essentially, or proto-concentration camps—in the eight main French ports, for holding blacks and people of color brought onto French soil or found to be living in France illegally. The idea was to circumvent the whole fifty-year tradition of freedom trials by refusing to allow blacks into France at all: the depots were on French soil but were explicitly extraterritorial, so that the freedom principle could not apply to them. The Police des Noirs also called for rounding up all slaves who could be found to have entered illegally before 1777, for removal to the depots and subsequent deportation.

Surprisingly, the Parlement of Paris did not take a stand against these new laws. Part of the problem was that the concept of race itself was still quite new: the high court had no tradition of defending the rights of blacks per se, except as either slave or free. Persecution based purely on skin color had not been examined judicially, or, like slavery, had been used widely as a metaphor for oppression. This was a concern to Parisian gentlemen of color like Thomas-Alexandre and Saint-Georges, because it meant their status could be legally revoked, with no recourse.

In 1778, the Police des Noirs laws were supplemented by two orders. One required "colored" subjects living in Paris to carry a special certificate, with name, age, and owner (if slave). The other forbade "white" subjects from marrying "blacks, mulattos, or people of color"—a longtime goal of the hard-core racist lobby. In 1780, as Thomas-Alexandre turned eighteen, the king issued a new law prohibiting people of color from using the titles *Sieur* or *Dame* ("Sir" or "Madame"). Saint-Georges remained a chevalier—and Thomas-Alexandre was a count—but neither could use "Sir" before his name without risking arrest.

Like so many initiatives in the last years of the *Ancien Régime*, the new race laws were poorly administered. In this sense, the rule of kings offered a kind of humanity in inefficiency. It would take the rise of a different kind of leader, two decades later—Napoleon Bonaparte—for the depots to become efficient. And by then blacks and people of color in France would have experienced true freedom and thus feel the full pain of knowing what it meant to lose it.

AMERICANS IN PARIS

THOUGH Thomas-Alexandre was dark-skinned and clearly of African descent, his looks were not disparaged by his contemporaries; rather, they were admired and celebrated. "One of the handsomest men you could ever meet," a 1797 profile would declare, whose "interesting physiognomy is accompanied by a gentle and gracious manner." His "dark—very dark" looks and non-European features were taken not as signs of primitive inferiority—as they would be in nearly every time and place over the next two hundred years—but rather as echoes of antiquity, when the great civilizations had been the melting pots of the ancient world. "His frizzy hair recalls the curls of the Greeks and Romans," the 1797 profile announced. In this period of neoclassicism, no compliment was higher.

His proportions were those of a Greek hero as well. wide shoulders, a slim waist, and powerful, well-shaped legs. He was "well built at a time when it was an advantage to be well built," his son would write. "At the time of his marriage . . . his leg was the same width as my mother's waist." (In a reversal of later eras, well-proportioned legs were then far more important for men, who went around in tights or breeches, than for women, whose legs were hidden beneath floor-length gowns.) Thomas-Alexandre was tall—nearly six foot one when the average height was around five and a half feet—and his strength would be compared to Hercules's, though his hands and feet were said to be as delicate as those of the ladies he escorted about town.

Thomas-Alexandre's looks were the perfect calling card for an age that regarded a man's physique as a sign of virtue as well as vigor, and when even a city man spent much of his time on horseback and might dance the evening away with a grace that can today be seen only onstage. His natural gifts allowed him to do all these things as well as or better than youths who had been born to the life.

"In the midst of the elegant youth of that period," his son would write, "among the Fayettes, the Lameths, the Dillons, the Lauzuns, who were all his companions, my father lived as a true gentleman's son." In addition to all the new skills he was picking up, many of the things he'd done as a boy in the Great Cove highlands now stood him in good stead. Though the animals and the terrain were different, the hunt was the favored sport of French gentlemen, being viewed as the best means of staying fit for battle. (It was Louis XVI's favorite activity, along with tinkering with clocks and door locks.) After a hunt there might be feasting at a neighbor's château, or even at a palace, where the menu could include a dozen hors d'oeuvres along with as many dishes of fish, fowl, and game and, of course, wines, soups, desserts, dessert soups, and more wines. The setting might be enhanced by waterfalls, topiary gardens, artificial lakes, fireworks, and outdoor theater, with the most beautiful music seeming to rise out of the earth itself, owing to the fashion for concealing orchestras in dug-out pits (the opposite of modern gatherings, where live music adds prestige).

Thomas-Alexandre was living a life that earlier Davys could only have dreamed of. When Antoine was his age, he—like his brothers—had learned swordsmanship not at a fencing academy but at war. None of his own father's generation had had an income that did any more than maintain the property in Caux.

Antoine fully supported his son's lavish lifestyle, perhaps in vicarious wish fulfillment. He may also have relished scandalizing his niece's stuffy husband, the Count de Maulde, whose former fortune Antoine and Thomas-Alexandre were now disposing of as quickly as possible. They had made it to Paris, the capital of the empire, of the world—of everything! Here they drank Dominguan coffee with Dominguan sugar out of cups plated with Peruvian silver and Guinea gold. Here was where all the products of the empire ended up, and here they'd ended up, too.

Thomas-Alexandre could enrapture his hosts with tales of the colonial frontier, of facing down alligators and pirates. Beyond his looks, his grace, and his charm, what may have made him most attractive in this rarefied world was that he was "an American."

In late-eighteenth-century France, the term "American" was usually used synonymously with "man of color." He was from the American sugar islands, and was thus a former slave or the son of a slave. Thomas-Alexandre was newly arrived, while the Chevalier de Saint-Georges had left the islands over a quarter century before, but it made no difference: both would always be "Americans" in Paris. The term was laden with implications, of adulation or contempt, but always denoted much more than a birthplace. From 1778 onward, it had a new meaning: "comrade-in-arms."

◆◀

A handful of white British colonists living in Paris were also "Americans" (though going strictly by the French definition they were Creoles), and in early February 1778 France entered into a formal alliance with them to help them win their independence from England. The alliance was negotiated by Benjamin Franklin, whom Parisians affectionately nicknamed the "electrical ambassador," and signed by young King Louis XVI, who thus became, with irony too delicious for anyone to mention, the world's prime sponsor of anti-monarchist insurgency and revolution.

Louis XVI's government supported the Americans to get back at England for France's humiliating defeat in the Seven Years' War—for the loss of French North America and humiliation in French India. To the ministers in Versailles, the American War of Independence was the latest battle in the global war for trade and colonial power that the two countries had been fighting for a century. England had knocked France out of the Americas in 1763. France hoped to return the favor in 1778.

But the aristocratic French officers who volunteered for the American cause—the Marquis de Lafayette being only the most prominent of many—had more personal reasons than geopolitics. There was a certain restlessness, since over a decade of peace had meant few chances to prove one's mettle; all that training at La Boëssière's wasn't meant merely for garden duels. The war in America might be their sole chance for the thrill of battle. Still deeper than their desire for combat was this generation's desire to experience the exciting political concept the Americans had practically made their own: patriotism.*

---

* Among the French forces fighting for American independence at the Siege of Savannah, Georgia, in 1779: a batallion of free blacks and men of color from Saint-Domingue that included future French legislator and ex-slave Jean-Baptiste Belley, and future king of Haiti, Henri Christophe.

To be a "patriot" was all the rage in Paris. And no one admired the American patriots more than the liberal members of the French aristocracy, who saw the proud colonists as standing up to the despotism of George III. The French nobles particularly identified with the American colonists' "antitax" message.* Like slavery, the American cause had become a metaphor for what Frenchmen felt about their own condition, another proxy for the struggle of the enlightened nobility against the backward monarchy. (This also marked the beginning of the French love/hate relationship with America.)

Suddenly Paris fashion—that bellwether for the French mind—had to be *à l'Amérique*: tailors manufactured "insurgent coats" and "lightning-conductor dresses" (in honor of Ben Franklin, with two wires hanging to the ground). Hairdressers created coiffures *à la Boston* and *à la Philadelphie*. The queen's milliner created a hat *à la John Paul Jones*—it featured the kind of showy plume the queen had declared she wanted to stick in the cap of the American naval hero—as well as one that was a fully armed sailing ship, perfect down to the rigging, masts, and cannon, in honor of a recent naval battle with the British. It was a small but telling sign of the growing cognitive dissonance when, by year's end, the Paris police forbade the name of the newest hairdo—*aux insurgents*—though not the coiffure itself. This only made the style more popular.

But while Versailles tried to suppress the mere word "insurgent" at home, in its support of insurgency abroad it never looked back. Only the full tonnage and firepower of the French navy made the American Revolution more than a glorious pipedream. While Americans view the Revolutionary War as a conflict fought from Maine to Florida, France actually forced Britain to fight the Revolution as a world war, defending its outposts in India, Jamaica,

---

* New England's patriots had a fair bit in common with the French nobility on the level of tax grievance—both groups felt overtaxed and underrepresented. But when one looks at tax rates in the British Empire of the 1760s and '70s, one sees that the New England colonists, the fiercest patriots, were actually among the most lightly taxed of all British subjects. They railed against "taxation without representation," but even that was not quite accurate, because, given the workings of the British parliamentary system, many royal subjects in England were no better "represented" than the colonists, and they paid much higher taxes. A similar paradox existed in France: nobles were taxed at a lower rate than the rest of the population and, because of the *parlement* courts, were better "represented" than most other French subjects. Yet they were France's fiercest patriots, doing as much as any single group to bring on the Revolution.

and Africa. The British had to divert most of their celebrated navy from the American coast to defend against French attacks elsewhere.*

Thomas-Alexandre and La Boëssière's other students could follow news of the adventures of France's finest on the battlefields of Massachusetts, New York, Maryland, and Virginia as the French navy terrorized the British from the West Indies to the Bay of Bengal. And when the young Viscount Louis-Marie de Noailles, a neighbor from Saint-Germain-en-Laye, was given a role by General Washington in negotiating the British surrender at Yorktown (alongside an American negotiator), it was a final emblem of the importance of French aid in winning the American Revolution.

Thus the oldest great monarchy in the West assured the establishment of the first great republic since ancient times. In the process, Versailles bankrupted itself. In 1781 alone, the Crown spent 227 million livres, a huge portion of its budget, on the American cause; its naval costs alone were five times their normal peacetime levels. No one has ever determined exactly how Louis XVI's government came up with the money, but clearly it involved borrowing on a massive scale.

The peace deal that ended the Revolutionary War was negotiated in Paris, but France got little more for its decisive help than Britain's return of Senegal. (Owing to some bizarre diplomacy, Spain received far more territory in the New World.) "France retained glory and ruin" from its American adventure, wrote the historian Michelet. The French monarchy's reputation was never higher than during the celebrations of the Anglo-American treaty in Paris in 1783.

President George Washington hung a full-length portrait of Louis XVI on his wall at Mount Vernon, and American patriotic commemorations featured toasts to the French king as "the protector of the rights of mankind," as well as to "the Count de Rochambeau and French army." For some years, the French king's birthday was even celebrated as one of the United States' first national holidays.

---

* Britain's only hope was for its navy to raid neutral ships supplying both the Americans and the French with matériel for their fleets. This hope was dashed in 1780, however, when Catherine the Great of Russia created the "League of Armed Neutrality," which united every major European power in keeping the American and French shipping lanes open; Prussia, Austria, Holland, and Spain, even the Ottoman Empire, joined the anti-British effort.

But there was something fundamentally off kilter about the most powerful monarchy in Europe being feted as the champion of "life, liberty, and the pursuit of happiness." It was not, as we now say, a sustainable situation.

The musket-toting patriot was the new chivalric knight, tilting at tyrannical redcoats. Fashionable Paris gentlemen joined Le Club de Boston ou des Américains, founded by the Duke d'Orléans, returning from a trip to England in a mood of revolutionary insouciance.

Yet, while the American Revolution would later come to be seen as a model of decorum—mainly because of its contrast with the bloody French Revolution that followed it—men like Lafayette worried that their countrymen would go wrong in revolution not by being too violent but by being too meek. "French affairs are harder to resolve because the people of this country seem in no way ready to turn to extreme measures," he wrote to Washington. " 'Liberty or death' is not a fashionable motto on this side of the Atlantic."

Eighteenth-century French intellectuals embraced the American Revolution in much the way twentieth-century French intellectuals would embrace the Russian Revolution and its offshoots—wholeheartedly. Just as their modern counterparts would talk away the oppressions of Communist regimes, so did eighteenth-century French intellectuals defend the new United States against charges—loudest from England, of course—of hypocrisy on the issue of slavery. What did it mean to declare all men free and equal if the patriots continued to keep slaves? Many of the Founding Fathers themselves foresaw that their compromise with southern states was a poison pill that would eventually lead to tragedy. But the French stalwarts of the new America found every way of glossing over the problem. Paris theaters staged plays about the idyllic life in Virginia, where black slaves and their masters sang songs of liberty as they worked together side by side.

►—◄

AS Thomas-Alexandre grew up, he spent ever more time in Paris, only a three-hour coach ride away. The City of Light must have offered many temptations after nightfall on its newly lit streets; in Saint-Germain-en-Laye, there were no streetlights at all, whereas Paris sported candlelit lamps and even brand-new oil lamps to defy the dark—even if the idea still outstripped the technology. At a distance the streetlamps "dazzle, but close to give little light, and standing underneath you can hardly see your hand before you," wrote the memoirist Louis-Sébastien Mercier, who recorded his observations throughout the 1780s. Where streetlights failed, there were lanternmen. The lanternmen—numbered, so the police could keep track of them—waited around the doors of townhouses in Paris whenever an entertainment was going on inside, and, for a few coins, one of them would accompany a reveler home, lighting his way even up the stairs and into his room. But, of course, any young gentleman like Thomas-Alexandre had a lackey to do this.

Every Frenchman of any quality had a lackey—a servant who accompanied him everywhere, attending to life's quotidian details. Dinner guests in the great houses were expected to bring their own lackeys to serve them. Ten guests meant ten lackeys, each pouring wine, ladling soup, and choosing hors d'oeuvres according to his master's preferences. This custom would not change with the Revolution, and behind even the loftiest French revolutionary was a devoted lackey. Thomas-Alexandre, though he would face every danger fighting for liberty, equality, and fraternity, would never again be without a lackey to take care of the mundane tasks. (When, years later and by then a war hero, he lost his lackey in a storm at sea, he would find himself in a true predicament: facing enemy attack was one thing; arranging his own clothes was quite another.)

Alexandre Dumas would make one of his most beloved characters, d'Artagnan, a handsome outsider from the south of France, his face "long and brown"; he also arrives in Paris knowing hardly a soul. But Thomas-Alexandre, a century and a half later, came into a far vaster, and louder, city than d'Artagnan did. Everywhere was a noise "so stunning [and] appalling that only the most superhuman voice can pierce it," Mercier wrote. Fishwives hawked mackerels, herrings, oysters: "Live, live, just arrived!" Other hawkers peddled old clothes, umbrellas, gingerbread, baked apples, liquor from barrels, sweet oranges from the south.

The biggest difference, of course, was that the boy from Saint-Domingue came to the city with his father's deep purse, even if it would later be revealed to have been filled mostly with IOUs. It's something of a mystery why Antoine indulged Thomas-Alexandre to the extent he did. "M. le Marquis

wasn't living on his holdings and only had your lifetime payments," the notary in charge of Antoine's estate would later inform the benighted Count de
Maulde, "having spent all his money paying the debts for a young Dumas
(mulatto) [*sic*] that is said to be the natural son of the deceased." The notary
underlined the point about Thomas-Alexandre's habits: "This out of wedlock
child has cost him enormously."

But a young gentleman in Paris could be forgiven for burning through
cash. A respectable gallant's party ensemble of embroidered silk, satin, brocade, and velvet might cost 4,000 livres, especially once gold buckles and
three-inch bejeweled pumps were figured in. Though Thomas-Alexandre
had witnessed dazzling finery among the dandies and hostesses of Jérémie,
Paris prices were on a different scale. As Louis XIV's finance minister,
Jean-Baptiste Colbert, supposedly once said, "Fashion is to France what the
mines of Peru are to Spain."

In Paris it wasn't just what you wore—it was what you rode that told
who you were. "A carriage is the grand object of everyone in the scramble
for wealth," wrote Mercier. "At the first fortunate event, a man will set up his
one-horse chaise, then a chariot, and afterwards a coach for himself." However, there was a good reason for this: Paris streets were narrow, crowded,
and dirty, and most lacked sidewalks. Mercier devoted pages to the mud of
Paris, which "is necessarily filthy, black with grit and metal fragments detached by the eternal traffic, but it is the domestic waste running into it which
chiefly accounts for the smell. This, no foreign nose can abide; it is sulphu-
rous, with a tang of nitric acid. A spot of this mud left on a coat will eat
away the cloth." Only those Parisians already covered in muck—the poor,
the workers—could afford to walk.

For long-suffering pedestrians who considered themselves gentlemen yet
couldn't afford to replace their bright silk trousers or stockings continually,
there was a solution that gave birth to the future of French fashion: all black.
An all-black ensemble of fine materials might cost as much as a colorful outfit
but, in the long run, was far cheaper to maintain. Meanwhile, women took
to defying the mud by wearing all white, "*à la bordelaise*"—i.e. in the style
of the port city of Bordeaux, whence the all-white trend had arrived from
the sugar islands. It hit Paris in 1782, when Thomas-Alexandre was twenty.
The queen herself pushed the style when she decided on dressing strictly *à*

la bordelaise. She dazzled Versailles in her white gowns and white diamonds, with her white hair and light-blue eyes.

Diamonds. Their sparkling whiteness hung everywhere in those days—from necks, cascading down décolletages, studding practically every surface a woman could find to place them on. Grande dames and demoiselles did not limit their diamonds to necklaces, rings, and bracelets but set them in hatpins, hair bands, bouquets, and snuffboxes. Some matched their necklaces with diamond "stomachers"—panels covering the front bodice of their gowns. Men wore precious stones, too—the masculine hand was even more bejeweled than the feminine one. Not to mention the masculine shoe buckle, sword knot, pistol butt, and pocket watch. Unfortunately for Thomas-Alexandre, the manly diamond bug bit his father hard, and he watched the man who'd lived for thirty years in the hardscrabble hills, who'd taught him to value a good cutlass and a working saddle, make ever more frequent visits to the jeweler.

Antoine's jeweler was in Rouen, in eastern Normandy, and, according to his records, the lost-and-found man from Saint-Domingue was his best customer. One day the jeweler sent a lackey to Saint-Germain-en-Laye to complete a transaction. Antoine's lackey led the jeweler's lackey to the second floor, where he found Antoine lying in bed. The lackey asked him if he was the Marquis de la Pailleterie. Antoine, apparently instinctively, from decades of covering his tracks, replied: "No, no, this is not me. I swear to you that I am not the Marquis de la Pailleterie." The lackey returned to Rouen to say he'd been unable to locate the client.

Father and son competed in their frivolous spending, but the old man's jewelry buying probably meant that he won. Antoine had never had as much fun in his life as he was having now, in his years "back from the dead." With the furor that sometimes accompanies imminent mortality, he seemed determined to spend his way into oblivion. He was soon deeply in debt. And in 1783 the sixty-nine-year-old Marquis de la Pailleterie was not only treating himself to this lifestyle but sharing it with the thirty-year-old Marie Retou, his housekeeper, to whom he had grown very close.

The marquis gave Thomas-Alexandre sufficient funds to go live on his own in the center of Paris.

BLACK COUNT IN THE CITY OF LIGHT

IN the spring of 1784, Thomas-Alexandre moved into his new rooms, on the rue Étienne, in the heart of Paris. He left home precisely as the son of an eighteenth-century marquis should—with a hefty allowance and lodgings just behind the Louvre.

Over the past century, Paris had undergone a vast remodeling. Louis XIV, who had deconstructed medieval Paris as he was constructing Versailles, had taken the first steps: he had new tree-lined boulevards built, where people could promenade and shop, and private gardens and palaces were opened to public use; this was how Thomas-Alexandre could practice his horsemanship in the Tuileries Gardens. And his new apartment was three blocks from an unprecedented real-estate development that symbolized the revitalization of the city, a unique complex of buildings and enormous courtyards called the Palais Royal.

"The Palais-Royal was the heart and soul, the center and preferred meeting place of the aristocracy of Paris," as one visitor of the time put it. It had originally been the palace of Cardinal Richelieu, who in real life spent more time plotting real-estate deals than assassinations. After his death, the Palais Royal went to the Orléans family, as a gift from Louis XIV, but it wasn't until the 1770s and '80s that they would invest the capital necessary to transform it from a private palace into the most vital public space in Paris.

Its colonnaded courtyards were now lined with shops, cafés, taverns, hotels, theaters, bookstores, and public baths. Anything might be bought here. "In a single day and without leaving its precincts one can buy as prodigiously much in the way of luxury goods as one would manage in a year in any other locality," wrote a visiting marquis in 1786. A dense canopy of ancient chestnut trees provided a natural roof over the complex. Poets and scientists alike read from their works, and one could learn to play the harpsichord or watch demonstrations of mesmerism, then all the rage. The year Thomas-Alexandre moved to his new digs, the Swiss anatomist Philippe Curtius and his niece Marie Tussaud opened an offshoot of their wax museum here, displaying likenesses of Voltaire, Rousseau, Benjamin Franklin, and various French royals.

In those days, most Parisian cafés didn't spill into the street but served their customers in great interior rooms with marble-topped tables, gilt walls, mirrors, and chandeliers. But in the Palais Royal, with its large, protected courtyards, the cafés could set up outdoor tables where customers could read or talk amid the throng. Nearby were open-air billiard tables, musicians playing bawdy songs, magic-lantern shows, displays of electromagnetism, and political satires of all kinds—often distributed by freethinking agents of the Duke d'Orléans—mocking the king. Men and women crowded into these courtyards day and night; at the tables sat groups of men in intense discussion on the matters of the day.

Anyone could read what they liked here and argue as loudly as they wished about it. The brilliant thing was that since the Palais Royal belonged to the duke, the entire space was off limits to the Paris police. Only the duke's own guards held sway within these walls, and the family had given strict instructions to allow the public a long leash. Philosophers, politicians, doctors, lawyers, workmen, and aristocrats all bumped up against one another, and many political clubs of the French Revolution began their debates here. (A little over half a century later, Karl Marx would first meet Friedrich Engels at a Palais Royal café, making this birthplace of eighteenth-century revolution that of twentieth-century revolution as well.)

Perhaps more on Thomas-Alexandre's mind, even in the age of Enlightenment, was the opportunity for admiring some of the loveliest women in the world. "The chairs, which are placed two or three deep all along the walks, hardly suffice to accommodate all these women who are so beautiful to look at in the waning light and who provide such a varied and tempting feast for the eyes," a German visitor raved. "The most beautiful, or at least the most elegant, saunter, with a natural grace that marks a Parisian woman, past those lined up along the paths. . . . The 180 lamps that hang from the 180 arches of the arcades surrounding the gardens, as well as the lights of the cafes, restaurants, and shops, bathe this promenade in a soft glow—a sort of twilight that makes the beautiful still more interesting and even improves what is ordinary. The half-light encourages decency but also desire, as its magical effect seems to fill the air with sensuality."

Thomas-Alexandre would surely have been conscious of his blackness—a black face in a sea of white—but along with stares of curiosity, the twenty-two-year-old found approving looks meeting his own "brown and mellow" eyes. Sexual adventure was trendy in 1784; the novel everyone had been reading was *Les liaisons dangereuses*, published two years earlier. The Chevalier de Saint-Georges was said to have known intimately as many fine ladies as its rakish protagonist, the Viscount de Valmont; and even if white divas balked at having an "American" order them about onstage, they might not resist being alone with him in a theater box after dark.

Much as the Palais Royal was the center of fashionable life during the day, the theater was the center of nearly everything else at night. At the Comédie-Française—where the aristocracy was then enjoying *Le mariage de Figaro*, Beaumarchais's takedown of all things aristocratic, just released from a three-year censor's ban—the action was on the stage. But for a rendezvous with a lady, it was better to go to Nicolet's Theater, in the nearby Boulevard du Temple.* At Nicolet's you would see women of fashion alongside courtesans, soldiers of ancient families alongside lawyers and public accountants. M. Nicolet had made a name for the place with audacious stunts (memorably replacing a sick leading man with a monkey, who turned out to have been the more impressive talent), but the theater's real draw was that no place was better than its darkened private boxes for an amorous rendezvous.

Thomas-Alexandre sometimes went to Nicolet's, and in September 1784 he had a fateful encounter there.

—◆—

---

* The Boulevard du Temple served as a raucous, downmarket extension of the Palais Royal. It was named not after a house of worship but a cavernous fortress that had once been the original European headquarters of the Knights Templar. In the 1790s, at the height of the Terror, the fortress would be turned into a prison, where Louis XVI, Marie-Antoinette, and their family would endure abusive treatment while awaiting execution—and where the lost boy-king, the unfortunate Louis XVII, would meet his mysterious end.

NICOLET'S was always packed—four hundred people in a space not much larger than a small restaurant, lit by torches and flickering tallow candles that gave off a distinct, acrid odor. The fashionable crowd had to take care that the torches didn't set their wigs on fire.

One evening Thomas-Alexandre was attending a performance, seated in a box with a lady in the flickering candlelight. The lady was later described as "a very beautiful Creole who had quite a reputation at the time"—which was not at all unlikely: white women from the islands were popular in Paris, reputed to possess a perfect combination of beauty and hot-bloodedness. Thomas-Alexandre might have felt a transgressive thrill at escorting such a woman—color lines were stricter for Creole women, who had been living in a world of increasing race legislation, than they were for enlightened Parisiennes—and surely he would have enjoyed company from his homeland.

The risks latent in their encounter suddenly materialized in the shape of a colonial naval officer, who approached them along with two armed companions. They closed in around the couple.

"You are quite beautiful; you have a nice figure and a nice bosom," Thomas-Alexandre later reported the officer saying, addressing the lady as if she were effectively alone. "I would be pleased to get your address, would you accept mine? Madame is a foreigner; would she like me to take her to Versailles?"

Thomas-Alexandre must have wondered how much of this forwardness was actual flirtation and how much was for his benefit. Given the two armed supporters, the officer's every utterance seemed meant to goad him into some unwise action.

Thomas-Alexandre recognized the officer, though he may not have known his name: it was Jean-Pierre Titon de Saint-Lamain, an ex-captain from an elite cadre in Martinique. Such men were known to hang around Versailles hoping to move up in the naval hierarchy while boasting of their exotic, dangerous commands, which in truth were often glorified slave-catching operations. But Titon had been a member of an elite grenadier unit, and by the look of him he was trouble.

Did the lady "like Americans?" he asked sneeringly.

In the sworn statement he later gave the police, Thomas-Alexandre said the officer made "a thousand other indecent proposals" to the lady, all the while acting as though Thomas-Alexandre himself were invisible.

As would soon become clear in his letters and his conduct, Thomas-Alexandre did not believe in race as a determinant of character. Moreover, half his family was white—he lived among whites, he had a white father, white friends, white lovers; except for Saint-Georges, his teachers were all white men. There would have been nothing so contemptible to him as this sort of colonial flunky. Since their status and livelihood depended on domination over blacks, all free blacks and mulattos posed a threat to them.

When the lady answered that she did like Americans, the officer congratulated her, his voice dripping sarcasm, and proceeded to make jokes about her choice of escort. At that point Thomas-Alexandre addressed Titon directly.

"Madame is respectable, please leave us alone," he said. He turned to his date and advised her to ignore the man.

Titon burst into loud, vicious laughter.

"Madame!" he said. "I thought you were with one of your lackeys!"

Thomas-Alexandre must have ached to reach for his sword. He had been training six hours a day for just such an insult.

"But, my friend, we know what a mulatto is," Titon said, addressing him directly for the first time. "In your country they put chains on your feet and on your hands. If you dare to say a word, I will have you arrested by the guard and taken to prison. You know who I am."

The manner in which he addressed Thomas-Alexandre showed the likely true purpose of his visit: not competition for a lady but to put the fancy colored man—a gallant about town with sword and fine waistcoat—in his place.

Thomas-Alexandre replied that he felt contempt for everything the officer was saying, and that he knew "what" he was: a clerk in the war office at Versailles, according to what he had heard. Titon lost his temper. One of his men raised his cane to strike Thomas-Alexandre and shouted to a theater guard to have the mulatto arrested. Thomas-Alexandre tried to leave with his companion, but the officer blocked their path.

Then the man's confederates grabbed Thomas-Alexandre and, in a move that must have burned in his memory, tried to force him to kneel before his attacker and beg for his freedom. This was to be the consummation of their taunting: to make the man of color beg for pardon on his knees, with the white woman looking on. Titon called on the guards of the theater to help "arrest this mulatto," and the guards asked him if he wanted Thomas-Alexandre taken away.

According to his own written account, Thomas-Alexandre broke free of the guards and Titon and his men and returned to his box. Thomas-Alexandre writes that the lady fled the scene. Without his audience, Titon told the guards to release Thomas-Alexandre. But he was not quite finished with his game.

"You are free! I give you pardon and you may go!" he called loudly, in a parody of manumission.

At that point, a police marshal finally approached to take both men into custody for disturbing the peace.

The details survive in both of their sworn statements, given to the Paris police the following day on parchments dated September 15, 1784. Thomas-Alexandre's, written in his own hand, as was the custom then, and in first person, recounted the events with surprising candor, while Titon's is written in the third person with a haughty chill. "Sir Titon de St. Lamain, formerly commander of the battalion at the fort St. Pierre Martinique where he owns a residence, and is currently attached to the infantry in France, is honored to explain that he was yesterday at the show of Mr. Nicolet with two of his friends, and that he noticed a demoiselle sitting in the box next to the bench he was sitting on. Which gave him the opportunity to strike up a conversation with her and after a few ordinary compliments Sir Titon was exchanging with the said demoiselle, a mulatto sitting next to her started getting involved." "Sir Titon" records that he was forced to call the guard because of the mulatto's "impertinence"—but, being a magnanimous type, he then forgave him.

The novelist Dumas was obsessed with the encounter at Nicolet's throughout his life, and his father certainly never forgot it; he must have told his future wife the story, and probably his intimate friends knew of it. I had first read about the incident many years ago, in my childhood copy of Alexandre Dumas's memoirs. Until now that was the only version that was known, and it ended completely differently from the police documents I found.

The novelist's version begins to depart from the police statements when

Dumas has the grenadier officer say, "Oh, I beg your pardon, I took monsieur for your lackey." From there it goes on:

> This bit of insolence was no sooner uttered than the impertinent musketeer launched, as if from a catapult, and crashed into the middle of the orchestra pit.
>
> This unexpected descent produced a great tumult in the crowd.
>
> It was a matter of interest not only to the falling man but to those onto whom he fell.
>
> In those days the orchestra was standing room only, consequently there was no need to get up; the section turned towards the box from which the musketeer had been hurled.
>
> My father, who was awaiting the consequences that such an affair would naturally have, left the box at that instant to wait for his adversary in the corridor. But instead he found a police officer.

Dumas not only makes his father triumph handily; he also makes the incident comic by having the bad guy land in the crowd.

I had always liked this scene, as terse and satisfying as a page from a picaresque novel. But, having read the police dossier—along with thousands of other documents relating to the society in which Thomas-Alexandre lived—I would now say that this action-hero account is perhaps the most misleading thing Dumas ever wrote about his father.

But beyond the memoir, Dumas would use the story's basic dynamic over and over. His novel *Georges* directly addressed a mixed-race man's lifelong struggle in the aftermath of a similar slight: its hero receives training very similar to Thomas-Alexandre's at La Boëssière's with the sole idea of returning to confront the white colonials who long ago insulted him and his family. *The Count of Monte Cristo* describes Edmond Dantès's planning, in his dungeon cell, to avenge himself against not one but many persecuting villains. And, of course, the character of the hotheaded d'Artagnan in *The Three Musketeers* draws on Thomas-Alexandre's youthful dishonoring at Nicolet's. Like him, d'Artagnan is from country nobility and he is certainly an outsider in Paris. Even so, he is a white man and thus, no matter how poor or provincial, can fight for his honor with abandon, deliriously.

In Dumas's memoir of the Nicolet incident, the novelist omits all reference to his father's race. And by dropping the fact that his assailant was a colonial officer he buries the racial aspect still deeper.* The slight becomes the same slight the provincial d'Artagnan constantly encounters—because of his clothes or his manner, mistaken for someone of a lower social rank. Slights can be so subtle, in fact, that, as the novel has it, the proud young Gascon considers "every smile an insult, and every glance as a provocation."

But what made Thomas-Alexandre an outsider was anything but subtle; despite liberty unimaginable outside France and despite the Parisian frivolity and license, he still lived in invisible shackles. Miraculously, within a decade, his shackles would be broken, in a France transformed by the orgy of emancipation that was the French Revolution. From his late twenties on, he would never again need to brook an insult from a white man without reaching for his sword.

><

THOMAS-ALEXANDRE signed his police statement "Dumas Davy," that fusion of mother's and father's names which he hadn't used since his first year in France. The incident was officially put to rest; the marshals wrote out a declaration certifying their acceptance of both his statement and Titon's and, along with a bit of legalese directed at preventing any possible future duels between the parties, were content to let the matter drop. The blessed inefficiency of the kingdom ensured that the man of color was not charged with violating the Police des Noirs and remanded to the naval police, technically in charge of such violations, for lacking proper registration. Given Sir Titon's extensive connections in the Naval Ministry, he could have made good his threat to have Thomas-Alexandre arrested, perhaps even sent to a depot and deported, but Titon chose not to persecute his victim further. Instead Thomas-Alexandre walked out a free man.

Still, the first record we have of his voice is in a police report.

---

* It was an odd late-eighteenth-century radicalizing trope that the class consciousness of future French revolutionaries was often awakened by being insulted at the theater. It happened to both Robespierre, founder of the Jacobins, and Brissot, founder of the Girondins, the leading competing group. Both were involved as young men in altercations in theaters with arrogant aristocrats—though more simply, in fights over seating, not involving women.

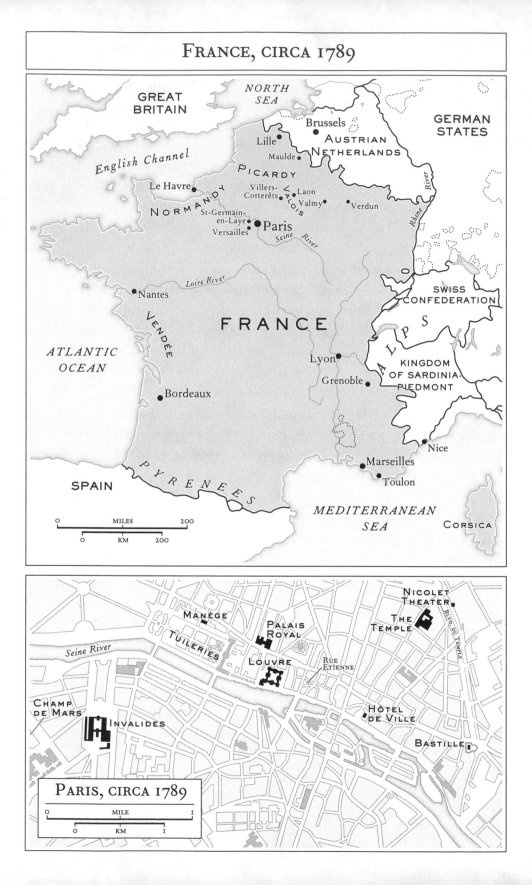

France, circa 1789

GREAT BRITAIN

NORTH SEA

GERMAN STATES

English Channel

Brussels

Lille

Maulde

AUSTRIAN NETHERLANDS

PICARDY

Le Havre

Villers-Cotterêts

Laon

Valmy

Verdun

VALOIS

NORMANDY

St-Germain-en-Laye

Versailles

Paris

Seine River

Rhine River

Loire River

Nantes

FRANCE

VENDÉE

A L P S

SWISS CONFEDERATION

ATLANTIC OCEAN

Lyon

Grenoble

KINGDOM OF SARDINIA-PIEDMONT

Bordeaux

Nice

P Y R E N E E S

Marseilles

Toulon

SPAIN

MEDITERRANEAN SEA

CORSICA

```
0        MILES        200
0         KM          200
```

Nicolet Theater

MANÈGE

PALAIS ROYAL

THE TEMPLE

BLVD. DU TEMPLE

TUILERIES

LOUVRE

Seine River

RUE ÉTIENNE

CHAMP DE MARS

INVALIDES

HÔTEL DE VILLE

BASTILLE

Paris, circa 1789

```
0        MILE         1
0         KM          1
```

A QUEEN'S DRAGOON

ON February 13, 1786, a contract of marriage was signed between Thomas-Alexandre's father—"Alexandre Antoine Davy de la Pailleterie, knight, former lord and owner of the parish of Bielleville [and other fiefdoms], gentleman in the former chamber of the Prince de Conti," and so forth—and his housekeeper, Marie Retou, who was, as the contract stated, the daughter of a vintner. The wedding took place on Valentine's Day.

Thomas-Alexandre appears not to have attended the wedding—he did not witness the marriage contract—and all indications are that he did not appreciate his father's newfound happiness. The novelist Dumas writes that the "marriage caused a cooling-off between father and son. The result of this estrangement was that the father tied his purse strings tighter . . . and the son discovered one fine morning that Paris life without money was a sorry life." Antoine had always supported his son generously, but his new wife was from a frugal lower-middle-class background, and perhaps she lacked the proper respect for a fashionable young man's expenditures. She had known Thomas-Alexandre since he'd arrived in Le Havre nearly ten years earlier, and she had watched him grow into a dashing Parisian rake with neither a trade nor obvious aspirations to one.

At twenty-four, Thomas-Alexandre was conversant with Caesar and Plutarch, well versed in contemporary theater and in Palais Royal gossip, and, of course, an expert horseman and fencer. But he had not worked a day since stepping off the ship. There was only one profession really suited to a man of his style, skills, and temperament. In France, as a contemporary visiting English nobleman observed, "it is very dishonorable for any gentleman not to be in the army, or in the king's service as they call it."

Less than two weeks after his father's marriage, Thomas-Alexandre made up his mind to enlist.

→ ←

ALTHOUGH there could be no more traditional career move for a young man of his station, Thomas-Alexandre's entrance into the military was fundamentally different from his peers': he enlisted not as an officer but as a common soldier.

The Queen's Dragoons, the regiment he picked, had flashy uniforms and a rugged, even reckless reputation. But, for the son of a marquis to enlist without a commission—as a private!—was unheard-of. The novelist recounts a conversation between his father and his grandfather:

[My father] told him that he had made a resolution.
"What is it?" asked the marquis.
"To enlist."
"As what?"
"As a common soldier."
"Where are you going to do that?"
"In the first regiment I come across."
"Marvelous," replied my grandfather, "but as I'm called the Marquis de la Pailleterie, am a colonel and commissioner general of artillery, I don't intend for you to drag my name through the lowest ranks of the army."
"Then you oppose my enlistment?"
"No; but you must enlist under a nom de guerre."
"That's fair," replied my father. "I will enlist under the name of Dumas."
"Very well."
And the marquis, who had never been a very tender father, turned his back on his son and left him free to do what he pleased.

The novelist Dumas got paid by the line, and so was always making up dialogue when he could. But whether or not this exchange took place as written, it conveys Thomas-Alexandre's insolence toward his father at that point.

—▶—◀—

ON June 2, 1786, Thomas-Alexandre signed the enlistment rolls of the Sixth Regiment of the Queen's Dragoons. The document still exists, and it is the first record of the name "Dumas, Alexandre."

Whatever combination of anger, pride, and determination caused him to give this name instead of any of the others he had been using since he came to France—"Thomas Retoré," "Thomas-Alexandre Davy de La Pailleterie," "Thomas Retoré (called Dumas-Davy)"—the young "American" had found his identity. Rather, he had invented it. Beneath that invention came another: "son of Antoine and Cecette Dumas."

Alexandre—he never again used the name "Thomas"—had with the stroke of a pen inverted his family's racial history: instead of the son of the Marquis de la Pailleterie and his black slave Cessette, he was now the son of Cessette Dumas and her husband, Antoine. He had made his father into a Dumas. It may have been expedient, but it was also a kind of poetic revenge. And it was the only concrete memorial he would leave his mother: to take her name. Next to his new name and family data was a description of Alexandre Dumas:

> Native of Jemerie [*sic*] in Martinique, 24 years old, 6 feet tall, with frizzy black hair and eyebrows . . . oval face, and brown skinned, small mouth, thick lips.

The enlistment officer mistook "Jemerie" to be in Martinique rather than Saint-Domingue; future records of the Sixth Dragoons would often simply state that their unusual recruit was "from Jeremie, in America."

Enlisting as a private in the dragoons was a bad place to start one's career: from that rank, Thomas-Alexandre was unlikely to ever rise above the rank of sergeant-major, the cavalry regiment's senior noncommissioned rank at the time.

A 1781 rule decreed that to qualify for an army commission, a candidate must "show proof of four generations of nobility on his father's side," certified by the royal genealogist. Thomas-Alexandre *had* such lineage—the Davy de la Pailleterie family tree went back to the 1500s—but the recently passed race laws made it hard for a man of mixed race to claim his rightful title or noble status. Infuriated as Thomas-Alexandre must have been to be held back by such restrictions, he must have felt relief to jettison the name of the man who had owned and sold him—and join up under a new name that was both his own invention and an homage to the slave mother he'd so thoroughly left behind.

Thirteen days later, on June 15, Antoine died. It was only four months after the old rogue's wedding. He was buried in the cemetery at Saint-Germain-en-Laye. Antoine's death certificate states that mass was sung and lists the witnesses: Alexandre Dumas was not among them. It was lucky that the son was living the life of a soldier by then and did not need his father's support, because the "fortune"—which had in fact been merely glorified support payments from the Mauldes in accordance with their arrangement regarding the Pailleterie estate—was revealed to be an illusion. A letter to the Count de Maulde written on the widow's behalf by a lawyer a few months later indicates the severity of the want:

> The death of M. le Marquis frees you of the life annuity . . . you were obligated to pay him I believe; please accept, sir, my compliments, but permit me to place before you the unhappy situation of an honest woman whom he had just married about 4 months ago, who had no possessions and on whom he meant to play a trick. In fact, the marriage contract . . . gave all the Marquis's possessions and all his movable and immovable property to his wife, who recognizes today that M. le Marquis wasn't living in his holdings and had only your lifetime payments, having spent all his money paying the debts for a young Mister Dumas (mulatto) who is said to be the illegitimate son of the deceased. This illegitimate child has cost him enormously, and he just ended up enlisting in the military as a dragoon. The poor widow has instructed me to make you aware of her sad state; she finds herself without bread; she relies on your bounty to assure a small pension for the rest of her days. Someone advertised your charitable sentiments and the small amount of resources you could give her would allow her

to avoid hiring herself as a servant; it would not look good for the family of the Marquis to have a titled widow forced to become a servant.

The Count de Maulde refused. That summer he sold off the Bielleville estate, definitively ending its four-century-long connection to the Davy family, along with eighteen other properties that had somehow belonged to the family. Maulde did not do this lightly. It was an indication of how much his association with Antoine had cost him that he was selling all the lands and buildings that, in recent years, he had gone to great pains to buy back after Antoine summarily sold them to a neighbor. Maulde had tried to bring a measure of respectability to a family that did not want it. He used the money from the current sale—a serious sum, 350,000 livres—to pay off the marquis's creditors and those of his widow, as well as his own.

➤◄

MEANWHILE, after presumably putting his silks and velvet waistcoats in storage, Alexandre Dumas threw himself into the life of an armed man on horseback. Dragoons were light cavalry, used mostly for reconnaissance, skirmishing, and raiding. They got their name from their short carbine muskets, which were known as *dragons* because they spat fire.

The first regular dragoon regiments had served Louis XIII and Cardinal Richelieu in the previous century. They were introduced at the same time as the musketeers, who specialized in assignments in and around the capital. Like them, the dragoons were organized specifically to provide elite military opportunities to the sons of minor noble families or of those who had fallen on hard times. (The musketeers were phased out by Louis XVI in 1776 for budgetary reasons.)

For the government, a big virtue of the dragoons was that they were expendable. They got poorer horses and cheaper weapons than the elite heavy-cavalry or royal-guard units. Dragoons did the toughest and dirtiest jobs. In offensive warfare, they went in ahead of other troops, scouted enemy positions, secured bridges, took out enemy snipers, defused traps; and during retreats they held bridges and walls until the regular troops had gotten through. In peacetime, the dragoons took on highwaymen and secured the roads for the king and other dignitaries during their travels. The dragoons also battled smugglers, fighting the Crown's constantly simmering war against dealers in illegal salt, which was then one of the most heavily taxed essential commodities in the kingdom.

Alexandre Dumas took to this rough-and-ready life, discovering a side of himself that the Palais Royal gallant would not have recognized. He trained hard on the northeast frontier of France's so-called iron belt of fortresses. "The liberty that he had known in the colonies had developed his skill and strength in a remarkable way," his son would write. "[H]e was a veritable American horseman, a cowboy. With his rifle or pistol in hand, he accomplished marvels that made St. Georges jealous. . . . And his muscular strength became legendary in the army."

Private Dumas was a showoff, and he loved doing tricks that displayed his strength and agility. His son captured these as well as anyone, since no one is bigger or stronger to a young boy than his father:

> More than once he amused himself in the riding-school [*manège*] by passing under a beam, grabbing it with his arms, and lifting his horse between his legs. I have seen him, and I recall this with a childish amazement, carry two men on his bent leg and hop across the room with these two men on [his back]. I saw him, in a painful motion, take a medium-sized rush in his hands and break it by turning one hand to the right and the other to the left. Finally, I remember, one day leaving the little château des Fossés where we lived, my father had forgotten the key to a gate; I remember seeing him get out of the carriage, take the gate crosswise, and at the second or third shake, break the stone in which it was fixed.

Another anecdote his son tells—and which was recounted throughout the nineteenth century by many others as though it were fact—involves a trick Alex Dumas performed with a bunch of military muskets. The novelist paints it a bit like a barroom dare:

> On the evening of his arrival, by the campfire light, he watched a soldier who, among other feats of strength, amused himself by putting his finger into the mouth of a heavy musket and lifting it up, not with his arm but on his extended finger.

A man wrapped in a cloak mingled among the onlookers and watched with them; then, laughing and flinging back his cloak, he said:

"That's not bad—now bring four guns."

He was obeyed. . . . He then put four of his fingers in the four gun bores and lifted the four guns with as much ease as the soldier had lifted one.

"There you are," he said, laying them gently on the ground, "when you want to get into tests of strength, that's how it should be done."

When [the witness] recounted this incident to me, he still marveled at how any man's muscles could bear such a weight.

At all times and in all places, tales of strength and power are prone to exaggeration. But no matter how much one exaggerates the feats of the strongest man in the barroom—or the barracks—he is still the strongest man, just lifting a little less weight. A French infantry musket of the period weighed at least ten pounds; it was not very likely that Alex Dumas lifted four quite like that, for it would have meant hoisting nearly forty pounds with only his fingers. The horse-lifting claim is even wilder: the dragoons' Norman horses weighed perhaps 1,500 pounds each. Even assuming Dumas could perform "many feats which might draw an envious groan from the strongest of professional 'strong men,' " it seems impossible that he actually lifted his horse by squeezing his legs around it and grabbing a beam, as he was reported to do.

This is how tales of strength were spread in a world before the *Guinness Book*. Private Dumas was clearly reputed to be one of the strongest men in the French army, but proof of his achievements would have to wait for real combat, real injuries, and real deaths.

Though duels were illegal in Paris, they could still be fought in the army without risking arrest. In fact, the aristocratic tradition of dueling for the "slightest offense" was maintained, and even encouraged, by the army, as a means of sharpening combat skills. This was especially true among the dragoons, who needed to be ready to grapple hand to hand with both enemy soldiers and ruthless highwaymen. Another oft-repeated story from Private Dumas's early days as a soldier was the one about his fighting three duels against fellow soldiers in a day and winning all three, despite being gashed twice in the head. During one of them, he received a blow across the brow that may have been responsible for terrible headaches he suffered later and for problems with his vision.

It was also common among the dragoons to fight group duels with other regiments. Such practice bloodshed could start with a disparaging remark about another regiment's skills or record, and nothing was thought better for esprit de corps than going up against rivals blade to blade. Raised on stories of these contests recounted by his father's retired comrades, Alexandre Dumas would transpose the fights to the early 1600s to create his tales of musketeer derring-do. In the memoirs he delights in presenting them with his tongue-in-cheek bravado:

> My father had hardly rejoined his regiment before an occasion for displaying his skill as a pupil of La Boëssière presented itself.
>
> The King's regiment and the Queen's regiment, which had always been rivals, both happened to be stationed in the same town. This offered the perfect opportunity for staging a small war; such worthy rivals were not about to let such a chance escape.
>
> One day a soldier of the King's regiment passed by a soldier from the regiment of the queen.
>
> The former stopped the latter and said, "Comrade, do you know something?"
>
> "No," replied the other, "but if you tell it to me I shall know it."
>
> "All right! The king f—the queen."
>
> "That's a lie," replied the other, "it's the other way round, the queen f—the king."
>
> One insult was as grave as the other, and they could only be erased by a recourse to arms.
>
> A hundred duels took place during the next twenty-four hours. My father fought three of them.

There is no evidence that anyone in the dragoons bothered Dumas about his unusual family history or his skin color. Records from his regiment indicate that at least two, possibly three, other "Americans" served in it at the time, though one of them was a bugler. If Dumas did get harassed about being a man of color, here he was free to defend his honor. Such duels would be only slightly more serious than the novelist's caricature of them suggests. But they would have given Alex Dumas's fellow soldiers a glimpse of what the tall black private might be capable of if circumstances required.

→—←

IN the summer of 1788, two years after Alexandre Dumas enlisted, France began falling apart. Although frequently at war with her neighbors, the country had enjoyed ten centuries of uninterrupted monarchy—the throne had stayed in the same family for eight hundred years—and king after king had, by monarchical standards, done a pretty decent job. For centuries, people shouted "*Vive le roi!*" when they meant "*Vive la France!*" And there was little reason to think this was bound to change. True, Louis XVI's coronation, in 1774, had coincided with the biggest grain riots in seven years. And pairing his rumored impotence with his outsize passion for traditional pursuits like hunting, his subjects often treated the king as a figure of fun. Even so, the idea that this Louis—who, unlike some of his predecessors, showed an obviously sentimental devotion to his people and the throne—could one day lose his head must have seemed unthinkable.

But the royal finance minister had by this point discovered that France was on the verge of bankruptcy, and had presented King Louis XVI with a famously brief "to do" list:

1. The present situation
2. What to do about it?
3. How to do it?

He presented one solution: a plan for comprehensive tax reform which would remove the old privileges that largely shielded the aristocracy from taxes.

As the American Revolution had been sparked by a tax revolt, the same would now be true in France, though the many heady ideas in the air obscured the heart of the matter: France was broke.

→—←

THAT June, crowds in Grenoble pelted royal troops with red roof tiles. The troops fired back, killing three people. At the time it seemed like a disturbing trifle, a crowd temporarily carried away by antiroyalist feeling, quickly dispersed. But in fact it was the first blood of the Revolution, a year before the fact, for the sentiment that animated the Grenoble crowds would soon overtake the country.

In July, a freak storm dropped hailstones so big they killed animals and destroyed nearly all the crops around Paris. Harsh weather hit almost every region in the kingdom, dooming the harvest.

In August, a new finance minister informed the king that the treasury was officially empty. Many people blamed the empty coffers on aristocratic frivolities and on their Austrian queen. The bitter irony was that the financial crisis had largely been caused by French support of the American patriots; in getting back at the English, Versailles had committed not only ideological but fiscal suicide. The finance minister brought the unwelcome news that something must be done to avoid default and that that something was raising taxes. The people burned effigies of him in the streets.

In order to satisfy one of the demands of the nobles, the minister advised the king to reconvene an ancient political body known as the Estates-General. The Estates-General, a kind of class-based legislature, was almost a mythical organization, however; nobody was clear about how it worked, since it hadn't been convened since 1614. Since then, one King Louis after another had simply ruled, albeit constantly vexed by the nobles and their *parlement* courts.

The Bourbon kings had fiercely resisted reconvening the Estates-General, but in this case Louis XVI finally conceded and the country breathed a sigh of relief. Slated to convene the following spring, the Estates-General would be France's salvation, everyone was certain. That 1788 was the hundredth anniversary of England's "Glorious Revolution" led to speculation that a Gallic version of such a bloodless shift to constitutional monarchy might be just around the corner.

Freakish weather returned in the winter of 1788–89: the Seine and other rivers froze, roads were blocked, and gristmills seized up. Bakeries baked no bread, and the penniless starved or froze to death. The remnants of the French economy ceased to function: shops were empty; Lyon's looms stopped weaving. A broke government was powerless to help.

When spring finally arrived, a desperate euphoria greeted the prospect of the Estates-General. Preparations included not only the election of representatives but also the compilation of *cahiers de doléances*—"complaint books," lists of grievances—stating all the things a local district's people disliked about how France was run and how they wished to see them changed. Any subject of the king could complain about anything, provided he was over twenty-five and entered on the tax rolls. (Some widows tried to add their complaints, insisting that there was no explicit gender requirement.) All across the country, people gathered in improvised town-hall-style meetings to decide what to complain about. The complaints could also be about the nation's empire, and some notebooks contained complaints about slavery and calls to end it. Educated nobles tended to dress up their complaints in philosophical rhetoric about citizenship and the nation, while members of the lower classes stuck to more down-to-earth concerns. Most complaints addressed the continuing domination of peasant life by relentless taxation, pitiful wages, and the remnants of feudalism, with its exploitation of cheap labor.

This public venting stoked participation in politics. It got ordinary people involved in government and made them hopeful—too hopeful—that once these complaints reached the king, he could make everything all right.

In a working-class district of Paris in April, one meeting caused a riot. A local wallpaper manufacturer's remark started rumors that he—along with other bosses—was trying to use the occasion to cut workers' wages. In fact, this manufacturer, who barely escaped with his life, was a proponent of workers' rights whose remark had been misunderstood. The French Guards, responsible for the city's policing, rode in to disperse the rioters. In their blue coats, red collars, and white breeches, they sported the colors that would be adopted by the Revolution but were in fact their age-old livery at Versailles, where they performed palace security along with the Swiss Guards, the mercenaries of European kings and the pope. The French Guards were elite troops, and, though recruited from all over France, they lived in Paris among the population. The king depended on them to restore order when crisis threatened. On that afternoon, they did not let him down. The French Guards fired into the crowd, ending the riot and killing at least twenty-five people.

A week later, on May 5, 1789, the delegations to the Estates-General gathered before the king at Versailles. The seat of the monarchy was transformed into a vast political carnival. Delegates came from every town and region in France, bearing the complaint notebooks of their local constituents, and as they met and mingled in the shadow of the legendary palace, they naturally split into smaller groups to eat, drink, and argue about what was to be done. A cluster of Breton deputies formed one little chat group that, once the carnival moved on to Paris and the Palais Royal, would become known as the Jacobin Club.

Before any representative governing could begin, a battle had to be fought over how voting would work. The Estates-General got its name from the traditional division of France into three "estates": clergy, nobility, and commoners. The way it had originally worked was that each of the three estates got an equal say: each had an equal number of "deputies" to represent it. This meant that the clergy and the nobility together could outvote anything that the rest, collectively known as "the Third Estate," wanted; the idea of proportional representation—or any meaningful voice for the people—was a sham.

The energized and emboldened delegates of the Third Estate, the "99 percent"—in reality, closer to 96 percent—of the French population who paid the bulk of the taxes, demanded that its number of representatives be doubled so that commoners' votes would equal the combined votes of nobles and clergy. In other words, the Third Estate was still demanding only half of the total political power. After weeks, the king was convinced to allow the doubling of the Third. But by this point a group of radical delegates had convinced a majority of commoners and liberal nobles that the entire archaic structure of the Estates-General should simply be thrown out and replaced by a national assembly in which there would be no estates and everyone would have an equal vote. This meant that the 96 percent who were neither clergy nor noble would dominate.

On Wednesday, June 17, 1789, France went from a system where only the nobility and the church had power to a system where, at least theoretically, the common people did. Europe's most renowned absolute monarchy was suddenly the widest system of suffrage in the world. But on Saturday morning, the deputies arrived at the hall of their new National Assembly to find that royal troops had blocked the gates and put up notices telling the deputies to return the next week for a special "royal session," at which Louis planned to inform them personally that their actions were illegal and invalid. But instead of dispersing, the infuriated deputies marched to a nearby indoor tennis court, where they swore an oath not to leave until France had a constitution. Frenchmen were finally taking the "extreme measures" of which Lafayette had not believed them capable.

The king ordered garrisons around Paris to be reinforced in case force was needed. As against a Parisian population of 650,000, the Swiss and French Guard regiments at the king's immediate disposal totaled fewer than ten thousand men. In ordinary circumstances, Dumas's unit, the Queen's Dragoons, might have been among those called to Paris. But in a crucial sign of the way things were going, a full third of the twenty thousand reinforcements summoned by the king were foreign mercenaries. The king's ministers feared that French soldiers might at this point be too easily turned to the patriot cause. Activists had been arrested for giving out pamphlets that read, "We are Citizens before Soldiers, Frenchmen before slaves." When news of the king's calling in foreign troops reached the Palais Royal, its arcades exploded. "The ferment at Paris is beyond conception," an observer reported. "Ten thousand people have been all this day in the Palais Royal . . . the people seem, with a sort of phrenzy, to reject all idea of compromise."

As if nature again were conspiring to foment revolution, northern France now ran out of grain completely. Bread riots swept from Normandy to Picardy and threatened Paris, too. Rumors grew that royals and aristocrats were in league to starve the patriots before attacking them with foreign troops.

Spurred on by such rumors, the crowds in the Palais Royal rushed to arm themselves, and suddenly all of Paris was on the move. On the night of July 12 and throughout the next day, people broke into shops and houses, grabbing every gun, sword, pike, dagger, and kitchen knife. They also raided bakeries, in a desperate search for scraps of bread. The mob secured thirty thousand Charleville muskets from the Invalides armory, but the government had prudently removed both shot and powder to the Bastille, the prison-fortress in the heart of Paris. By 1789, it housed only a handful of prisoners and was actually slated for demolition (its most prominent prisoner, the Marquis de Sade, had just been moved). For most people, though, it remained a hated symbol of oppression. On Tuesday, July 14, crowds stormed the Bastille and, after negotiating the prison governor's good-faith surrender, stabbed him to death, shooting the corpse for good measure and parading its severed head around the city streets on a pike.

The day would become France's version of July Fourth, though Bastille Day commemorates a far bloodier, more contested event than the signing of a Declaration of Independence.

One fundamental development that made the storming of the Bastille— and indeed the entire Revolution— possible was, with a mysterious alchemy, the advance revolutionizing of the French military. Three months earlier, in that first riot, the French Guards had followed orders and fired on the rioters. Yet on July 14, instead of doing their job and defending the Bastille, the French Guards *joined* the rioters, and would soon declare themselves the *National* Guard. The war minister informed the king that he could no longer guarantee the loyalty of any French soldier or junior officer. Without its army, the royal government collapsed.

At the Hôtel de Ville—the city hall—on July 17, the cornered king met the new Paris municipal government and gave General Lafayette his blessing as official head of the new Paris National Guard. The king acknowledged his acceptance of the Revolution by allowing Lafayette to pin a cockade—the showy round fabric ornament by which revolutionaries recognized one another—on the royal hat. The assembled patriots cried, *"Vive le roi!"**

▶—◀

WHILE Paris rioted, Alex Dumas and his regiment remained in their garrison, awaiting orders. He had spent the last year of the *Ancien Régime*, with the Sixth Dragoons, stationed in the provincial town of Laon, a hundred miles northeast of Paris, with a long view over the Picardy plain toward the French border with the Austrian Netherlands. This was one of the poorest regions of

---

*Initially cockades were various colors—the crowds storming the Bastille may have been wearing green ones in their hats—but this historic meeting at the city hall marked the christening of the cockade as a red, white, and blue symbol of the Revolution. Red and blue were chosen because they were the colors of the city of Paris, though they were also the colors of the House of Orléans. White was the color of the Bourbon monarchy. It is said that when the mayor first presented the cockade to the king, it was only red and blue. Then Lafayette stepped in to propose adding the Bourbon color white to acknowledge the king's gesture of accepting the Revolution.

the country, and a hotbed of patriot sentiment; Picardy had sent more soldiers and junior officers to fight in the American Revolution than any other place in France.

Yet it was hard to find a more surreally calm place in the summer of 1789—less than a hundred miles from Paris but centuries removed from the events taking place there. Perched on a hill above the plain, Laon uncannily afforded views for miles from almost every spot in town. While Paris had undergone a century of remodeling, breaking down medieval walls and creating boulevards and public spaces—currently packed with revolutionary mobs—Laon remained surrounded by one big wall, with gates for horsemen to ride through to defend the towns and cities below. Since the days of the Roman Empire, Laon had protected northern Gaul from the Vandals, Alans, Huns, Burgundians, and Franks, until the Franks eventually broke through and became its new landlords. After that, for another thousand years, it had protected France. Walking around this perfectly sited fortified town today, one may picture a scene from *The Lord of the Rings*. A stone city on a hill—a spot of magnificent, even desolate, beauty.

On August 15, the Sixth Dragoons at last received their orders. They were to ride down to the town of Villers-Cotterêts, to defend the château of the Orléans family—princes of the blood still, though patriots—against mobs of brigands. The soldiers were also to protect the townsfolk. The order had come via the regional headquarters at Soissons but had not originated in Versailles's war office or, indeed, with any officer of the kingdom. It came instead from a common innkeeper named Claude Labouret, who had just been elected commander of the Villers-Cotterêts National Guard.

SUMMERS OF REVOLUTION

IN the weeks that followed the taking of the Bastille, a wave of violence known as the Great Fear swept across the French countryside. Rampaging mobs attacked châteaus and burned the papers recording their feudal obligations to the local nobles. In the process, they sometimes burned down the châteaus themselves. Some rampagers made the local lord offer them a feast as he watched his belongings go up in flames.

No one has ever fully explained these events, though many later put it down to the rumors spreading of a so-called famine pact between royal bureaucrats and noble speculators to hoard goods and manipulate prices while peasant children starved to death. Tens of millions of people were living on the edge of destitution, and even in normal times a peasant family could spend nearly half its income on bread; in a year of poor harvests, a spike in bread prices could raise that figure as high as 90 percent. The compiling of local complaint petitions that spring had raised expectations of an improvement in conditions. Instead, the summer had brought only more shortages—exacerbated by commodity speculation—and no help at all from the government, which had collapsed.

On the other hand, it would seem that, like many actions in the French Revolution, there was a backstory of opportunism: many of those burning feudal records were not the genuinely destitute but rather what we would now call small business people, using a moment of public disorder to reduce their tax burden. In the last years of the *Ancien Régime*, clever lawyers had encouraged their noble clients to mine their records for all sorts of fees they could charge the enterprising commoners who used their land. Commoners already paid the lion's share of national taxes and, because of these old feudal records, they now also paid a whole host of other duties to their local nobles (who, further inspiring anger, were exempt from most national taxes). Like the American Revolution before it, the French Revolution began as a tax revolt, and there were even rumors that King Louis XVI himself authorized the burning sprees because he felt the taxes on his people were unjustly high.

Social conflict was fueled by mass confusion. All across France that summer, bells tolled to warn villages and towns of approaching brigands. Such roving criminal bands had long been a problem in the countryside, terrorizing travelers, villagers, and peasants alike. But fear far outpaced the actual threat. People whispered that noblemen had organized gangs of looters to harass the commoners. Few waited for proof before taking up arms. No one could really be sure who was a brigand and who was defending against one. When villagers armed themselves and went out to confront the supposed brigands, they were in turn taken for brigands by villagers in the next town over, who then rang their bells and went out armed to meet the brigands.

The bells also rang in Villers-Cotterêts, where the innkeeper Claude Labouret was responsible for the town's defense. Labouret was one of many locals who had prospered over the past decades by serving the needs of the Orléans family and their hangers-on. The House of Orléans had brought not only debauchery and progressive politics to the town but also a brisk aristocratic tourist trade, especially for those who liked to hunt. The Retz Forest had the best hunting in France—stag, partridge, pheasant, and wild boar—and wealthy visitors built country places in the vicinity. (There was a brief family embarrassment in the early 1780s, when "Louis the Fat," the father of the current Duke d'Orléans, grew so obese he could no longer mount a horse to lead the hunt and had to surrender that role to the next in line to the royal throne.) Around the Orléans château a number of inns and hotels had, over the past decades, also built up a thriving trade. Some local peasants who had served in the château—even, according to local lore, gathering up unfortunate debauchers who had passed out in the gutter after a wild night—set up as independent hotelmen. Claude Labouret was among the most successful.

Since Villers-Cotterêts was on the Paris-Soissons road, the town had good sources of Parisian news by coach and, this being a progressive town in a patriot province, the residents were early in forming a National Guard unit and pinning tricolor cockades on one another. But Claude Labouret was levelheaded enough to know his ragtag militia would be no use in defending the town, with its many fine houses and hotels, not to mention the Orléans château, if a mob of brigands actually descended. He was also concerned about the town's granaries and the food in its marketplace. And so he sent for the dragoons.

—◄

ON August 15, twenty dragoons, clad in scarlet and white, their horses draped with the queen's blazon, rode into the main square of Villers-Cotterêts. One in particular caught everyone's eye: the remarkable black-skinned man nearly half a head taller than the rest, with broad, powerful shoulders. Though a private, he had the bearing of an officer in the saddle, as well as the high cheekbones, imposing brow, and almost disdainful look that would have made one sure he was an aristocrat if his uniform and coloring did not say otherwise.

"He was an object of curiosity and general admiration," a descendant of one eyewitness would recall of the day Alex Dumas first rode into town.

Since there were no barracks in Villers-Cotterêts, the dragoons were billeted with the townsfolk. As the National Guard commandant, Labouret had first choice of which soldier he would host, and this was particularly convenient, since he owned a hotel. He invited the handsome black soldier who made such a favorable impression. The following night his daughter, Marie-Louise, wrote to her friend Julie Fortin:

> Dear Julie—
> The dragoons that we expected arrived the day before last at eleven in the morning. They were to be housed at the château and at the hunting lodge, our Lord had bidden Germain, but only the horses will be there for now and later the men, because for now, they are being generously received by one or another family in town. My father set his heart on taking in a man of color who belongs to the detachment. He is very nice. His name is Dumas. His companions say that it is not his real name.
> He is said to be the son of a lord from Saint-Domingue or somewhere in those parts. He is as tall as Prevost, but he has better manners. You see, my dear and good Julie, he is a fine figure of a man.

The Labourets learned from his commanding officer that "Alexandre Dumas" was in fact Count Thomas-Alexandre Dumas Davy de la Pailleterie (if he had claimed his inheritance, he would technically have been a marquis by this point, since Antoine had died), and though the title might be legally disputed in Paris or Saint-Germain-en-Laye, in Villers-Cotterêts it made quite an impression. Though a masterly swordsman and equestrian, as they would see, he could also enchant Marie-Louise and her parents with stories of life in Saint-Domingue and descriptions of the Parisian theater, the amazing diversions of the Palais Royal. Here was a young man with breeding, bearing, intelligence, and a life of unbounded romance and exoticism. The entire family was beguiled. As for Marie-Louise, Dumas was the most dashing man she had ever laid eyes on.

Dumas lived for four months at the Hôtel de l'Ecu with the Labourets. They spoiled him and treated him like a beloved member of the family. They would learn that, despite his aristocratic training, he was a man of deep republican convictions and believed in the Revolution fervently.* This mattered a great deal to a commander of the National Guard in the summer of 1789. Indeed, if Dumas had not had such convictions, his noble background might have been a mark against him in a France where all previous distinctions were being upended.

—◆—

ON the night of August 4, the National Assembly, in an attempt to halt the fires being set on thousands of estates, declared the total abolition of feudal rights in France. Patriot aristocrats voluntarily renounced their noble privileges and took advantage of the peasant uprisings to push for social reform far beyond what any peasant could have imagined. The

---

* Republicanism was an ideology—radical in the eighteenth century—that opposed the divine right of kings and favored representative government based on a constitution, elected leadership, and a free, responsible citizenry. It was not only about liberty and personal freedom, but also duty and sacrifice to the nation. The French republicans looked back more than two thousand years for their model, writing speeches, giving plays, and making art that glorified the ancient republics of Greece and Rome. But they also glorified the ancient "Frenchness" of the Celts and Franks. They considered more recent French history to be a period of dissolution and decline in the nation's moral character, brought on because the formerly free French citizen-warriors had become decadent "subjects" of a falsely deified king.

Viscount de Noailles, victor at Yorktown and Alex Dumas's old neighbor in Saint-Germain-en-Laye, was the first to renounce his privileges, calling for a universal income tax to accompany the end of feudal rights. The Duke de la Rochefoucauld-d'Enville, a cofounder of the Society of the Friends of the Blacks—the powerful French abolitionist society whose members included the cream of patriot nobility—rose with his fellow "friend of the Blacks," the Marquis de Lafayette, to call for the Assembly to consider abolishing slavery before the night was through.*

French aristocrats had many reasons to voluntarily cast off their rights and privileges. In some ways the night of August 4 was the apotheosis of Enlightenment principles—a "moment of patriotic drunkenness," as the Marquis de Ferrières put it—that allowed these nobles to put the ideals they'd been imbibing for two decades into practice at last. It was their chance to bring the most thrilling experience of their young manhood—fighting for revolution in America—home to France. In another way, though, these voluntary renunciations merely bowed to the inevitable: in practice, feudalism had long been on its way out in most parts of the kingdom. By voluntarily casting off their rights and taking on the mantle of commoners and freedmen, these nobles grabbed the reins of the Revolution and took control of its direction—for the moment.

By late August, "the representatives of the French people, formed into a National Assembly, considering ignorance, forgetfulness, or contempt of the rights of man to be the only causes of public misfortunes and the corruption of Governments, [had] resolved to set forth, in a solemn Declaration, the natural, unalienable and sacred rights of man." These words were written by Lafayette, with the help of Thomas Jefferson, then serving as American ambassador in Paris, and formed the preamble to the Declaration of the Rights of Man and of the Citizen, approved by the National Assembly in that tumultuous month. This greatest document of the French Revolution was a

---

*Along with La Rochefoucauld and Lafayette, some of the Enlightenment's leading lights—Brissot, Condorcet, Grégoire, Mirabeau, Raynal, and Volney, to name the most illustrious—would become members of this French "abolitionist international." Incredibly, it would meet its goal of ending slavery after only six years of activism. The group would then operate as a sort of think tank, planning a post-slave economy for the colonies. During the Revolution, its mostly white membership would also include almost every major black and mixed-race activist in Paris.

conscious homage to the American Declaration of Independence. It enumerated the rights article by article:

Article 1

Men are born and remain free and equal in rights. Social distinctions may be based only on considerations of the common good.

Article 2

The aim of all political association is the preservation of the natural and imprescriptible rights of Man. These rights are Liberty, Property, Safety, and Resistance to Oppression.

Other important ones included Article 6, assuring that all citizens, being equal, "shall be equally eligible to all high offices, public positions and employments, according to their ability, and without other distinction than that of their virtues and talents." And Article 9 prohibited torture: "As every man is presumed innocent until he has been declared guilty, if it should be considered necessary to arrest him, any undue harshness that is not required to secure his person must be severely curbed by Law."

The Declaration of the Rights of Man and of the Citizen was a heady achievement, but it was followed by that year's October Days, when a mob of furious women marched on Versailles to avenge an insult a royal officer had supposedly made against "the Nation." Such mobs—which became emblematic of the violence of the Revolution as it broke down all conventions, even those of gender—were driven as much by bread shortages as anything else. This mob stormed through the palace, furiously shouting for Marie-Antoinette: "Where is that villain? We need her guts to make cockades! No, first we've got to burn her alive and fricassee her liver!" The queen fled through a secret passageway leading from the king's chamber but ran into a locked door and, for many terrifying minutes, stood pounding on it—the king had gone to save their children—until finally some National Guard troops came to her rescue. The mob returned to Paris with huge carts full of flour and grain, along with the heads of two bodyguards on pikes—men who had been unfortunate enough to stand between them and the royals.

The National Guard forced the king and queen to accompany them back to Paris as their virtual prisoners. Thanks to some fancy intervention by General Lafayette at the head of the Paris National Guard, the royals were not murdered but rather recast—tenuously—as people's monarchs, who would henceforth reign in the people's capital.

The monarch-prisoners were moved into the Tuileries Palace, which had not been used as a royal residence for more than a century. Since Versailles's construction, this palace in central Paris had been used as office space and even, occasionally, as a performance space for the Comédie-Française and other theatrical companies. Now it was revived as a setting for the monarchy, and Versailles lay abandoned, the ghost palace of the Revolution.

The National Assembly also relocated to the Tuileries, installing itself in the Manège—the cavernous indoor riding hall where Thomas-Alexandre had taken his lessons; it was the only building in Paris big enough to hold upward of a thousand deputies, along with the members of the public who would come to observe their proceedings. (Jefferson worried about the size of the body, writing in a letter to Tom Paine, "I have always been afraid their numbers might lead to confusion. Twelve hundred men in one room are too many.") The hall's strange, narrow design, with tiered seating on both sides, caused the deputies to divide themselves according to their political opinions: radicals to the left of the Assembly's president, conservatives to his right, the origin of the political terms "left" and "right."

Days after the Manège opened for business, it received a delegation of free men of color who came to petition for the right to serve as representatives in the colonial legislature as well as the National Assembly. They had on their side the Society of the Friends of the Blacks and the principles expressed by the Declaration of the Rights of Man and of the Citizen. On the other side of the aisle, rich colonial planters created the "Club Massiac" to oppose the extension of rights to blacks, arguing that it would be "the terror of the colonists" and the ruin of France. Charles de Lameth, one Friend who also owned vast plantations on Saint-Domingue, declared that he preferred "to lose everything rather than mistake the principles that justice, humanity and eternal truth have consecrated."

But the National Assembly was no legislature in any ordinary sense. Rather, it was a sort of meeting ground for the clubs, those odd political bodies that had sprung up during the Estates-General and for the next five years would wield the real power in France. The largest and most prominent was the Jacobin Club.

At first, the Jacobin Club was not the most radical club. It was known for its lively, collegial debates and for attracting diverse and prominent revolutionaries to its ranks. Though it would one day command the loyalty of the Paris "street," its initial membership was largely professional and bourgeois, mainly because it charged hefty subscription fees to join. The Duke d'Orléans's son Louis-Philippe—who in the nineteenth century would become king of France—joined; so did the Viscount de Noailles.

The Jacobins debated revolutionary issues among themselves, then took their impressive collective brainpower to the immense chamber of the Tuileries riding academy to argue them with deputies from the other clubs. Any issue—from the future of women's rights to the conferring of vending permits—could be the subject of fiery altercation. This is what constituted French democracy in the fall of 1789—fierce, idealistic conversations about how to impose universal ideals and fairness in society. But even as the deputies were having these lofty debates, courts were adjourning, government offices were shutting down, schools were closing. Many government officials simply gave up and went home, and the *parlements* and other judicial organs folded, many never to reconvene. (The *parlement* courts were suspended and then officially abolished in 1790 as part of the introduction of an entirely new judicial system.) The right to vote was given to all "active citizens": men over twenty-five who were French or had "become French," whose residency had been established for at least a year, and who paid a sum worth the value of three days' labor. Despite the vociferous objections of a few deputies, women were not considered active citizens.

Out of a system where all administrative positions were appointed or bought sprang a system where nearly every position—down to the lowest level, practically to the file clerks—would be elected. Nearly a million positions now needed to be filled, and though the government was still broke, hundreds of thousands volunteered for service. Despite the economic crisis and the continuing shortages, and although nobody was really in charge, the entire country seemed to pull together and run on the fumes of enthusiasm.

➤◄

AT the Hôtel de l'Ecu in Villers-Cotterêts, Marie-Louise had been confirmed early on in her first impressions of the handsome soldier who was taking shelter under her roof.

Three years in the army, living in the rugged garrison town of Laon, with its medieval air and eternal silent vistas, had changed Dumas. He had a cavalryman's swagger and the convictions of a republican revolutionary. If in Laon Alex had lived in a world where time stood still, he'd ridden from its gates into a world where time had accelerated—where changes that might have taken decades, or even centuries, were happening over weeks or days.

It must have been with some trepidation that he approached Monsieur Labouret to ask for his daughter's hand. But Monsieur Labouret responded positively to Dumas's proposal. Here, in this provincial place—as in the French army, too—race actually appears to have been a nonissue. Dumas's whole picaresque life so far belied the idea that fortune could be determined at birth. The tricolor cockade pinned to both his and his future father-in-law's hats told that it was a new day, when all men would be equal before the law.

On December 6, Alexandre Dumas and Marie-Louise Labouret were engaged. Claude Labouret had a single request: that they postpone the wedding until Dumas had been promoted to sergeant. This could also have been a father's test of a suitor's fidelity, to be sure he'd remain loyal once he was away in the wide world, among all the other women he was bound to meet.

Ten days later, Dumas and the Sixth Dragoons rode out of Villers-Cotterêts to do their duty and find their place in the Revolution. Surely Claude Labouret had doubts about how long it might take Dumas to make sergeant. But he could not have imagined how far his request would be surpassed.

➤◄

THE summer of 1790 was the second—and sunniest—of the Revolution, metaphorically anyway; in fact, it rained a lot. It was a summer of nonstop public parties and festivals celebrating the momentous changes under way in the country, feted at mass banquets and galas nationwide. The largest of these took place in Paris on July 14—the first anniversary of the fall of the Bastille—on the Champ de Mars, the "Field of Mars," named for the Roman god of war because it was a military parade ground. (It is now a public park accommodating armies of tourists visiting the Eiffel Tower.) The government declared the day the Fête de la Fédération.

In preparation for the event, thousands of volunteers of all social classes donated their labor, joining more than twelve thousand hired workers, to prepare the field to accommodate the hundreds of thousands of expected revelers. They created the world's longest set of bleachers, out of compressed earth. (The earthen tiers were so well built that they lasted until the mid-nineteenth century.) The volunteers built an ornate triumphal arch at one end. This orgy of labor culminated in what was dubbed the Day of Wheelbarrows, on July 13, when the final preparations for the events were made. By now, the former military practice grounds had been transformed into a stadium of pharaonic proportions.

On July 14, under a driving rain, before hundreds of thousands of people, Bishop Talleyrand stood at a specially erected "Altar of the Nation" to bless the assemblage. A massive orchestra played a religious hymn arranged for military instruments. Both bishop and altar were symbolic of a melding of state and religion that was already becoming one of the Revolution's hallmarks. On the side of the altar was inscribed:

> The Nation, the Law, the King
> The Nation, which is you
> The Law, which is also you
> The King, who is the guardian of the Law

General Lafayette, still the hero of the American Revolution, swore an oath and was followed by King Louis himself. For the first time Louis used his new title, "King of the French"—not "King of France"—thus symbolizing his duty to the people. His sworn oath was "to employ all the power delegated to me by the Constitution to uphold the decrees of the National Assembly." A cry went up from the crowd, pronouncing the theme of the summer: "Frenchmen, we are free, we are brothers! Long live the nation, the law, and the king!"

Banners from National Guard regiments around France colored the field, and amid them all flew the first American flag ever displayed outside the

United States—carried by a U.S. delegation led by John Paul Jones and Tom Paine.

Then came feasting and public balls that went on for days and nights with performances by thousands of actors, opera singers, and musicians. Huge banquets took place around the city where members of different classes and political factions broke bread together. (They passed out their leftovers to thousands of eager Parisian poor; the underclass was not actually invited to dine with them.) Many individual Parisians were moved to demonstrate their fraternal enthusiasm by inviting visitors to stay at their homes and share their tables. That July, the revolutionary dream seemed momentarily to be coming true, with people of every class and background joining in celebration. As extraordinary as everything else about the day was Louis's apparent enthusiasm for it. He permitted National Guards from all over the country to browse his library and stroll in his botanical gardens; a week before the Fête, he showed up at the Champ de Mars in person to inspect the progress of the preparations. Instead of a prisoner of the Revolution, in the summer of 1790 Louis was an active participant in it. This was not to last.

➤—◄

THE previous summer, even before the Bastille had fallen, Louis's younger brother, Charles, escaped the country and took refuge in the territory of his father-in-law, the king of Piedmont-Sardinia. Piedmont-Sardinia, lying on France's southeast border and controlled by the House of Savoy, was the most powerful of the many small kingdoms that would eventually become modern Italy; its territories included rich, important cities like Milan, much of the French Alps, and also parts of modern France, including Nice. Over the next few years, hundreds of thousands of aristocratic émigrés—this is the origin of the word—would arrive in Piedmont-Sardinia and neighboring monarchic states, eager to raise a counterrevolutionary force to restore order in France. But the émigrés had no power without the backing of a European state with an army. And their appeals for help from the great powers largely fell on deaf ears.

No matter what sympathy they felt personally for Louis and the Bourbons, none of the European states yet saw any compelling reason to intervene in France's internal affairs. Most thought that, according to traditional balance-of-power politics, France's weakness would be their own strength. The idea that the Revolution might cross international borders and threaten their own cozy monarchies did not occur to them. Even that arch-opponent of the French Revolution Edmund Burke believed the French had "done their business for us as rivals, in a way which twenty Ramilies or Blenheims could never have done"—that is, had weakened their own country's ability to project power more than any defeat on the battlefield had ever done. No one yet conceived that a state "weakened by revolution" could pose a serious military threat to its neighbors. The idea that revolution might actually make a state *stronger* was not even considered.

France's archrival England was certainly not inclined to help the Bourbons, and while British politicians on the left praised the Revolution, others expressed undisguised schadenfreude about Louis XVI's plight. It served him right for supporting the American Revolution—that its ideology had come back to bite him showed that God was Protestant. Preoccupied in eastern Europe, neither Russia nor Prussia showed any interest in intervening. Spain was too weak to act alone or to lead a coalition, as were smaller monarchies like Piedmont-Sardinia. These states would take in émigrés but were not about to launch an attack on revolutionary France.

Louis's last, best hope for help was his wife's brother, Emperor Leopold of Austria. After Louis himself, Leopold was the most powerful monarch in Europe. In the eighteenth century, Austrian territory still made up the bulk of the "Holy Roman Empire of the German Nation"—a vast multilingual conglomeration of states that traced its origins to the high Middle Ages and included some of the wealthiest parts of modern Germany and Italy, as well as other territories in both eastern and western Europe. In fact, many of these principalities were along the French border, and while Vienna did not directly control them, it had a close alliance with their rulers, as was the case with Piedmont-Sardinia. This long frontier was one reason the French and Austrians had fought so many wars over the last several centuries. But since the 1750s, and the marriage between Louis and Marie-Antoinette, Austria and France had been in an uneasy alliance. If there was any monarch who should have come to King Louis's aid, it was Leopold. The Austrian emperor,

however, also bowed out of attacking France. Like the other European powers, Austria was shaken by the Revolution and feared it would spread, while
also being happy to see France, that perpetual boss of European affairs,
knocked down a peg or two.

In the late spring of 1791, after a year of growing frustration and isolation
in the Tuileries, the royal family decided to flee to the border of the Austrian Netherlands—the modern country of Belgium—where they believed
that Emperor Leopold could protect them, and perhaps even launch their
restoration to full power. Louis also held the delusional belief that once he
was out of the Parisian hotbed of revolutionary extremism, his people would
embrace him. On the night of June 20, the king, in a coach and disguised
as either a valet or a merchant traveling with his family—the story is told
both ways—made his "flight to Varennes." There his identity was discovered, because he stopped the entourage to dine and the man serving him got
suspicious: he supposedly checked the king's face against the image on a coin
or banknote and called the guards to arrest him. (Many accounts of this in
the popular press lampooned the king's gluttony, saying that he'd been too
hungry to make it to the border without stopping for a snack.) The king and
his entourage were arrested and returned to the Tuileries Palace under guard.

The king had, in fleeing, publicly spurned the Revolution, but most revolutionaries were still not ready to spurn him and be without a monarch. The
government crafted a cover story to explain Louis's flight—the royal family had been kidnapped by counterrevolutionaries, who were to use them as
pawns in a complex plot, until the patriots happily discovered the plot and
liberated the royals. Nobody believed it for a second. Before fleeing, the king
had left an angry denunciation of the Revolution behind at the Tuileries
Palace. A petition was drafted denouncing Louis as a lying traitor and demanding that he make his attempted abdication formal. On July 17, a score
of demonstrators brought their petition to the Champ de Mars, where a year
earlier Parisians had come together harmoniously, in far greater numbers, in
the Fête de la Fédération.

What happened next has always been disputed. (If a crowd of thousands
can obscure the truth behind mayhem caught on video at a rock concert today,
how much more obscure must things have been before there were cameras of
any kind?) It seems clear that angry shouting, then pushing, broke out in the

crowd. Some would later say that the entire event had been infiltrated by foreign conspirators—or the ever-useful "brigands"—who had lured Parisians
there to do them harm. Supporters of the petition would say that the violence
arose from a royal plot to destroy republicanism.

One thing is certain: the political throng on the field suddenly found itself
joined by military units, mostly National Guardsmen, streaming in from all
directions. At Lafayette's importuning, the government had declared martial law: the factions denouncing the king as a traitor were being answered
by an ugly mood in the street, and the constitutional monarchy was looking
increasingly fragile.

Alex Dumas and the Sixth Dragoons also rode onto the field. Policing
public events was one of their jobs, and they were good at it. They knew how
to keep their cool in such situations better than regular soldiers. They were
armed with their usual sabers and short muskets but also light cannons.

General Lafayette, commanding the Paris National Guard, rode in on his
white horse. The "hero of two worlds" ordered the rioters to calm down and
go home, in his self-important, involuntarily aristocratic manner. The crowd
jeered and threw rocks at his guardsmen.

Seeing his orders emphatically disobeyed, Lafayette commanded the National Guard to fire, either above the heads of the crowd or—as some reports claim—directly into it. In one version, the mob attacks the guardsmen,
causing them to panic, and they fire mostly to protect themselves. In any
event, the day became known as the Champ de Mars Massacre. The number
of dead is uncertain: the estimates range from twelve to around fifty. But such
violence from the revolutionary government was at that point shocking: the
guillotine had yet to make its debut on the political stage.

Soon, though, the July 1791 violence would be overshadowed by revolutionary killing on an unimaginable scale. If in July 1790 the Champ de Mars
Fête symbolized where the Revolution had come from, the Champ de Mars
Massacre of July 1791 symbolized its future. By the spring of 1794, when the
Revolution had turned to the bloody period called the Terror, Alex Dumas
would be threatened with the guillotine for his mere presence on the field that
day. By then, however, the association with a previous government, in any
capacity, could be grounds for immediate execution.

"REGENERATION BY BLOOD"

"REMEMBER those crusades in which Europe armed herself for a few superstitions," wrote Jacques-Pierre Brissot, leader of one of the most powerful revolutionary factions, in his paper *The French Patriot*, on December 13, 1791. "The time has come for another crusade, and it has a far nobler, and holier, goal. This is a crusade for universal freedom."

Maximilien Robespierre, leader of a rival faction, objected that trying to turn the Revolution into a universal, military crusade for freedom would not work. France's neighbors would not accept liberation at the hands of foreign troops, any more than France would have. He advocated maintaining peace with surrounding nations, and focusing on imposing ideological purity at home.

France's enemies had given the war faction a great boost: in the wake of Louis's unsuccessful flight and arrest the previous summer, a coalition of royalist powers led by the Austrian emperor had issued a declaration threatening to summon "the forces necessary" to come to the king's aid. It was actually a weak threat—the language was left purposefully vague so that no one had to commit to any concrete action—and any normal eighteenth-century government would have realized that and ignored it. But France did not have a normal government: it had a collection of caffeinated intellectuals conducting passionate nonstop shouting matches in the former royal riding school of the Tuileries Palace. The threat of foreign invasion now made the agenda of preemptive, revolutionary war seem sensible, even inevitable.

"It is a cruel thing to think, but it becomes more striking every day: we are regressing through peace," fumed one of Brissot's followers. "We will be regenerated only by blood. Shallow character, corrupt and frivolous morals:

these basic qualities, incompatible with liberty, can only be overcome by adversity."

Jacques-Pierre Brissot knew adversity firsthand. Though the son of a pastry cook, he knew what it was to go hungry. In the years before the Revolution, he had lived as a kind of freelance foreign correspondent and pamphleteer, recording his observations of events in the Austrian Netherlands (Belgium), England, Switzerland, and America, and finding paid work as he could. He served time in a debtors' prison in London. He was short and slight, with a scribbler's stooped shoulders and an awkwardness that ranged from timidity to belligerence. But his main character flaw was that of so many French revolutionaries: a zeal for human rights so self-righteous that it translated into intolerance for the actual human beings around him. Brissot had spent more time abroad than most of the other revolutionaries. During his travels in the brand-new United States, in 1788, he had become infatuated by the American republic and its spirit of "simplicity, goodness, and that dignity of man which is the possession of those who realize their liberty and who see in their fellow men only brothers and equals." Brissot had determined to bring the American ideals to Europe.

The one thing he rejected about the American Revolution was its perpetuation of slavery. On this issue, the poverty-stricken journalist made common cause with Lafayette and La Rochefoucauld, working alongside these wealthy aristocrats in the Society of the Friends of the Blacks. Traveling through Virginia, Brissot met with General Washington and tried to convince him to start a new revolution for racial emancipation; Washington demurred, telling his French visitor that Virginia was not yet ready for such a thing. But Brissot insisted that racial liberation must respect no borders. Now he applied the same logic to the French Revolution.

Brissot was still passionate about the abolitionist cause, but in the winter of 1791–92 the slaves that concerned him were not the actual enslaved blacks in the colonies. Rather, Brissot and his followers now talked about metaphorical "slaves." These slaves were the white European soldiers of all France's enemies: Austrians, Prussians, Sardinians, Russians—it did not matter. So long as they marched against revolutionary France in the name of a king or emperor, they were slaves, pitted against the land of liberty. Thus the revolutionaries both belittled enemy soldiers and held out the prospect that they needed help and liberation. The rhetoric of slave armies attacking the Revolution implied a newly urgent task. France naturally needed to defend itself, but the attackers could not just be repulsed: they also needed to be liberated from their own masters, so as to spread the Revolution. In this way, the line between defense and offense was hopelessly blurred. France could not defend its revolution without attacking.

This essential idea would be captured in the words of the Revolution's greatest song, which would eventually become France's national anthem. The "Marseillaise" was originally titled "The War Song for the Army of the Rhine" and was penned in these fevered months to inspire Frenchmen to fight off the royalist armies massing on France's eastern borders. The second verse told of the slave soldiers marching under their royal masters to crush the Revolution and put the freed French people back in chains:

> *What do they want, this horde of slaves,*
> *of traitors, of conjured kings?*
> *Meant for whom, these vile chains,*
> *These irons long prepared?*
> *Frenchman, for us, ah! what outrage!*
> *What fury it must inspire!*
> *It is for us that they dare plan*
> *A return to the slavery of old!*

As the Assembly's most fervid warmonger, Brissot called for immediate action against the Revolution's foreign enemies. "We cannot be at ease until Europe, and all of Europe, is in flames!"

Along with the French deputies, the Manège now contained various professional dissidents who had arrived from around Europe to join in the excitement. These international revolutionaries were followers of Brissot's universalist creed. "It is because I want peace that I am calling for war!" shouted Anacharsis Cloots, a German baron who had shown up in Paris and taken to calling himself "Orator of the Human Race." He vowed that the French flag would fly over twenty liberated countries within a month.

IN the 1750s and '60s, when Alexandre Dumas's uncle Louis de la Pailleterie was serving as a captain, and then a colonel, in the artillery, French warcraft was in a dreadful state. As one French commander lamented, "I lead a gang of thieves, of murderers fit only for the gauntlet, who turn tail at the first gunshot and who are always ready to mutiny . . . The king has the worst infantry under heaven, and the worst-disciplined, and there is simply no way to lead troops like these."

Until the late eighteenth century, the "professionalizing" of the military had proceeded in fits and starts. For hundreds of years, professional military standards existed only among mercenaries, and these men fought alone or in small groups. Throughout the seventeenth century, European soldiers were still only slightly removed from thugs; they raped, robbed, and pillaged civilians as assiduously as they fought the enemy. Whole towns would be massacred without much thought, and even when soldiers attempted to behave with a measure of humanity, they still pillaged wherever they went, because pillaging was the only way to support their operations, especially on long campaigns. Since most of Europe lived harvest to harvest, an army often left famine in its wake.

After the horrors of the wars of religion, during which nearly a third of central Europe's population was wiped out, various innovations were introduced to make armies less randomly destructive. Discipline was introduced in the form of drills, regimentation, uniforms. Most important, armies began clothing and feeding soldiers, so they'd have no need to pillage, and paying them in lieu of booty. As a result, European armies became less destructive. Ironically, less destructive wars could be fought more often—could in fact be fought more or less constantly, with short breaks for minor changes in coalitions. Europe thus remained in a near-constant state of low-level conflict between 1700 and 1790; during that time, the various powers fought more than fifteen different wars, with France almost always involved on one side or the other.

In previous centuries, the idea of joining an army to "serve one's country" would have seemed ludicrous (though traditional national hatreds and rivalries could be a useful spur to those who'd joined). Soldiers fought because they feared not doing so. While an officer's commission was a perquisite of the aristocratic class, soldiering was work for the dregs of society, and little more was expected of soldiers than to follow orders and not desert; every army had devised elaborate horrors to keep its men in line, like the "wooden horse" favored by the British—a stiff wooden board that a recalcitrant soldier would sit on for hours, muskets weighing down his legs—or the Prussians' infamous "running the gauntlet," where a delinquent soldier was forced to run between two lines of his comrades, who flogged him as he passed. In seventeenth-century France, it was still possible for a captain to cut off the nose of a soldier who had deserted before a battle, and branding as a punishment was common.

Officers fought for the glory and honor of their rank and family name. Until the mid-1700s, an officer's commission had been seen as a social and monetary sinecure, an object of inheritance, favoritism, or sale. For the old "sword nobility," supposed descendants of the chivalric knights, a commission was a means of keeping up family tradition; for the newly wealthy, it was a means of fabricating status. For the monarchy and the state, it was a means of collecting revenue—effectively, a tax. The most prestigious French commissions sold for what it would cost to build a great château and required even more funds, because a commission came with a regiment of soldiers, which the purchaser had to equip and pay. A businessman who'd saved the necessary pile could make his adolescent son a colonel or his ten-year-old a captain, although he first had to purchase his family's noble rank.*

An entire army held together by common training, discipline, values, and purpose had long been a theoretical dream—widely contemplated in ancient Greek and Roman texts but not to be found on the battlefield. But then France benefited from its overwhelming defeat in the Seven Years' War, which brought not only the loss of the French Empire in North America but humiliation by the Prussians. In the can-do spirit of the Enlightenment, a small group of scholar-officers became determined to reform the military.

Most Enlightenment intellectuals regarded warfare with contempt, as an atavistic remnant of mankind's irrational past and medieval values, along with plain old-fashioned brutality, greed, lust, and cruelty. They thought that as society matured into a more rational, scientific age such barbarism would

---

* The system of adolescent officership did not preclude talent—France's brilliant general Maurice de Saxe displayed audacious courage at twelve and commanded a regiment by seventeen—but it left little clear opportunity for men of mere ability and initiative.

wither. But alongside these pacifist philosophers, France also produced a generation of military philosophers dedicated to remaking the French army into an invincible tool of conquest. At the forefront of these was Count Jacques de Guibert, who—in 1770, at the height of the Enlightenment—called on the French army to resurrect the lost spirit of the Roman legions and predicted great things if it could be done: "Now suppose there arises in Europe a vigorous people, with genius, resources, and government; a people who unite austere virtues and a national militia with a fixed plan of military expansion, who would not lose sight of this plan, who, knowing how to wage war at little cost and subsist on their victories, are not reduced to laying down their arms because of financial calculations. One would see such a people subjugate its neighbors, and overthrow our feeble constitutions, as the north wind bends the frail reeds." Much as Rousseau advocated stripping human life down to a "natural" state, Guibert called for sweeping away the decadence of the foppish eighteenth-century French officer to discover a neo-Roman ideal. He imagined an army of self-sacrificing, physically courageous citizen-style soldiers. Guibert and his fellow military philosophers laid the groundwork for patriotic warmongers to come. Their reforms of the French army transformed it, preparing it for the revolutionaries' extreme ambitions.

Guibert and his colleagues focused on professionalizing the officer corps through education and created Europe's finest military academies. They also took the first steps toward endowing soldiering with dignity and regularity. They built barracks, so that soldiers constantly trained with their regiments, instead of haphazardly coming and going from their houses. They introduced uniforms for officers as well as soldiers, though some officers still resisted wearing them—why would an officer dress in livery, like a lackey or coachman? They provided the French army with the plans and the tools for melding France's infantry, cavalry, and artillery into Europe's first modern army. And they created written orders and maps, both high-tech innovations in an age when armies arrived days late for battles and rarely had a clear idea of the terrain they crossed.

The French military philosophers created a whole new generation of guns, designed to be lighter and more accurate than anything anywhere. These new guns would allow a new kind of offensive warfare—based on mass, maneuverability, and the ability to strike quickly over long distances.

France's budget crisis in the 1780s kept many of these weapons from going into production in the monarchy's last years, but the technology was there, waiting for a government with the wherewithal and drive to use it.

France, which had long had Europe's largest population, now had the unique power of the revolutionary idea to create citizen soldiers. Since France's most entrenched aristocratic officers had defected to the émigrés, the field was unusually wide open for brains, bravery, and enthusiasm.

＊＊

THE revolutionary government began its universal crusade for liberty with a preemptive strike on the Austrian Netherlands, as a way both to protect its frontier and to attack its great royalist enemy and the émigrés' supporter. The men in Paris believed this would mobilize the French-speaking population there against their German-speaking overlords. The Austrian Netherlands had exploded in an American-and-French-inspired revolution only two years earlier: six months after the Bastille fell, Brussels patriots proclaimed "the United States of Belgium" and declared their nation's independence from the Austrian Empire. But then the emperor sent in more Austrian troops and claimed the region back. The French now hoped that their incursion would spark a renewed uprising.

Alex Dumas, recently promoted to corporal, accompanied one of three columns that were to carry out the attack. Dumas was still just one of thousands of faceless soldiers, only one rank above a private, so no other records survive of his presence. His column of ten thousand men was led by the Duke de Biron, another member of the 1776 generation who had served with Rochambeau in America. The column met with initial success, taking a key strategic town on the border and continuing deeper into Austria's Belgian territory. Later that day, April 29, the column was attacked by Austrians but successfully beat them back. However, the inexperienced among the French soldiers panicked, and that evening two cavalry regiments actually mounted their horses and rode off. General Biron rode after the deserters himself, alone, and eventually caught them and, by argument rather than orders, persuaded most of the men to return to the camp.

Meanwhile, on the same day, another French general, Théobald Dillon, was less lucky. Dillon was leading ten squadrons of cavalry across the frontier at a different point, to the north, and, coming under Austrian fire, these soldiers panicked, fled back into French territory, and barricaded themselves inside the walled city of Lille. When General Dillon came looking for them, a mob of his own troops shouted that he had betrayed them to the enemy. They seized him and tore him to pieces. In Paris the Assembly tried to organize a court-martial to investigate the incident, but Robespierre, a mastermind of mob mentality, in a chilling foreshadowing of the course he was to follow, congratulated the troops who had murdered their commander. (Members of Dumas's own Sixth Dragoons were recommended for court-martial for the incident.) Though generals like Biron and Dillon supported the Revolution—they had become émigrés, after all—they were still nobles and moderates, hence, suspect. To a man like Robespierre, only the lowest soldiers could really be trusted. Lucky for Dumas that he was still only a corporal.

With the French troops a danger more to their own officers than to their enemies that spring, the Austrians and Prussians easily gained the advantage. But then, in late July, the Austrian-Prussian coalition blew this advantage by issuing another threat: once again it warned of retribution should any harm befall King Louis or his family. Like its declaration almost a year before, the July 1792 manifesto backfired, only this time more severely.

On August 10, pike-wielding mobs stormed the Tuileries Palace, massacred the Swiss Guards, the last troops loyal to the king, and turned the neighborhood around the Palais Royal—now called the Palais Égalité—into a charnel house. The king and his family survived only by running to the Manège and begging refuge from the deputies of the Assembly who were gathered there. That day, the French monarchy effectively ended, and the Assembly immediately began preparing to declare a republic. The royal family, under arrest, would henceforth live in the Temple—the old Knights Templar headquarters, now a revolutionary prison—just around the corner from the Nicolet Theater.

━━◆━━

CORPORAL Alex Dumas remained on the Belgian frontier, far from Paris. Here among bleak hedgerows and turnip and bean fields, the Austrians and the French fought a war of cross-border raids. The most important French cavalry base in the region was at a little town called Maulde, where they created a large armed camp.

Dumas worked out of the camp at Maulde. His job was to lead small units of dragoons and other cavalry, usually four or eight horsemen, on scouting missions to forestall enemy incursions. Most of the time, the scouts saw more cows and sheep than Austrian troops. But on August 11 they ran into a raiding party. Dumas spotted the enemy riders, a force considerably larger than his own. But rather than try to escape or evade, Corporal Dumas led his little band in a charge on the startled Austrians. The Austrians, perhaps stunned at the mere sight of a six-foot-one black man riding full tilt out of a Belgian bean field, quickly surrendered to him en masse. His son the novelist would take evident delight in describing the incident:

> Spotting them, despite his inferiority in numbers, he gave the order to charge in an instant. The [Austrians], who were unprepared for this sudden attack, retreated to a small meadow surrounded by a ditch large enough to stop cavalry. But, as I've said, my father was an excellent horseman; he mounted a good horse that he called Joseph. He took the reins, spurred Joseph on, leapt the ditch, . . . and in an instant found himself alone in the midst of the thirteen chasseurs, who, stunned by such audacity, handed over their arms and surrendered. The victor piled up the thirteen carbines in a stack, placed them on his saddle-bow, made the thirteen men march to meet his four dragoons, who had stopped on the other side of the ditch which they could not cross, and, being the last to pass over the ditch, he led his prisoners to the camp.
>
> Prisoners were rare in those days, and the sight of four men leading thirteen produced a major sensation in the camp. This proof of the young officer's courage was much discussed; General Beurnonville wanted to see him, made him sergeant, invited him to dinner, and mentioned his name in the day's report.
>
> This was the first distinction to fall on this new name, Alexandre Dumas, adopted by the son of the Marquis de la Pailleterie.

That the father's heroism was equal to the son's description was confirmed by the *Moniteur Universel*—the paper of record in revolutionary France—in its edition for Saturday, August 18, 1792. Corporal Dumas, the newspaper states, "cut [the enemy riders] off so deftly and fell upon them with such alacrity that they all surrendered with their rifles loaded, without having had time to so much as fire a shot." His son gave Alex Dumas thirteen adversaries, while the newspaper mentions only twelve.

Three months later, the newspaper was still talking about Dumas's exploits, and was particularly impressed by his decision to donate his portion of the spoils to the French nation: "Citizen Dumas, American, who offered as a patriotic gift the sum of 12 livres, 10 sous, his share of the proceeds from the captured rifles, taken by him and his companions from the 12 Tyroleans whom they took prisoner." A suitably grand, patriotic gesture for an army that seemed to offer limitless possibilities for glory.

"THE BLACK HEART ALSO BEATS FOR LIBERTY"

A FEW hundred miles south, a far bigger border raid was under way. A combined force of tens of thousands of Prussians, Austrians, and Hessians—along with several hundred counterrevolutionary émigrés—crossed the frontier in wooded country east of the French border fortress of Verdun. France's defenses crumbled before the advancing Germanic force. The commander of the Verdun fortress committed suicide.

As news of the invasion reached Paris on the second of September, conspiracy theories swept the city. Since the people's armies were invincible, the only way the Germans could have crossed the frontier was . . . Treason! Betrayal by the enemy within! A monstrous aristocratic conspiracy must have sold out the revolutionary armies.

Mobs stormed the city's prisons and turned on the inmates, "enemies of the state" rounded up over the preceding two weeks. Starting with priests, they moved on to former servants of the royal family, nobles, and finally petty criminals, too—prostitutes, beggars, and thieves. Impromptu "street trials" were followed by beheadings without the guillotine's swiftness; the mobs used old swords, pikes, even kitchen knives, to murder at least 1,200 men, women, and children.

The September riots turned many foreign supporters of the Revolution against it, especially in England. The London *Times* published accounts that upped the death toll from 1,200 to 12,000 and exhorted Englishmen to "ardently pray that your happy Constitution may never be outraged by the despotic tyranny of Equalization." Appalled by the events in Paris and with a warrant out for his arrest, General Lafayette himself defected across enemy lines.*

But along with bloody-mindedness, the German invasion also inspired a new sort of patriotism—a bold sense of citizenship as soldiering. Recruiting offices were swamped. Thousands of new French citizen-soldiers signed up to receive a weapon and a uniform, or at least a scrap of tricolor fabric, and a pass authorizing them to proceed to the front.

The French volunteers met the Germanic invaders at a little village called Valmy, not far from the fortress of Verdun, and at Valmy a new legend of French invincibility was born. French gunners used some of their newest weaponry, showing what twenty years of innovation in cannon design could do. They also showed what true patriotism from below could mean for an army defending its homeland: troops taunted the invaders with cries of *"Vive la nation!"* and *"Vive la Révolution!"* The revolutionary songs and chants they let loose echoed down the wheat fields and defied the battle's torrential rains. "Here and now a new epoch in world history is beginning,"† remarked the poet Goethe, observing the French armies with amazement from behind the Prussian lines.

As part of the patriotic orgy in the wake of Valmy, the deputies in the National Assembly dissolved themselves and called for a new body to be elected directly by the People. This "National Convention" immediately voted to abolish the monarchy—the end of a 1,350-year journey—and to declare France a republic.

➤◄

BY the middle of November 1792, the new French Republic had conquered territories all along its frontiers. Flush with a power that could, conceivably,

---

* Lafayette was arrested by the Prussians, and when he protested that he had left the French army and was traveling on his honorary American citizenship, the "hero of two worlds" was thrown into irons. Lafayette spent the next five years as a common prisoner in a series of Prussian and Austrian fortresses. General Washington wanted to intervene on his behalf, but the monarchist states of Prussia and Austria did not recognize the revolutionary United States—any more than they recognized the revolutionary government of France—so Washington was powerless to help his friend.

† On the eve of World War I, over a century later, French leaders would still be invoking this battle, in the hope, ultimately false, that the French would always beat back the Germans.

even liberate the world, the republic pushed its perceived military advantage in all directions. It invaded the Austrian Netherlands, first liberating Brussels and then the whole of Belgium from the Austrian yoke. It then liberated a series of independent German states along the Rhine, long in the Austrian orbit, getting as far as Frankfurt. On the Republic's southern border, its troops invaded Piedmont-Sardinia and captured the city of Nice.

The government issued the Edict of Fraternity, offering military support to any nation that wanted to fight for its freedom. It was an open invitation to radicals across Europe to overthrow their governments. In order to live up to this offer, France needed to increase the size of its army. Fast.

The government had already begun experimenting with a new system for recruiting fighting men based on an archaic French model dating back hundreds of years: the "free legions," units independent of the regular army that could be called up in war and disbanded during times of peace. The formations would not replace but would exist alongside the regular army and the National Guard.

The legions were an eye-catching bunch, owing largely to the political refugees who had streamed into France during the first years of the Revolution and begged to take up arms in the fight for European liberty. Few of the refugees had actual military training. The government simply separated them out from the military mix by allowing them to form their own legions: soon there was a Belgian legion and a Germanic legion, and even an English one.* Baron Anacharsis Cloots offered to raise a legion of "Vandals," his term for his fellow Prussians, though it didn't come to anything.

And, on September 7, a delegation of free blacks from the colonies went to the Manège to lobby the government to approve a legion of their own. The group was led by Julien Raimond, a well-to-do planter born in Saint-Domingue to an illiterate white Frenchman and wealthy mixed-race

---

* The English legion was created by the poet John Oswald, a Scots officer in the British army who'd developed a militant form of Jacobin vegetarianism, tinged with Hinduism, while stationed on the Malabar Coast of India. He pioneered the cause of vegetarianism in the West with his book *The Cry of Nature* before dying in a battle against royalists in western France in 1793.

mother native to the island. The result of their petition was the Légion Franche des Américains et du Midi—the "Free Legion of Americans and of the South." And though most legions had the word "free" in their names, to indicate that they were independent of the regular army, in this case the word had a double meaning: every member of this legion was a free man of color. It would soon become known as the Black Legion.

The new Black Legion was also known by the name of its commander— the Légion de Saint-Georges. Saint-Georges had lived high in the last years of the *Ancien Régime* but had, like all noblemen of color, experienced the increasing racism of those years. In his midforties when the Bastille fell, he volunteered for the National Guard the following year; he was made a captain in 1791. Hearing about the new legions, Saint-Georges leapt at the chance to command a legion of mixed-race and free black men, and to get Alex Dumas into the formation.

The problem was that another officer, Colonel Joseph Boyer, had already recruited Dumas to a legion called the Hussars of Liberty and Equality, or the Hussars of the South. (The paperwork on these legions, which I experienced in all its florid immediacy in the old Château de Vincennes military library, reveals that they didn't pay much heed to consistency: many legions had multiple names.) With his recent success on the Belgian frontier, capturing those twelve prisoners single-handedly, Dumas's reputation now preceded him. Any legion forming in the fall of 1792 would want to have the hero of Maulde riding with it. It was not that different from drafting players for a football team.

A kind of bidding war ensued, with the two legions offering higher rank instead of higher pay. Dumas had agreed to be first lieutenant of the Hussars of Liberty and Equality when Saint-Georges topped that with an offer of the rank of lieutenant colonel, and also offered Dumas second in command of the Free Legion of Americans—the Black Legion. So Dumas joined up with the Americans and the Chevalier de Saint-Georges.

The date at the top of Dumas's commission (which I found in the safe at Villers-Cotterêts) provides a fascinating snapshot of the tumult of that time:

Paris, October 10, 1792. Year IV of liberty, and Year I of equality *and of the French Republic*

While the official "republican calendar" was not introduced until late 1793, the War Ministry had started printing letterhead and forms in revolutionary time much earlier. "Year IV of liberty" referred back to the taking of the Bastille and the declaration of the National Assembly. "Year I of equality," also printed, referred to the establishment of the Republic, just one month before. But the words "and the French Republic" were not even printed but scrawled beside the printed header. Events were moving so fast the stationers could not keep up.

The document itself is addressed to "Alexandre Dumas, Lieutenant Colonel," and reads:

> Sir, I am giving you notice that you are appointed to the vacant post of lieutenant colonel of the cavalry in the Free Legion of the Americans. . . .
>
> It is imperative that you join your post within one month at the latest, from the date of this letter, otherwise we will assume you have relinquished this position and it will then be given to another officer. You will be attentive enough to let me know when you receive this letter and forward me the original papers documenting the service you may have in the troops of line, in France or with the Allied Powers. These documents are necessary to expedite your certificate [*brevet*]. I will ask the Colonel to inform me of your arrival at the Regiment.
>
> Acting War Minister
>
> Le Brun

＋━＋

IN October 1791, the Friends of the Blacks had persuaded the king to sign a law reaffirming the freedom principle and banning all distinctions of color in assigning citizenship rights in France proper. But the plantation owners continued to resist any extension of the Rights of Man and of the Citizen to blacks in the colonies, whether free or not. The richest planters mostly lived in Paris, and those who didn't hired lobbyists to work the deputies in the Assembly.

Ironically enough, this was exactly how Julien Raimond, father of the Black Legion, had first become involved in politics. For all the similarities between his background and Dumas's, there was one crucial difference. Like his parents before him, Raimond was a successful slave owner who outfitted his Saint-Domingue plantation in sophisticated luxury; he spent his money on everything from books and sheet music to silver, crystal, and a slave who had been specially trained as a pastry chef. When he arrived in France in 1786 to claim an inheritance left to his wife, Raimond pushed for specific racial reforms that would have benefited him as a free black property owner of two indigo works and hundreds of slaves. He made the case that free blacks should be considered as whites' natural allies against potentially rebellious slaves—a point he stressed by referring to light-skinned people like himself as "new whites."

In a short time republican ideals and the fervor of the times turned Raimond from a member of the slaveholding faction to an increasingly committed—if practical-minded—abolitionist. As a member of the Jacobin Club, he campaigned for men of color born to free parents to be able to vote in colonial elections, an achievement that, when it was passed into law on May 15, 1791, presaged even greater changes. But Raimond's pragmatic bent led him to make common cause with fiery white radical allies like the Abbé Grégoire, a member of the Friends of the Blacks, who railed against the colonists' demand "that there will be no change in the status of the people on our islands, except at the colonists' request":

> The National Assembly will not stamp out injustice except at the request of those who feed on the situation and want to prolong it! . . . Put another way, these men will be the victims of oppression until their tyrants agree to lighten their fate.
>
> The volcano of liberty that has been lit in France will soon bring about a general explosion and change the fate of the human species in the two hemispheres.

Grégoire's words pointed to the sugar islands, and especially to Saint-Domingue, where by 1791 the volcano of liberty was already erupting. Since the summer of 1789, the Rights of Man and of the Citizen had been clashing head-on with the Code Noir. It was now two years into the Revolution and black slaves were still toiling and dying in the fields. Many had had enough. Also, as the French colonies got word of the mother country's revolution, the islands had been filling with rumors. One was that King Louis had invoked the universal rights of man and freed all slaves. Another was that he had merely abolished the whip and ordered that slaves be given three days off from work. Much as rumors of another mythical royal order had contributed to the Great Fear in August 1789, now slaves throughout the sugar islands felt they had royal sanction to rise up.

Reports reached Paris that the Saint-Domingue slave uprising, by far the largest slave revolt in history, had already taken thousands of white lives and set fire to tens of thousands of acres of sugarcane. The death toll was exaggerated, but many deputies in Paris panicked at the thought of losing France's economic backbone and supported repressing the rebellion by any means. French national security seemed to call for sacrificing principle, and the planters' lobby argued for repression of all the islands' blacks and people of color, both free and slave. The revolutionary government sent in troops to suppress the slave revolt, even though that revolt proclaimed itself part of the wider French Revolution: for the next decade, the black insurgents of Saint-Domingue would demand nothing so consistently as to be accepted into the new world of free French citizens.

By the end of 1791, slave insurgents had managed to take control of the northern half of Saint-Domingue. But when they confronted the heavily armed and trained white French army and colonial militia, the results were disproportionate casualties on the black side—ten insurgents killed for every white death. In the wake of this repression, the deputies in Paris furiously debated what to do about slavery. One of the few things Brissot's followers and Robespierre's followers agreed on was support for racial equality and disapproval of slavery. But both sides feared taking any step that could economically weaken the Republic during wartime.

"The black heart also beats for liberty!" Brissot cried to the Assembly in December 1791 in one of a series of fiery speeches defending the rights of the colonies' black and mixed-race people. It was the white planters who had sown the seeds of unrest, Brissot said—perhaps the one point on which he and Robespierre would remain in perfect agreement.

On April 4, 1792, eight months after full-out rebellion exploded on Saint-Domingue, the National Assembly extended full citizenship to free blacks and "men of color"—people with some European blood—in the colonies as well as the kingdom, but took no action against slavery itself.

The extension of full citizenship to mulattos and freed blacks was not the same as ending slavery outright, but it put France and its colonial empire in the vanguard with regard to racial emancipation. The French multiracial citizenship act had the effect of setting the British abolitionist movement back a decade, since now any political gesture on behalf of blacks was taken as evidence of crypto-French beliefs.

Within the French Empire, the declaration definitively turned most planters against the Revolution in all its facets. A decree passed by Saint-Domingue's Assembly the month after the citizenship act prohibited the "sale, impression, or distribution" of any coins or medals depicting or commemorating "the politics and revolution of France," as if stomping out republican paraphernalia could curtail the Revolution itself.

On the other side, France's free black population now felt an even more fervent allegiance to the nation and the government. Dumas's ardent republicanism and devotion to the tricolor put him in perfect sync with the nation taking shape around him. France's citizens of color now wanted to express their devotion by risking their lives to defend the Revolution. The legions would give them a chance to make that sacrifice while claiming the full privileges and dignity their newfound political status afforded them. Raimond handed an eloquent statement to the president of the National Assembly—"If Nature, inexhaustible in its combinations, has differentiated us from the French by external signs, on the other hand it has made us perfectly similar in giving us, like them, a burning heart to fight the enemies of the Nation"—and placed 125 livres in notes on his desk. This was the first contribution toward equipping and training what would become the Black Legion.

The president's reply is worth noting:

> Sirs, Virtue in Honor is independent of color and climate. The offer that you make the Fatherland of your arms and your strength for the destruction of its enemies, in honoring a great part of the human species, is a service rendered to the cause of all humankind.
>
> The Assembly appreciates your devotion and your courage. Your efforts will be all the more precious since love of Liberty and Equality must be a terrible and invincible passion in the children of those who, under their burning sun, have groaned in the irons of servitude; with

so many men gathered to harry the despots and their slaves, it is impossible that France will not soon become the capital of the free world and the tomb of all the thrones of the Universe.

—►◄

CITIZEN Claude Labouret must have been the proudest man in eastern France. The unusual soldier who had swept his daughter off her feet in the summer of 1789 had now returned, in the fall of 1792, to claim his bride, not an officer of some minor unit but the lieutenant colonel of a free legion. The little town had its hero of the Revolution, and he was about to be Labouret's new son-in-law.

On November 18, 1792, a Sunday, a notice went up on the main entrance of the Villers-Cotterêts town hall announcing:

> The future marriage between Citizen* Thomas-Alexandre Dumas Davy de la Pailleterie, 30 years and 8 months old, Lieutenant Colonel of the Hussars of the South [*sic*], born in La Guinodée, in Jérémie, in America, son of the late Antoine Alexandre Davy de la Pailleterie, former Commissioner of the Artillery, deceased in St. Germain en Laye in June 1786 & of the late Marie Cessette Dumas, deceased in La Guinodée near Jérémie in America in 1772, his father and mother, on one side. And Citizen Marie-Louise Elisabeth Labouret, grown daughter of Citizen Claude Labouret, Commander of the National Guard in Villers-Cotterêts and owner of the Hotel de l'Ecu & of Marie-Josèphè Prevot, her father and mother, on the other side.
>
> The said parties are domiciled as follows: the future husband in garrison in Amiens, the future wife in this town.

---

*Among the most ubiquitous changes imposed in the first days of the French Republic was the use of the words "Citizen" and "Citizeness" to replace all previous titles, including the most basic "Monsieur" and "Madame." The National Convention "will not suffer the title of 'Monsieur' in its midst; we will substitute that of 'Citizen,' " fumed an article from Brissot's *French Patriot* newspaper in the fall of 1792. "Citizen is a sacred word." The text goes on to explain that the ultimate revolutionary goal should be to emulate the Romans, who did not use any honorifics at all, not even the sacred word "citizen."

The Revolution had brought many changes to Villers-Cotterêts. In 1791 the Orléans' magnificent château, originally built for Charles de Valois in the thirteenth century, had been turned into an army barracks. As commander of the National Guard, Claude Labouret had overseen the conversion. More recently he'd been busy turning part of the grounds into a public sheep meadow. The current Duke d'Orléans, who had renounced his family title to become Philippe Égalité, or "Philip Equality," had not protested.

As was the revolutionary custom, Villers-Cotterêts' Church of Saint-Nicolas had been desacralized. Its cross was swapped out for a weather vane in the shape of a cockerel, the French national symbol, and the nave was now being used for meetings of the local Jacobin Club.

The couple were married in a civil ceremony at the town hall on November 28. It is not clear if they eventually had a Catholic ceremony—if so, it would have been for the benefit of Marie-Louise, since Lieutenant Colonel Dumas had no faith besides republicanism. (Ten years later, when their son Alexandre Dumas was born, the church had been resacralized, and the future author was duly baptized there.)

The ceremony was witnessed by two of Dumas's old comrades from the dragoons, including "Citizen Louis Augustin Brigitte Espagne, lieutenant colonel of the 7th Hussars Regiment," who would go on to serve under Dumas (and eventually rise to become "Count of the Empire" under Napoleon). But the most interesting witness was Marie Retou, "widow of the late Antoine Alexandre Davy de la Pailleterie, residing in St.-Germain-en-Laye." Her presence implied an attempt by Dumas at reconciliation with his past and his father's memory, not to mention with his stepmother herself.*

The marriage contract details the financial conditions of the marriage—neither spouse assumed any debts incurred by the other prior to the union,

---

* Mademoiselle Retou, now Madame de la Pailleterie, would keep up cordial relations with the Dumas household, but practically the only mention I ever found of her by Alex Dumas was in a letter he wrote home from the front to Marie-Louise in 1796, when they were having grave money troubles after the birth of their second daughter, in which Dumas cursed the old inheritance fiascos in his family: "I would not have believed my father unnatural to such an extent; I had not done him . . . anything so ridiculous . . . I have just written to Madame de la Pailleterie to discover in whose hands lies my uncle's fortune." It is impossible to decipher the details of the inheritance squabbles at that point, but the letter mainly complains about other people, such as Antoine's lawyer, making only that passing reference to "Madame de la Pailleterie."

and, in the event that either died, "The one person remaining of the two will take from their part of the contract and before dividing the assets, as far as personal property is concerned, clothes and linen for his/her own use and a fully furnished bedroom with decoration at his/her discretion, moreover if the bride survives she will take her jewelry and rings, as for the groom he will take his horse, weapons and luggage."

The honeymoon was brief and involved no exotic travel—but it left Alexandre Dumas and Marie-Louise expecting their first child.

━━

WHILE Dumas was getting married, the National Convention had been debating what to do with the former King Louis XVI, who, after titles were abolished, was now simply called "Louis Capet"—a mocking reference to his distant ancestor Hugh Capet, who had assumed the throne in the year 987. The Convention put Louis Capet on trial. Representative Philippe Égalité voted with the slim majority to send his cousin to the guillotine, though he himself would follow before the year was out. On January 21, 1793, Louis Capet was decapitated.

Lieutenant Colonel Dumas, having meanwhile returned to his post following his honeymoon, may have felt that the Revolution had sent him back in time: on January 11, the Free Legion of Americans was stationed at Laon, the dragoons' old garrison town.

There were about two hundred free men of color and former slaves in the Black Legion, including a number of junior officers older than Dumas who had last fought with colonial regiments in Saint-Domingue or the other sugar islands. It was Dumas's job to train them all, lead patrols, and, as his plentiful correspondence with Paris shows, fight for weapons, rations, uniforms, and horses. There was also the matter of their pay, which now seemed to have slipped the government's mind.

Dumas may have soon wished that he'd taken the offer to join Boyer's Hussars of Liberty and Equality instead of Saint-Georges's legion. He was left to command the legion largely by himself, for Colonel Saint-Georges and the legion's other senior officers often went on "recruiting missions" to Paris—where it seems likely that they spent their time drinking and carousing. While Saint-Georges had seemed filled with genuine zeal about the legion's creation, a socialite whose hardest riding had been in the Tuileries Gardens did not transform easily into a soldier.

In February 1793 the government ordered the legion to defend the Belgian frontier a hundred-odd kilometers north of Maulde. Despite France's early victories, it was still a war of frontier raids. Dumas knew this kind of fighting well, and he led the Americans to a succession of victories. His son the novelist offers a colorful description:

> As the head of the regiment, my father saw a vaster field open for his courage and intelligence. . . . Once, for example, [the American legion] was in the vanguard when it suddenly stumbled upon a Dutch regiment hidden in the rye, which at that season and in that country grew as high as a man. The regiment's presence was given away by the movement of a sergeant who was barely fifteen paces from my father and raising his gun to fire. My father saw this movement, understood that at such a distance the sergeant could not miss, drew a pistol from his holster, and pulled the trigger with such rapidity and luck that before the [sergeant's] weapon was leveled its barrel was pierced clean through by the pistol bullet.
>
> This pistol shot was the signal for a magnificent charge, in which the Dutch regiment was cut to pieces.
>
> My father picked up the bullet-pierced rifle from the battlefield. It was held together by two scraps of iron. I had it for a long time in my possession, but in the end it was stolen during a move.
>
> The pistols which had wrought this miracle of precision had been given by my mother, and came from the workshops of Lepage. Later, they acquired a certain celebrity in the Army of Italy.

An encyclopedia entry from the 1820s, written decades before the novelist's account, provides a more sober confirmation of Alex Dumas's heroism with the Black Legion:

> [Dumas] led his young warriors into action every day. Constantly sent to the outposts, [Dumas] distinguished himself in particular

at Mouvian, near Lille, where, at the head of a patrol of 14 men, he swooped down on the post of 40 Dutch soldiers, killing three by his own hand, taking 16 prisoners and dispersing the rest.

Though Saint-Georges was frequently absent, when he was around he continued to carry out his duties, and his conduct in April 1793 showed that he was still devoted to the Revolution: that month, the army's commander-in-chief, General Dumouriez, attempted a coup d'état. Saint-Georges and Dumas refused an offer to join it, and instead rallied the Americans and another legion to defend the city of Lille from the pro-coup forces.

But the Black Legion was dogged by problems. Neither the officers nor the men had received their pay, and some of the men lacked boots. Lieutenant Colonel Dumas even had trouble finding them weapons. His letters show he was becoming exasperated with the situation.

Then, in June, Saint-Georges disappeared again—some reports said to Paris, some to Lille—and when he surfaced, the Ministry of War accused him of running a horse-trading scheme. The charge was that he had purchased good horses with government money, sold them at a profit, and then bought cheap mounts to give his soldiers. According to the novelist Dumas, seconded by many other writers, when Saint-Georges was summoned to Paris to explain himself, he put the blame on his second in command:

> As Saint-Georges's books were very badly kept, he hit on the idea of throwing the blame upon my father by saying that it was Lieutenant Colonel Dumas who had been charged with the regimental mounts.
>
> The minister of war therefore wrote to my father, who immediately proved that he had never ordered a single requisition, nor bought or sold a single horse.
>
> The minister's response entirely cleared my father. But he didn't give up his grudge against Saint-Georges, and . . . he resolved to fight a duel with his former colonel.

The novelist Dumas has a great deal of fun with the grudge between the two old comrades in arms, the former teacher and his pupil, ending it with a scene where Saint-Georges comes to call on Dumas after the latter had challenged him multiple times to a duel. "Saint-Georges, brave though he was with pistol or sword in hand, much preferred to choose his duels," the novelist comments, then paints the scene as occurring when his father was sick at home in bed, recovering from an operation, being nursed by his old adjunct Dermoncourt:

> [O]n being told of the indisposition that kept him in bed, [Saint-Georges] was about to leave his card and withdraw, when Dermoncourt, who had heard much about him, seeing an admirably handsome mulatto who stuttered while speaking, recognized Saint-Georges, and, running after him:
>
> "Ah! Monsieur de Saint-Georges," he said, "it's you! Do not leave, I beg you; for, ill as he is, the general is quite capable of running after you, so eager is he to see you."
>
> Saint-Georges at once made up his mind what would be best.
>
> "Oh! dear Dumas!" he cried, "I certainly believe that he wants to see me; and so do I! We were always such good friends. Where is he? Where is he?"
>
> And, darting into the room, he flung himself upon the bed, took my father in his arms, and embraced him almost to the point of suffocation.
>
> My father wanted to speak, but Saint-Georges did not give him time.
>
> "Ah," he said, "but you wanted to kill me? To kill me—me? Dumas, kill Saint-Georges? Is it possible? But aren't you my own son? When Saint-Georges is dead, could any other man replace him? Come on, get up! Order me a chop, and let there be no more question of all this foolishness."
>
> My father was strongly inclined to pursue the affair to the very end; but what is there to say to a man who throws himself on your bed, who embraces you, who calls you his son, and who demands some lunch?
>
> This is what my father did; he held out his hand and said:
>
> "Ah! you brigand, you are surely happy that I am your successor, as you say, and not that of the last minister of war; for I give you my word that I would have you hang."

"Oh! you would guillotine me at least," said Saint-Georges, forcing a laugh.

"Not at all, not at all. Honest people are guillotined these days; but thieves are hanged."

In the memoirs the incident ends with the two friends trading a few more threats and then being interrupted by lunch. In fact, there is no record of any letters showing that Saint-Georges tried to place the blame on Dumas, or that Dumas was ever questioned by the war minister about the horse-trading scheme. On the contrary, when the Black Legion was disbanded, he received neither a reprimand nor a summons to trial. Instead, on July 30, 1793, Alex Dumas received a letter signed by the minister of war informing him that he had been promoted to the rank of brigadier general of the Army of the North.

"MR. HUMANITY"

IN the space of a year, Alex Dumas had gone from lowly dragoon corporal to one of the army's highest ranks. A month after his appointment as brigadier general, he was promoted to general of division. He now had not a hundred or even a thousand men under his command, but *ten thousand*.

Revolutionary opportunities came with revolutionary risks: it took a special sort of courage to accept a general officer's commission in the summer of 1793. While Dumas had been serving with the Free Legion of Americans, a profound change had occurred. In addition to the possibility of murderously insubordinate troops, a French general now had to worry still more about the danger of being murdered by his political masters, who controlled every aspect of military affairs.

That spring France's official foreign-enemies list had mushroomed: Spain, Portugal, Naples, Holland, Great Britain. The government had taken every reversal on the battlefield as an excuse to arrest and purge more internal counter-revolutionaries, finding them especially in the officer corps. The truth was that revolutionary France had simply attacked or antagonized too many countries. A decade earlier, the American revolutionaries had been supported by nearly all of Europe in their war; now the French revolutionaries were in the opposite situation. They faced a devastating combination of Britain's grip on the seas, and on the land the might of the Austro-Germanic forces. Saint-Domingue and the other French sugar colonies were raided, and their ships looted, along with French ships in the Mediterranean and elsewhere. In Paris, hyperinflation—the price of bread reached half a million francs—sparked riots. The Austrians surged back into Belgium and once again threatened France's northeastern frontier. And Dumouriez attempted his coup d'état.

It was this last event, in April 1793, that provided the excuse for forming within the government a new, elite body with an ominously innocuous-sounding name: "the Committee of Public Safety." This panel of nine deputies set out ostensibly to protect the Revolution from subversion, foreign and domestic, and to bring ruthless order to the chaos of revolutionary politics. Soon they would begin sending their own members to the guillotine, along with civilian counterrevolutionaries, aristocrats, priests, and sundry other enemies of the people. But the Committee's original and ongoing mission was to ensure the military's—particularly military officers'—loyalty to the Revolution. To this end, civilian "commissioners" were sent out to every army and division to monitor the generals and exercise the government's new control over the war effort.

The Committee member in charge of this task was Louis de Saint-Just. The son of an army officer, and only twenty-four, Saint-Just soon earned the nickname "the Archangel of Terror": his specialty was threatening officers at the front with the guillotine if they did not deliver victory, and he was known to have officers executed in front of their troops as an example, "to encourage the others." Before he went to the guillotine himself in July of 1794, scores of generals would be murdered by his commissioners for disappointing expectations. "You no longer have any reason for restraint against enemies of the new order," Saint-Just said, elucidating his theory of applied terror. "You must punish not only traitors but the apathetic as well; you must punish whoever is passive in the Republic." (Dumas would have run-ins with the commissioners, though luckily he did not run into Saint-Just.)

Along with the Archangel of Terror, the Committee's other and more senior military mastermind was the brilliant engineer Lazare Carnot, called "the Organizer of Victory." Carnot was one of two techies on the Committee of Public Safety. He had published important papers in the fields of mathematics, physics, and engineering.

Carnot had determined that in order to counter the vast coalition against it, France needed to capitalize on its manpower edge over its rivals, to exploit its surplus of young, able-bodied men. Last year's strategy of volunteers riding around from one front to another, looking for glory, must be replaced by massive, centrally directed columns hurtling themselves at the enemy in a vast patriotic carnage of blood and sacrifice. Nothing less would do. To this end, Carnot instituted an innovation that would transform the history of war: the *levée en masse*—the first military draft in modern history.

In under a year, from February 1793 to December 1793, Carnot's draft increased France's troop strength from 178,000 to approximately one million men. France would field fifteen separate armies, totaling 800,000 active-duty soldiers, to defend or expand every possible inch of its frontiers.

In order to arm such a mass of conscripts, Carnot brought back an old weapon: the pike. The last time pikes had been issued to French soldiers was in 1703. But they were the iconic French revolutionary weapon. As early as the battle of Valmy, Carnot had incited the Assembly to distribute pikes to every soldier and citizen in the land, and ordered local blacksmiths to drop all other tasks to make more of the long thrusting spears. "The pike," declared Carnot, "is the arm of liberty."

His colleague Brissot had gone even farther: "Pikes began the revolution, pikes will finish it," he intoned—before falling to the Revolution's other iconic edged weapon, the guillotine.

The nostalgia for this medieval battlefield weapon had been present well before the Revolution, as advocates had invoked its power in the hands of supposedly passionate French soldiers as a way of channeling the Frenchman's primal, tribal past, and of allowing for individuality and impetuosity in combat.* A musket fusillade, conversely, required a high degree of coordination and unity among troops. What's more, the pike was the anti-aristocratic weapon par excellence. In the waning Middle Ages, pikes had helped end the dominance of the aristocratic knights, who were unhorsed and overwhelmed by throngs of lower-class foot soldiers wielding deadly thickets of pikes.

Finally, in the neoclassical spirit of the times, pikes represented a return to the bravery of the ancient Greek warriors, who confronted overwhelming enemies with their close phalanxes of spears. "If we have not been either Spartans or Athenians, we should become them!" fumed one furious deputy when someone challenged the pike-making effort.

The romanticizing of primitive blade weapons over firearms was a

---

* Of course, there was a newer weapon that did the same thing—the one that had made the pike obsolete in the first place: the bayonet. Frenchmen were thought also to have a particular love of and propensity for bayonet fighting. But pikes did not require attached firearms, which were still expensive to make and difficult to learn to use.

peculiar strategy for a nation capable of producing the finest guns and artillery pieces in the world. But the French army in 1793 instead received hundreds of thousands of freshly forged pikes. If a general complained that these weapons were useless, his name could be put on a commissioner's list for suspect counterrevolutionary conduct. He could receive a letter from the Committee of Public Safety summoning him to Paris.

Along with pikes, Carnot ramped up all French arms production at an exponential rate: the main French armory, which produced 9,000 muskets in 1793, would produce 145,000 muskets a year later.

The French recruits of the *levée en masse* were inexperienced and ill-trained, and to avoid a repetition of the panics and disorderly routs that had plagued the first few months of the war, revolutionary songs and music were played constantly to inspire them. Carnot and the Committee issued a never-ending stream of decrees, many restating the obvious with obvious impatience, such as Carnot's directive number one: "Strike en masse and always offensively."

►◄

UNTIL the Committee's downfall, in 1794, Dumas would be forced to correspond with it on a regular basis about nearly all logistical, tactical, and strategic matters of his command. He received many letters a week signed by Carnot and the other members of the Committee.

He must have been aware of the situation when he received his promotion, but Alex Dumas was brave, self-confident, and stubborn. Also, his own zeal gave him the kind of protective faith that true believers have. Dumas had thrown his life and soul fully behind the Revolution, even though he was not inherently a political man. For him, there was no going back. Unlike many others, he couldn't emigrate if pushed too far—where would he go? In a world where men of his color were slaves, revolutionary France was his promised land, even if he had to share it with some unsavory characters.

In any event, Alex Dumas's general politics were close enough to the political inquisitors' that he felt immune to intimidation. The military hero above worrying about political assassins is a story common to many revolutions and wars, though the story does not always work out well for the hero.

It was no coincidence that no one had yet heard of the brilliant artillery captain born Napoleone Buonaparte, though the Revolution would facilitate his military career just as much as Dumas's. If the *Ancien Régime* had not fallen, the energetic young cadet from Corsica might well have ended up as a highly decorated junior officer, well respected in the War Ministry but nothing more.

The Revolution opened up huge opportunities for young Napoleon. But until the summer of 1793, he remained studiously aloof from events in France. This allowed him to stay away from Paris at a time when performing marvelous military feats under one political faction might lead to having one's destiny cut short by another. At one point, in 1791–92, he was actually dismissed from the French army for failing to return from a three-month leave; he was in Corsica, involved in local revolutionary events as a volunteer. (A notation at the Ministry of War actually recorded that Lieutenant Bonaparte "has given up his profession, and has been replaced on February 6, 1792.")*

Dumas, on the other hand, had the recklessness of a man who has discovered a cause worth dying for—a cause that has redeemed his world and given unlimited hope and meaning to his life. He would have many moments of reckless courage in his career, emboldened by each act of bravery to go on to greater ones.

On September 10, a week after his appointment as general of division, Marie-Louise had their first child, a daughter they named Alexandrine Aimée. Dumas rode to Villers-Cotterêts to be by their side. But after spending only four days with his wife and new child, he found himself appointed commander-in-chief of an entire army and had to depart. He was to head the Army of the Western Pyrenees, which had been skirmishing with Spanish forces on the French side of the border since it had been formed the previous April.

Things weren't going well: in five months of conflict, the army had gone through four generals, each yanked by the Committee of Public Safety after

---

* The young artillery captain was back in Paris, however, on June 20, 1792, to witness the storming of the Tuileries Palace, which provided him an important political lesson. As his companion and later secretary Bourrienne would remember, he and Napoleon watched from the street as the king came to the window of the palace with a red revolutionary cap on his head. "What a fool!" Napoleon scoffed. "How did this rabble gain entrance? If four or five hundred of them had been shot down by a volley of grapeshot, the rest would have run."

another Spanish victory. "This appointment will afford you fresh opportunities for showing your devotion to the public welfare by beating down its enemies," the war minister wrote now. "The zeal for the Republic you have hitherto displayed is a sure guarantee that you will not spare her enemies." He affirmed that Dumas's "sense of patriotism and his courage render him worthy of the confidence of the nation."

Claude Labouret, who had begun referring to his son-in-law as "the General," must have been equal parts astonished, proud, and intimidated by the rapid transformation of young Alex from mounted cavalryman to commander-in-chief. On September 20, he wrote to a family friend:

> The General arrived here on the 15th, and left us yesterday, the 19th, by stagecoach. In a few days' time he will be in the Pyrenees. The little girl is well, as, too, is Marie-Louise. She behaved with great courage in the presence of her husband, and shed tears only after he had gone. Today she is once more mistress of herself. She finds consolation in the thought that all these sacrifices must be for the good of the Nation.

It was the one-year anniversary of the founding of the Republic—and the establishment of the National Convention—and, to celebrate, the government declared the Christian calendar officially overthrown and a new revolutionary calendar in force. The revolutionary dating system used on documents written before then had taken 1789—the proclamation of the Rights of Man—as Year I of Liberty. But now 1789 was associated with the "false revolution" of the aristocratic patriots—the compromisers, the moderates—and anyway liberty was no longer the issue. The new calendar was only one of countless utopian measures the ruling Jacobins initiated in 1793–94, but it is notable because, apparently, not a single person had to be murdered to carry it out.

Dumas arrived in Bayonne with a ten-page memo outlining the many goals the War Ministry had for the Army of the Pyrenees. He should lose no time in making an inventory of "the most important passes, ports, and highways, and if they are occupied by the Spanish, use his best endeavors to expel them and take possession of them." He also had a reminder from the war minister, whose own career and life were on the line, that he "must maintain an accurate correspondence with the minister of war independently of that with [the Committee]."

Bayonne was a fortified city, and when General Dumas's coach reached the gates, he was informed that the new commander-in-chief could not enter until the local representatives of the people, apparently out of town at the moment, had arrived. Only after much negotiation did General Dumas and his aides-de-camp receive permission from the political guard to go to their lodgings.

The rooms Dumas and his aides took overlooked the town's main square, where the People's Representatives had set up their guillotine. A small but telling episode then followed, for which the only source is his son's memoir; it's the kind of story the novelist loved to tell about his father—and loved to shape for maximum effect. Still, it sounds like Alex Dumas.

When the terrible hour arrived, and all other windows were filled with spectators, my father would close his, pull down the blinds and draw his curtains.

Then, beneath his closed windows, a terrible commotion would begin; all the sans-culottes of the countryside would gather below and yell at him:

"Hey! *Monsieur de l'Humanité* ["Mr. Humanity," the *de* making it sound as if weakness were compounded by aristocracy], come to your windows! Show yourself!"

Despite these catcalls—which often took on a character so threatening that my father and his aides-de-camp stood, sabers at the ready, pistols in their hands, readying themselves more than once to respond with arms to an attack—not one of the windows was opened, nor did one of the officers belonging to my father's staff appear at the balcony.

As a result, the new general . . . ceased to be addressed as Citizen Alexandre Dumas, he was thenceforth known only by the name—strongly compromising at that time, especially among the people who had given it to him—of Mr. Humanity.

That winter, as France continued to languish under the dark spells of the Committee, Dumas got word that he was being transferred yet again, into what was one of the toughest and most challenging theaters of the war—in ways having to do as much with the natural surroundings and terrain as it did with the enemy. The soldier from tropical Saint-Domingue had orders to report to a glacier, 7,300 feet above sea level, to assume command of the Army of the Alps.

＞－＜

HIS orders from the War Ministry were a model of revolutionary understatement: since it was assumed that General Dumas would "live up to his reputation as a patriot and a great soldier," he should arrange his affairs and ride to the Alps as soon as possible, to "ensure the protection, the brotherhood and the indivisibility of the Republic, as well as its continued liberty and equality." No "or else" needed to be added. Commissioners of the Committee of Public Safety were everywhere, as were civilian representatives of other government departments who could sometimes mimic them in brutality. A bloodthirsty "political agent" of the Foreign Affairs Ministry who visited the Army of the Alps, one Pierre Chépy, had recently suggested that morale might be boosted only when every general who'd been condemned to death was beheaded "in the midst of the army he may have betrayed, [and] his body . . . hanged by its heels in the enemy's territory, with the inscription, 'This monster sold himself to the enemies of the country. The vengeance of the French people, which has taken his head, abandons his remains to birds of prey and to tyrants.' "

Dumas was the fourth commander-in-chief the Army of the Alps had had in a year. On accepting the post, he reported to Paris that he was taking along as adjuncts two old comrades from the Sixth Dragoons, Piston and Espagne. In the small world of revolutionary soldiering, this was a felicitous reunion. Espagne had served as a witness at Dumas's wedding and was a personal friend. Piston was eight years older than Dumas, and an especially shrewd and reliable officer in a jam. Both men were happy to be reunited with the ever-adventurous Dumas and to follow their new commander-in-chief into mountains that promised more glory than did their current post.

The Army of the Alps was dispersed throughout five huge departments, all of them mountainous and difficult to traverse, making communication and logistics particularly challenging. When I went to visit the battlefields there, I had to wait until June for the highway to get to them to become passable. As I drove up into these snowy peaks—a surreal sight in summer—and got dizzy as I drove higher, my mind reeled imagining how Dumas and his men, without proper winter boots or gear, had made it through here in January on horseback. But they had done it. I had just spent hours examining a room-size oil painting of the scene, which hung in the bell tower of the town hall of Bourg Saint-Maurice, a ski resort. It was off-season when I arrived, but a friendly functionary took pity on my eccentric request and unlocked the town hall to let me stare at the painting, which showed thousands of republican and royalist forces fighting and marching around a glacial amphitheater, and, in the center, accepting the surrender of the Sardinian commander, was Alex Dumas.

The novelist Dumas told a story about his father's stop at Saint-Maurice. In the memoir, he said the anecdote came from his father's longtime friend and aide-de-camp Paul-Ferdinand Dermoncourt:

> My father passed through the village of Saint-Maurice during a bout of particularly harsh weather. The first thing he saw on the main square of this village was a guillotine, fully erected and ready to perform its function. He had learned that four unfortunate men were about to be executed, for having hidden a church bell to keep it from being melted down. The crime did not seem to my father worthy of death, and, turning to Captain Dermoncourt, soon to become his aide-de-camp, he said: "Dermoncourt, it is very cold, as you can see and very well feel for yourself. We may not find any wood where we are going; therefore, have that devilish red-painted machine you see there pulled down and cut up to make wood we'll warm ourselves up with."

I have no doubt that the novelist heard some such tale from the old warhorse Dermoncourt, long since a general.* But that he willfully burned a

---

* Dermoncourt would stay by General Alex Dumas's side for years, sharing with him the most perilous and glorious combats, especially in Italy and the Tyrol. Dumas trusted him completely, probably more than any other officer, and Dermoncourt looked up to Dumas.

guillotine—in January 1794, with the Terror raging across France—seems unlikely. By now, thousands of independent Jacobin clubs existed in municipalities throughout France—a bit like local franchises of the Terror business, getting guillotine kits and denunciation guidelines from the central office in Paris. One did not cross these local clubs— "popular" societies, they were called—lightly. The novelist Dumas here portrays his father facing the Terror with a spirit that matches his way of regularly facing death in battle, with a soldier's fatalism. But while General Dumas was certainly one of the bravest men in the French army, there is no evidence to suggest he was suicidal.

The writer Dumas clearly thought his father the purest, noblest man who ever lived, incapable of understanding intrigue—an Edmond Dantès before his education in the dungeon transforms him into the Count of Monte Cristo. Alex Dumas had the confidence that accompanies a life of physical exploits, along with an unwavering faith in the rightness of his actions that made him tough to intimidate. But to survive the treacherous waters of the time, which claimed the lives of hundreds of respected, patriotic officers, he needed more than naive bluster and love of justice.

General Dumas would in fact have a number of confrontations with the Committee of Public Safety over the coming months, beginning with one involving an incident that by then belonged to another time entirely.

>—→

ON their way north, General Dumas and his adjuncts passed through Lyon, Piston's hometown. In October, after a two-month siege, the government had retaken Lyon from a group of moderates who had overthrown the local Jacobin club the previous spring; the government carried out reprisals intended to punish the entire city, destroying many of its finest buildings and

---

But Dermoncourt would outlive General Dumas by more than forty years, and go on to a career full of status and honors in its own right, becoming an officer of the Légion d'honneur and a Napoleonic "Baron de l'Empire." In his retirement, in the 1830s, Dermoncourt got to know his former comrade's son very well when he hired the writer Alexandre Dumas to help him complete his own memoir, *La Vendée et Madame*. This collaboration was the perfect chance for the young writer to pick the old general's brain for everything Dermoncourt remembered about his father.

murdering nearly two thousand of its residents. The Jacobins then proceeded to rename Lyon—with no apparent irony—"Liberated City."

We don't know what Dumas and Piston said to each other in Liberated City—or what cruel sights they saw there—but Dumas did not pass through unnoticed. The People's Representatives in Liberated City warned Dumas to be careful: there were traitors all around. And someone denounced him as one of the soldiers who had been on the Champ de Mars in July 1791 when troops fired into a crowd of stone-throwing protesters. Dumas's mere presence among the government forces that day meant he was suspect, in all likelihood a patriot of the old, Lafayette variety—an upper-class-liberal enemy of the true Revolution.

Dumas mailed his response to the denunciation both to the "People's Commission of Liberated City" and to the Committee of Public Safety in Paris.* He freely acknowledged having been at the Champ de Mars with the dragoons that day. But rather than suppressing the demonstration, Dumas said, he and his comrades had risked their lives to enter the fray and, he believed, saved "up to 2,000 people" who could have been massacred. (They presumably did this by keeping the conflict between the crowd and Lafayette's National Guard from escalating further.) He went on:

> Even though it infinitely repulses me to speak of my exploits, I cannot hide from you the truth of the adventures of which they are trying to [accuse me] and against which I am only fully supported by my love for the community and the common interest. You know the absurd manner in which I was denounced to you. Now they blame me, and they denounced me in front of you. They accuse me, perhaps, of having ordered two cannons to the Champ de Mars on 17 July 1791. Yes, I ordered them, and I thank heaven I did, because my comrades and I not only had neither the intention nor the idea of shooting at our fellow citizens, but at the risk of our lives, we threw ourselves into the fire to

---

* This letter, which I picked out from among the stacks of his military dispatches, reveals Alex Dumas's presence at that major event of the early Revolution. His son's memoir glosses over the whole period with the sentence "My father took no part in the earlier events of the Revolution." The rather poor condition of the letter might explain why it was overlooked before, but the infamous date—17 July 1791—grabbed my attention.

stop it, and by these acts of humanity, of which we try not to boast, we may perhaps have saved the lives of 2000 people, who would have perished victims of the deeply treacherous designs of the perpetrators of that awful day. At the time everyone involved congratulated me and my men for our conduct.

It is impossible to know exactly what he and his men *did* do that day, since this letter is the only evidence that they were there at all. But no matter how the Jacobins interpreted his explanations, Alex Dumas's heart would have been with the protesters that day. In all his adventures, the main thing that set Dumas apart was his refusal to countenance the bullying of the weak by the strong. This meant that whenever a unit he commanded seized a thousand prisoners or the wealth of a town, he told his fellow officers and his men, perhaps too often for their taste, that they must restrain themselves from taking the slightest advantage. Dumas was unrestrained when outnumbered and outgunned, just as he was unrestrained when he disagreed with his superiors. But toward anyone less powerful than he was, Alex Dumas showed nothing but self-restraint, and a kind of violent love. It would have been typical of him to have pointed his artillery directly at the National Guardsmen if he thought they were about to fire again, or, by the same token, at out-of-control rioters.

But even Alex Dumas could not bury the dark anxiety that overcame him as he faced the denunciation. He makes clear in his letter that he expects nothing to result from his defense other than his death—he particularly mentions poisoning, a fate that has recently befallen one of his colleagues who ran afoul of the Committee. He concludes with an uncharacteristic burst of anguished foreboding:

> Without entering into too many details, I will submit to you some observations which will perhaps be striking to you. Three of us, among others, we were together in the Faubourg St. Marceau. And we were unvarying in our principles, and we've been happy enough to have an impact on the great revolutionary movements; Lazowsky, Basdelaune, and I. The first was poisoned to death. The second, brigadier general in the army of the Alps, was just assassinated in Chamberry, and as for me, I am being slandered, and I am expecting poisoning or assassination;

but whatever fate awaits me, I will serve the Republic none the less right up to the last moment.

> General Commander of the Army of the Alps
> Alexandre

It seems the Committee found his explanations sufficient for the current moment, perhaps because it wanted to avoid having to search for yet another replacement to command the Army of the Alps. Dumas was allowed to go on to the mountains, but it was not by any means the last he would hear from the Committee of Public Safety.

➤◄

SINCE the previous spring Dumas, Saint-Georges, and other elite men of color had sometimes found themselves under suspicion as potential counter-revolutionaries. (In September 1793, Saint-Georges and ten of his officers from the Black Legion were arrested for having "counterrevolutionary designs," according to the recently passed Law of Suspects.) But even as the Jacobins and the Committee pushed the Revolution further into terror, Alex Dumas saw growing evidence around him that the French Republic—his nation—remained a land unparalleled in the opportunities it gave to people of color.

In June 1793, five officers of the Black Legion presented the Convention with a petition calling for "American liberty"—freedom for all black people in the islands. A group of "citizens of color" marched to the Hôtel de Ville carrying a banner that read THE RIGHTS OF MAN AND OF CITIZENS OF COLOR: LIVE FREE OR DIE. After a vigorous debate on what to do, members of the government escorted the petitioners to the Champ de Mars and officially saluted as they "renew[ed] their oath to spill their blood for liberty."

And in the first days of February 1794, a remarkable three-man delegation arrived in Paris after an arduous journey from Saint-Domingue: Jean-Baptiste Belley, a black native of Senegal and a former slave; Jean-Baptiste Mills, a free Saint-Dominguan of mixed race; and Louis-Pierre Dufay, a white Frenchman who had worked for years as a clerk in the colony and now proudly identified himself as a "commoner." Before the Jacobin-controlled Convention,

Dufay made a passionate argument for the abolition of slavery—and the Convention unanimously acclaimed it. Then, in a single vote, the government became the first in history to abolish slavery.*

At last Alex Dumas's self-identification as a French republican and a soldier of the French Revolution had been wholly ratified. The vote seems to have given him a rare occasion to reflect on his roots. A letter he penned to the soldiers stationed at "Liberated City" on Ventôse 16, Year II—March 6, 1794, as France celebrated the abolition decree—shows Dumas swept up in the momentousness of the event. The letter is less a specific or practical military order than an emotional and highly uncommon reference to his own racial origins and their relevance to the Revolution. In it, Alex Dumas speaks of himself in the third person:

> Your comrade, a soldier and General-in-Chief, is counting on you, brave brothers in arms. . . . He was born in a climate and among men for whom liberty also had charms, and who fought for it first. Sincere lover of liberty and equality, convinced that all free men are equals, he will be proud to march out before you, to aid you in your efforts, and the coalition of tyrants will learn that they are loathed equally by men of all colors.

---

* In fact, slavery had already been abolished in Saint-Domingue's Northern Province, the locus of the rebellion, in August 1793 by Léger-Félicité Sonthonax, a French commissioner who had been sent to quell the revolt. A few months later, in an effort to win support from former slaves, Sonthonax declared that the government in Paris had abolished slavery in all the colonies—a risky move, considering that at the time he had no news of the Convention's vote.

THE BATTLE FOR THE TOP OF THE WORLD

ALEX Dumas had never even seen snow until he got off the ship in Normandy when he was fourteen. Now he found himself in a world of it: the glacier of Mont Cenis, high in the French Alps, with its two strategic passes that guarded the route from France to Italy. The local people, the Savoyards, had been annexed into the new French nation. But the Kingdom of Piedmont-Sardinia, Austria's ally, which had joined the anti-French coalition, held the key mountain passes in the region. Dumas was supposed to dislodge them and their Austrian allies and open the Alps, and the Italian territories beyond them, to French invasion. (Italy did not yet exist as a single nation—and would not until 1861—but instead was a collection of independent kingdoms, and of territories, some held by the Austrian Empire, others by the pope.)

Dumas would be fighting against the Austrians, who had trained their whole professional lives amid ice and glaciers. The Piedmontese were also used to defending the Alpine country. Dumas had approximately fifty-three thousand men under his command, of varying quality and spread over a large and rigorous terrain. "The enemy he needed to get at were bivouacking in the clouds," his son puts it aptly in his memoirs. "It was a war of Titans: the heavens had to be scaled."

The war in the Alps was symbolic—the French Republic wanted to conquer the highest peaks in Europe. But it was also strategic: the Army of the Alps was to prepare for a major invasion. For the first time in three hundred years France would invade the Italian kingdoms, and strike directly at its chief enemy, Austria. A great deal was at stake for the Republic, as it was for General Dumas. The post was vastly more important than any with which he had previously been entrusted and would make or break his career.

General Dumas vigorously set about whipping his army into shape, a task made difficult by the fact that his battalions were stationed on different peaks that, depending on snow conditions, could take up to a week to reach from his headquarters in Grenoble. Dumas himself often went on two-week-long inspection tours, which could be further delayed by snowdrifts.

Dumas arranged the formation of an elite company of Mont Blanc guides to handle the most difficult passes and provide basic logistics to the other troops. But high winds made movement around the peaks all but impossible that January. Making things worse, the weather was not quite cold enough to produce a solid top layer of ice; anything attempting to move immediately sank. One of Dumas's generals of division sent him a report on the condition of the roads: "Mont-Cenis is currently covered in snow, as is Mont Saint Bernard." Mont Saint Bernard was another objective. "As it did not frost vigorously, the snow is not holding up" (i.e., to the weight of men and horses), "and the wind which is called in this country 'the Torment' has filled all the hills with snow and has made the roads and the trails impassable." The general also informed his new commander that he had deployed spies in the area, disguised as merchants: "I have two spies of which one is currently at Turin, and the other at the frontier, selling butter, cheese, and cattle to our enemies."

Nothing in Dumas's experience had prepared him for the challenges of mountain fighting. Among his first requests were maps. "I cannot procure those of the Alps at any price," he wrote the war minister. "I am obliged to rest, arms folded, until they arrive." Dumas also asked for rifles, cannon, saddles, gunpowder, bandoliers, howitzers, and mules, horses, and lots of hay to feed them. To feed his men, he requested hunting gear, including game bags, and encouraged the men to hunt chamois, the goat-antelopes that pranced through the mountains, which was also good practice tracking in the snow. (Dumas himself went on hunting expeditions with the local chamois hunters and, in addition to some fine pelts, in this way he acquired the trust and friendship of some of the mountains' best guides.)

The hundreds of pages of field reports, memos, and orders Dumas wrote just in January and February of 1794 reveal that, remarkably, the natural fighter had a gift for logistics and planning. Days after establishing his base in Grenoble, Dumas had worked out an elaborate operation that—as per instructions—he kept secret from all but his most trusted right-hand men. He wrote long letters on organizing communications as well as on ordnance and intelligence. He successfully brought off the movement of hundreds of horses and their food supply. When the army sent him horses that were too small to walk through the snowdrifts, he had them sent back, requesting taller ones. He mastered every detail, down to equipping fifteen thousand of his men with special snowshoes and placing an order to his commissary for "four thousand iron cleats made according to the mold I gave him." Though desertion had been a problem, after General Dumas's arrival it became less of one.

On January 27, Dumas received an order from the minister of war, referring to a decree by Citizen Carnot and the Committee of Public Safety telling Dumas to launch a major campaign to take the passes as soon as possible.* The order amounted to insisting that General Dumas break the stalemate that had prevailed ever since the French had occupied the region two years earlier—and it contained a rebuke, with the sort of impatient language common to Committee letters:

> We want the conquest of Mont Cenis and Petit Saint Bernard without delay. We know as well as you do that the earth is covered with snow; that's precisely why we want a prompt attack. You want to wait until it's melted and that's a true way to fail. . . . The National Convention wants its generals to obey the orders of the Committee; you will answer with your head for their implementation.
>
> Signed, Carnot and Barrère

Dumas wrote back to the Committee that "these parts are very difficult to maneuver, and Nature's insurmountable aspects are for now thwarting our plans." As if to reasonable men, he explained that the passes could not

---

* The military correspondence in this period, winter and spring of 1794, was more voluminous and complex than usual, since the war minister wrote to generals but so did the Committee itself, which was clearly running the show. The war minister himself was a pawn of Carnot, Saint-Just, and the other Committee members and worked closely with them; often they wrote almost the same letter to Dumas, necessitating two replies, and they also jointly signed orders to him.

be crossed until either the weather got colder and the snow froze, or it got warmer and the snow melted. "The snow's massive quantities and little firmness have opposed us." Then, with the enthusiasm of a new general, Dumas suggested a productive use for him and his men while they waited to attack the passes. He knew the great value of the upper Po River Valley, which lay below them, the key to the city of Turin in the Kingdom of Piedmont-Sardinia. Dumas suggested they find an alternative way of getting there and attacking it. He went on to report, after some investigations, that if his army could gain permission from the local Swiss—which he thought possible— there was a pass at Saint-Gothard they could use to outflank and surprise the Piedmontese-Sardinians.

See p. 188

St. Gothard is Switzerland See p. 188

Then he added: "The Republic can count on me to battle its enemies. . . . Offensive war suits the passionate character of the French, but it is the responsibility of the man in charge of leading them to prepare with caution and wisdom everything that leads to victory."

The letter received a prompt reaction, but instead of writing directly to Dumas, the war minister wrote a sarcastic critique about Dumas to the Committee of Public Safety. "I never imagined, Citizen representatives, that the expeditions stipulated in your decree from the 6th pluviose for the Army of the Alps could prove so difficult to execute," wrote the minister.

General Dumas, from the depths of his apartment in Grenoble, has judged impossible an operation which men placed at the foot of the mountains deemed very doable. You will notice with astonishment the rambling ideas of his letter: he wants to cross the Alps, plant the tricolor flag on the banks of the Po, pass through Switzerland to go to Milan, penetrate via Mont Saint-Gothard to bring war into Italy.

The following day, the Committee of Public Safety sent Dumas an angry letter full of rebukes and also a veiled threat:

You say that the Republic can count on you, but the Republic counts only on the nation. . . . it cannot be concerned with a single citizen. The provisional executive council is waiting for you to explain your conduct.

The Committee goes on to wonder whether Dumas is "a Republican as firm as he is enlightened"—and demands to know where he got the crazy idea of violating Swiss neutrality.

In Paris the Reign of Terror was approaching its cruelest phase, with hundreds being executed daily on lesser charges than insubordination to Citizen Carnot's wishes. Dumas had had reports of what was happening in Paris, and he brooded on the fate of the generals who had preceded him in his command in the Alps.

On February 26, he called a council of war with his generals (with the government's representatives attending, as well) to prepare for an attack on the passes held by the enemy, especially the ones on Mont Cenis and Mont Saint Bernard. Dumas believed that the snow was simply too soft to assure the safe movement of troops and horses, but he gave the generals their assignments:

> Each general will try to surprise the enemy and, once established on Mont Cenis and Petit Saint Bernard, he will take all necessary measures to hold his positions and take full advantage of the equipment the enemy will have left in its defeat and flight. . . . He will hasten . . . to re-orient the artillery the enemy has abandoned on them, construct entrenchments on the enemies' route, and destroy those [entrenchments] that the Piedmontese constructed and which served against us.

Dumas emphasized the need to keep the operation a secret from enemy spies by conducting a campaign of planted misinformation and rumors.

The operation was ready to move, but then it snowed hard. Dumas knew this made the plan impossible—the soldiers would die of exposure before the Piedmontese guns ever got them. On March 1, he wrote a careful letter to the war minister, emphasizing the weather and the difficulties the terrain involved.

In the face of potential execution for *incivisme*—"lack of civic consciousness," the Revolution's version of treason—or for defeatism, Dumas shows surprising firmness and calm. He explains that he has been unable to write for the last two *décadis*, or twenty days—in throwing out the backward twelve-month calendar, the Revolution had also done away with the seven-day week, replacing it with this ten-day increment—because he was touring the outposts to see the snow conditions for himself. He reiterates that he is "looking for the most favorable opportunity to execute the offensive projects you prescribed to me . . . on Mont Cenis and Petit Saint Bernard." But he maintains that he is not ready to risk his army in the current conditions.

Penned in the margins of this letter was a note, presumably written by someone at the Ministry of War, mentioning "attacks against the Sardinian king" by local patriots and that "400 trees of liberty have been planted." The note also mentioned in two places that "liberty bonnets"* had been spotted on flagpoles in downtown Turin. This, the note said, was a very good sign of the rout of the "local aristocrats."

In his correspondence with the Committee, Dumas also insisted that it take into account and address what provisions his men would need to make the operation come off; he even detailed how the quartermaster should store and transport everything in the extreme climate of the mountains. Dumas requested 300,000 cartridges, "cannons firing 500 shots each, 2,000 firing pins, and around twenty rockets." He also said he desperately needed materials for hideouts, caissons for the artillery, twelve thousand rifles, and lots of gunpowder.

Finally, as if to defend himself against the inevitable charges of disloyalty, Dumas even told the Committee of Public Safety something about his writing style:

> In speaking to the Minister in this way, it was not my intention to re-
> spond evasively to your decree. I am too frank by nature to speak any

---

* The red felt liberty bonnet and the liberty tree were two of the most ubiquitous symbols of the French Revolution, along with the cockade and the tricolor flag. (Sometimes they were combined, in effect, by placing the red bonnet on top of a liberty *pole*.)

The bonnets were actually an adoption from, or homage to, ancient Rome, where they had been called Phrygian bonnets and had supposedly been worn by freed slaves. Both the French and the American revolutions used the Phrygian bonnet as a symbol of liberty. (Though its use in the United States has been forgotten, throughout the late nineteenth century it was common on U.S. coins and patriotic paraphernalia—usually either worn by "Miss Liberty" or perched atop a flagpole flying the Stars and Stripes—and it continued to appear on U.S. half-dollar coins until 1947.)

The liberty tree was a French homage to the American Revolution—to the famous elm tree near Boston Common that had been a rallying point for the American patriots in their escalating resistance to British oppression in the 1760s and 1770s.

other way but bluntly. I meant to tell the truth and not shy away from your orders.

━━

DESPITE the good news about the liberty bonnets and trees in Turin, most of the surrounding Piedmont countryside was less interested in French patriotism. Many locals remained fiercely loyal to monarchism, for territorial as much as political reasons: first of all, they did not like being invaded, and, second, many were religiously conservative. The nobility and priests here were some of the fiercest critics of the French Revolution, and counterrevolutionary feeling pervaded the upper classes, who had welcomed King Louis's brother and many aristocratic French émigrés.

Dumas's letters to the Committee in March and April talk of his belief that the émigrés and various other hostile groups—brigands, armed anti-revolutionary priests—were trying to sabotage the French war effort, spying on French troop movements for the enemy, all the while milling back and forth over the border transporting weapons and other contraband. As well as being preoccupied with these threats, Dumas needed to look over his shoulder constantly to make sure the local Jacobin clubs did not have him arrested and sent to Paris to be guillotined. Fortunately nothing satisfied the Committee of Public Safety better than talk of conspiracy—especially ubiquitous, insidious conspiracy all around.

Since the Army of the Alps was spread out over hundreds of miles of remote terrain, the French troops actually needed to cultivate local goodwill to operate. As commander-in-chief of an occupying army, Dumas was responsible for the impression they made on all the locals, including the nearby Swiss. Dumas proved a skillful and conscientious diplomat.

But Dumas's diplomacy did not extend to the local Jacobins, and later that spring, he would learn he'd been denounced again, by the Popular Society of Chambéry. He had sense enough to be cautious with the Committee of Public Safety in Paris, but he drew the line at kowtowing to a bunch of hick mountain radicals. "An enlightened society must know that generals cannot and must not make their operations public without danger to the safety of the army," he wrote to this particular "enlightened society," and requested the names of his accusers so he could confront them personally.

Dumas survived these clashes largely owing to the fact that he'd charmed the commissioner who, since his arrival in the Alps, had been charged with watching over him. This man, "People's Representative" Gaston, apparently took a liking to the unorthodox republican general and sent a glowing report addressed to "my colleagues" on the Committee of Public Safety in Paris, backing up what Dumas said about the military situation:

> The General in Chief and I have reconnoitered all of the positions on our frontier. We have climbed on foot through the snow to the base of Mont Cenis and Petit Saint Bernard pass. As of today the snow is not hard and will not support the weight [of a man]. We hope that the snow conditions will soon be as you require, and that we will be able to accomplish your objectives and ours.

But in the same letter Gaston demonstrated his revolutionary zeal vis-à-vis everyone else in the Alps:

> I have seen all of the constituted authorities of this country and talked to them in the language of fervent Republicanism. Some of these authorities are weak, others are misguided. Several, however, are committed to serving the Revolution well. . . . In the towns where inhabitants were too moderate, I thought I had to take action to warm them up to the interests of the Republic. Leading by example, I had them choose between victory or death. Everyone signed . . . and declared on their blood an eternal war with the nearby petty tyrants [and] declared their readiness to plunge a dagger in [the tyrant's] breast at the first chance they got.

＞－◄

AS April approached and the weather began to turn warmer, Dumas ordered preparations for full-out assaults on the passes. Although generals didn't usually do their own reconnaissance, Dumas led forty-five men out on a multiday mission to gain intelligence on the enemy positions on Mont Cenis.

On the night of 16 Germinal, Year II—April 5, 1794—the operation against the enemy positions on Mont Cenis began in earnest. Dumas's plan was to move against the passes on the north and south sides of Mont Cenis at the same time, with about four thousand men. One force, of 2,100 men, would attack Mont Cenis, while another force, about equal in size, would move against the Saint Bernard Pass. In a rare break from style, General Dumas did not go at the head of his troops but left two subordinate generals to take field leadership of the mission. He gave the Mont Cenis column to a trusted subordinate with long experience, General Sarret—a decision he would come to regret.

Since reconnaissance reports had indicated that the redoubts atop Mont Cenis were lightly manned or abandoned, the enemy not expecting an attack this early in the spring, the French assumed they would have the advantage of surprise. Commanded by General Sarret, the main column left the French base at 9 p.m. The plan was to reach the Piedmontese redoubts before dawn, but fierce weather conditions slowed its pace; a number of men slipped on the icy trail and fell into the gorge. When the trail became too slippery and treacherous for the column to continue at all, they were forced to retrace their steps, losing precious hours and energy, until they'd found another trail and resumed their ascent.

When General Sarret's column finally reached the first redoubt below Petit Mont Cenis pass, after dawn, they found it not unmanned but "full of so many people and [so] many small cannons [that] it was impossible to turn them because of the steep hillside. Despite the obstacles, General Sarret decided to take them by force. He left his column and took over the advance guard."

After climbing all night from the valley to the pass near the summit, Sarret's troops were exhausted and suffering the effects of cold and lack of food and water. Now they found themselves suddenly engaged in a fierce battle, with the enemy making short work of them, as their blue coats made them targets against the snow. Artillery rained fire on them all day. But General Sarret pressed on with his hopeless attack. Another general who witnessed what befell General Sarret and his men described the scene this way:

> Those who came were killed or wounded, the hillsides . . . were so steep, the snow made it impossible to walk [and] whoever attempted to [walk across] fell down the precipice. General Sarret was only 110

feet from the summit when he was fatally wounded. Several grenadiers were killed or wounded at the same time. This scene frightened many within the division; there was a moment of terror.

With their commander dead and the subfreezing temperatures of the night approaching, the surviving soldiers began the long and treacherous descent, leaving behind red-stained heaps in the snow and "the horrible sight of the wounded who fell down the crevasses."

In the aftermath of the operation, General Dumas wrote a report to the Committee citing the high winds and the fact that the Piedmontese had apparently been tipped off: "Two Piedmontese deserters assured us that [local villagers] had warned the Piedmontese of our march and that it was by means of this warning that Mont Cenis was reinforced by 2,500 men," he wrote. In short, General Sarret and his men had walked into not only a trap but an overwhelmingly well-defended one. One can only imagine the anguish Dumas felt personally at the suffering of Sarret and the men. He would spend the rest of the campaign trying to avenge them.

Meanwhile Representative Gaston remembered the threat not only from the enemy but from Paris. Bold talk was needed to save the general's head as well as his own. "The enemy was not surprised," Gaston wrote the Committee. "It seems that they were rather certain of the attack, since they had brought forces to all points, and their batteries kept up extensive fire."

"The War Office is infested with corrupt men," his letter to the Committee went on, describing how these supposed double agents had sent "extraordinary couriers to the court of Turin to warn them of our plans for Mont Cenis and Petit St Bernard." Without accusing the minister of war himself of being in on the plot, Gaston managed to cast suspicion back at Paris, rather than leaving it with himself and Dumas in Grenoble. Gaston then tried swagger: either trust us or arrest us, he said in effect, but don't expect us to do our duty under a cloud of suspicion. "Either the Representatives of the People who are close to the Armies have your confidence or they do not," he wrote.

Gaston's brashness worked. One of the savviest things Dumas did in the course of his service was to cultivate the friendship of this decent

Jacobin official. It was a savviness, alas, that he would soon fail to apply to an up-and-coming general who would hold far more control over his fate.*

➤─◄

APRIL turned luckier for the French, and after a bloody assault Dumas's forces were able to capture the smaller of the two main objectives, the Petit Saint Bernard Pass, as well as a Piedmontese fort lower down the mountainside, which yielded them a fresh supply of captured cannons and guns. Along with his letters to the Committee of Public Safety, Dumas also wrote a jubilant note to his loyal adjunct, Piston, who had stayed behind in Grenoble:

> Victory, my dear Piston! Our intrepid Republicans . . . seized the famous post of Petit St Bernard . . . the obstacles of nature ceded to their valor, all the redoubts were taken. The enemy lost many people, our brave brothers in arms worked miracles. Cannons, howitzers, ramparts, rifles, and lots of prisoners, are our trophies, and we only have to regret sixty men wounded, who are as many heroes.
>
> One with a hand blown off was climbing the redoubt with his bloody arm, another, with a broken leg, consoled himself by saying it's nothing. Victory is ours. Each, in a word, gave dazzling proofs of valor during this day, and all fought like Frenchmen!
>
> Salute and Brotherhood!
>
> Alex Dumas

Pressing the advantage, Dumas prepared for a final assault on Mont Cenis. On May 14, he set off with a force of approximately three thousand, who donned woolen socks and fastened iron crampons over their boots for

---

* In fact, it was from this month, March 1794, that I discovered what seems to have been the first contact between General Dumas and the man who would one day do him so much harm. It was a trivial contact, and the name Napoleone Buonaparte—as the Corsican still called himself—meant nothing to General Dumas at the time. But when I saw the name on one of Dumas's orders, it of course jumped off the page at me. Napoleon had just been appointed commander of the artillery corps of the Army of Italy, the poorer sibling of the Army of the Alps, and he had sent Dumas's army a request to borrow some cannons. These being in very short supply, General Dumas had simply denied the request, writing that no guns should be sent to "the artillery General Buenaparte [*sic*] employed in the Army of Italy."

the occasion. Dumas also had the troops put on white hunting smocks over their blue coats in order to disguise themselves against the snow the way the chamois hunters did. Their weaponry was the usual assortment of sabers, knives, grenades, clubs, blunderbusses, pikes, and bayoneted Charleville muskets, including some of the better model 1777s, which could take down a man at up to eighty yards.

Mont Cenis could be assailed from only three sides because the fourth was "defended by nature"—by a set of ice cliffs. The Piedmontese had not even bothered to put a battery on this side but merely a stockade. The battle for this peak was the first time General Dumas was written into history books outside France. An account of it appeared in *The Naval and Military History of the Wars of England*, a general English military history book published in 1795, just a year after the events, and it begins: "Dumas, commander in chief of the army of the Alps, obtained a most decisive victory at Mount Cenis. On this celebrated mountain the Sardinians [Piedmontese] had doubled their forces; and on this account the French general, who seems to have acted with great ability, formed a system of vigorous diversions, extended over all the line."

The English account states that Dumas and his men "ascended the mountain, and amidst volumes of fire, they carried all the redoubts with fixed bayonets." Nothing could better evoke the "French fury" than a bayonet charge across a glacier against entrenched artillery batteries firing all manner of shot and ball. A Scottish history book that repeated this account some years later added the blustery line: "How harmless may volumes of fire be when French Republicans have occasion to pass through them!"

There was nothing harmless about such a barrage. The "bullets" of the time were musket balls two-thirds of an inch in diameter that moved far more slowly than modern bullets, often colliding with just enough force to penetrate a soldier's jacket and vest and enter his chest cavity, where they would get stuck, ricocheting off ribs and doing the damage of later dumdum bullets. The iron cannonballs the Piedmontese were firing obliterated soldiers where they hit and then continued along down the field like bowling balls, killing or maiming anyone in their path. There was nothing worse than when they bounced at about chest or head height, and artillerymen were trained to place them so that they would. (The one thing Dumas could benefit from was the difficulty the enemy artillery had in calculating their bounces on uneven mountain terrain; eighteenth-century artillery was deadliest on flat ground.)

"Torrents of fire rolled down on our brave brothers in arms," reads the account General Dumas sent to Paris immediately after the battle. But though the barrage was fearsome, Dumas's men continued to surge the Piedmontese positions, chanting "Long live the Republic!"; and soon "the mouths of fire are turned against the enemy, I have the drums beat the charge, and bayonets in front of us, we took all the redoubts, [turning] the enemy toward the horrible precipices."

Their own guns turned against them, beset by chanting, fanatical French blues on one side and the fearsome ice cliffs on the other, the white-jacketed Piedmontese "fled before the brave, conquering Republicans," as General Dumas put it, "abandoning their superb and numerous artillery, their equipment, and their immense storehouses." Dumas led his men in pursuit down the other side of the pass and chased them three leagues from Mont Cenis. "We took 900 prisoners, killed many men, and our losses, unbelievably, rose to only seven or eight dead and around 30 wounded. Europe, astonished, will learn with admiration of the great deeds of the intrepid Army of the Alps. Long live the Republic!"*

Later French accounts of the battle raised the number of those captured considerably. An account published in 1833 said that General Dumas led his troops "from position to position, and arrived at the foot of Mount Cenis crowned by a large artillery fortification. But the obstacles did nothing but increase his courage; he climbed the rocks, captured the fortification. The Sardinian troops defeated, cut to pieces, gave us 1,700 prisoners and forty pieces of cannon."

What was undisputable was that the Piedmontese had been routed and Mont Cenis belonged to the French Army of the Alps. General Dumas had captured the seemingly impregnable mountain passes, which opened up not only Piedmont but the riches of the entire Italian peninsula waiting down below.

---

* To top his report, Dumas could not resist adding another compliment about his troops that reflected his own meticulous standards for treating local populations: "The French soldier conducted himself with intrepidity and heroism, he honored misfortune and shared his bread with the inhabitant ruined by the scourge of war."

DUMAS'S conquest of Mont Cenis lifted him to a new place in the pantheon of the heroes of the French revolutionary war. Until then, his heroics had been a kind of soldiers' legend: the great horseman with incredible dueling skills and a knack for capturing enemy outposts at the head of a small band of dragoons. It was a legend of the kind of man whom men liked to follow, a warrior's warrior—but the kind of thing mostly told over a few glasses too many by other soldiers. Now, General Dumas had led thousands of soldiers to a great strategic victory, while still facing enemy fire in front of them and risking his life alongside them.

Among the hundreds of battle reports sent regularly to the Committee by Dumas's colleagues, I occasionally came across one that really captured the way men talk about their commanding officers. In a June 28, 1794, letter, an officer named Jean-Jacques Rougier—who served under Dumas all that spring— wrote,

> At each place, the slaves bit the dust and we took lots of prisoners. Only a few republicans lost their lives. Brave Dumas is tireless, he is everywhere, and everywhere he shows up, the slaves are defeated.

Rougier wrote that the troops felt a new spirit sweeping over the region in the wake of General Dumas's conquests:

> Dozens of deserters come here every day: recently, a captain and an artillery lieutenant have been among them and told us the revolution was starting in Turin: patriots . . . are jailed by force. But far from having such a tyranny block the progress of reason, tempers flare, minds are electrified. And soon the Italians will be worthy of their ancestors.

The Committee of Public Safety displayed almost equal enthusiasm in addressing the Army of the Alps, in a proclamation letter signed by the Organizer of Victory, Lazare Carnot, himself:

> Glory to the conquerors of Mont Cenis and of Mont Saint Bernard. Glory to the invincible Army of the Alps and to the representatives

who have guided it on the road to victory! We cannot tell you, my dear colleagues, of the enthusiasm that has been created here as a result of the news you have announced. . . . We place the greatest confidence in you and in the energy and talents of the brave General Dumas.

Dumas had fulfilled the mission demanded of him. He had secured the top of the world for the French Republic of Liberty and Equality—the highest point it would ever reach.

13

THE BOTTOM OF THE REVOLUTION

O N June 24, 1794, Dumas received a letter, signed not only by Carnot but by Robespierre, ordering him to come immediately to Paris to appear before the Committee of Public Safety.

It was the height of the Great Terror. Two weeks before Dumas received his summons, the Committee had passed a law formalizing the informal policy of executing "enemies of the people" suspected of "abusing the principles of the revolution." Trials were superfluous, since suspects were presumed guilty and the concept of self-defense was not granted to "conspirators"—and the penalty for every political offense was death. The atmosphere was so murderous and irrational that even the greatest victory could no longer protect a general from "the national razor" if his name came before the Committee.*

"I have received, Citizens, your letter," Dumas wrote back. "I will leave for Paris immediately, in accordance with the Committee's orders."

However, that letter has a line crossing out part of the text, indicating that Dumas probably did not send it, and I found a second letter dated the same day showing that he thought better of leaving "immediately." Citing some personnel decisions he needed to make, Dumas wrote, "I anticipate that I will only be able to leave around July 8." The delay may have saved his neck.

Two days later, all Paris celebrated the news of a glorious victory against the Austrians at Fleurus, on the Belgian frontier. It was the capstone to a

---

* Perhaps feeling it couldn't execute the living fast enough, the previous summer the Committee had decided to attack the dead: it ordered the systematic desecration of the royal tombs. The kings and queens of France had been interred in the Abbey of Saint-Denis, just north of Paris, since the sixth century, but in a frenzy of historical obliteration, each royal corpse was exhumed, tossed in a common grave, and covered in quicklime. A "Committee of Jewelers" seized and inventoried the jewels and precious metals found in the coffins.

few months of good military news—including Dumas's victories in the Alps, which had secured the southeastern frontier—and Fleurus was a place that had been the fulcrum of the revolutionary war, a source of great invasion fears.

War had made the Terror possible. The ongoing military crises on France's frontiers had fed the mood of retribution and justified any kind of conspiracy theory the most extreme Committee members chose to invent. Now that the military situation was steadily improving, Carnot and other less fanatical members wondered about the pace of legislated murder.

By mid-July, as Dumas settled in Paris to wait his turn before the Committee, paranoia stalked the government: every deputy eyed his neighbor and feared for his own head. Anyone might reasonably expect to receive a letter in the mail or a knock on the door. Any appearance before the Committee might result in decapitation.

Then, on July 27, the 8th of Thermidor, the solution suddenly became clear: the heads that must fall to the guillotine were those of the chief hangmen themselves. Robespierre's colleagues in the Convention, who had cheered his every whim, now declared him to be "outside the law," which implied their right to imprison and execute him. Robespierre took shelter in the Hôtel de Ville, and when a mob of armed men and soldiers stormed the room, he shot himself. No one knows whether he was trying to commit suicide or whether the pistol went off accidentally, but in any event he aimed badly. France's chief executioner had no experience with firearms. The bullet shattered his jaw, and he lay on a desk all night, attempting not to choke on his own blood. The next morning, a surgeon dressed his wounds, and he was given a clean shirt and tie, apparently his only request, and was led off to the guillotine. He was joined there by Saint-Just and the other ultra-radical members of the Committee.

With that, the Terror ended. The Committee was not abolished, but a new law restricted its powers to war making and diplomacy. It would no longer run France, nor would it be in the execution business. Lazare Carnot, who had helped plot the coup against Robespierre, became the Committee's most powerful member.

◦—◦

THE newly reconstituted Committee appears not to have known what to do with Alex Dumas. To his chagrin, they did not send him back to the Alps. Instead, in early August they shuffled him around among temporary assignments, until they finally settled on a grueling new command that must hardly have seemed a reward for his performance in the spring. In mid-August, the Committee decided to send "the hero of Mont Cenis" to lead the Army of the West, whose mission was to combat a bloody royalist rebellion—some called it a civil war—in the Vendée, in western France.

While the majority of the revolutionary armies fought external enemies, a few targeted internal rebellion and counterrevolution. The Army of the West was particularly notorious in this respect: its task was to suppress the motley collection of aristocrats and peasants who called themselves the Catholic and Royal Army. Many factors had made the Vendéeans rebels: many of them opposed the Revolution from the beginning or were alienated by the persecution of priests and the confiscation of Church property or by the 1793 execution of the king. But the biggest cause of the rebellion seems to have been Carnot's implementation of the *levée en masse*.

The draft was wildly unpopular among the region's peasants. A year in the army for a farmer meant that his family might not be able to bring in the harvest and might starve. In the spring of 1793, angry peasants vandalized hundreds of town halls and local republican officials' homes across western France. They killed or chased off officials, attacked National Guardsmen, whom they often murdered in gruesome fashion, and formed a "brigand army." Victor Hugo would later describe it thus: "Invisible battalions lay in wait. These unseen armies snaked beneath the republican armies, sprung from the earth for an instant, then disappeared; they leapt into view, uncountable in their numbers, then vanished . . . [they are] an avalanche that turns to dust . . . jaguars with the habits of moles."

The repression the Republic imposed in the Vendée escalated to a level of surreal violence that dwarfed the Parisian Terror. Here the most extreme rhetoric of revolutionary war became reality—the idea of "exterminating angels of liberty" that came to earth and left miles of corpses in their wake. "We burned and broke heads as usual" was a typical report from a brigadier. What this meant in sheer numbers was, by eighteenth-century standards, almost unimaginable: up to a quarter of a million men, women, and children perished—one out of four residents of the Vendée region. (When historians quote figures for the number of people who died in the Terror, the majority of the deaths always come from the mass executions the army carried out in the Vendée, along with epidemics and starvation in the wake of that war.) Among many signature atrocities perpetrated there were those of the army's "hell columns": approximately thirty thousand soldiers, divided into a dozen equal columns, marching through the countryside in a grid of destruction that wiped out everything in its path—men, women, children, animals, trees, and any other living thing that could be shot, stabbed, or burned to death. In Nantes the army saved costly lead musket balls and time by organizing mass drownings. As Thomas Carlyle described it, "Women and men are tied together, feet and feet, hands and hands; and flung in: this they call *Mariage Républicain*, Republican Marriage." The Army of the West carried out most of its mass drownings using specially constructed barges that they floated into the middle of the Loire, loaded with approximately 130 victims each, and scuttled by opening special trapdoors designed for the purpose. (Many details of this atrocity came from the trial testimony of one of the carpenters in charge of building these "floating coffins," who described how they worked and how his first one was used to drown a boatload of priests.)

A decent man could not last long in the Vendée without becoming either a bloodthirsty killer or a victim. This was the case for Dumas's old commander General Biron. Biron had been sent to the Vendée in May 1793 to fight the insurgency. He had achieved immediate military successes, but the insubordination and continued violence toward civilians on the part of his troops caused him to resign. Another general then accused him of *incivisme* because he had been too lenient with the insurgents. This was enough to land Biron on the guillotine in December 1793, the very month that the Army of the West declared provisional victory over the insurgency.

Though the Vendée was no longer in open revolt, it was still a problem for the central government. The bloody crew that the Army of the West had become needed to be taught how to be a proper army again. General Dumas was a useful man for the job because he was a "good republican" without being a Jacobin fanatic. He inspired respect among subordinates, was known for both his sense of fair play and his toughness, and had shown keen organizational abilities in the Alps.

Dumas arrived in the Vendée in September 1794 and was appalled at what he found. "The Vendéeans no longer needed the pretext of religion or royalist sentiments to take up arms," he later wrote. "They were being forced to defend their homes, their women who were being raped, their children who were being put to the sword." His first order, on September 7, was to the chief of staff of the Army of the West:

> The chief of staff will . . . establish a police force that is as strict as it is fair in the location of the General District. [He will] assure that no soldier, no matter his rank, will be there without being attached there or without a mission. It will be the same for all the agents employed in the army, and no one will leave his camp or quarters, for any reason and without a formal order.

Dumas threw himself into cleaning up the republican forces under him. The Army of the West was living high off plunder. Dumas set about making it relearn the simple soldier's virtues, like sleeping outdoors. He was always hardest on fellow officers: "The officer must provide an example to the soldier . . . and sleep like him in a tent."

His orders here show his trademark attention to detail and concern that his army receive its fair share of provisions and matériel. But whereas in his other commands Dumas had habitually praised his men and written as their advocate, in his letters from the Army of the West he sounds less like the general of a professional army and more like a new principal brought in to fix a particularly bad school. A selection of his typical orders, in reference to a junior officer, gives an idea of his assignment:

> He will tell me why there are 288 men in the garrison . . . If they are not necessary there, [he] will give them the order to rejoin their battalion.
>
> . . . I have received information that soldiers are selling their cartridges to bandits. You will mention that fact in the order of the day, with the expression of my indignation about such an offense. To [ensure that] it does not happen again, you will order daily inspections and . . . punish all those who are proven to have sold their cartridges or to have lost them due to negligence.

. . . Any soldier who crosses the boundaries of the camp except for military reasons will be considered a deserter; the reading of the penal code will take place every ten days. The General Officers and the Corps Chiefs are personally responsible for carrying out this order.

Dumas showed no shortage of his usual zeal, but his efforts went toward a thankless task. Throughout September and October of 1794, he inspected thousands of republican troops, from the great slave-and-sugar port of Nantes to the hamlets and wheat fields where so many villagers had stories of atrocities and mass graves. An official report by General Dumas summing up his observation of the Vendée command, reproduced by his son in the memoir, captures this good man's feelings about this very ugly conflict:

I have delayed my report on the state of the army and the war of the Vendée in order to base it on sure facts, seen by my own eyes. . . . It has to be said that there is no part of the Army of the West, either military or administrative, that does not call for the stern hand of reform. . . .

You must judge from this, by the numbers of their new recruits, by the utter incompetence of these battalions, of which the fit portion finds itself paralyzed by the majority's inexperience, even as the officers themselves are so undisciplined that there is no hope of training new recruits.

But there is a greater evil than this.

The evil lies deeper, in the spirit of indiscipline and pillage that rules throughout the army, a spirit produced by habit and nourished by impunity. This spirit has been carried to such a point that I dare to tell you that it is impossible to repress, except by transferring these corps to other armies and by replacing them with troops that have been trained in subordination.

[The] soldiers have threatened to shoot their officers for trying at my orders to stop the pillaging. You may at first be amazed at these excesses; but you will cease to be shocked when you realize that it is the necessary consequence of the system followed up to present in this war. . . . You will not find even among the general officers the means to remind the rank and file of a love of justice and upstanding comportment. . . .

And yet military virtues are never more necessary than in civil warfare. How, in their absence, can we carry out your orders? . . . [For] I wholly believe the war could be ended quickly if the measures I have proposed are adopted. They are:

1. The reorganization of the army;
2. The reorganization of the general officers;
3. A carefully vetted selection of officers destined for the Vendée . . .

While matters remain in the same state it is impossible for me to respond to your expectations and assure you of the termination of the war in the Vendée.

In late October, Dumas was transferred out of the Army of the West. The official *Moniteur* gazette printed a statement by local representatives in the Vendée that thanked General Dumas for bringing a new discipline to the Army of the West and for "deploying a character of justice and inflexibility whose effects are already being felt." The representatives regretted his departure after such a short time but affirmed that even that short time had made a difference.*

Dumas's indictment of the atrocities would not be forgotten, especially not by the chroniclers of their victims. In the following century, as the memory of the Vendée would continue to divide French society, as civil war memories do, Dumas would have the rare distinction of being praised for his conduct both by enemies of the Republic and by its supporters. "Fearless and irreproachable," wrote a pro-royalist historian of the region nearly a century after the terrible events there, General Dumas "deserves to pass into posterity and makes a favorable contrast with the executioners, his contemporaries, whom public indignation will always nail to the pillory of History!"

▸—◂

---

* An 1823 biographical dictionary of French generals quotes from "General Dumas's memoir from the Vendée campaign," which claimed that he was forced out of the position: "I wanted to discipline the army and put the principles of justice and humanity into practice on the field. . . . Villains, whose power was brought to an end by the anarchy [they caused], denounced me: they slandered me with the design of wanting to stop the bloodshed." But I have never located such a memoir and this 1823 entry is the sole reference to it.

THE Vendée posting took its toll on the victor of Mont Cenis, both mentally and physically. Dumas began reporting severe headaches, and also trouble from a cyst above his left eye—the leftover scar from his duel back in the Sixth Dragoons. In early December, the Committee gave him leave to return home to Villers-Cotterêts to recuperate. There, he divided his time between doting on his little daughter Alexandrine Aimée and hunting in the forests.

Compared to the past years, France was quiet in the fall and winter of 1794–95. The government benefited from continued military success, and though the Committee continued to govern, sober men now sat in place of fanatics. The guillotine was once again reserved for something like actual crimes—more or less the equivalent of any other public method of execution, but supposedly more painless, as Dr. Guillotine had intended.* In the Vendée the government agreed to exempt peasants from the normal draft laws.

Meanwhile, Napoleon Bonaparte, who had been lying low in Marseilles the past few months, moved to Paris and cultivated relationships with members of the government, especially Carnot. By summer Napoleon wrote to his older brother Joseph that he was "attached to the topographical bureau of the Committee of Public Safety."

In the summer of 1795, most of the powers in the anti-French coalition had pulled out to concentrate on other issues—Prussia, the Netherlands, and Spain all signed truce agreements with Paris—and Austria was left to conduct the land war against France virtually alone. Austria's one stalwart ally against revolutionary France was Great Britain, whose navy continued to harass French ships on the high seas and block colonial trade with the sugar islands. (It also continued to provide cash to whatever other power wanted to challenge France.)

Carnot decided that France should use the dissolution of the antirevolutionary coalition to attack Austria. If the Hapsburg Empire fell, or was greatly weakened, the affairs of Europe would be dictated from Paris. To this

---

* In fact, a lively debate in the press concerned the unanswerable question of whether people died instantly upon being guillotined. Witnesses to the execution of Charlotte Corday, the prim Girondin assassin who had stabbed Marat to death in his bathtub, said they saw Corday's severed head flush when it was slapped by the executioner. A famous surgeon published an article stating that severed heads may continue to live for some minutes and have "a perception of [their] own execution."

end Carnot launched the great Rhineland offensive of 1795. He was determined to beat the Austrians in their own imperial backyard.

Dumas, who was not cultivating his career very carefully but was always eager for action, got himself a posting with General Jean-Baptiste Kléber and the Army of the Rhine. General Kléber was a stoutly framed builder's son from Strasbourg, with a wild head of curly hair, a huge jaw, and a love of fighting. He'd actually gotten his start in the military when as a boy he had helped a pair of nobles in a tavern brawl in Munich, and his first commissions had been in the imperial Austrian army. But like so many others of low birth, Kléber had seen his opportunity in the French Revolution and enlisted in the Fourth Battalion of the Upper Rhine.

Dumas and Kléber understood each other perfectly and this would be the beginning of an important friendship for Dumas. In September 1795, they crossed the Rhine together and attacked Düsseldorf in the name of liberty, equality, and fraternity. The *Moniteur* reported, "The loss of Frenchmen during this great expedition was calculated to be 400 men, including both dead and wounded. General Dumas is numbered among the latter."

It isn't known what injury Dumas suffered during the battle, but it was not life-threatening. He spent the rest of the fall shuttling between various postings on France's eastern frontier, both in Belgium and along the Rhine. Meanwhile, in Villers-Cotterêts, his beloved was pregnant with their second child. In January 1796, Marie-Louise wrote him:

> My good friend,
> The military post that stops here today on its way to Germany . . . will bring you this note which will convey our most tender wishes and which will tell you that the due date is coming soon and that I want to have you with me then. Don't delay and bring me the courage I need. Everyone here congratulates you. Marie-Aimée [i.e., Alexandrine Aimée, their first daughter] sends you a thousand fond kisses, I add another thousand and I'm longing for you.
> Marie-Louise Dumas.

Their second daughter, "Louise Alexandrine," was born shortly after, and though it's not clear if Dumas was able to attend the birth, his letters from that spring show he had more time to bounce this child on his knee than he had when Alexandrine Aimée was born, during the frenetic months of fall, 1793, just after his promotion to general's rank. Not enough time, as fate would prove.

━━

THROUGHOUT 1795 the government's pursuit of stability ran into a roadblock: the rotten state of the French economy. Three years of war had brought on hyperinflation, since the government printed ever more paper to pay for the pikes, the muskets, the modern artillery pieces. The hyperinflationary cycle had been disguised somewhat by the intensity of feelings that attended the war fever, and then the Terror, but now that France had returned to something more like normalcy, the economic crisis drove politics.*

The current Committee members' lack of extreme ideological convictions also made it a target for all sides, and Paris was rife with plots against the middle-of-the-road government. In spring hyperinflation and bread riots had sparked a rise in what was called "neo-Jacobinism," and in May these far-left radicals staged an uprising; it was brutally suppressed. But the repression of the neo-Jacobins on the far left created an opening for the neo-royalists on the far right.

On October 5, 1795, the royalist-leaning sections of the city erupted in insurrection against the central government. Thirty thousand insurgents marched on the government, which had at most six thousand troops to defend it.

---

* The French economy ran on a bizarre kind of money called the *assignat*. Since a debt crisis had sparked the Revolution in the first place, one of the revolutionary government's first goals had been to provide capital. It did this by nationalizing the property of the Catholic Church—monasteries, convents, churches, bishops' tea sets, and jewelry collections—and issuing a new sort of circulating bond backed by nationalized Church property: the *assignat*. But the government issued more *assignats* whenever it felt like it, and the ensuing hyperinflation caused food riots, which increased instability, which caused the government to print more *assignats*, which increased hyperinflation. The paper bills had long since ceased to represent anything, except perhaps the belief in world revolution. Finally on October 19, 1795, the floor literally fell out from under the *assignats*: in Paris, at the printing house that manufactured them, someone simply piled too much worthless paper currency in one spot and the wood floor collapsed under the weight.

The government called on a man of influence, a provincial noble named Paul Barras—*Viscount* Paul *de* Barras—who was promoted overnight to command the Army of the Interior. Barras looked to the army and specifically to an up-and-coming general living in Paris. Napoleon Bonaparte did not disappoint him.

Napoleon's use of canister shrapnel shells on the crowd—the "whiff of grapeshot" in Carlyle's famous description—revealed the sour-faced artillerist's chilling efficiency. Hundreds of royalists lay dead in the streets of Paris, hundreds more wounded. By comparison the Champ de Mars Massacre had been a bar fight. The counterrevolutionary uprising was suppressed.

In recognition of his services, Napoleon gained the patronage of Barras, who emerged from the crisis as France's new strongman. The government was reorganized yet again: at the top was a five-man executive branch called the Directory, which swore itself in on November 3, 1795. The top "Director" of the French state was now Paul Barras. Among his four colleagues—*plus ça change*—was Lazare Carnot. There was also an oddly enormous new legislative body called the Council of Five Hundred.

Though the so-called Directory government that ran France in the mid- to late 1790s is usually derided as a low point in the Revolution—a time of cronyism and corruption—it is rarely credited with an amazing, quiet accomplishment: this period saw the French movement for racial equality persist not only in the colonies but in Paris itself. One emblematic example was the election and acceptance of black and mixed-race legislators in the Council of Five Hundred. Belley and Mills were the first, but at least ten more would hold political office in the 1790s, including the mixed-race men Jean Littée, Joseph and Jean-Louis Boisson, Louis-François Boisrond, Jean-Baptiste Deville, Jean-François Petitniaud, Pierre Thomany, Jacques Tonnelier, and the doyen of eighteenth-century black activism, Julien Raimond. Former slaves Etienne Mentor and Jean-Louis d'Annecy also served as representatives. Annecy held the position of secretary in the Directory's Council of Elders.

Perhaps one of the most touching of the forgotten stories from this period was how revolutionary France, under the outwardly soulless Directory, instituted the world's first color-blind elite secondary school. It gave the sons of former slaves—alongside the sons of privileged mixed-race and white abolitionists—one of the world's finest educations at a time when the English-speaking world still considered it a crime for black children to learn to read.

It began in the mid-1790s, when, at the invitation of prominent members of the Society of the Friends of the Blacks, revolutionaries "of color" in the French colonies began sending their children to school in Paris. The government responded by creating an elite boarding school, the National Colonial Institute, which would be the world's first experiment in integrated secondary education. Among its founders were leading civil rights activists like Julien Raimond, the Abbé Grégoire, and Léger-Félicité Sonthonax, the man who had first ordered abolition in Saint-Domingue.

The headmaster was a revolutionary preacher close to the Society of the Friends of the Blacks. Pupils included the children of deputies Belley, Dufay, and Thomany, Sonthonax's own mixed-race children, and the son of Henri Christophe (the future King Henri I of Haiti). In this it mirrored the revolutionary colonial elite but did not reflect the growing political rift between blacks and mulattos in Saint-Domingue: in Paris, the children of black general Toussaint Louverture and mulatto general André Rigaud were classmates at the Institute, while in Saint-Domingue their fathers were bitter enemies in a civil war.

The Directory passed a law mandating that "every year, in each department, for the 1st of Germinal (the Festival of Youth), six individual children will be chosen . . . without distinction of color, to be transported to France and looked after in special schools, at the cost of the government, during the time necessary for their education." The Institute therefore took in not only children of the elite but also many black scholarship students.

The minister of the interior also mandated that students be recruited from places other than the West Indies, such as Egypt and East Africa. In addition to scholarship tuition for children of black or mixed-race heritage, the government also funded some white children, especially the sons of prominent revolutionary abolitionists such as Brissot. (Interestingly, among the non-scholarship students at the school in this period were a number of openly racist planters' sons.)

The Institute was not merely an experiment in race mixing. It provided its black and white students with one of the most rigorous educations in the world, and the school's best students, of whatever complexion, could take the examination for the École Polytechnique, then France's most elite military academy. From the perspective of early 1796, Alex Dumas might well have assumed that his son, when he had one, would attend this school or a similar one. He could not have known that his son Alexandre, brilliant as he would be, would instead be unable to attend any secondary school at all, because of a man whose name was still unknown to all but a small circle in the government and the War Ministry but who would soon remake France, and the Revolution, entirely.

In early 1796, Director Carnot opened a new front against the Austrians in Italy, and he gave the post of general-in-chief of the French Army of Italy to a talented Corsican artillery man, Napoleon Bonaparte, who had recently done the government a favor. At the time, many saw it as an insult because the Army of Italy was known to be decrepit and underfunded. Napoleon knew it was an opportunity.

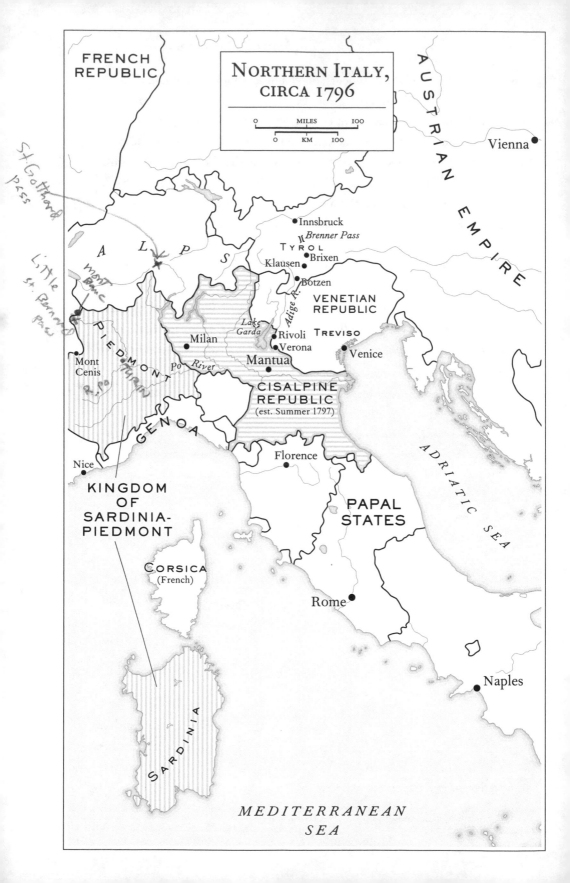

NORTHERN ITALY, CIRCA 1796

MILES
0 — 100

KM
0 — 100

FRENCH REPUBLIC

AUSTRIAN EMPIRE

Vienna

St. Gothard Pass

Little St. Bernard Pass

A L P S

Mont Blanc

Innsbruck

Brenner Pass

TYROL

Brixen

Klausen

Botzen

Adige R.

VENETIAN REPUBLIC

TREVISO

PIEDMONT

Mont Cenis

Milan

Po River

Lake Garda

Rivoli

Verona

Mantua

Venice

R. Po

GENOA

CISALPINE REPUBLIC
(est. Summer 1797)

Nice

Florence

ADRIATIC SEA

KINGDOM OF SARDINIA-PIEDMONT

CORSICA
(French)

PAPAL STATES

Rome

SARDINIA

Naples

MEDITERRANEAN SEA

THE SIEGE

A T the fortress city of Mantua, the moss-covered walls are still riddled with bullet holes from the battles Dumas and his comrades fought here. This was the most important siege of the Italian campaign. Here the French challenged the forces of the Austrian Empire who held northern Italy in their grip, and the ground for Italian independence was laid.

Fifty miles north of the fortress city, where the misty hilltop plain of Rivoli guards the approaches to Lake Garda and the Alps, the French army fought its most famous battle. In a little village dotted with poplar trees, a tiny museum celebrates the revolutionary army's most glorious campaign—the last, history would show, that it truly fought as republican brothers-in-arms. Among the endless portraits and trinkets celebrating Napoleon, I discovered a framed sheet of miniature engravings of the other French generals of the Italian campaign. Each portrait showed a general encased in a little oval frame, as if in a locket.

The portrait of General Dumas leapt out from the rows of his lighter-skinned comrades, with their romantic pompadours and bushy side-burns. Dumas's hair was trimmed close and neat, his head turned in three-quarter view, one eyebrow cocked high. Most of the other generals looked off to the right or left or into the distance, in a pose of destiny calling. Others presented themselves in full antique profile or looked straight at the artist with a self-satisfied air. But Dumas peered out with an open, almost quizzical expression, and I had that uncanny feeling that while the others were frozen in their lost worlds, he was alive within his little oval—impatient, curious—staring right back at me from the two-hundred-year-old paper.

▸—◂

DUMAS arrived in Milan in November 1796 to join the Army of Italy. The very name the French had chosen—"the Army of Italy"—could be seen as a provocation to the various authorities who controlled the Italian peninsula. The capital of the army's semimythical Italy was not on the peninsula at all—Rome was the capital of the Papal States—but in Paris, the beacon of light for the nascent Italian patriots.

Many international dreamers after liberty had drifted in and out of Paris since the early 1790s —Belgians, Germans, Poles, Saint-Dominguans—but the cause of the "Italians" was among the most far-fetched. Italy had not been a united nation since the fall of Rome. Since then, Italians had experienced independence only in the form of self-governing city-states, each of which had developed its art, commerce, and political power independently. The extreme geographical separation of the north and the south, from which deep cultural, political, and economic separations followed, helped keep a unified nation from emerging.

In the late eighteenth century, "Italy" was a concept few Italians understood or cared about. There were historical antecedents: Dante had spoken of Italy in a poetic sense and Machiavelli in a political one when he imagined a liberator to deliver his country from foreign occupation (at that point, Spain). But 250 years after Machiavelli wrote *The Prince*, Italy was more than ever under foreign domination—at the moment by the Austrian Empire.

Formerly powerful independent cities in the north, like Florence and Milan, had become Austrian imperial cities, like Vienna or Salzburg. Resentment of the Austrians provided much of the impetus for the nascent Italian patriotism and provided a terrific opportunity for the French: the Florentines and Milanese had fewer rights than the American colonists had had and a much greater sense of their own history. The American Revolution inspired them, and the spirit of 1789 brought a new sense of cohesion and urgency.

The French Army of Italy, under General-in-Chief Napoleon Bonaparte, burst across the western frontier of the Kingdom of Piedmont-Sardinia, the most powerful Italian kingdom allied with the Austrians, in April 1796. After a series of lightning victories that caused the Sardinians to surrender and the Austrians to retreat, the French were welcomed into Milan on May 15 with revolutionary songs and adulation. Napoleon then paused the campaign, as would become his habit, and proceeded to overhaul the society and politics of northern Italy. He announced that more than a dozen ancient city-states would be incorporated into two new "independent republics": the Cispadane Republic, south of the Po River, and the Transpadane Republic, north of it. These insta-republics amounted to a new kind of franchising of the Revolution: with this model, a "liberated" population would not need to wait more than a few days before a representative government sprang up fully formed in their capital, mimicking whatever style was then fashionable in Paris. Because this was 1796, the new Italian republics each got a version of the Directory—the fashion of republican government in Paris since the previous year—and its own French-style legal code. By July of the next year these two French-sponsored Italian republics had merged into one larger one called the Cisalpine Republic. Nobody much remembers these strange names today—but they were the political taproot of modern Italy.

They were also the model for how Napoleon would adapt and export the French Revolution at the head of his conquering armies. He understood how to use the rhetoric and spirit of the Revolution to advance his interests. The constitution for the Cisalpine Republic shows his approach; it begins with a statement justifying the French invasion and advertising its benefits to the local people:

> The Cisalpine Republic was for many years under the domination of the Empire of Austria. The French Republic succeeded in its place by right of conquest; she renounces her claim from this day on, and the Cisalpine Republic is now free and independent. . . . [France] now gives to the Cisalpine people its own Constitution, which is the result of the most enlightened minds of the most enlightened nation in Europe. . . . No republic has existed in Italy for many years; the sacred fire of liberty had been snuffed out, and the most beautiful part of Europe lived under the foreign yoke. It is up to the Cisalpine Republic to show the world, by its wisdom, its energy, and the good organization of its armies, that modern Italy has not degenerated, and that it is still worthy of freedom.

Dumas was troubled by Napoleon's approach. In Milan Dumas glimpsed the first signs that Napoleon was being treated less like a general and more like a potentate, wrapping himself in the Revolution in order to extend his own influence.

━━◆━

WHEN Napoleon took command of the Army of Italy at the end of March 1796, it was the worst equipped and the most demoralized of all the French armies. Many of its forty-two thousand troops marched without shoes, not to mention boots, and dressed in rags stolen from local peasants; its officers actually wore goatskins. Morale was so low and discipline so poor that it was said its soldiers sang royalist songs and one company had renamed itself "Dauphin" in honor of the murdered King Louis's son. The government had withheld its limited resources from the Army of Italy because it felt that the more important war with the Austrian enemy was on France's German frontier, or in Belgium. Italy was seen as a sideshow, and also a dangerous place to launch an offensive: France had not won a major victory here in centuries. Napoleon's strategy for reviving the Army of Italy was based on making it self-sustaining. To make an army self-sustaining is not a pretty thing.

"Soldiers, you are badly fed and nearly naked," Napoleon declared in March when he arrived in Nice, then the Army of Italy's headquarters, to take its command. "I am going to lead you into the most fertile plains in the world, where you will find great cities and rich provinces; there, you will find honor, glory and riches."

Inspiring words, but what did they mean? "The art of making war feed on war is totally unknown to us," the military philosopher Guibert had written, arguing that armies needed to free themselves of their lumbering supply trains by living off the land and making the enemy bear the cost. "But if a general appeared who had such a talent, would we give him the power to put it into execution?" In fact, European armies spent most of the eighteenth century weaning themselves off this style of warfare, which had decimated much of the continent the previous century, in the Thirty Years' War. States had built up complex logistical infrastructures that could transport in vast wagon trains everything an army needed to live and fight. This was how the Austrians, the Prussians, the Piedmontese, and all the *Ancien Régime* armies fought. Since 1793, the French revolutionary armies had revived the old tradition of pillage in a highly organized way; it was designed to avoid inflicting extreme suffering and starvation, which could cause revolt, while maximizing the profits of war for the republican liberators. Parisian art lovers benefited from each campaign, as the Louvre galleries filled with new works from around Europe.

But after taking command of the Army of Italy in 1796, Napoleon took organized theft to a new level. He began by raising his soldiers' back pay with a freedom fee imposed on the city of Milan—the price for its independence from Austria—to the tune of 20 million francs in cash. He followed this with liberation levies on every state, city, and principality the army invaded. The French also stole art at a new level: Napoleon requested that the government send him experts qualified to judge which paintings his men should steal; priceless canvases by Titian, Raphael, Rubens, and Leonardo da Vinci were shipped to Paris. The army also took precious manuscripts, books, and scientific instruments. Napoleon charged every local duke a ransom in artwork for an armistice, and the ransom was five times the usual rate for the pope, who had the best collections of anybody. In small towns that could not supply artwork, jewels, cash, or gold, the requisitions came in the form of sacks of flour or rations of meat and casks of wine.

From bare subsistence the soldiers of the Army of Italy suddenly began to live like kings; where they were hungry, they now commandeered thousands of steaks and bottles of wine from their liberated hosts. The hard-bitten bunch had more cash than it knew what to do with. One sergeant described how the officers bought jewelry: "The watchmakers and jewelers saw their shops emptied in twenty-four hours, and everyone strutted around with two watches decorated with chains and ornaments that fell halfway down their thighs, just as the fashion was in Paris at that time."

An inventory taken in December 1796, the first full month Dumas was on duty with the Army of Italy, put the official estimate of cash collected to that point at 45,706,493 francs and the amount collected in gold, silver, and precious jewels at 12,132,909 francs. Liberated Italians were beginning to wonder whether French freedom was worth the heavy price.

Throughout his time with the Army of Italy, Dumas clashed with Napoleon on the issue of how to treat civilians. As in the Vendée, Mr. Humanity found himself again in the role of trying to keep his troops from exploiting the local population in the permissive atmosphere of war. He wrote countless letters of reprimand to his cavalry officers for infractions such as "constantly going to the inns, eating and drinking without paying." He ordered that a certain officer be relieved of command and placed under arrest for being "unworthy to be called a Frenchman" because he confiscated cattle supposedly under Dumas's authority. At the bottom of the arrest order Dumas added:

> P.S. You will also warn the hussars of that detachment that all the requisitions that they had the impudence to make in my name are void, and that all the cattle which have been taken must be returned immediately to their owners. . . .   —Alex Dumas

Where most other generals were coarsened by their time in the Vendée, Dumas seems to have been made even more sensitive to the need for maintaining correct relations between troops and the civilian population. He treated the occupied population the way he insisted his own soldiers be treated: as deserving of his respect and—at least when they were not actively fighting him—protection.

When Napoleon ordered the evacuation of the civilians in a battle zone Dumas controlled, Mr. Humanity bristled at the order to confiscate all of their property that could be useful to the French forces. He was careful not to directly contravene one of Napoleon's orders, but his conduct amounted to a conscientious objection to the policy of plunder. He wrote to his brigadier to "soften the order" and to make sure people were not abused or cheated by the troops:

> You will appoint two officers or more, clever and worthy of your trust, to conduct an inventory of grains, hay, straw, oats, carriages, horses and oxen, and [you will] leave the inhabitants enough to feed themselves and their cattle. . . .
>
> When we need to make use of carriages, they will be driven by the inhabitants to whom they belong, but always escorted by the number of necessary soldiers who will make sure that the drivers are never separated from their carriages, [since] once we don't need them

anymore, they will be driven back to where they were taken from, by the same escort.

You will give the strictest orders [to ensure] that the houses these inhabitants will leave are subject to no misappropriations by the soldiers, by prescribing that whosoever be caught committing one, will be punished to the extent of the laws. In the same way, you will have [your troops] make sure that the inhabitants leave their homes in the greatest safety. . . .

Alex Dumas

Receiving orders that all women must leave a certain brigade within twenty-four hours, presumably to forestall rape and prostitution, Dumas does not object to the order but speaks to headquarters on the women's behalf: "Where will these women who are three hundred leagues from their home go? The law commands, but humanity demands. I enlist you, therefore, to postpone the execution of this order until General Masséna has proposed a gentler method."

Dumas attempted to avoid clashing with the commander-in-chief directly by adopting the time-honored strategy of pretending that the man on top must be shocked at any abuses, which surely happened without his knowledge. While complaining about the plunder of his men, he attributes some of their behavior to the greed of their officers.

General-in-Chief Bonaparte:
Daily, General, I receive complaints from inhabitants who are forced to contribute to our soldiers because of the carelessness of our military commissaries and our administrators, who reduce [our men] to going without the most basic necessities. . . . Obliged to resist the ravages of the weather, to which he is exposed for lack of shoes, of clothing, he must also battle with hunger and the deprivation of the other things in life, because a Commissary, a quartermaster, have preferred their pleasures, their own affairs instead of providing for his subsistence. Thus I am pained, General, to see him [this soldier] indulging in excesses unworthy of a Republican, and that because he has been two or three days without meat and without bread. . . .

Alex Dumas

After all, Dumas reasoned, the French could not claim to be liberating the Italians if they were at the same time pillaging their property and abusing their women. And indeed, as the campaign wore on, the policy of systematic pillage would undermine the initial widespread goodwill the Italian patriots felt for the French.

Dumas had been a general of division when Napoleon was still a captain, and he had continued to outrank the Corsican until December 1795. But the man still known as General Bonaparte was convinced he was destined to rise above his contemporaries to be much more than a general. To Dumas, the Republic's generals stood together on the same plane and should be proud of the fact. Along with liberty, the Revolution's two other commandments were equality and brotherhood. "The French Revolution stamped a peculiar seal upon our army," Dumas's son the novelist later wrote:

> When I come across it I treasure the imprint as one would that of a precious medal that will soon be lost to rust, whose worth one wishes to impress upon one's contemporaries, its characteristics upon posterity. . . . We shall misjudge all these men of the Republic if we judge them only by those who survived and whom we knew under the Empire. The Empire was an era of powerful pressures, and the Emperor Napoleon was a brutal coiner of metal. All money had to be stamped with his image, and all bronze smelted in his furnace.

The campaign for Italy was the beginning of Napoleon's reminting the republican generals in his own image. General Alex Dumas refused the new stamp. From the beginning of their relationship, Dumas failed to recognize the special reverence in which Napoleon expected to be held. While this must have piqued Napoleon, he was enough of a pragmatist to keep an eye on General Dumas to see what he could contribute. As he would discover in the conquest of Italy, Dumas could contribute quite a lot, so Napoleon would tolerate his troublesome manner and annoying egalitarian values—up to a point.

➤◄

THE Austrian Empire's main line of defense in northern Italy was a chain of fortresses built along the ancient trade routes running up into the Tyrol region and across the Alps at the Brenner Pass. Since Roman times, this has been the main non-sea route connecting the Italian peninsula to the rest of Europe. Most of the route is densely wooded hilly terrain that, just south of the romantic city of Verona, opens up into the flat marshy plain surrounding the southernmost link in the fortress chain: Mantua.

By controlling Mantua, which stands almost in the center of northern Italy, guarding not only the route up to the Alps but also the crucial east-west axis linking the Mediterranean and Adriatic seas, the Austrians effectively controlled northern Italy. They fortified and garrisoned Mantua, and after Napoleon's victories against them, thousands more Austrian troops retreated into its fortress. The city was admirably protected by geography: by lakes on three sides and an impenetrable marsh on the fourth, southern side. The marsh, almost a swamp, produced one of the unhealthiest climates in northern Italy—flat, stale, and, at that time, miserably malarial—and it made direct assault on the fortress, which was reachable only by long causeway bridges, almost impossible. Napoleon instead decided to lay siege to it, counting on starving into submission the twenty-three thousand Austrian soldiers inside.

Six weeks after arriving in Milan to report to the Army of Italy, Alex Dumas was assigned to command the first division maintaining the siege at Mantua. Dumas's two immediate predecessors in this post had resigned for medical reasons, overcome by the unhealthy climate; when Dumas arrived, his senior commander was ill.

Perhaps because he had grown up in a tropical climate, Dumas was not affected by the swamp air—and he was determined to come up with a way to break the Austrian grip on the city. He reviewed all aspects of the siege, inspecting the guard posts and gun emplacements, and interviewed all the officers under his command. He increased the number of patrols, especially at night.

Less than a week later, Dumas's strategy bore fruit.

On Christmas Eve, his patrols arrested three men trying to cross through the French lines to enter the city. When they were brought to him in the middle of the night, he was particularly interested in one of them. The man's bearing seemed to betray both intelligence and the fact that he was hiding something. Dumas suspected he might be in charge of a mission of some kind. He pressed the man, telling him that he knew he was on a mission to the Austrians and must have some sort of papers on him.

The man protested his innocence, claiming he was the son of a Veronese lawyer and had merely gotten into the wrong place at the wrong time. When nothing was found in his clothes or his books, Dumas accused him of having swallowed a message. At this point, he decided to frighten the man into a confession. Dumas's son wrote a memorable account of the incident (based on Dermoncourt's recollections) that accords with the official version:

> Among my father's favorite books were Caesar's *Commentaries*. A volume of the *Commentaries* of the conqueror of Gaul lay open on the table placed near his bed, and the passage my father had been rereading before going to sleep was where Caesar relates that in order to get his lieutenant through to Labienus with valuable information, he had encased his letter in a little ivory ball about the size of a child's toy; the messenger, when he came to the enemy's posts, or to any place where he feared attack, was to carry the ball in his mouth, and to swallow it if he had a close call.
>
> This passage from Caesar came back to him as a beam of light.
>
> "Very well," said my father; "since this man denies it, he must be taken out and shot."
>
> "What! General!" [he] exclaimed in terror. "Why am I to be shot?"
>
> "To cut open your stomach and find the dispatches you have swallowed," said my father with as much aplomb as if the thing had been revealed by some familiar spirit.

After the man confessed that he was a spy and that he did swallow the dispatches, it became a matter of how to get them out of him, short of disemboweling him. In the novelist's account, Dumas dispatched Dermoncourt to find a pharmacist and have him prepare a purgative. When he returned, they gave the purgative to the spy; "then they took him to Dermoncourt's room, where two soldiers kept him in sight, while Dermoncourt passed a very bad night, woken by the soldiers each time the spy put his hand anywhere near the button of his underclothes. Finally, around three in the morning, he delivered up a little ball of wax the size of a filbert."

General Dumas's letter to Napoleon the next day (Christmas, 1796) tells essentially the same story in a deadpan style. Dumas told the man, "if he did not want to be shot on the spot, to have me warned every time he needed to relieve himself." And he concludes:

> He did not fool me, he abided by my orders. Several times he asked for me, and several times I went through futile steps, until at last today he gave birth to the letter that I am having one of my aides-de-camp deliver specially to you.

There were in fact two letters inside the wax tablet, written on vellum.

One was from the Austrian emperor: the emperor told the general inside the fortress that "his valor and his zeal make me expect him to defend Mantua to the last extremity"; but, if the relieving army came too late and the men inside Mantua fortress started dying en masse from starvation and lack of supplies, they were to destroy everything in the city that could be used by the French—especially the fortress's cannon—and then break out of siege over the marshland to the south to head toward the Papal States, where he and his men would find sanctuary. This was an interesting piece of information, because the French had always assumed that, were the Austrians to evacuate the fortress, they would head back north, toward their homeland. That the pope was offering the Austrians sanctuary was actionable news for the Army of Italy, for Napoleon had been looking for a reason to attack the Vatican.

General Dumas and his officers had been concerned, wrote the novelist, that "the dispatch might be in German, and no one in the area spoke German. . . . Great was the joy of the two officers when they saw that the letter had been written in French; it might have been said that the emperor and his commander-in-chief had foreseen the chance of the letter falling into my father's hands."

The other letter was from the Austrian general who was leading a twenty-eight-thousand-man army down to relieve the fortress. It explained that he would be coming down from the Tyrol but did not know exactly when his army could arrive.

Napoleon sent Dumas congratulations and sent a favorable note about the counterintelligence coup to the government in Paris. He then assigned Dumas command of a division at the fortified camp of San Antonio—Saint-Antoine, as the French called it—a village which guarded the approaches to Mantua from the north, the direction of the Alps.

+—+

THE siege wore on—a dull, nerve-racking affair, made worse by freezing rain, the constant lack of supplies, among the besiegers as well as the besieged, and mysterious, oddly spaced cannon fire that Dumas and his officers took for some sort of enemy signaling. In fact, they learned, it was only the "Venetian scoundrels"—officially neutral in the conflict—firing their weapons in celebration of the New Year. The French troops could barely sleep through the racket.

There were constant rumors of Austrian breakouts. Dumas often stayed out all night on horseback circling the perimeter, either alone or at the head of a few horsemen, looking for signs that the Austrians were on the move. In addition to all the fretting about when a breakout might happen, the dozens of letters Dumas wrote and received daily dealt with all the usual issues of functioning in a camp of some thousands of armed men. He requested thousands of soup rations and extra clothing, and suggested ways they could use the local river system to transport flour for making baguettes.

Finding that thousands of pairs of shoes were missing, Dumas became convinced that the commissaries, who were civilian contractors, were selling his troops' supplies for profit. He wrote this letter to one he suspected in particular:

> Citizen:
> For a long time now, the troops want for rice, salt and many essential items; I would have thought that the first warnings I already gave you would have sufficed to compel you to employ any means necessary to put an end to this penury. I warn you that I am beginning to tire of such carelessness, and if you do not hasten to pull yourself out of it, I'll know what needs be done.
> Alex Dumas

Wading through hundreds of pages of correspondence on such matters— the eighteenth-century version of office e-mail but elaborately penned and watermarked—I imagined what a hard-charging warrior like Dumas must have felt like, sitting around using only his quill for twelve hours a day. Sometimes he and his immediate superior, General Serurier, would produce an entire correspondence on something like a gun emplacement, or even horse feed—all dated the same day, the messenger having ridden from the south of the city to the north and back as the generals debated the details. The monotony of the correspondence evoked the monotony of the siege, in the chilly, fetid air of the Mantua swamps, waiting for something to break.*

On January 13, 1797, word came that the new Austrian divisions—the ones referred to in the wax-tablet messages—had been spotted north of Verona. These were 43,000 crack troops, heading straight for a French force of 10,300 men, which had retreated to Rivoli after early skirmishing. Napoleon sent in reinforcements, but the French were still outnumbered and outgunned.

Most of the Austrian troops would be pinned down in the Battle of Rivoli, but two columns of cavalry avoided the trap and headed straight for Mantua. In fierce fighting before dawn, the Austrians easily overwhelmed the smaller French divisions that guarded the northern approaches to the city.

General Serurier sent Dumas desperate letters—he seems to have written more than one an hour—wondering if they should retreat or regroup.

In what came close to insubordination, Dumas—from his position in the fortified village of San Antonio—told Serurier, stationed at Roverbella, that he could do what he pleased but that Dumas and his men were not moving and would stand and fight the Austrians. (Serurier was used to Dumas's brash intensity by now; in a note typical of their correspondence, from four days earlier, Dumas wrote to his commander: "I am about to mount my horse. Tomorrow I will give you an account of the reasons that drive me to stay there

---

*I found another way of reliving the siege: when I was visiting Mantua and walking around the fortress, I met an interesting guide—a medical-parts salesman who became an eighteenth-century French infantryman on the weekends, his role in the local Napoleonic reenactors society. No casual weekend warrior, Massimo Zonca had spent years studying the northern Italian campaign of 1796–97 and had self-published a number of books on its battles, complete with elaborate maps and references. He showed me around the battlefields, gravesites, and redoubts where the fighting had occurred. He also showed me his costumes, including an authentic Charleville musket, which was so heavy I could barely heft it, and whose bayonet was the length of a small sword. We went to a meeting of his reenactment group's "historical fencing society" in Verona, where old combat styles are practiced as a martial art, with real, bladed weapons.

all night.") Dumas had only about six hundred men with him. In his memoir the novelist uses Alex Dumas's mocking of Serurier's concern as the basis for a conversation between Napoleon and his father in which Napolean pretends to reprimand him while privately approving:

> "Ah! There you are, monsieur," said Bonaparte, giving him a dark look.
>
> My father could not let such a look pass without demanding an explanation.
>
> "Yes, it's me! Well, what is it?"
>
> "General Serurier wrote you two letters yesterday, monsieur."
>
> "Well! What of it?"
>
> "In the first he warned you of the possibility that he would retreat . . . What did you reply?"
>
> "I replied, 'Retreat to the devil, if you like; I couldn't care less; but as for me, I'll get myself killed, but I won't retreat.' "
>
> "Do you know that if you had written me a letter like that, I would have had you shot?"
>
> "Maybe; but you would probably never have written me the kind of letter General Serurier wrote me!"
>
> "That's true," Bonaparte said simply.
>
> Then, turning to Dermoncourt:
>
> "Go and form the troops into three columns, and report back when it's been done."
>
> Dermoncourt left. Turning to my father, who was about to return to his room, [Napoleon said]:
>
> "Stay here, General; I had to speak to you like that before your aide-de-camp; damn it! When a man writes such letters to his chief, he should at least write them himself, and not dictate them to his secretary. But we will say no more about it."

The long-awaited breakout from the fortress came on the morning of January 16. If the troops from the fortress united with the Austrian troops coming to rescue them, Dumas's force would be sunk. He would be outnumbered about ten to one.

But for now, it was only a little worse than three to one—the sort of odds that got Dumas's blood going. Also, Dumas had heard that a few French units returning from the Battle of Rivoli had been spotted coming down the high road from Verona. He leapt into the saddle and rallied his men. They would ride to meet these French units and return together to confront the Austrians. So Dumas led the six hundred cavalrymen away from the position they were guarding and up the road toward Verona. The Austrians must have been pleased when they arrived at San Antonio and were able to take it without firing a shot. But their pleasure there was short-lived. After only an hour's ride Dumas met the French units, and after brief introductions, they whirled around and all rode to San Antonio to face the Austrians.

As Dumas charged into town with the new troops at his back, the Austrians still outnumbered him—but now only about two to one.

Dumas always performed best when the odds were against him, and this morning proved no exception. As the white-jacketed Austrians charged from all sides, Dumas on his horse towered above the fray in his blue uniform with the red-white-and-blue sash, raining down saber blows. His sword arm was so powerful he could unseat a horseman with one blow, a great advantage in this sort of combat, and he had an intuitive sense for fighting multiple opponents at once. The chaos of battle was his home.

At one point, his horse was shot out from under him. But Dumas rose, found another horse, mounted, and continued slashing away at the Austrians. A cannonball landed directly in front of him, his new horse fell, and he went down a second time, only to rise again. By the end of the morning Dumas was still cutting down enemy troops without having sustained a single serious wound. His combined forces succeeded in driving the Austrian columns back—not only out of San Antonio but down the lakeside, across the bridge, and back through the gates of the citadel they'd just escaped.

━◆━

DUMAS'S actions in beating back the Austrians' breakout that morning prevented the uniting of the Austrian forces that could have broken the siege. By the time the large Austrian army finally arrived from the north, they found themselves trapped outside, isolated, unable to perform their mission. They fought the French in the fields, but at this point the rest of the French forces were returning victorious from the Battle of Rivoli. The hapless Austrian general who had made it all the way to Mantua now found himself squeezed by an accumulating catchall of French troops led by some of the finest commanders in the French army. After a couple of hours' bloodshed, he surrendered. Two weeks later, Mantua finally caved: the Austrians raised the white flag of surrender over their main fortress in Italy. In Paris, Rivoli was celebrated as the greatest victory of the Italian war. But the whole point of Rivoli was to keep the Austrian reinforcements from rescuing and uniting with the army trapped inside Mantua, and it had been Dumas, at the head of his little force, who had saved the day at the fortress.

It was no wonder, then, that Dumas lost his temper when he read the official report of the battle, compiled by Napoleon's aide-de-camp General Berthier, and saw that his role had been diminished to one of "in observation at San Antonio." Berthier did include a phrase about Dumas's fighting the enemy "well," but this did nothing to make Alex Dumas reconsider what he was about to write into the official military record of the Army of Italy. Dumas picked up his quill and wrote to Napoleon a letter of such fantastical insolence it would be cited in every historical account of him as an example of his legendary temper:

> January 18, 1797
> GENERAL,
> I have learned that the jack ass whose business it is to report to you upon the battle of the 27th [the 27 Nivôse, i.e., January 16] stated that I stayed in observation throughout that battle. I don't wish any such observation on him, since he would have shit in his pants.
> Salute and Brotherhood!
> ALEX. DUMAS

The Army of Italy was a tough-talking lot, but this was not a wise move. General Berthier was Napoleon's right-hand man (he would later become his chief of staff). I made my way through Berthier's report looking for the sentence that had infuriated Dumas. It comes on page 15 of what is a densely packed description of the entire campaign of the Army of Italy relating to the

Siege of Mantua. It covers vast actions, such as the Austrian emperor's rede-
ployment of his forces from all around Europe to the Mantua effort, in just a
paragraph. Given the scope of this report, obviously assembled from many
sources and with an eye to being a strategic overview, Berthier's description
of Dumas's role during the last day of the siege, while not correct, is not
nearly so insulting as Dumas perceived it to be.

In the aftermath of great victories, Napoleon had a habit of reorganizing
his forces and handing out promotions and spoils. Berthier sent out these ap-
pointments and, not surprisingly, Dumas got some bad news: he was not even
being given his own division; rather, he was to command a subdivision under
General Masséna, whom he did not like.

> On Nivôse 28.
>
> To General Bonaparte.
>
> I have received your order, General. . . . I will not hide from you the
> surprise that the news of my transfer caused me. That on the day after
> a battle whose success I contributed to with all my power, I would see
> myself so dishonored! . . . and [that] you, General, who have always
> seemed to grant your esteem to the brave republicans in your army, you
> could, without even meeting with me, take [your esteem] away from
> me when I did everything to deserve it. I should have hoped for a little
> more consideration; after having commanded several armies, never
> defeated, finding myself the oldest general in this army at the moment
> when I believed I had [earned] new rights to the confidence of my chief
> and my comrades . . . I am sent to command a subdivision!

The letter went on quite a bit longer, and of course did nothing to improve
his situation or get him what he calls, further down, "the justice I deserve."

In a poignant coda to the incident, I discovered in Dumas's military
file the following testimony, written and mailed to Bonaparte one day later,
signed by twenty-five members of "the 20th Dragoon Regiment, 1st Division, of the Mantua Blockade":

> We, Commander, officers, noncommissioned officers and Dragoons,
> members of the 20th Regiment, attest that Division General Dumas,

in whose Division we [serve], took all possible measures and took all the actions in his power to get the Job done, that to our knowledge the General visited the outposts for three or four consecutive nights and gave himself no rest whatsoever. . . .

Moreover, we confirm that in the last affair of the 27th of this month, leading us, he acted as a Republican, full of honor and courage. Therefore we are signing the present declaration.

When Napoleon sent his January battle report to the Directory, he praised every other officer involved in ending the Siege of Mantua. General Dumas's name was not mentioned once.

THE BLACK DEVIL

THE demotion that humiliated Dumas proved to be an opportunity. By being denied his place as a general of division in charge of thousands, he was freed from administrative and political duties and thrown back into the role in which he had originally made his name: at the head of small mounted bands running reconnaissance missions and riding in to engage the enemy, in terrain too rugged or dangerous for the main army to reach yet.

In January 1797, Napoleon reorganized the French Army of Italy into three main columns, with the goal of driving the Austrians up into the Alps and out of Italy. If the French columns succeeded in this, they might even follow their enemy and burst down into the heartland of Austria itself, from which the enemy's capital, Vienna, would be just a day's ride away.

For the first two weeks of February 1797, Dumas and a small band of dragoons under the command of General André Masséna advanced relentlessly, driving the Austrian army ever farther north toward their own border. "[Dumas] flies from one city to another, from one village to another, hacking everything to pieces," runs one account, "capturing two thousand prisoners here, one thousand there, he performs truly fantastic charges." The Austrians came up with a name for the relentless French general who stalked them through the snow: *die schwarze Teufel*, the "Black Devil."

Dumas arrived in Italy too late to be part of the core group of generals who were calling themselves "the men of Italy." Dumas proved his mettle to these generals many times over, but he always kept himself a bit aloof. He was disturbed by the generals' growing idolization of General Bonaparte. Without authorization from the government in Paris, Napoleon had started having honorary swords made to his own specifications, with his name and dedication engraved on them, and handing them out to officers for bravery after battles. He also gave out hefty cash rewards to the men of Italy to thank them personally for their service. The men of Italy talked a little too much of themselves and their brilliant commander-in-chief for Dumas's taste, and too little of the goals and values of the Republic. The words of the "Marseillaise" were no mere martial lyrics to Dumas; they burned in his consciousness.

One of the generals greatly admired Dumas's integrity. General Barthé-lemy Catherine Joubert desperately wanted to recruit Dumas to serve in his column. Joubert was also a true republican—a patriot in the 1790 style. Some lines he had written to Dumas as part of an update on siege preparations in late December read almost like a platonic love letter from one revolutionary general to another: "I have no less impatience for the moment, General, when I will meet a republican as good as you are. I gather up all personal glory to merit his esteem."

Joubert had command of twenty thousand French troops facing an even greater number of the enemy dug into the rocky terrain running up along the Adige River into the Tyrol, the alpine borderland between Austria and Italy. It would be some of the toughest fighting the French had yet faced. The area was defended not only by Austrian regulars but by Tyrolean mountain militias, and both groups knew this country far better than the French blues ever could.

At the end of February, Joubert got his wish: Napoleon transferred Dumas to his column. Joubert briefed Dumas on the mission: to chase the Austrians all the way to the Brenner Pass, "the great gate" of Italy, through which countless barbarian invasions had passed—only this time the French invaders would be going in the other direction, north up through the Italian Tyrol, over the Alps, and down into the Austrian heartland.

Dumas must have been greatly relieved at being out from under Masséna and given a place with his fellow republican Joubert. On his first week with his new comrades, Dumas led a small force up a tributary of the Adige to outflank the Austrians. The enemy was camped out along the river, guarding every bridge. He took them out, one by one. In this close-in fighting, where the horses and men had to keep their footing sometimes in the torrent itself, Dumas's imposing skills—lunging, jumping, unhorsing opponents with a single whack of his saber, or even a fist—did much to break enemy morale and cheer his own troops. Over and over again Dumas charged larger groups of Austrians and forced a surrender or put them on the run.

An official army report from the first week of March, describing the taking of a strategic point on the river, captures Dumas as an almost cinematic war hero: "The battle was uncertain, until General Dumas, commanding the cavalry, rushed into the village of Tramin, took six hundred prisoners, and captured two cannons; as a result, the enemy column . . . was blocked from entering Botzen [a key city in the Italian Tyrol], and was forced to scatter into the mountains." Dumas went on to save General Joubert himself shortly thereafter, when his new commanding officer was ambushed on a maneuver by a larger Austrian force. Dumas snuck around the enemy soldiers and struck at them from behind, as Joubert described it to Napoleon, always with a faintly breathless admiration for the powerhouse who had been assigned to serve under him.

Dumas's own battle reports describe the hot violence of the encounters with matter-of-fact professionalism: "I charged the enemy cavalry that was advancing on me, they were thoroughly routed although superior in number: I cut the face of a commander and the neck of a cavalryman; the regiment I was in command of killed, took and wounded several Austrian cavalrymen." But he was careful to credit fellow officers as well: "The adjutant general Blondeau showed great courage. General Belliard's column aided by the 8th Dragoon Regiment took 1,200 prisoners: this general again showed great distinction."

Throughout February and March, despite the bitter cold weather, Dumas chose to camp by the banks of the Adige with his dragoon bands rather than settling into one of the captured Austrian towns and fortresses that the French had taken alongside it. As Dermoncourt observed, the campaign Dumas was fighting was "more like a race than a war." He had never fought better.

→—←

YET behind Dumas's frenzied battling lay not just the desire for glory but the deepest anguish. On March 3 he wrote Marie-Louise: "My beloved, for the past nineteen days I haven't received any of your precious news; I don't know to what I should attribute this damnable delay. Our worries are at their peak, and I think I have more than one reason."

Two days later, he wrote again, finally having heard from her. The letter Marie-Louise sent him has been lost, but in it she seems to have hinted that his fears were justified. A terrible event had befallen their younger daughter, Louise, a toddler of thirteen months.

To the only one I care about in the whole world

My virtuous friend, you have told me about an event that tears away half of my existence and I think I have been confirmed in my fear that something even more awful has happened; if it was unfortunately so, you must reveal everything . . . (the truth, that is)

. . . my poor Louise, my unfortunate child. It is perhaps in vain that I call out to you! . . . My divine friend, I will not live in peace until I receive a letter from you that tells me the truth (but I am still trembling) . . .

Adieu my love, your letter has distressed me too much to have the strength to say any more, give a big kiss [to] my, I don't dare say children—or my child and our respectable parents, and above all you, forever.

It isn't clear whether it was an illness or accident, but Dumas would soon learn that little Louise was dead. If anything his sense of loss and grief over the next weeks and months seems to have driven him to fight harder. The man the Austrians called the Black Devil continued to rout them out of the Adige River Valley. Dumas's efforts were so effective that Joubert at one point began to refer to him as General of Division Dumas, even though he had no division. Joubert officially gave Dumas control of a few regiments, but whenever he could, Dumas rode out ahead with his small bands of dragoons.

Some twenty-five miles north of Botzen, the Austrian forces were dug in "in a terrible position," as Dumas reported to Joubert, at Clausen, a small Tyrolean city of quiet church squares and streets that end in sheer cliffs, set dramatically against snowcapped peaks nearly as high as the Swiss Alps. The Austrians had artillery emplacements above the town and thousands of troops protecting it. Hundreds of Tyrolean fighters hid in the woods and in rock formations, sniping at any French troops they saw. It was a shooting gallery in which the Austrians and their local allies had all the high ground.

On the morning of March 23, Dumas and Dermoncourt rode into town at the head of about thirty dragoons and "crossed Clausen under enemy fire," as Joubert would report to Napoleon, even as the bulk of the French forces were pinned down nearby. On the far side of the town stood a strategic bridge, across the Eisack River, which at this point alternated between narrow streams and raging torrents, all pitched at preposterously steep inclines. The French could not advance farther north to pursue the Austrians toward the border without crossing this bridge. The Austrians were as determined to hold the bridge as Dumas was to take it. They scattered carts filled with heavy stones all over it, Dermoncourt recalled, against which Dumas "did more alone with his Herculean strength than the twenty-five of us put together. When I say twenty-five I exaggerate; the Austrian bullets had done their work, and five or six of our men were disabled."

The troops received reinforcements, and as soon as they had pushed the last of the carts into the river, Dumas crossed the bridge into the town of Brixen. Dumas and Dermoncourt found themselves alone there. The enemy was firing at them from high positions in the boulders by the banks and from the far side of the bridge. Troops faced them in hand-to-hand combat. Dermoncourt recalled watching Dumas "lift his saber, as a thresher lifts his flail, and each time the sword was lowered a man fell." Trapped himself by a trio of Austrian cavalrymen, Dermoncourt received a serious shoulder wound, severing the tendon. The Austrians "continued to hack at me with saber-swipes, and soon would have entirely skewered me, if I had not managed to draw a pistol out of my holster with my left hand."

Early in the battle Dumas's horse was shot out from under him and fell in such a way that the Austrians were sure it had killed him. "The Black Devil is dead!" the cry went up. But then Dumas rose from the dead, or, rather, from behind his horse, which he then used as cover to stage his own counter-fusillade. He had discovered a small cache of loaded Austrian guns, which he now used to return fire.

As Dermoncourt lay in a bleeding heap, he later recalled, "I managed to turn toward the general; he was standing at the head of the bridge of Clausen and holding it alone against the whole squadron; and as the bridge was narrow and the men could only get at him two or three abreast, he cut down as many as came at him."

Bleeding from the arm, thigh, and head, Dumas slashed and stabbed with unrelenting fury, and with such power that most every Austrian touched by his blade fell mortally wounded or took a deadly dive over the bridge into the river below. When he was finally relieved on the bridge by a few dozen French cavalry and the Austrians retreated, Dumas did not rest but leapt on a horse to pursue the fleeing enemy nearly ten miles into the alpine woods.

"I must make a full report about the conduct of General Dumas," Joubert wrote to Napoleon after the battle, "who charged three times at the head of the cavalry and killed several cavalrymen with his own hand; he contributed not a little by his courage to the success of this day."

The final outcome of the day, according to Joubert: "we have taken fifteen hundred enemy prisoners, our loss has been about a thousand give or take."

Meanwhile, of the man who had been at the very front of the action, surrounded by enemy soldiers shooting and hacking at him: "[Dumas] has received two light saber wounds during the time he was fighting off the Austrian cavalry, alone, on a bridge." Another account says that musket fire pierced his greatcoat in seven places, though Dumas somehow emerged unscathed.

In the safe at Villers-Cotterêts lay a letter Dumas had written to friends from the headquarters of the Army of Italy. In it, he describes leading the cavalry into the Tyrol and how "these victories were necessary to dissipate a little the stinging grief of the irreparable loss which I had of my unfortunate Louise . . . cherished and adored child, who was always before my eyes and accompanied me day and night." Then, as always, his thoughts quickly return to his beloved wife: "What worries me still more, is the state in which my wife finds herself, because this event will make itself felt."

➤━

THIS time, Napoleon did not expunge Dumas's heroism at Clausen in his report to Paris:

> General Dumas at the head of the cavalry has killed with his own hand several enemy cavalrymen. He has been twice slightly wounded by enemy sabers, and his aide-de-camp Dermoncourt has been seriously wounded. This General held a bridge all alone for many minutes against

the enemy cavalry who were trying to cross the river. By doing so, he was able to delay the enemy advance until reinforcements arrived.

At the end of March, Dumas received a letter from Napoleon announcing that "as the General-in-Chief wants to show his satisfaction to General Dumas for his valorous conduct in the recent actions in the Tyrol, he therefore grants him the command of all cavalry troops in the divisions stationed in the Tyrol."

As a further sign that Napoleon was ready to forgive Dumas fully, he added this line to the following week's report: "I request that General Dumas, who, along with his horse, has lost a pair of pistols, be sent a pair of pistols from the armament manufacturer at Versailles."

Napoleon also gave Dumas a new nom de guerre, hailing him as "the Horatius Cocles of the Tyrol"—high praise indeed in that era. "Rome was in great hazard of being taken, the enemy forcing their way onto the wooden bridge," Plutarch recounted, and "Horatius Cocles . . . kept the bridge, and held back the enemy." Dumas was referred to as the "Horatius Cocles of the Tyrol" in all subsequent writings about him down to the early twentieth century, when classical allusions fell out of favor.

During the rest of 1797, Napoleon concluded the victory over the Austrians by forcing them to negotiate and sign a humiliating peace treaty, the Treaty of Campo Formio, which acknowledged all the new French-sponsored Italian republics, ceding various non-Italian Austrian territories to Paris, including the Austrian Netherlands as well as key islands in the Mediterranean. Napoleon also forced a laundry list of other concessions on the emperor. (One of these endeared him to liberal-minded people everywhere: General Lafayette, still held by the Austrians after deserting from the French army and attempting to flee the continent with his honorary American passport, was at last set free.)

While the treaty negotiations were going on, Napoleon appointed General Dumas military governor of Treviso, a wealthy province and city of the same name twenty-five miles outside Venice and filled with rich vineyards and residences built by Venetian merchants over the centuries. Dumas helped the residents rebuild their lives under the new order, taking part in local hunting expeditions and, if their letters to him are any guide, generally showing an evenhandedness that shocked civilians under his jurisdiction. A folder in the safe at Villers-Cotterêts contained these letters to General Dumas from the citizens of Treviso province, who mix flattery and thanks with fulsome attempts to prove that they, too, were true-blue republicans in the highest French style:

> In this state of revolution, so new to us, and in a Democracy developing from Italy's own regeneration, we had the greatest need to find in you, Citizen General, a Father, who would guide our steps, and support our efforts to consolidate ourselves in this state of cherished Liberty that we owe to the generosity of the French. Here we are, freed from a most hideous slavery, and here we are under the protection of your justice and selflessness.

LEADER OF THE EXPEDITION

RELYING on the memories of old Dermoncourt, the novelist described the period after his father's greatest triumph, when he was treated like the savior of Rome and celebrated even by Napoleon, as one of his most melancholic.

He had no sooner won his heart's desires than he conceived a profound disgust for them. When the energy he had expended in obtaining his desires had died down . . . he sent in his resignation. Happily Dermoncourt was at hand. When he received these letters of resignation to dispatch, he slipped them in a drawer of his desk, put the key in his pocket, and quietly waited.

At the end of a week or two weeks, or even a month, the momentary cloud of disgust which had swept over my poor father's spirits would disappear, and some brilliant charge or daringly successful maneuver would arouse enthusiasm in his heart, ever eager to aspire after the impossible, and, with a sigh, he would say: "Upon my word, I believe I did wrong to send in my resignation."

And Dermoncourt, who was on the watch for this, would reply:

"Don't worry yourself, General; your resignation—"

"Well, my resignation—?"

"It's in that desk, ready to send off on the first chance; there is only the date to alter."

After leaving his post as military governor in Italy, Dumas returned on furlough to Villers-Cotterêts for three months, to be with his wife and daughter, and also to perfect his hunting skills at the expense of the wild boars and stags in the Retz Forest. At the end of March 1798, he received orders from the minister of war to report to Toulon, in the south of France, to assume a new command. As happy as Dumas must have been during his time at home, the new assignment probably came as a relief to him, or so his son came to believe: his father, he thought, could not really thrive away from the action (hence his fit of melancholy after the Italian campaign). He now rewrote his will, kissed his family, and rode off for the south. He was thirty-six years old and in vigorous health, with dreams of greater glory.

On coming into Toulon, Dumas found the port in chaos with the provisioning of what appeared to be a great armada in formation. There were thousands of soldiers, sailors, animals, guns, and all the supplies needed not only for a military campaign but for maintaining a small city. (When fully assembled, the armada would consist of thirteen large warships and another forty-two smaller ones, along with 122 transport vessels. On board were 54,000 men, including 38,000 soldiers and 13,000 sailors, who brought 1,230 horses, 171 field guns, 63,261 artillery shells, 8,067,280 rifle rounds, and 11,150 hand grenades.) A military campaign of major proportions was clearly being planned, yet the destination was a closely held secret. Neither Dumas nor the other officers or men in Toulon had any idea what it was.

"The object of this grand voyage is not known," wrote one of the other participants in an April 11 letter intercepted by British intelligence. "It is . . . certain that they have an immense amount of printing equipment, books, instruments, and chemical apparatus, which suggests a very long absence." The identity of this letter writer was a clue to the expedition's unusual character, for he was neither a soldier nor the sort of civilian who usually accompanied military adventures. Déodat de Dolomieu was one of Europe's leading geologists. In 1791 he had discovered a mineral, which was named in his honor (dolomite), and later an entire mountain range in north Italy (the Dolomites) would also bear his name.

Yet Dolomieu was not the only eminent scientist and man of letters in Toulon waiting to board the ships. There were dozens of others, including, as he observed, "geographical engineers, military engineers, mathematicians, astronomers, chemists, doctors, artists, and naturalists of every sort; two professors of Arabic, Persian and Turkish." Drawn from the cream of the French intelligentsia, the sheer number of "savants"—as they were designated on the expedition's rosters—was as surprising as their renown. "And all have gone aboard without knowing where they are going."

The mystery of the expedition's destination had precisely the desired effect: the enemy was flummoxed. Having learned about the massing of the French armada, the British Admiralty had sent their best man to investigate. Rear Admiral Horatio Nelson, though at thirty-nine relatively young for the British navy, had an outsized reputation for tactical brilliance and bravery in harassing and sinking French vessels. He was also an arch-traditionalist who despised the French Revolution.

Nelson had been sent into the Mediterranean commanding a small squadron of just three large warships and three smaller frigates (scout ships) with orders to determine the French armada's destination. Arriving south of Toulon on May 19—only one day before the armada's departure—he positioned his squadron "exactly in a situation for intercepting the enemy's ships." By chance Nelson captured a small French corvette sailing from Toulon and interrogated the crew. But the French sailors could not tell Nelson anything about the armada's destination because, like everyone else, they had no idea themselves. They managed instead to provide some bits of misinformation, including that Napoleon was not planning to sail with the expedition himself. Then Nelson's luck failed him: gale-force winds, careening waves, and driving spray pummeled his warships for nine hours, damaging all three and demasting his flagship. The winds had blown his frigates out of sight. The British squadron was forced to retreat to neutral Sardinia for repairs—sans frigates, which effectively blinded it.

In the meantime, Napoleon's vast armada had departed Toulon, missed the gale, and was safely cruising down the west coast of Italy. Back near Toulon on June 5, Nelson was overjoyed to see a fleet of eleven British warships arriving to join his command. This new firepower would give him fighting odds, if he could catch the French fleet in a vulnerable position. But where had Napoleon's armada gone? And where the devil was it going?

The top British admirals surmised that the French expedition was planning to break out of the Mediterranean, sail up the Atlantic coast, and invade Ireland or England. The risk of invasion was seared into British consciousness, part of the heritage of an island nation whose very identity rested on a succession of transformative invasions, such as those of the Romans in

AD 53 and the Normans in 1066. But beginning with the failed Spanish armada in 1588, at least a half dozen other attempted foreign invasions, most recently in 1759, had been thwarted by the British navy. In response to rumors the French government had planted of an imminent French assault across the Channel, panic seized the British public.* The *Times* of London called for emergency preparations—"barricades for each street"—against the Jacobin hordes who would soon swarm the city.

The French actually *had* been planning to attack England that spring. This was the mission the government had chosen and assigned to General Bonaparte after Italy. Command rolls for the invasion of England were drawn up at the end of 1797: Alex Dumas had been appointed commander of the dragoons and "Chief of Staff of the Cavalry." His nemesis Berthier— the general Dumas had said would "shit in his pants" if he were exposed to danger—had been appointed chief of staff of the "Army of England." In February 1798 Napoleon toured Calais and Dunkirk while General Kléber toured the beaches of Normandy. But Napoleon then held secret meetings with the government to dissuade them from the British armada plan. Napoleon was not ready to attack England; he would return to that idea in the following decade. In the spring of 1798, he had another idea. He had set his sights on invading Egypt.

➻➻

EUROPEANS had always coveted Egypt. It symbolized all the power of the ancient world—an imperium almost three thousand years older than Rome's. Egypt was thought to be as rich in grain as in mythology; imperial strategists imagined that control of its croplands would feed populations and armies. These are the reasons Alexander the Great conquered Egypt in the

---

* Terror over rumors of imminent French invasions would continue to haunt Britons for seventy years. Napoleon seriously planned to conquer the island in the years between 1801 and 1805, but the British naval triumph at Trafalgar finished that hope for good. Invasion panics later returned with a vengeance, especially during the reign of Bonaparte's nephew, Napoleon III (1848–70). When a unified Germany occupied France in 1871, it also replaced that defeated country as the object of British invasion panics. The German invasion never arrived, but the fear of it proved inspirational for British novelists, whose visions of it eventually produced the modern spy thriller. And when H. G. Wells turned the invaders into Martians in *The War of the Worlds*, modern science fiction was born.

fourth century BC to establish his dynasty there. Napoleon dreamed of following in his footsteps and establishing his own.*

Today the *Expédition d'Égypte,* as the bloody venture is still called in France, is widely seen as among the most delusional of Napoleon's globe-conquering fantasies. But the French had long viewed Egypt as a land of adventure, opportunity, and riches, and a stepping-stone out of Europe into the wider world. The rise of literacy and the spread of printed books throughout the eighteenth century fed the public a slew of travelogues of the Near East. "The Nile is as familiar to many people as the Seine," wrote one observer in 1735. The expedition, with the help of the savants, would discover the famed Rosetta Stone, excavate tombs in the Valley of the Kings, and catalog countless ancient artifacts—and, in the name of scholarship, haul many of them away.

In 1769, Louis XV's foreign minister tried to get him to strike at Egypt—"to replace the [French] colonies in America, in case they should be lost, with colonies offering the same products and a more extensive trade." Perhaps products like indigo, cotton, and, most important, sugarcane could be grown in Egypt as well as in Saint-Domingue. One of the best sources of information on Egypt was a polemical travelogue by the utopian philosopher "Volney," who had chosen his name in homage to Voltaire. Volney traveled to the Middle East from 1783 to 1785, where he learned Arabic, adopted native dress, and lived among the Egyptians. His *Travels in Egypt and Syria* offered a thorough description of the Egyptian economy, society, government, and strategic forces. In Volney's view Egypt, though ruined by oriental despotism, was full of potential and ripe for conquest—a tempting target for French colonization. France could gain control over a primary sea route to Asia and incredible prestige by resurrecting the ancient Egyptian past.

Volney came to prominence in 1791 as a star philosopher. His book *The Ruins: A Meditation on the Revolutions of Empires* was the toast of English Romantic poets like Shelley and political activists like Tom Paine; Thomas Jefferson translated it into English. Volney's writings influenced a generation of radical democrats, but he arguably had the most impact on an altogether

---

* Alexander of Macedon's pharaonic dynasty, the Ptolemies, ruled for the next three centuries. The suicide of Cleopatra, the last of the Ptolemies, marked the end of Alexandrian Egypt in 30 BC.

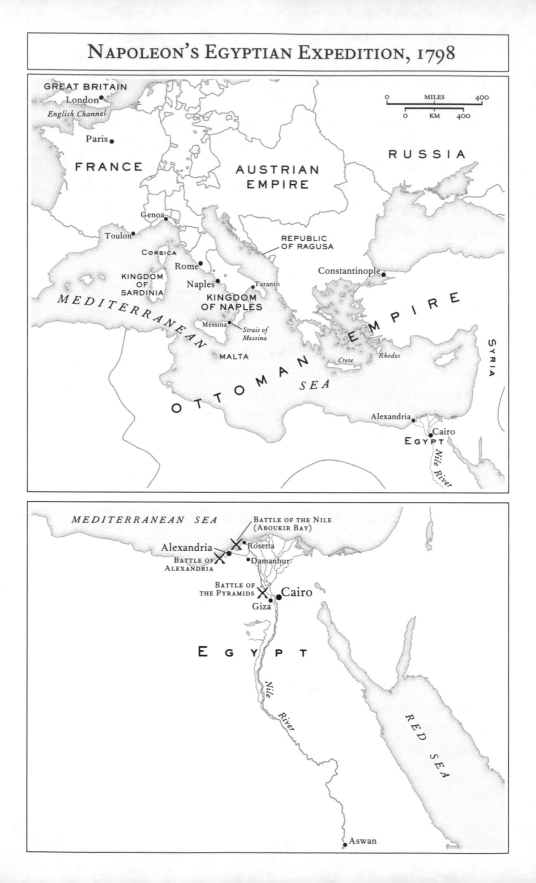

NAPOLEON'S EGYPTIAN EXPEDITION, 1798

different sort of man. Napoleon met the philosopher personally in 1792 when Volney bought an estate on the island of Corsica. Young Napoleon Bonaparte was spending that year back in his native Corsica, avoiding the dangerous turmoil in France. Napoleon served as Volney's informal guide to the island, while picking his brain about Egypt.

Napoleon had developed an identification with Egypt from the time he was twelve, reading about Alexander the Great. At the end of his life, having gained and lost control of Europe, he would remember his heady time in Egypt. "I dreamed of many things and I saw how I could realize all my dreams," he mused. "I imagined myself on the road to Asia, mounted on an elephant, a turban on my head, and in my hand, a new Koran that I had written myself for my own purposes. I would have combined in my enterprises the experience of two worlds, scouring the terrain of all world history for my profit." Though the general had absorbed Volney's extensive knowledge of Egypt, he ignored his most important lesson: that his dream of a Middle Eastern empire was a mirage.

Almost immediately after describing the riches to be gained in Egypt, Volney warned France's leaders against trying to seize it. Any invasion would bring on an unwinnable three-front war with the British, the Turks, and the Egyptians themselves. The locals will quickly come to loath us, he told his readers: "Even our officers would take that arrogant, exclusionary, and contemptuous tone that foreigners can't stand about us." Volney predicted that a third of French troops would perish from disease, a few venal Arab collaborators would get rich, and eventually, the whole venture would collapse into the desert dust. France would do much better to invest its energies at home.

For Napoleon, this warning only pointed to greater glory if he could pull it off.

After securing the conquest of northern Italy in the summer of 1797, Napoleon began laying concrete plans for his Egyptian expedition. While busy overseeing the transport to Paris of Venice's artistic treasures—including the bronze horses of St. Mark's Cathedral, which the Venetians themselves had looted from the Greeks during the Fourth Crusade—Napoleon's thoughts were already with the upcoming mission. In one of the more memorable bits of secret advance preparation he had done while in Italy, Napoleon sent his agents throughout the peninsula looking to secure an Arabic printing press, so he would be able to print revolutionary tracts and edicts for the Egyptians. (They at last located one to seize in the papal propaganda office at the Vatican.)

In his meetings with the government in Paris to discuss the invasion of England, Napoleon emphasized that by taking Egypt instead, he could cut off the British overland trade routes to India, her most valuable possession. He probably did not reveal the full extent of his dreams of founding a vast Franco-Afro-Asian empire stretching from the Barbary Coast cities of Tunis and Algiers in the west to India in the east: after seizing Egypt, the "Army of the Orient" would conquer Syria, cut across Iraq, Iran, and Afghanistan, and cross the Khyber Pass into India—all in the name of liberating the despotic East. Napoleon hoped to enlist the support of local insurgents like Tippoo Sahib, the sultan of Mysore, in south India. Tippoo was a great fan of the French Revolution and England's most formidable enemy in India. He had gone as far as to cofound, in 1792, the Jacobin Club of Mysore and referred to himself as "Citizen Tippoo Sultan." Napoleon attempted to get a message to the Citizen Sultan promising that the French army would fight side by side with him for a new republican India (once the French had conquered Egypt and marched across Mesopotamia, Iran, and Afghanistan, that is), but Tippoo would fall in battle against the British, in 1799, before he could receive it.*

On May 10, 1798, Napoleon inspected the troops in Toulon and gave a famous departure speech:

> Soldiers, the eyes of Europe are upon you. You have a grand destiny
> to fulfill, battles to fight, dangers and trials to overcome. . . . The ge-
> nius of Liberty that has made the Republic, since its birth, the arbiter of

---

* Tippoo's plucky army was famous for its "rocket brigades," which fired special long-range rockets out of steel and bamboo tubes. In one battle in April 1799, Tippoo's rocket fire disoriented the normally unflappable Colonel Arthur Wellesley, future duke of Wellington, and forced a retreat. ("So pestered were we with the rocket boys that there was no moving without danger," wrote one British officer.) But the British army gained the upper hand when a shot struck a magazine of Tippoo's rockets, causing a massive explosion. The victorious British hauled away hundreds of rocket launchers and fire-ready rockets, and four years later they began their own rocket program at the Royal Woolwich Arsenal in England, under the direction of William Congreve. It was the so-called Congreve rockets, improvements on Citizen Tippoo Sultan's rockets, that provided "the rockets' red glare" when the British bombarded Washington, D.C., in 1812.

Europe, desires that it also be the arbiter of the seas and of the farthest lands.

He promised each man six acres of land if the mission succeeded. The soldiers, sailors, and engineers still had no idea where the land was to be situated—did he mean an Irish farm, an Indian orchard, or a Levantine olive grove? When the French first laid eyes on the Egyptian desert, they would coin one of the bitter catchphrases of the campaign: "Voilà—the six acres of land they promised us!"

—

IN his memoir, Alexandre Dumas writes of an encounter between his father and Napoleon before the expedition's departure. Yet it's possible the meeting is invented: his father's relationship with Napoleon as the writer wishes it had been. According to his account, Napoleon ran into General Dumas shortly after arriving in Toulon and invited him to visit the next morning, as early as he wanted. Accordingly, at 6 a.m. the next day, General Dumas met up with his aide, Dermoncourt (the primary source for all of the novelist's stories about his father, except presumably his mother).

"Where the devil are you off to, General, this early?"
"Come with me," said my father, "and you'll see." They set off together.
Approaching their destination, Dermoncourt said:
"You're *not* going to see Bonaparte, are you, General?"
"I am."
"But he won't receive you."
"Why not?"
"Because it is too early."
"Oh! That doesn't matter."
"But he'll be in bed."
"Quite likely."
. . . In sum, [Dermoncourt concluded] my father must have a special audience scheduled, and followed him.

My father ascended a stair, walked down a hallway, opened a little door, pushed back a screen, and found himself, along with Dermoncourt, who had been following him the whole time, in Bonaparte's bedroom.

He was in bed with Josephine, and, as the weather was very hot, both of them were covered by no more than a sheet, upon which were drawn the outlines of their bodies.

Josephine was weeping, and Bonaparte was trying to wipe her tears away with one hand, while with the other he laughingly beat a military march on her body.

"Ah! Dumas," he said, catching sight of my father; "your arrival is well timed; you must help me make this crazy woman listen to reason. Ought she to wish to come to Egypt with us? Would you take your wife there?"

"My word, certainly not," says Dumas, and the two proceed to have an excruciatingly arch exchange in an attempt to jolly the tearful wife out of her distress, which is only redoubled when Napoleon says the expedition may last several years. He again enlists Dumas, telling Josephine that, if that does turn out to be the case, she and Madame Dumas can both travel by convoy to Egypt together. (" 'Does that suit you, Dumas?' 'Perfectly,' replied my father.") And there, the famously childless Napoleon goes on, the reunited couples can dedicate their efforts to producing male issue, since "Dumas . . . has only daughters [*sic*], and I . . . have not even those." If successful, he exultantly tells Josephine, they will all be godparents together, and he concludes: "There now, that's a promise; stop crying, and let's talk business."

Then, turning to Dermoncourt, Bonaparte said:

"Monsieur Dermoncourt, you have just heard a word drop which indicates the goal of our expedition. Not a soul knows of this goal: do not let the word 'Egypt' escape your lips; you understand, under the circumstances, the importance of a secret."

Dermoncourt made a sign that he would be as dumb as a disciple of Pythagoras.

In reality, Dumas had never been a confidant of Napoleon, and he had probably not been invited to know the great secret of the expedition, though in a farewell letter to Marie-Louise he guesses correctly (or perhaps gives away the secret he was in fact told?):

> In great haste— via Paris
>
> To the Citizeness Dumas, in her home.
>
> . . . I embark in one hour but I will write to you more at length on board, farewell I am in a terrible hurry, my father [maybe a priest, taking money to her?] left this morning with 115 Louis in gold, I think we are going to Egypt, farewell, eternal friendship to everyone.
>
> Alex Dumas

Dumas and Dermoncourt boarded their vessel, a midsized ship called the *Guillaume Tell* (the "William Tell").* (Napoleon sailed on the *Orient*, a gargantuan vessel that was the largest ship of any navy on earth, boasting 120 cannons mounted on three decks.) The armada set sail for its first rendezvous point, the island of Malta, off the coast of Sicily. Britain's Nelson, meanwhile, lost an important tool for tracking them when he became separated from his two main frigates in a sudden storm. The loss of these fast, nimble scouting vessels—the closest thing to radar in those days—meant that Nelson now had little chance of finding the French armada: even on a clear day, intelligence was limited to the twenty miles visible through Nelson's Dolland telescope, the most advanced available. Naval warfare in the late eighteenth century was the ultimate game of hide-and-seek: it could take days, weeks, or months to locate your enemy at sea.

Malta was a heavily barricaded outcropping that had withstood every invader since the sixteenth century. The Ottomans once lost fifty thousand men besieging Malta before giving up. Napoleon's plan was to take the island and

---

* William Tell, the national folk hero of Switzerland, loomed large over the French Revolution. The national myth goes that Tell, an uncannily fine marksman, assassinated an Austrian tyrant in the fourteenth century and gave birth to Swiss democracy and independence. It heightened French fascination with him that the tyrant he assassinated was Austrian. During the Revolution, Paris was subdivided into administrative "sections"; one of the more radical was named for William Tell.

make off with a king's ransom in treasure—this, plus the booty from the Italian campaign, would finance the invasion of Egypt.

Since ancient times, Malta had been ruled by a dizzying array of conquerors—Phoenicians, Byzantines, Carthaginians, Romans, and Arabs. But the island's name is synonymous with its most colorful and enduring conquerors: the Knights of Malta. First banded together as the Order of St. John in Jerusalem in the eleventh century, the Knights were as fundamental to the world of real-life chivalry as King Arthur and his knights were to its legend. In return for support from the pope, the Knights swore to take on the defense of pilgrims and the sick and to defend the Faith in territories that the crusaders had conquered from the Muslims. They began calling themselves "holy knights" and wearing their trademark insignia: an eight-pointed white cross, made up of four V-shaped arms joined in the center, on either a red or a black field.*

Since the Middle Ages, the Knights had been based in Malta, which they turned into the most impregnable fortress island in Europe. Would-be holy Knights showed up from everywhere, hoping to win fame and glory for God by fighting Islam in a sunny climate. But the island was also a refuge for adventurous scoundrels of every variety, such as the Italian Renaissance painter Caravaggio, who, after committing murder, fled to Malta in 1607 and was made a knight in return for painting his masterpiece *The Beheading of St. John the Baptist*. (According to some sources, Sir Caravaggio then got into another violent altercation, with a fellow knight, and left Malta in disgrace.)

In spite of the order's vows, including chastity, Malta also became

---

* When the crusader kingdom fell, the Knights lost their castles in Syria and Palestine, but rather than return to Europe, they relocated to the Greek island of Rhodes, where they built a powerful fleet to fight sea battles with the infidels. They held Rhodes for nearly one hundred years until the Turkish sultan Suleiman the Magnificent finally ousted them; it took a fleet of four hundred ships and 200,000 soldiers to do so.

But as the last line of defense between Christian Europe and the world of Islam, the Knights got a new home from the Holy Roman Emperor: a hilly, barren island of olive groves called Malta, which then belonged to the Kingdom of Sicily, itself a possession of the emperor. The only condition was that the Knights of St. John become official vassals of the king of Sicily and pay him annual feudal dues that included one "Maltese falcon." This was the inspiration for the enigmatic statue that so upends the world of Detective Sam Spade—a treasure that men covet and kill for—just as a different kind of Maltese treasure would soon upend the world of Alex Dumas.

renowned for the beauty and laxity of its prostitutes, with the best ones going to the Knights and their guests. And fighting the infidel on the high seas, they took in so many galley slaves and so much booty that they began to seem like a Christian version of the Barbary pirates. The pope heard of the Knights' lax morals and sent an inquisitor to the island in 1574; he set up shop in a mansion in the shopping district.

The Knights had once been swashbuckling crusaders riding the waves for Jesus; now their island bastion was more like some crusaders' version of Palm Springs, where elderly Knights lived off a carefully fixed income of hoarded treasures, along with taxes and feudal dues collected from their native lands. This latter source of income was the most important, and since many of the Knights were from French noble families, the dues supporting the order's lavish lifestyle came disproportionately from France. When the French National Assembly abolished feudal dues in the summer of 1789, it hit Malta hard. Aristocrats across Europe were incensed, but the Knights of Malta were ruined. Given their aristocratic and religious heritage, the Knights would have opposed the Revolution in any case, but since it had wrecked their livelihoods, they regarded it with a special loathing. They made overtures to ally with France's enemies Austria and Russia, as well as plotting with their traditional feudal landlord, the Bourbon Kingdom of Naples.

All this provided the French armada with the perfect justification to intervene. On June 9, 1798, the ships approached the harbor at Valletta, the island's capital. To the Knights, it must have looked as if the entire world was descending on them. They said they would let four ships into the harbor at a time. It was then that Napoleon learned that the geologist Dolomieu had a special relationship with them: as a young man, he had been a member of the Order of St. John but had gotten into trouble for killing a fellow knight. However, after serving a nine-month prison sentence, Dolomieu attempted to run for a leadership office, an effort that stalled due not to his criminal record but to his liberal politics. In fact, the head of the Knights of Malta, the Grand Master, had been trying to contact him. "The Grand Master wrote to me, . . ." Dolomieu recorded in a later report, "and asked me to use my good offices with [Napoleon]." Before Dolomieu could do so, Napoleon ordered him to row ashore to carry his terms to the Knights.

"Tell the Knights I will grant them most advantageous conditions," Napoleon commanded the scientist, "that I will pay what they want, whether in cash or by the treaty I will make with them; that all the French can return to France and enjoy their political rights; that those who wish to remain in Malta will be protected; that the Grand Master can have a principality in Germany and anything he wishes."

The negotiation was successful, but once the Knights opened up the gates of the harbor and let the armada in, Napoleon announced an entirely different plan. He commanded the Knights to abandon their island in three days, with no compensation. "After demanding that Malta be sold to him," recalled Dolomieu bitterly, "Bonaparte could not have gotten it cheaper."

The French were surprised to find themselves suddenly inside the legendary fortress without a fight. "No one who has seen Malta can imagine that an island surrounded with such formidable and perfect fortifications would have surrendered in two days," wrote Napoleon's personal secretary, who also recorded that, upon inspecting the fortifications, the expedition's chief military engineer exclaimed, "Upon my word, General, it is lucky that there is someone in the town to open the gates for us!"

Napoleon sent ashore in Malta the same experts who had appraised the Vatican for him, to catalog the treasures of the order's monasteries and warehouses. They efficiently inventoried 1,227,129 francs' worth of loot and had it stowed aboard the *Orient*.

But the primary thing Napoleon did in Malta was to lay down a new social order dictated by revolutionary principles. He abolished feudal privileges and declared religious freedom and political equality; he closed the Inquisition's offices and abolished torture. He gave Jews full government protection from persecution and fulfilled the Revolution's rejection of slavery by freeing more than two thousand North African and Ottoman galley slaves, planning to use this as propaganda in Egypt. He drew up plans for hospitals, schools, police stations, pawnshops, and post offices—not to mention street lights, rent-control regulations, and excise taxes. He treated the island like some medieval Lego set that could be taken apart and rebuilt overnight. He established a legal code that over time he would hone into the Napoleonic Code—an updating of Roman law that would later be established in France and around Europe, and that to this day is the basis for nearly all modern European law and administration.*

The actions Napoleon took here were a dry run for his reshaping of Europe and they foreshadowed his maddeningly contradictory legacy. He betrayed the Knights and pillaged the island, but he also transformed it into a modern meritocracy. He was a dictator, a destroyer, and a harbinger of totalitarian leaders to come; he was also a liberator from a tyranny that had stalked Europe for a thousand years.†

━━

ON board the *Guillaume Tell*, still anchored in Valletta harbor, Dumas was once again overtaken by a dark melancholy. Perhaps the southerly voyage reminded him of his childhood in the tropics, for he wrote to Marie-Louise that he felt trapped on a journey that felt "more like a deportation than an expedition." The voyage seemed to him full of bad omens. One of these was that his lackey, Nicolas, fell overboard and drowned (although, in keeping with the ethos of the time, Dumas's laments are focused as much on the personal inconvenience this causes him as on sorrow for the lost life):

> I did not want, my good friend, to afflict you in my letter here by telling you that poor Nicolas, by his imprudence and being drunk while

---

* The Napoleonic Code would impose and codify French revolutionary principles of law, politics, family, and society on the rest of Europe in ways that would never be undone, despite the eventual defeat of Napoleon at Waterloo and the reestablishment of the old monarchy. The Code established equality before the law, meritocracy in education and civil service, economic liberalism and modern property rights, and, perhaps most important, the secular control of most institutions of society, such as education and marriage.

† Though the Code would form the basis of modern life in almost every European country Napoleon subsequently invaded, the Maltese quickly threw off the new order. In 1800, the British took Malta from the French and made it the headquarters of the Royal Navy's Mediterranean Fleet.

During World War II, Malta withstood another incredible siege   this one by the Nazis. Knights or no Knights, the Maltese showed they could hold out against the fiercest enemy. The king of England awarded the George Cross to "the island fortress of Malta . . . to honor her brave people," a rare instance of the British Empire's highest civilian award for gallantry going to a group rather than an individual. Franklin Roosevelt called Malta "one tiny bright flame in the darkness" of Nazi Europe.

playing with the servant of Lambert, fell into the sea at 9 in the evening and drowned before there was any way to save him. I assure you that I suffered a great deal from this event. One cannot be more distressed. I am without a servant; all my affairs are in disorder and I don't know what to do.

I cannot tell you what my morale and my body have already suffered. But what does it matter. I always think that it is for the good of my country. This idea will make me patiently suffer everything that I have yet to undergo. . . . Remember me to my child and our dear parents. As soon as I can send you money, I will do so. When you can, you should give 100 ecus to the father of Nicolas. It is impossible for me at the moment.

Adieu. I cannot recall your attention enough to our interests and the education of our darling child. We are leaving in half an hour for I don't know where. Tell our neighbor, your cousin and all our parents and friends a thousand sincere wishes. I embrace you all, and above all, I am and will always be your best friend.

Dumas also brooded over the fact that he still had no official command. In fact, unbeknownst to him, Napoleon had dictated to his chief of staff, Berthier, two weeks before: "General Dumas will command the cavalry of the entire army." Napoleon had evidently decided to reward the Horatius Cocles of the Tyrol, though Berthier (who no doubt had not forgotten Dumas's insults) made no effort to convey this to Dumas.

➤—◄

BY now Admiral Nelson had learned, in Naples, that Napoleon had taken Malta. After Malta, Nelson guessed, Napoleon might attack Sicily, but otherwise the French fleet would be heading for Egypt. Nelson would soon prepare a letter of warning for the British consul at Alexandria: "I think their object is to possess themselves of some Port in Egypt, and to fix themselves at the head of the Red Sea, in order to get a formidable Army into India; and, in concert with Tippoo Sahib, to drive us, if possible, from India." But guessing at the armada's destination was not the same as knowing either when it might arrive or where it was at the moment. As it happened, just at the very moment when he was about to stumble upon Napoleon's fleet, Nelson picked up a false trail.

In his freshly repaired flagship, the *Vanguard*, Nelson was heading south toward Malta with his squadron in the early morning of June 22—it was 4:20 a.m., according to Nelson's logbooks—when one of his ships, the *Mutine*, sailed within shouting distance of a merchant vessel. It was from the Republic of Ragusa (in present-day Croatia), a neutral country enjoying trade with both France and its enemies. Shouting back and forth, the Ragusans informed the British that the French had seized Malta on June 15 and had departed the next day, on the 16th. But the Ragusans were wrong: Napoleon had ordered the armada to depart on the 19th, leaving the messy details of reorganizing Maltese society to a handful of administrators. At the very moment this exchange was occurring, another of Nelson's ships sighted four unidentified ships in the distance. Nelson sent the *Leander* to investigate. By 6:30 the *Mutine* had reported to Nelson the misinformation about when the armada left Malta. Nelson was certain its target could no longer be Sicily; he had just been there on June 20. At 6:46, Nelson got a signal that "the strange ships are frigates"—light warships. The fifty-gun *Leander* would have had difficulty catching a thirty-six-gun frigate. Should he investigate them further and risk separation from the *Leander*, or make haste to chase the French, who were apparently already three days ahead of him on the way to Alexandria? Lacking his own fast frigates to pursue the ships on the horizon, Nelson ordered the *Leander* back into formation.

Nelson had two reasons to choose to ignore the four unidentified frigates: he wanted to keep his vessels together precisely to keep from losing any more of his squadron, and he had also just received word leading him to believe that the armada itself was halfway to Egypt by then. He brought his officers to confer with him on the *Vanguard*, and by 9 a.m. they had received the mandate to steer for Egypt.

The four strange frigates were the outriders of the French armada, which lay just over the horizon.

On June 23, a day after almost bumping into Nelson's squadron, Napoleon finally announced to the fifty-four thousand men under his command—sending orders ship to ship—the real object of the expedition. Dumas would now learn of his top command position: he would be supreme cavalry commander of the Army of the Orient.

Dumas's satisfaction at the seniority of the assignment must have dispelled his gloom somewhat—along with the message Napoleon now imparted, that the French would be liberating Egypt from the tyrannical Mamelukes, a caste of hereditary foreign warriors who were originally slave-soldiers serving the local Egyptians. (Like other "slavs" of the high Middle Ages, the Mamelukes were white, and to this day some of the elite families of Egypt have the pale skin and blue eyes indicative of that ancestry.) The fearsome slave-soldiers had been imported by Egypt's rulers in the thirteenth century from the lands around the Black Sea and the Caucasus Mountains to enhance their power. But the Mamelukes had then overcome their masters and seized control, until forced in turn by conquering Ottoman armies a few hundred years later to share power in a kind of uneasy partnership.

The Mamelukes had actually seized power in 1250 as a result of the previous French invasion of Egypt, that of the French king Louis IX, known as "Saint Louis." They had built a new capital, Cairo, to replace the ancient capital of Alexandria, and by the late eighteenth century, they still held Egypt in an iron grip and lived a life governed by elaborate military rituals. Their primary interactions with the native Egyptians were extracting taxes and using them as servants.

The Egyptians would welcome the French as liberators, Napoleon assured his men, and they would find riches in Alexandria and Cairo to beggar the greatest cities of Italy.

━━

APPROACHING Egypt on July 26, Nelson dispatched one ship to sail ahead of his squadron. It arrived in Alexandria harbor at sunset on June 28 to scout out the town; an officer went ashore for intelligence, but he returned with news that nobody had heard of any French fleet or spotted even a single French ship on the horizon. When the vessel reconvened with Nelson's flagship the next morning, Nelson regretfully admitted that he'd been wrong—that Napoleon was not invading Egypt after all—and ordered his ships to proceed away from Egypt, toward Turkey. Just three hours after the British left Alexandria harbor, the first advance ship of the French armada arrived there. Somehow, to cap off the string of near misses, the last British ship and the first French ship had passed just within spyglass distance but did not see each other. Nelson would spend the next two months searching the Mediterranean, squinting at the horizon for the French tricolor flag, and cursing the loss of his frigates.

Toward midnight, the longboats from the *Orient*, the *Guillaume Tell*, and the other French vessels set out for the Egyptian shore, storm winds whipping them in the darkness. Some longboats capsized, and the screams and shouts of the sailors carried over the howl of the winds and the crash of the waves. Seamen and soldiers of that era generally could not swim. The official report to the Directory said twenty-nine men drowned; other reports put the number at over one hundred. By the predawn hours of July 2, after two days of ferrying, about four thousand Frenchmen stood on the beach outside of Alexandria, while perhaps eight times that number remained on the ships. The men on shore had no artillery, no siege equipment, no horses, little food, and less water. Napoleon gave the order to march.

Slinging his rifle over his shoulder, General Dumas marched to Alexandria by Napoleon's side. The deputy commander-in-chief of the expedition's infantry was with them—Jean-Baptiste Kléber, who had briefly been Dumas's commanding officer in the Rhine campaign. Though Kléber's native Alsace could hardly be farther removed from Dumas's Saint-Domingue, the two men were cut from the same rugged republican cloth—fearsome to the enemy, often in trouble with the brass. Dumas would come to admire Kléber and confide in him.

The distance from the landing point to the city's walls was approximately ten miles. Though he was commander of the cavalry, Dumas marched with no horses—just as the commander of the artillery marched with no cannon. The storm had made it too difficult to unload them. Also, the Army of the Orient had transported only about 1,200 horses to Egypt, and many were in poor shape after a six-week sea voyage; this total number included horses to pull artillery and supply wagons as well as officers' personal mounts. Only a few hundred horses were left for the cavalry, and each cavalryman normally needed more than one horse. It was the equivalent of the D-day forces arriving without jeeps, trucks, or tanks. Based on travelers' accounts, Napoleon had believed as many as twelve thousand horses could be easily procured in Egypt, which turned out to be false.

The sheer size of the French force provided some protection. Still, before sunup, a few hundred Bedouin tribesmen attacked the French columns as they marched toward the city. When the French returned fire, the Bedouin retreated quickly, but not before kidnapping a few unfortunate Frenchmen and disappearing with them into the desert.

Inside the city, Alexandria's *sherif*—a kind of local nobleman, who controlled the city for the Mamelukes—was panicking. Alexandria was poorly garrisoned. He had only a few scores of Mameluke warriors to rely on for defense. The *sherif* sent a dispatch to Cairo, to one of his two supreme Mameluke overlords: "My lord, the fleet which has just appeared is immense. One can see neither its beginning nor its end. For the love of God and of His Prophet, send us fighting men." But Cairo, the Mameluke capital, was more than a day's ride away.

At dawn Napoleon ordered the bugles sounded and the French charged. Though the city walls seemed imposing at first, when the French began to scale them the old structures crumbled in many places, and soon the attackers poured into the city. Dumas led the Fourth Light Grenadiers over the walls with his rifle. The Alexandrians defended their city fiercely, house to house, but by the next day it was in French hands. General Kléber took a musket ball to the head but survived. Dumas escaped the fighting without a scratch.

>--

DUMAS'S appearance made quite an impression on the Egyptians—a tall black man in a general's uniform at the head of an army of whites. Napoleon had this in mind when, a few days later, he ordered Dumas to make contact with the Bedouins to try to ransom back the men they had kidnapped. He gave Dumas two dozen of his own elite guard to take along on this mission, telling him, "I want you to be the first general that they see, the first leader they deal with."

Dumas's mission was successful. But by the time he arranged the prisoners' ransom—100 piasters a head—the Bedouins had killed a handful and left the rest in almost worse condition. Napoleon interrogated one soldier who cried and could not bring himself to outline the treatment he'd received, though it was eventually pried out of him—all the men had been raped, a fate the French soldiers would come to know and fear in Egypt, a land where European sex norms did not apply.

General Dumas apparently stood out from the beginning of the campaign—and not in a way Napoleon would have enjoyed. In the rare, unpublished third volume of his memoirs, the expedition's chief medical officer, Dr.

Nicolas-René Desgenettes, vividly recalled the impression the expedition's top commanders made on the local population:

> Among the Muslims, men from every class who were able to catch sight of General Bonaparte were struck by how short and how skinny he was. . . . The one, among our generals, whose appearance struck them even more . . . was the General-in-Chief of the cavalry, Dumas. Man of color, and by his figure looking like a centaur, when they saw him ride his horse over the trenches, going to ransom the prisoners, all of them believed that he was the leader of the Expedition.

"THE DELIRIUM OF HIS REPUBLICANISM"

"THE French people—may God thoroughly destroy their country and cover their flags in ignominy—are a nation of obstinate infidels, of unrestrained evildoers," declared the Ottoman sultan and caliph of Islam when he learned of the French invasion. "Rivers of blood have watered the earth and the French have finally succeeded in their criminal designs over the nations that succumbed to them. They are sunk in a sea of vice and error; they gather under the flag of the Devil, and they can only be happy amidst chaos, taking their inspiration from Hell itself . . . may almighty God whom we worship turn their Satanic plots against them!"

"With the Prophet's powerful protection," he added hopefully, "these armies of atheists will be scattered before You and exterminated."

Napoleon ordered an immediate march on Cairo. His plan was to capture the smaller cities of Damanhur, Rosetta, and El Ramaniya along the way. With the Nile Delta in their hands, the French would drive the Mameluke warriors out of their capital city and seize control of the country. General Kléber, who needed to recover from his head wound, would stay behind as military governor of Alexandria. Admiral Brueys stayed with the fleet, which he had anchored in Aboukir Bay, just east of Alexandria at the mouth of the Nile.

The last of the groups to leave the ships were the savants. While the army marched on Alexandria, France's most distinguished scientists, scholars, writers, and artists had been left on board, forced to beg moldy biscuits and brackish water from the remaining crew. At last a frigate was sent to bring them to shore. It dumped them, along with their belongings and the elaborate instruments of their trades, on a beach near some remnants of marble columns and they straggled into town.

Vivant Denon, the artist-archaeologist whose magnificent sketches would help create the discipline of Egyptology, recalled his brutal entry into Alexandria: "I was assailed by packs of wild dogs, which came at me from the doorways, the streets, the rooftops, their cries reverberating from house to house. I left the streets and tried to cling to the shoreline. . . . I jumped into the sea to get free of the dogs, and when the water became too deep I scaled the walls themselves. Finally, soaked to the skin, covered in sweat, overcome with fatigue and frightened out of my wits, I reached the soldiers on guard at midnight, convinced that the dogs were the sixth and most terrible of the biblical plagues of Egypt."

Except for Napoleon's favorites, who lodged with him, the rest of the savants went essentially homeless in Alexandria. The general who was supposed to be in charge of them was busy preparing the march on Cairo. He told the savants to make do as best they could. France's most illustrious minds found themselves with fewer comforts than the lowest soldier.

Napoleon would attempt to remake Egyptian society from top to bottom in a manner as extreme as what he had done so quickly in Malta. But the Egyptians would prove much more resistant to their makeover, and in trying to bludgeon them into accepting foreign rule in the name of "rights for all," the French would unleash storms that are still igniting conflict between East and West to our own day. In a sign of future troubles, when the French tried billeting some of their troops in Alexandria's old city, a number had their throats slit, so the policy was jettisoned.

►–◄

THE vast infantry caravan left for Cairo first, dragging their artillery pieces behind them like stones. The thirty-six-mile march from Alexandria to Damanhur crossed brutal, arid desert, filled with Bedouin who made a sport of hunting stragglers, whom they decapitated or kept for ransom and abuse. The French tried to retaliate with artillery but with little effect: the tribesmen merely withdrew to a safe distance and then returned, always taking the opportunity to strike the endless caravan at points where the men looked weak, tired, or crazed from thirst. Despite the dire water shortage on the road to Cairo, Napoleon had made no significant arrangements for water-carrying vehicles.

It was July. Temperatures during the day went over 110 degrees. One of the reasons the British had not thought the French armada was heading for Egypt was the lunacy of invading the country in the middle of summer. But calculated lunacy—the defying of conventional wisdom and prudence in order to gain advantage—was one of Napoleon's favorite tactics.

The French troops wore dark-colored woolen uniforms and carried forty-pound packs. When not crossing bare ground or desert, they marched on a cragged, rocky camel trail along the abandoned Nile-Alexandria canal that was little better. One of Dumas's fellow generals captured the deadly conditions of the march from Alexandria: "Leaving that city behind to follow the Nile upriver, you find a barren desert, naked as your hand. Every dozen miles you run into a bad well of bitter, salty water. Imagine an army forced to cross these arid plains, with no escape from their unbearable heat. Dressed in wool and bearing five days of supplies on his back, after an hour's march the soldier is overcome by the heat and the weight he carries. He unburdens himself, throwing down his rations, focusing only on the present with no thought of tomorrow. When thirst comes, he finds no water. That is why, in the horrors of this scene, you saw soldiers die of thirst, of starvation, of heat, while their comrades, on seeing this suffering, blew out their own brains."

Dumas, along with Napoleon, had remained in Alexandria for some days, presumably trying to buy mounts for his men. But Alexandria was too poor a town to offer a significant number of horses. On July 4, Napoleon offered all cavalrymen who were unmounted a choice: they could either join the march to Cairo carrying their saddles or they could accept temporary reassignment to infantry brigades and march with less weight. Those who carried their saddles would have first dibs at horses in the future.

On July 7 the cavalry evacuated Alexandria to join the army marching southeast toward Cairo. Only a small contingency force under Kléber remained to garrison the city. Dumas and a small group of officers who, like him, had horses accompanied Napoleon. The rest had to proceed on foot, with or without their saddles. Dumas and Napoleon made the trip from Alexandria to Damanhur in under twenty-four hours. Here they met the army that had suffered the same journey over three hideous days, and here the real troubles for Dumas in Egypt began.

—•—

WHEN the first French troops reached the outskirts of the town of Damanhur—"a pile of huts, resembling dovecotes"—only one thing mattered: there was water. The officers and enlisted men fell over one another to get at it. They jumped into the cisterns and doused their uniforms and splashed and danced and laughed and sang. One officer drank twenty cups in a row. That stop by the cisterns, he would recall, "remains etched in the minds of every soldier in my division as one of the good memories of his life."

Having ignored his generals' urgent dispatches during their march from Alexandria to Damanhur, Napoleon was hardly embraced when he arrived at the front. Dr. Desgenettes, the chief medical officer, whose job kept him close to everyone, from the general-in-chief to the lowest ranks, recalled the mood: "When someone shouted in distress: There's no more water!—the army answered with deep sighs or in tones of fury. Despair went so far that men took their own lives, reminding themselves with bitter irony that they had their six acres that Napoleon had promised them. The feeling of collapse that hit the soldiers, or that excited them to fury, also overtook their leaders." Napoleon himself would recall "seeing two dragoons leave their ranks and, running as fast as they could, drown themselves in the Nile." One particularly promising young brigadier shot himself out of despair after going on a bitter rant about the expedition's poor planning and deadly cost so far.* Later, reflecting on the Egyptian campaign while in exile on Saint Helena, Napoleon would put the blame for its failures on the men: "This kind of warfare was even harder on them, because it contrasted the more with the comforts of the Italian piazza and casinos."

---

* At twenty-eight, General Étienne-François Mireur had been the youngest of Dumas's cavalry brigadiers and also a doctor. Six years earlier, barely out of France's finest medical school, Mireur had volunteered for the revolutionary army in Marseilles, where he achieved an odd renown: he'd supposedly been the first to lead his fellow volunteers in renditions of the recently penned French revolutionary anthem, and he sang it so enthusiastically that the song was forever after known for the place where Mireur and those volunteers had sung it—the "Marseillaise." But whatever remained of Mireur's enthusiasm had failed him on the march from Alexandria, and one day in early July, as a memoirist of the expedition bluntly described it, Mireur "got on his horse . . . before dawn, rode into the desert, and blew his brains out." Other accounts said Mireur had recklessly endangered himself and been shot by Bedouins in a virtually suicidal way.

Without mounts, the cavalry felt especially bereft and angry. They resented the haste and the lack of preparedness. Dumas's mood grew particularly dark, and Dr. Desgenettes remembered how Dumas "threw [his] trimmed hat on the floor, trampled [it] underfoot and, amid a flow of exclamations of frustration, told the troops that the [government] had deported them out of hatred for their leader, because they were afraid of him." There was certainly some truth to these words—though Dumas may have later wished he had not spoken so freely.

One evening while camped in Damanhur, Dumas procured a few ripe samples of a local fruit so bountiful, delicious, and thirst-quenching that the men had taken to calling it "Saint Watermelon." He invited some of his fellow generals—Lannes, Desaix, and the young firebrand Joachim Murat—into his tent to share them. The talk turned to the existential problem at hand: What were they doing there? Had the government intended to send them into a trap of disease and privation in the desert? Was Napoleon a victim or an architect of the plot? There was talk about declaring to the general-in-chief that the army would not go any farther than Cairo.

As Dr. Desgenettes would later report in his memoirs, one of Napoleon's many informants somehow heard everything at this meeting. Alexandre Dumas would piece together a fairly accurate version of the incident, assembling details of the evening from old soldiers who had been there when his father stepped dangerously out of line:

> Eating three watermelons was the only purpose of the get-together in my father's tent, but the gathering quickly took on political overtones when the generals began to air their frustrations.
>
> What had we come to do in this accursed country—a place that had devoured every would-be conqueror from Cambyses II to Saint Louis? Were we here to found a colony? Why leave behind the warm, gentle sun, great forests, and fertile plains of France for this fiery sky, this shadeless desert, these scorched plains? Was Bonaparte hoping to carve himself out a new monarchy, as the ancient Roman governors had done? He might have at least asked the other generals if they would be content as the heads of this new satrapy. That might have appealed to the freedmen and slaves of the ancient armies, but it wouldn't to the

patriots of 1792, who weren't the satellites of a single man, but the soldiers of a nation.

Was there anything to these criticisms beyond the harmless grumbling that emerges under stress? Or was this already the beginning of a rebellion against the ambitions of the future leader of a coup? The generals themselves might have been hard-pressed to answer, but that is exactly what was reported to Bonaparte as a serious attack on his authority by the general who had been the most vocal in declaring my father's watermelons delicious and Napoleon's motives rotten.

＞－＜

THE French army continued southeast toward Cairo. Reaching the Nile the next day, the troops slaked their thirst and were soon beset by dysentery. Worse was the affliction that began to affect their eyes: as they marched over the parched Nile basin, thousands of soldiers began experiencing a redness, burning, and swelling in one or both eyes, often with a discharge of pus. This, they realized, was why so many of the locals had one or two opaque, milky eyes. The French called this condition the Egyptian blindness, and it became the most widespread scourge of the expedition, as thousands of soldiers became partially or even fully blind.* Despite Bonaparte's admonition that "the Mamelukes are your enemy, not the inhabitants," troops began to ignore the orders against looting. Commanders did not object, since all notion of supply had broken down.

"You cannot imagine the fatigue of the marches," Dumas would write to his friend Kléber in Alexandria, "most of the time without food, forced to glean what the preceding divisions had left behind in the horrible villages they had pillaged."

Strangely enough, none of the villagers greeted them as liberators. Everywhere the population seemed prepared to put up resistance. General Berthier himself witnessed a peasant woman, who approached holding her

---

* Some French doctors mistakenly assumed Egyptian blindness (which they named "Egyptian ophthalmia," or "ophthalmia militaris") was caused by the desert climate. The debate over the true cause of the condition—later joined by British doctors—helped found ophthalmology as a separate field of medicine.

baby, suddenly stabbing an aide-de-camp in the eye with a pair of scissors. Dumas wrote to Kléber that they were "harassed during the whole march by this horde of thieves called Bedouins, who killed our men and officers twenty-five paces from the column. General Dugua's aide-de-camp, Géroret, was assassinated the day before yesterday in that way, while carrying orders to a platoon of grenadiers, within gunshot of the camp."

The French army soon encountered the official enemy in a test skirmish on July 13, dispatching some three hundred Mamelukes and chasing off another four thousand. Napoleon imagined that they wouldn't fight again until after the French seized Cairo. But on July 21, after a thirteen-hour march that began at 2 a.m. and ended the next afternoon around three, the French at last arrived at the place they were to fight their decisive battle: thousands of Mameluke horsemen stood facing them, their sabers flashing in the mid-afternoon sun.

"The Mamelukes have a great deal of spirit," Dumas would write dryly to Kléber after the battle was over.

The horsemen were clad in an array of brightly colored embroidered silk jackets, the sleeves encrusted with ivory beads and precious stones. Each man carried pistols in his belt, a blunderbuss, daggers, and the renowned Mameluke sword, a curved saber that could cut off a human head at a single blow.*

One of the French officers present marveled at these men who are "covered in sparkling armor, enhanced with gold and gems, dressed up in varied, brilliantly multicolored suits, their heads adorned with feathered turbans, and some wear gilded helmets. They are armed with sabers, spears, cudgels, arrows, muskets, blunderbusses, and daggers. Each is outfitted with three pairs of pistols . . . The wealth and novelty of this spectacle made a vivid impression on our soldiers; from that moment on, their thoughts were set on booty."

The Mamelukes, for their part, could not take this new threat seriously. They had beaten back the Mongols when no other military force could. Every Mameluke warrior had practiced martial arts since childhood, learning a tradition nearly ten centuries old. To them, these French soldiers were nothing more than godless lackeys in matching uniforms.

---

*The Mameluke sword was considered such a perfectly balanced weapon that, during the fifty years after the Egyptian expedition, it was adopted as the official cavalry weapon by almost all major Western armies and to this day is the official sword of the U.S. Marine Corps.

The French numbered about twenty-five thousand. Estimates of how many Mamelukes faced them vary greatly, though historians often quote the numbers recorded by Napoleon: twelve thousand Mameluke warriors, each with three or four armed servants, eight thousand Bedouin, and twenty thousand janissaries (Ottoman foot soldiers). The Mameluke warrior's military servants accompanied him into battle, reloading his pistols and passing him appropriate weaponry, rather like a golf caddy selecting his player's clubs. The warriors were also trailed by musicians playing flutes and tambourines, as well as crowds of women and children following along to watch the unbelievers be dispatched.

The French soldiers formed themselves into squares, six ranks deep; it was a formation designed to resist and frustrate cavalry charges. The rows of infantry formed a kind of human fortress. At the center of each square Dumas and Murat distributed the cavalry, along with the ammunition and supplies. The artillery was placed at the four corners.

The Mameluke riders attacked the French squares in powerful but disorganized charges, each warrior hurling himself like a tank at the enemy. If they had been able to isolate groups of five, ten, or even a dozen French soldiers, one of these ultimate human fighting machines would have easily won. If they had coordinated themselves into a modern cavalry charge, they might have broken the squares. But, as it was, they could not penetrate even one. The French, despite their poor morale and the fact they had not slept all night, showed remarkable discipline in holding their fire as they watched hundreds of terrifying warriors charging at them, legendary blades poised to chop off their heads, waiting for the precise moment when the volley could be loosed to maximum effect. "The flaming wads from our muskets penetrated their rich uniforms, floating and light like gauze, embroidered with gold and silver," recalled a soldier from one of the squares.

The Mamelukes had never seen one of their cavalry charges fail. Now they failed repeatedly. When French soldiers were hit, they were simply pulled into the center of the square and replaced. The French squares never broke, while the Mameluke horsemen kept attacking with futile bravery. Meanwhile the French artillery shelled their rear with howitzers, and another division attempted to cut the Mamelukes off from their fortifications and any possible retreat.

Realizing that the French were trying to trap them, the Mamelukes determined to make one final all-out charge on two of the five French squares. Thousands of warriors rode at the two at once, but both divisions held. The French countercharged with bayonets and drove the Mamelukes by the hundreds into the Nile, where more than a thousand are said to have drowned. Still, thousands of Mamelukes did ride off into the desert, where, though they were pursued by Dumas and Murat, most escaped south, into Upper Egypt, to regroup. After the French left, the Mamelukes would try to regain their former power over the country, ultimately in vain. Napoleon's invasion had sounded their death knell—just as, ironically, Saint Louis's crusader invasion in 1248 had marked the beginning of their reign in Egypt.

The French would call this the Battle of the Pyramids, though the pyramids at Giza were just far enough away that they likely were not visible during the battle at all. (Illustrations that show the Great Pyramid looming over the combat were either propaganda, which Napoleon went to great lengths to encourage, or orientalist fantasies.) Despite the implications of the Mamelukes' defeat, in the battle's aftermath Napoleon himself seemed mainly dazzled by the souvenirs they had left on or near the battlefield: "carpets, porcelain, silverware in great abundance. During the days following the battle, the soldiers busied themselves fishing in the Nile for bodies, many of which had two or three hundred gold pieces on them."

◆━

LATE-eighteenth-century Cairo was a city of about 250,000 inhabitants, but the French marched in to find empty streets, since, without the Mamelukes, the people were too scared to come out to face their conquerors. The first to emerge were the Europeans. An Italian pharmacist told a French officer that the Mameluke leaders had warned the inhabitants of Cairo that "the infidels who come to fight you have fingernails one foot long, enormous mouths, and ferocious eyes. They are savages possessed by the Devil, and they go into battle linked together with chains." Instead, as the Arab chronicler Al Jabarti (whose account of the expedition remains the most reliable non-French source on it) was shocked to discover, "the French soldiers walked the streets of Cairo unarmed and molested no one." And the French wanted to be welcomed: "They joked with the people and bought whatever they needed at very high prices. They paid one [Egyptian] dollar for a chicken, fourteen *paras* for an egg—in other words, what they would have paid in their own country . . . Thus the shops and coffee houses reopened."

As usual, Napoleon ordered a whirlwind of social and political reforms. Within weeks, the French organized garbage collection, established hospitals, and illuminated the streets by requiring that each house keep a lantern lit outside every night. They constructed mills and bakeries so Egyptians could learn that most basic culinary glory—how to bake French bread. The savants and the engineers set to work mapping the city and making drawings of all the monuments and important buildings. They measured the Sphinx and poked around inside the Great Pyramid, disturbing thousands of sleeping bats.

While in Italy and Malta he had trampled upon religion, in Egypt Napoleon adopted a new strategy. Here Napoleon cynically calculated that he must be seen as an emissary of the Prophet, so he issued his elaborate and peculiar proclamation to the Egyptian people, printed on the Arabic printing press looted from the Vatican. Four thousand copies were printed in Arabic, Turkish, and French; the proclamation went to great lengths to impugn "that gang of slaves," the Mamelukes, as usurpers, and to prove that Napoleon's glory and the glory of the prophet Muhammad went hand in hand.

In French the proclamation read: "Tell the people that the French are . . . true friends of the Muslims! The proof is that they have been to Rome and have destroyed the throne of the Pope, who always incited the Christians to make war on Muslims." In the Arabic leaflets, however, "true friends of the Muslims" had been rendered simply as "true Muslims"—an audacious provocation that Arabic readers would not fail to condemn.

Napoleon's proclamation and subsequent communiqués were translated by the Arabist savants, who had trouble because many revolutionary political concepts simply had no equivalent in Arabic. To make matters worse, these intellectuals were assisted in their translations by several Maltese Arabic speakers who had signed on to the expedition. But Maltese Arabic was an anachronistic and unique island dialect that had little in common with the Arabic spoken in Egypt, and various translation quirks and errors rendered the French proclamations ridiculous to Egyptians.

The local Cairo clergy offered to issue a fatwa recognizing Napoleon as the legitimate ruler of Egypt—provided the entire French army formally convert to Islam. Napoleon actually considered the offer, but when it became clear that the muftis' demand included mass adult circumcision and total abstinence from wine, the conversion plan was scrapped.

→ ←

FOR the thousands of French officers and enlisted men occupying Cairo, the situation hardly promised glory. They missed everything about their old life: Europe, the Revolution, the campaigns in Italy and on the Rhine, Malta—all of it was better than being stuck in a disease-ridden city surrounded by unfathomable people who most likely hated you.

"We have arrived at last, my friend, in the land we had so much desired," Dumas wrote to Kléber. "But for God's sake, it is so far from what we imagined. This wretched town of Cairo is inhabited by a lazy rabble squatting all day in front of their miserable huts, smoking and drinking coffee or eating watermelons and drinking water. One can easily lose oneself for an entire day in the stinking narrow streets of this famous capital."

Cut off from wine shipments, the occupying army made beer and distilled spirits from local figs and dates, but many also took to the local custom of smoking hashish and drinking hash-infused juices and teas. The perpetual hash haze would become such a problem for the occupation that the French would eventually impose their own drug laws and begin confiscating and burning bales of hashish.

One day, without warning, the general-in-chief stormed into Dumas's quarters. Napoleon himself, when he dictated his memoir on Saint Helena at the end of his life, recalled with apparent relish how he'd dressed down the man whose chest was level with his nose: "You have preached sedition. Beware that I don't fulfill my duty, for your six feet and one inch would not prevent you from being shot in two hours."

Napoleon never forgot a slight, and he'd been furious about the rumblings against him ever since Damanhur, when he had perceived Dumas to be inciting mutiny. Even in a crowd of cavalry officers, Dumas's temper and bluster were legendary, and he was the most imposing as well as possibly the most respected of the officers.* Napoleon may have calculated that bringing Dumas into line would silence the other generals in Cairo. But the fact that he recalled the incident decades later, after his empire had fallen, also suggests that Dumas had gotten under his skin.

In fact, he was wrong to assume the disloyalty of Dumas. Generals like Dumas led by inspiration and, like Washington's Continental Army, they fought better with a reason to fight. Blind discipline was not necessary when one fought for a righteous cause.

But Dumas's dedication to his republican ideals, to his nation, and to his comrades left the general-in-chief cold. To him, there was only one kind of loyalty that mattered—loyalty to him. Napoleon was not Cincinnatus—he was Caesar.

Though Napoleon would later abandon Egypt without so much as a warning to his fellow generals—leaving them to face hell in the desert while he returned to France to pursue his destiny—he expected them to achieve a far higher standard of loyalty. The logic of the imperial relationship was taking over, even though Napoleon was still officially only one general among equals.

Some days after Napoleon confronted Dumas, he summoned him to his quarters and bolted the door. Alexandre Dumas gives this account of the scene (related afterward by his father to his confidant, General Dermoncourt):

> "General, you conduct yourself poorly with me and you are trying to demoralize the army," Napoleon told him. "I know everything that happened at Damanhur. . . . I will shoot a general as soon as a drummer-boy."
>
> "Possibly, General," said Dumas, "but I think there are some men whom you would not shoot without thinking twice about it."
>
> "Not if they get in the way of my plans!"
>
> "Look here, General: a moment ago you spoke of discipline; now,

---

* As fate would have it, the leaders of the group opposing Napoleon's conduct on the expedition were all very tall men: along with Dumas, General Kléber, the geologist Déodat de Dolomieu, and the political savant Jean Tallien were over six feet tall, which was remarkable for the time. Napoleon's normal sensitivity about height must have been increased by the stature of his opponents.

you speak only of yourself," said Dumas. "Yes, the Damanhur meeting took place . . . [and] yes, I said that, for the glory and honor of my country, I would go around the world, but if it was for the sake of your whim, for you I would stop at the first step. . . ."

"Thus, Dumas, you divide your mind into two parts: you put France on one side and me on the other."

"I believe that the interests of France should come before those of a man, however great this man may be . . . I believe that the fortune of a nation cannot be subdued to that of an individual."

"Thus, you are ready to separate yourself from me?"

"It is possible, but I don't agree with dictators, not Sulla any more than Caesar."

"And you ask for . . . ?"

"To return to France at the first opportunity that presents itself."

"I promise to put no obstacle in the way of your departure," said Bonaparte.

"Thank you, General, it is the only favor I ask of you."

As Dumas was leaving, Bonaparte muttered, "Blind is he who does not believe in my fortune."

A different recollection of the conversation comes from Dr. Desgenettes, who had it from Napoleon. Napoleon's account is interesting for its keen description of the psychological nuances at play, as he figures out quickly how the purity of Dumas's idealism has made him vulnerable. Dr. Desgenettes recalled that Napoleon had begun their conversation by asking him what *he* thought of General Dumas.

"That he shows a mixture of the sweetest and kindest nature and all the fierceness that a soldier is capable of," the doctor answered. To which Napoleon, recalling what he believed was Dumas's subversion of his plan, said he'd told Dumas that if he "had been unlucky enough to notify me not to go further than Cairo, I would have shot [him] with no further formality." He went on, "Dumas, in a respectful attitude, took it very well; but I added, 'When that had been accomplished, I would have had you tried by the grenadiers of the army, and I would have covered your memory with opprobrium.' Then [Dumas] started to sob and shed floods of tears." Napoleon told Dr.

Desgenettes, however, that he recalled "that beautiful deed of arms where [Dumas] stopped on his own and cut down, at the head of a bridge, a column of cavalry, and I felt at peace right away." But, Napoleon said, he did not oppose Dumas's leaving Egypt—"Let him carry elsewhere both the delirium of his republicanism and his passing furies."

—◄

ON the high seas, in the meantime, the mystery of the French fleet's location had brought Admiral Nelson to a fury of his own. It had made him the laughingstock of England. A London newspaper reflected the mood: "It is a remarkable circumstance that a fleet of nearly 400 sail, covering a space of so many leagues, should have been able to elude the knowledge of our fleet for such a long space of time." Nelson already despised Napoleon and the revolutionary French, as all good British seamen did, but the harm to his reputation caused by losing the French armada made his desire to locate and destroy it more intense than ever. On July 28, tracking false rumors of a French attack on Crete, the British finally got hold of solid intelligence from Crete's Ottoman governor: Napoleon was now in Alexandria. Nelson's fleet set sail at once.

The frigates that had gotten separated from Nelson's squadron in May had wandered the Mediterranean on their own since then. The French had sighted them off Alexandria just eight days before the Battle of the Nile—an ominous warning that might have saved them had they not ignored it. At 2:30 p.m. on August 1, 1798, as the French army was settling into the daily routine of occupying Cairo, a cheer went up on Nelson's ships as the men finally caught sight of Napoleon's fleet, lined up at anchor in Aboukir Bay.

A French lookout had actually spotted Nelson's ships first, at about 2 p.m., as they began to round the tiny Aboukir Island marking the endpoint of the coastal shoals. Admiral Brueys reasoned that the British would not have enough ships in the bay by sundown to safely mount an attack. Naval warfare still operated at a glacial pace in the late eighteenth century, and ships took long hours to prepare for battle. Among other problems was that, in these last days of square sails, ships were good at sailing across the wind or downwind but bad at sailing into the wind. That was one challenge the British ships faced as they made their way into Aboukir Bay. The other challenge was to line up their ships in an advantageous position in relation to the French fleet. Eighteenth-century naval firepower was concentrated on the sides of each ship, where multiple decks of heavy cannon were arrayed. Ships were measured by the number of heavy guns and also the number of decks that housed them. The biggest ships in Nelson's squadron had 74 guns; the French ship the *Guillaume Tell*, on which Dumas had come to Egypt, had 80 guns, about average for the armada; the massive flagship the *Orient* had 120 guns. To sink or capture the French armada, Nelson's somewhat outgunned fleet would need to find the best position from which to fire.

As the British ships continued to enter the bay, many of the French officers and sailors were still on shore digging wells to supply water to the fleet. The French admiral had anchored his ships very close to the shoals, sure that the enemy would not risk maneuvering his ships into the shallow, narrow gap between the French ships and the shore, so as to fire from the landward side. Most of the French ships' guns on the shore side had therefore not even been mounted for battle. Brueys also thought Nelson would not be reckless enough to try anything in treacherous conditions in the failing light. To avoid friendly fire, navies of the era usually delayed combat until dawn. Like Napoleon, however, Nelson cared little for caution and still less about conventional tactics. He called his captains the Band of Brothers and expected them to carry out their mission creatively.

After several hours of tense maneuvering and cannon shots through the smoke-filled sea air, one of Nelson's captains found a gap between the anchors of two French ships and decided it was the right size to sail through. Several of the lead ships of the French fleet, including the *Orient*, would find themselves surrounded as British battleships were able to maneuver into position between the French line and the dangerous shoals. Brueys must have realized his mistake, but it was too late.

The French fired first in this particular face-off, and cannon blasts lit the night sky over Aboukir Bay. The formidable French fleet put up a tremendous fight—Nelson himself was nearly killed when a piece of French shot struck his head. But the French position was poor, and the wind had turned in favor of the British, giving them more dexterity than the French, whose sails faced the opposite direction.

After a firefight of several hours, the *Leander*, Nelson's smallest ship, moved into a gap opened when the French *Peuple Souverain* retreated from the British onslaught. The *Leander* then managed, without running aground, to slip into the narrow strip of water separating the French fleet from the shoals. From there it sent a barrage of cannon fire at the towering 120-gun *Orient*, battering in the process the French ship that sat between them, the *Franklin*, named for the electrical ambassador himself. Two other British ships joined the *Leander*, and together the three surrounded the *Orient*.

Even with much of its crew absent and half of its cannons unmounted, the *Orient* was so much larger and more heavily gunned than any of the British ships that it did well against them at first. "The *Orient* had nearly demolished two of our 74-gun ships, namely *Bellerophon* and *Majestic*, and would no doubt have done much more serious mischief," recalled a British midshipman, but the French sailors "had been painting the ship, and with true French carelessness had left the paint oil jars on their middle deck." The oil from the paint cans, along with turpentine, caught fire as British shot rained down on the deck. When the British saw the wild flames dancing across the great ship's stern, they concentrated their blasts toward the flammable target. The fire spread rapidly, and sometime around 10 p.m., it found its way to the great cache of powder and ammunition in the *Orient's* magazine.

The biggest ship in the world exploded like a giant bomb. Wood, weapons, and bodies flew so high into the night sky that time seemed suspended before they fell back down. Nine miles away in Alexandria, General Kléber saw a bright flame shoot toward the stars. ("When the *Orient* went up, we could make out men in the air, covered in flames, the cannons, the sails, the rigging; the whole harbor was on fire; and at the moment of the explosion, Alexandria was lit up," recalled a French officer with a clear view from a terrace in the city.) And the treasure seized from the Knights of Malta, accumulated over a thousand years—gold bullion, priceless gems, and antiques, riches Napoleon had counted on to fund the expedition—sank to the bottom of Aboukir Bay. Coins and jewels rained down along with the cannon, burning timber, and severed limbs on the decks of the French and English warships as their crews ran for cover. Nothing else of the treasure would be seen again until divers began to bring up coins from Malta, Spain, and France exactly two hundred years later.*

One of the few French ships to survive the day was the *Guillaume Tell*, which had carried General Dumas to Egypt. It was later captured by the British off Malta.

---

* A limited exploration of the *Orient*'s wreckage was conducted in 1983, but the first thorough study of the site began on August 1, 1998, precisely two hundred years after the Battle of the Nile. Of the fabled Maltese treasure, marine archaeologists found coins minted in Malta, Venice, Spain, France, Portugal, and the Ottoman Empire, suggestive of Malta's central place in Mediterranean trade. But there have been no reports of a large trove of riches being recovered. Was it ever there? Although the dominant understanding has long been that Napoleon's looted Maltese treasure had sunk with the *Orient*, some scholars hold the dissenting view that much of the treasure had already been moved ashore and melted down before the battle.

DREAMS ON FIRE

THE Battle of the Nile was one of the most decisive victories in naval history, and it instantly broke the communications and supply chain between France and Egypt.

When he was informed of the destruction of the French fleet, Napoleon called his fellow generals together and said, "We now have no choice but to accomplish great things . . . Seas that we do not rule separate us from our homeland—but no sea keeps us apart from either Africa or Asia."* But survival rather than conquest was on the immediate agenda. Cut off from supplies, the men of the infantry and cavalry suddenly learned a new deference for the two hundred civilians in their midst: the savants. Before, the savants' special quasi-military uniforms had been mocked by the regular soldiers, but now that they were all marooned in Egypt, the motley crew of scientists, professors, engineers, and artists became the Army of the Orient's best hope in a hostile land.

Among the most brilliant and dedicated of these men was Nicolas Conté, a forty-three-year-old self-taught engineer, physician, painter, and inventor, who, among his many patriotic accomplishments, had founded the world's first air force—the French army's "Aerostatic Brigade." He had converted one of Louis XVI's old palaces into an air base, from which the brigade launched military balloons that hovered over battlefields on France's frontiers in the mid-1790s, spying on troop movements. Napoleon had engaged Conté to run the Aerostatic Corps of the Egyptian expedition, but most of its

---

* The governors of the British East India Company reached a different conclusion about the impact of Aboukir Bay. They awarded Admiral Nelson a large cash bounty after his victory, having concluded that he had just saved India for them.

military balloons had gone to the bottom of the bay, along with much of the savants' other technical equipment, when the fleet sank.

Conté's trademark look was a scarf that covered one eye, which he had lost in an explosion while experimenting with hydrogen to replace his balloons' hot air. Undaunted by the current situation, he scurried around Cairo, offering to build the army and the city's civilians whatever they didn't have but needed. He built a foundry and recast the tools and instruments they had lost; he built machinery, factories, bakeries, windmills, and metal-stamping equipment for making weapons and minting coins; and he trained local workers to staff all his enterprises. Another savant recalled that Conté "had all the sciences in his head and all the arts in his hands."

He also constructed new balloons from scratch, as part of Napoleon's plan to impress the residents of Cairo with grand displays of French technological prowess. Egyptians were curious about the first launch, but were nonplussed to see that it was being used to drop copies of one of Napoleon's proclamations over Cairo. The second launch left a distinctly poor impression. "The machine was made of paper and had a spherical form; the tapering panels which formed its surface were patriotically colored red, white, and blue," recounted *Le Courrier d'Égypte*, the expedition's official newspaper, describing how, "when [the Cairenes] saw the great globe rise of its own accord, those who were in its path ran away in fright." Unfortunately, once it was aloft, with a reported 100,000 spectators watching, this cutting-edge piece of technology caught fire—it was, after all, a device made of paper being fueled by an onboard fire—and came crashing back to earth in flames. Luckily it was unmanned. The chronicler Al Jabarti expressed the Arab view: "The French were embarrassed at its fall. Their claim that this apparatus is like a vessel in which people sit and travel to other countries in order to discover news . . . did not appear to be true. On the contrary, it turned out that it is like kites which household servants build for festivals and happy occasions."

Aside from supporting the troops and the colonization effort, the other reason the savants had been brought along—and the main reason the expedition is remembered to this day—was to increase the West's knowledge of antiquity and Near Eastern culture. Though they were only two hundred among the fifty-thousand-strong French force, Napoleon saw the savants' ongoing mission as so crucial that in the fall of 1798 he decreed that Conté, Dolomieu, and the rest of the learned men must have a permanent headquarters in the heart of Cairo, dedicated to "progress and the propagation of enlightenment in Egypt." The Institute of Egypt, as it was called, researched and published works of archaeology, natural science, and historical data. Napoleon, who styled himself an intellectual and was proud of his membership in the French Academy in Paris, showered the Institute with problems both great and small: How do we purify Nile water? Which would be more practical in Cairo, windmills or watermills? What is the civil and criminal law in Egypt and what elements should we keep or throw out? Is there a way of brewing beer without hops?

When I went to Egypt looking for what remained of Dumas and the expedition, I found that while all traces of the vast military enterprise had disappeared into the sands, the legacy of the savants' cultural and scientific mission was still oddly alive, carrying on quixotically in the heart of modern Cairo. Behind the high iron gates of the French Institute of Oriental Archaeology, guarded by tricolor-clad soldiers, lay a perfectly groomed garden of Cartesian order and neoclassical architecture. Here, I met young Egyptian men who printed orientalist books on a room-sized press, using movable-type alphabets—which included little lead hieroglyphs—and I watched old men sewing the books together with long needles and spools of thread the size of bowling pins. A few blocks away, I found the Institute of Egypt itself, in its original revolutionary era building, stuffed with nearly 200,000 works of history, geography, science, and art, all of which had survived world wars and revolutions, putting the study of the ancient world above the modern world's strife, and giving Napoleon's ill-fated attempt at founding a colony in Egypt a positive legacy—at least until December 17, 2011. On that day, as Arab Spring fighting between protesters and police spilled over from nearby Tahrir Square, the Institute caught fire, the flames fed by thousands of priceless books, manuscripts, and maps. By the end of the day, the most significant legacy of the French expedition in Egypt had been destroyed.*

---

*A record of the savants' work was preserved in the monumental twenty-three-volume *Description de L'Égypte*, published between 1809 and 1828. Its merger of languid orientalist landscapes with Pharaonic renderings and desert battles between revolutionary soldiers and the medieval Mamelukes, all of it bedecked with imperial eagles reminiscent of Rome's, produces an effect almost of science fiction—as though these tomes had been left by space aliens whose life span traversed both the ancient and the modern periods of humankind. An original copy of the *Description* was among the books burned in the 2011 destruction of the Institute.

＞—＜

THERE is no record of how Alex Dumas reacted to the destruction of the French fleet, with the loss of at least two thousand men, but it isn't difficult to imagine. Concerned with maintaining order in Cairo and dealing with the continuing Bedouin threat, Dumas in the weeks after the disaster concentrated on finding mounts for his men. He dealt with stables and dealers and Bedouin sheikhs, and bought both horses and camels. The dragoons and cavalry were gradually outfitted, and some were given magnificent Arabian steeds abandoned by the Mamelukes.

Napoleon considered the cavalry vital to impressing the Egyptians, who had for centuries been ruled by mounted soldiers. Sometimes Dumas rode far into Upper Egypt chasing Mameluke insurgents or Bedouins. Other times he made forays into the delta, where the roads and paths along the Nile were still treacherous. Anywhere outside the two cities of Cairo and Alexandria, French soldiers and civilians were prey for kidnappers, insurgents, and bandits.

The letters General Dumas wrote in Egypt showed that he felt growing heartache. A letter to Marie-Louise that had been stowed in the safe in Villers-Cotterêts read:

> Cairo, the 30th Thermidor, Year VI [August 17, 1798]
> Be happy if it is possible for you, because for me all pleasures have died here, unless I can one day see France again, but when? . . . I deeply desire to tell you everything that is in my heart, but one must be silent and choke on one's pain. Embrace my dear, dear child, mother, father [his in-laws, the Labourets], and all our relations and friends.

The only other letters from Dumas that I could find from the fall of 1798 were to General Kléber in Alexandria. Kléber—who shared Dumas's opinion of Napoleon—memorably summed up his command by stating that Bonaparte was "the General who costs 10,000 men a month." Kléber detested the way he used people as mere instruments and was ready to send thousands to perish if it would give him the smallest advantage. "Is he loved? How could he be?" Kléber scribbled in a notebook. "He loves nobody. But he thinks he can make up for this with promotions and gifts." Like Dumas,

Kléber truly believed in the ideals of 1789. To them Napoleon was leading the great revolutionary French army into the gutter.

But the situation in Egypt—the ersatz "Republic" meant to assuage the economic losses from the abolition of slavery in the sugar islands—must have been especially painful for Dumas. He had overcome the legacy of slavery by embracing an ideal of brotherhood and liberty. Yet walking around Cairo, Dumas would have seen black Nubian slaves laboring in homes and fields and being sold in the markets. Though the Arab trade in black Africans was far older than the European one, it had never been questioned in a society like Egypt's. "The caravan from Ethiopia arrived in Cairo by land along the Nile, carrying 1200 black slaves of both sexes," one French corporal wrote. "Humanity is revolted by the sight of these victims of Man's ferocity. I shook with horror when I saw the arrival of these poor souls, almost naked, chained together, wearing a look of death on their dark faces, reduced to being vilely sold like cattle."

Egypt had been built on slavery at every level, right up to the top, since even the Mameluke ruling class had originally been brought there as slaves. It was hardly in Dumas's brief to set free the thousands of African slaves who lived in misery wherever he turned. Yet wasn't it the army's stated mission to liberate mankind and enforce the laws of 1794? "We have seen how slavery like a vast cancer covers the globe," one revolutionary had declared. "We have seen it spreading death shrouds over the classical world and the modern one, but today the bell of eternal justice has rung, the sacramental words have been read out by the voice of a powerful and good people—slavery is abolished!"

And yet here was slavery, alive and well in the new French colony of Egypt, and the general-in-chief had no interest in doing anything about it. Liberating slaves was one thing in Malta, where Napoleon intended to subvert the local order, and the galley slaves were part of that order (it also made a good impression on the Muslim world to free Muslim slaves in advance of the landing in Egypt). It was another thing entirely in Egypt, where he wanted to use the local order to prop up his power. Some French soldiers even bought their own black slaves in the markets here, a violation of the Republic's law, a law Napoleon flouted with impunity in this remote country. At one point he himself even ordered the procurement of two thousand slaves to be incorporated as soldiers. These slaves could not be obtained, but some 150 black Africans did enter the French military in Egypt as part of a special brigade.

They were eventually scattered to diverse postings, and grouped with black soldiers from the Caribbean, a type of racial segregation that also violated the Republic's constitutional guarantee of racial equality.

━━

IN August 1798, in an episode that could have come straight from one of his son's novels, General Dumas happened upon a treasure of jewels and gold—but there, alas, the similarity to *The Count of Monte Cristo* ends.

He discovered the abandoned stash, likely the property of some Mameluke warrior, buried beneath a house whose repair he was supervising in central Cairo. Although Dumas had protested the widespread pillaging of jewels and money in northern Italy, now he took a different sort of principled stand regarding this treasure, whose owner, after all, had fled into the desert, if he was even alive.

There is no evidence that Dumas had compunctions about taking the treasure—to the French, it was easy enough to see the Mamelukes as the aristocratic oppressor class and foreign usurpers of the local Egyptians.* But he turned the treasure over to the army in full, and sent, according to his son, the following note to Napoleon:

> The leopard cannot change his spots, nor can I change my character and principles. As an honest man, I must confide to you the fact [of a treasure] I have just discovered. . . .

---

* Nevertheless, Napoleon had actually decreed, on September 7, 1798, after the destruction of the fleet, that all young Mamelukes between the ages of eight and sixteen would join the French expeditionary army, along with all Mameluke slaves and servants of the same age, and over the next months some two hundred Mamelukes were integrated into the French army. They wore a rigid red or green hat with a white or yellow turban wrapped around the base, a kind of cross between an infantry hat of the period and a fez; it looked a lot like a birthday cake. Eventually they would follow Napoleon back to France, and in the years of his empire, the immigrant Mamelukes would serve with outstanding valor at the Battle of Austerlitz and during the Russian campaign (where they gave the Cossacks as good as they got). Strangely, the Mamelukes who went to France became fiercely loyal to Napoleon—the man who had destroyed their culture and ended their rule. By the Battle of Waterloo there were only forty-one of these "French" Mamelukes left, yet on that day they made a futile charge at the British cavalry squares—an eerie mirror image of the original charge at the Battle of the Pyramids—to defend "their emperor."

I abandon it to your disposition. reminding you only that I am a father and without fortune.

Napoleon was glad to accept the treasure, for that fall the army would urgently need all the funds it could get, with its Malta plunder sunk and the lifelines to France cut. I never found any acknowledgment by him of Dumas's self-restraint—beyond this brief note, sent to one of the savants, on August 23, 1798:

To CITIZEN POUSSIELGUE
Headquarters, Cairo, 6 Fructidor, Year VI
General Dumas knows the house of a bey where there is a buried treasure. Consult with him to arrange for its recovery.
    Bonaparte

The other great service Dumas did Napoleon that fall was to aid him in putting down the Cairo revolt. The revolt centered on the Al-Azhar Mosque, Cairo's main mosque, where for days the mullahs had been preaching that the French were worse oppressors than the Mamelukes, since they were unbelievers to boot. Revolt was therefore sanctified and indeed required by God and the prophet Muhammad, they said. Despite Napoleon's pro-Muslim statements and his attempts to write himself and the Revolution's other deists into the Koran—or perhaps because of them—many average Egyptians were ready to fight the invaders. The revolt ignited on October 22, and for three days terrifying scenes of murder, pillage, and arson bloodied the city.

After rescuing some savants at the Institute, where they had barricaded themselves against the mobs, Dumas set his hand to dispersing the main rebel groups, which had holed up in the Al-Azhar and turned it into their headquarters. In some versions of the events, Dumas charged into the mosque itself on horseback, while scattering rebels cried, "The Angel! The Angel!"—apparently believing the black rider was the Angel of Death from the Koran. Alexandre Dumas repeated the story in his memoirs, along with the following exchange, in which his father was greeted warmly by Napoleon after the rebellion was put down:

"*Bonjour*, Hercules," he said. "You have struck down the hydra." And he held out his hand.

"Gentlemen," he continued, turning towards his retinue, "I shall have a painting made of the taking of the Grand Mosque. Dumas, you have already posed as the principal figure."

Yet eleven years later, when Napoleon commissioned the painter Girodet to paint his celebrated picture *The Revolt of Cairo*, which depicted the epic melee inside the mosque, the "principal figure" of General Dumas was erased—or, rather, it was replaced by a blond, blue-eyed dragoon atop a rearing steed, saber raised, in a mocking echo of Dumas's trademark heroism. In another painting of the incident, the officer entering the mosque, saber drawn, is Napoleon himself.

►—◄

NAPOLEON would leave Cairo without notice or fanfare the following summer and would sail back to France, leaving Kléber, who had for so long yearned to return home himself, to assume command and mop up the failed Egyptian operation. Napoleon would not even tell Kléber directly that he was turning over supreme command to him; he sent him instructions by mail. Learning that Napoleon had left in the night and put him in charge, Kléber is said to have responded with the sort of blunt language that endeared him to his friend Dumas: "That bugger has left us here, his breeches full of shit. We're going to go back to Europe and rub it in his face." But Kléber did not live to fulfill this oath: he was stabbed to death on a Cairo street by a Syrian student hired by the Ottomans. (The assassin's skull was taken back to France where generations of phrenology students studied it for indications of "murderousness" and "fanaticism.")

General Dumas got out of Egypt in March of 1799—no doubt full of grave misgivings at leaving Kléber behind. Reversing the steps of the previous spring, he rode from Cairo to Alexandria, there to find a ship to take him home. By his side was General Jean-Baptiste Manscourt du Rozoy, who had first served with him at the Siege of Mantua. Manscourt was about fifteen years older than Dumas, and an aristocrat, but he was an amiable and good-hearted companion. Together they rode toward the harbor and made inquiries about hiring a ship. There were no military ships going to France, but passage was now considered possible on a civilian ship—the less impressive, the better.

This was how Dumas, Manscourt, and another illustrious passenger, the savant Déodat de Dolomieu, came to hire passage on an old corvette called the *Belle Maltaise*. The vessel's condition did not inspire confidence, but it had a reputation as one of the best ships remaining in the Alexandria harbor, and besides, they had little choice. Dumas gave its captain, a Maltese sailor, funds for whatever repairs might be necessary for the journey, but he would later find out that the captain had simply pocketed the money.

In Cairo Dumas had sold most of his possessions and bought eleven Arabian horses; he also bought four thousand pounds of Arabian coffee, which he planned to sell back in France. He loaded his horses and his coffee, along with a collection of Mameluke swords, onto the boat.

Besides the generals, the horses, and the geologist, the ship was packed with Maltese and Genoan passengers, and about forty wounded French soldiers. All the French military men had been beaten down mentally and physically and were looking forward to nothing more than going home. They could not weigh anchor soon enough.

Immediately before sailing, Dumas was approached by four young Neapolitan naval officers who said that their ship had been sunk by the English and that they were trying to find any passage back to Europe. He arranged for them to join the ship's party.

The *Belle Maltaise* departed Alexandria on March 7, 1799. In Villers-Cotterêts, I found a note Dumas had written two weeks earlier to "Citizeness Dumas":

> I have decided to return, my beloved, to France. This country, with its rigorous climate, has altered my health a great deal. . . . I hope to follow [this letter] very closely.
>
> My desire is but to escape the English so as to embrace what will never cease to be dearest in the world to me.
>
> Your friend for life,
> Alexandre Dumas

It was the last word anyone would hear from him for over two years.

PRISONER OF THE HOLY FAITH ARMY

THE *Belle Maltaise* departed Egypt on the night of March 7, 1799. The ship seemed to be well armed and well provisioned, and thanks to the pitch-dark night and brisk winds, she avoided British cruisers and made about forty leagues by morning. In the account Dumas later wrote about his ordeal—I found the stained parchment pages in the safe in Villers-Cotterêts, with line after line of his elegant, furious words etched on them with a quill pen—he recalled discovering that in fact "the ship was dilapidated." This, he noted dryly, "surprised us early on the first night of our navigation as it began taking in water from all sides." There was one lifeboat on the vessel that could accommodate perhaps twenty people; nearly 120 were registered aboard.

"Having already found ourselves 40 leagues from the Egyptian coast, with the wind absolutely against our returning," Dumas wrote, there was nothing to do but to jettison everything of weight, including provisions, cannonballs, fresh water, and the ship's anchors and cables. Dumas sacrificed his four thousand pounds of Arabian coffee to the waves, and even most of his prized Arabian horses. (In a letter, Dolomieu would later blame Dumas for weakening the ship by cutting a beam in order to fit the horses.) "I saw the necessity, so as not to sink, of throwing overboard ten pieces of cannon successively, and nine of the eleven Arabian horses I embarked with," General Dumas wrote.* "Yet despite this lightening," he added, "the danger only

---

* As evidence of what these men valued, however, the passengers didn't throw their own personal weapons overboard, for, based on a later inventory I found of the ship's remaining contents, everyone was still personally very well armed, even as they foundered and bailed and fought the sea for dear life: at least thirty-seven double-barreled rifles, forty sabers,

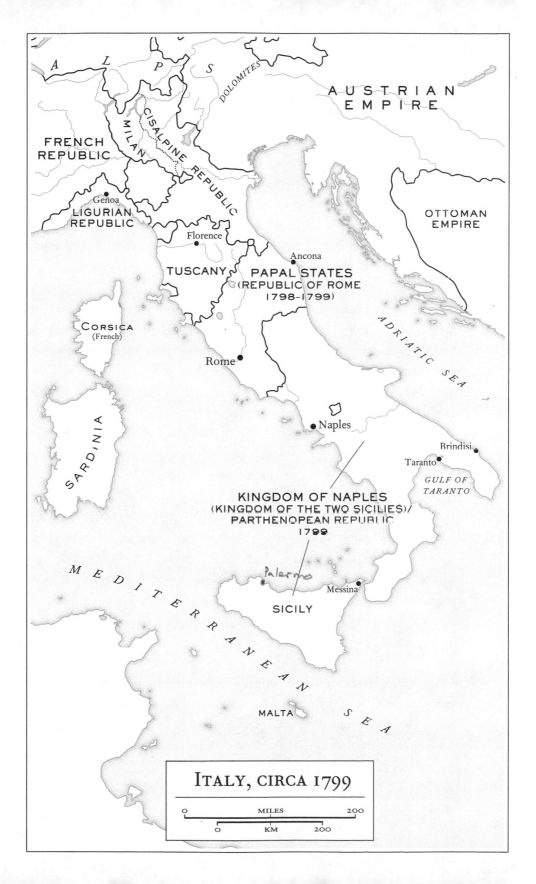

A L P S

DOLOMITES

AUSTRIAN
EMPIRE

FRENCH
REPUBLIC

MILAN

CISALPINE REPUBLIC

Genoa

LIGURIAN
REPUBLIC

OTTOMAN
EMPIRE

Florence

Ancona

TUSCANY

PAPAL STATES
(REPUBLIC OF ROME
1798–1799)

CORSICA
(French)

ADRIATIC SEA

Rome

SARDINIA

Naples

Brindisi

Taranto

*GULF OF
TARANTO*

KINGDOM OF NAPLES
(KINGDOM OF THE TWO SICILIES)/
PARTHENOPEAN REPUBLIC
1799

M E D I T E R R A N E A N

Palermo

Messina

SICILY

S E A

MALTA

Italy, circa 1799

0   MILES   200

0   KM   200

worsened." The leaky corvette continued to take on water at an alarming rate, especially after a ferocious storm began, lashing the ship with rain and high waves.

An old Maltese sailor told them of a technique for securing the hull that Dumas and Dolomieu at first mistrusted but eventually agreed to let him try. The man charged money to perform it, even though it would ostensibly save his life as well as everyone else's. It involved diving into the ship's hold and finding the holes to fill them, continually, with bits of straw and debris. The sailor reported that the ship was leaking not just in one place but along many seams of the hull. Somehow his technique worked to get the water levels down and to slow the influx.

The leaking vessel sailed on stormy seas for over a week in that perilous condition. The men faced not only drowning but a dwindling supply of food and water. Dolomieu brooded about how their deaths would go unmarked and undiscovered. Reflecting late-eighteenth-century meteorological science, he later noted that "it had been a long time since the equinox had influenced the weather to such terrible effect."

A meeting was held among "the French seamen and the foreigners," and the captain convinced everyone that the only thing to do was head for the nearest port. And so the *Belle Maltaise* limped into the Gulf of Taranto, which separates the heel from the toe of Italy, and followed the ancient shipping lanes once plied by Greek and Roman galleys. The city of Taranto had once been the lone colonial outpost of the warrior state Sparta on the Italian peninsula. Even today, the ruins of the ancient Spartan temple of Poseidon are among its most picturesque sites, lying below a great gray fortress of more recent vintage.

◆—◆

"I dispatched the captain of the ship with a letter for the governor of the city, in which I explained the reasons that had forced me to approach their territory," Dumas recounted. "I asked for help in our unfortunate situation and for hospitality until we could get repaired and continue on our way."

---

twenty-seven bayonets, twenty-one blunderbusses, twenty-six pistols, two combat axes, several Mameluke swords, and four wooden crates that contained thirty iron hand grenades each.

Until two months earlier, the city of Taranto had belonged to the Kingdom of Naples, ruled by a king and queen: Marie-Caroline—"Maria Carolina"—Marie-Antoinette's older sister, and her husband Ferdinand, who hated the French Revolution as fiercely as any other monarch. But they had then been driven out by a French-inspired revolt of liberal patriots, and a French-backed republic had been installed in their place. News of the event had reached Egypt by mid-February. Dumas and his men therefore felt sure of safe passage and expected a warm welcome.

"After a series of extremely violent gales, one after the other without respite," as Dolomieu recalled it, "we were overtaken by flights of joy knowing that we had arrived home in Europe, believing we were out of all danger, and thinking that we would soon be seeing other Frenchmen, who we assumed were the masters in Taranto."

The captain returned to Dumas with the news that the governor of the city would welcome them into the port but that they would first need to be quarantined. The request seemed benign; a plague epidemic had been decimating the French in Alexandria, and a passenger on the *Belle Maltaise* had just become its latest victim.

But even as the longboats brought the passengers of the *Belle Maltaise* ashore, the Frenchmen began to feel twinges of unease. It must have hit Dumas like a blow that he was not, after all, in friendly territory. "Instead of the tricolor flag," Dolomieu recalled, "we saw Neapolitan banners on all the towers." The flags in the harbor bore not only the symbols of the overthrown Kingdom of Naples but a new, hybrid symbol none of the Frenchmen could have seen before: the fleur-de-lis, the old device of the Bourbon kings, superimposed on a cross. It was an emblematic merger of the two powers the Revolution had overthrown: the Crown and the Church.

The travelers were subjected to a rough search, followed by questions from an endless tribunal of bureaucrats, factotums, attorneys, and men armed with pikes and assorted weapons, all acting under orders they would not reveal. "We were interrogated, searched, disarmed, and, to quarantine us," wrote Dolomieu, "we were locked, 120 of us, in a big storage room." The anti-French hostility was palpable. A student of Dolomieu's who had accompanied him believed the quarantine saved their lives: "If the plague hadn't claimed one of us," he wrote to the librarian of the Institut d'Égypte, "we might have been massacred that very night." (The men in charge struck him as "savages.") So far, the travelers were allowed to keep their money.

Many, of course, had wounds and all were malnourished from their days at sea; they were packed so tightly together that no man could lie down without dislodging another. But the following day, their jailers took Dumas, Manscourt, and Dolomieu from the common holding room and gave them private cells. Like everything, this was effected by a cash payment. Dumas also explained to the officials that his remaining two horses needed food and care, and the officials agreed to do this if he provided more money. Bribes were the order of the hour, for everything. Dumas paid the guards in advance for his horses' upkeep—though he would learn later that the animals had been seized and would never be returned to him. (Remarkably, even as the guards' conduct became balder and more aggressive, removing all doubt as to whether they were jailers rather than hosts, they never simply confiscated all Dumas's belongings and money outright. Perhaps the culture of bribery was simply too deeply ingrained for anyone to want to cut the cycle of requests and extortion short.)

"We had all been delighted by what we thought was a sincere welcome," Dumas remembered, "but under the mask of humanity ran evil designs and crimes worthy of the Neapolitan government." They were indeed being held by men with "evil designs," yet unbeknownst to Dumas even later, these men did not represent the "Neapolitan government" at all, at least not in the usual sense of the term.

The Kingdom of Naples had a strange and violent history, and rarely had life in the kingdom been as strange or as violent as it was now, in the spring of 1799. In fact, of all the places in Europe for Dumas, Manscourt, and Dolomieu to have landed, they'd happened upon one of the most dangerous.

The Kingdom of Naples encompassed all of southern Italy, right up to the border of the Papal States (in 1799, the French-backed Republic of Rome). It was a fairly recent monarchy: Ferdinand had been its sovereign for most of its existence, preceded only by his father, Charles, who had come onto the throne in 1759. Before that, the area had been ruled since the fall of the Roman Empire as a colony or possession: first the Byzantines, then the Muslims, then the Normans, the Germans, the French, and finally the Spanish had all taken a turn at running southern Italy, or trying to. Since the sixteenth century it had been the Spanish, whose armies conquered southern Italy at the same time Cortés was conquering Mexico. Even today, many people, especially northern Italians, remark that the south reminds them more of a Latin American country than of any place in Europe, and though they often mean something insulting, the comparison is based on a very real shared history (symbolized by that South American novelty, the tomato, which so transformed southern Italian cuisine). From the 1500s to the early 1700s, the Spanish ruled Naples and Taranto much as they did Buenos Aires and Bogotá. Under them, the capital, Naples, briefly rivaled Paris as the largest city in Europe.

But at the beginning of the eighteenth century Madrid lost its southern Italian colonies, and then, at mid-century, came an obscure inheritance battle that gave a relative of the king of Spain a chance to trade up from a dukedom and turn the former southern Italian colonies into a new kingdom: the Kingdom of Naples. It was as if a junior Sun King had taken over a banana republic. Naples nevertheless became a center of the Italian Enlightenment; the scientific and cultural enthusiasm aroused by the nearby excavations of ancient Pompeii made Naples one of the high points of the European Grand Tour.

In 1759, the kingdom's founder got bumped up the royal ladder to inherit the throne of Spain and left his little start-up kingdom to his eight-year-old son, Ferdinand, who took the keys to the kingdom and, at seventeen, married Marie-Antoinette's sister. As politically savvy as her younger sister was frivolous, Queen Maria Carolina bore Naples some eighteen royal offspring while guiding its geopolitics in a radical direction. At the end of the 1770s she invited a British expat named Sir John Acton to be secretary of the navy of the Kingdom of Naples, with the understanding that, as an Englishman, he would know how to build a navy from scratch. Sir John also became Naples's secretary of war, secretary of finance, and so on, until he was running many of the functions of the state.

At this point, Neapolitan banana-republic absolutism entered its disturbing second phase—the one Dumas haplessly sailed into. When Marie-Antoinette was guillotined in 1793, Queen Maria Carolina swore an eternal hatred of France and instructed Acton to devote the kingdom's every resource to keeping out French ideas, French printed matter, and French people. But "French ideas" took root despite the censorship, especially in the educated upper class. Then, when the French army of Italy liberated the north in 1796–97, a wave of revolutionary sentiment swept down the Italian peninsula. The tree of liberty was planted in Rome's notorious Jewish ghetto, and its residents were set free. Naples was ablaze with revolutionary speeches and calls to action. When, in the spring of 1798, Napoleon's armada passed by Italy's southern shores on its way to Malta, the French seemed to Ferdinand and Maria Carolina to be closing in on all sides.

But the *Expédition d'Égypte* provided Neapolitan royals with a real opportunity to strike at the French: along with Acton and the British ambassador Sir William Hamilton, the monarchs furiously arranged the kingdom's affairs in opposition to French power. The linchpin in Anglo-Neapolitan relations was Hamilton's young wife, Lady Emma Hamilton, whose torrid affair with Admiral Nelson—by then Lord Nelson of the Nile—kept the British navy close at hand.* With an alliance solidified not only by geopolitics but by Nelson's constant need to visit his lover, Ferdinand and Maria Carolina felt invincible. That fall, while Dumas was tamping down unrest in Cairo, Naples attacked the French-sponsored Republic of Rome. However, when confronted by the crack battle-hardened troops of the French Army of Italy, the Neapolitan soldiers panicked, dropped their weapons, and ran before the French. (The rout did nothing for the reputation of Neapolitan troops. When his son had their uniforms changed, King Ferdinand disparaged the move, quipping, "My dear child, dress them in white or dress them in red, they will run just the same.") The French army chased the Neapolitan troops home, enabling the creation of one more Italian republic and eradicating (for the moment) the peninsula's last vestiges of monarchy. Ferdinand and Maria Carolina drained the royal treasury and, with Acton, fled to Sicily.

With King Ferdinand gone, strange days arrived in the former Kingdom of Naples. No one was clearly in charge. On the one hand, the forces of the French Revolution had arrived. When the French army entered Naples, the Neapolitan patriots emerged from hiding to proclaim their own French-sponsored Parthenopean Republic on January 21, 1799, less than two months before Dumas reached Taranto. Patriots planted trees of liberty and

---

* Passing through on one of his tours, Goethe wrote that Sir William Hamilton "has now after many years of devotion to the arts and study of nature, found the acme of these delights in the person of an English girl of twenty with a beautiful face and a perfect figure. He has had a Greek costume made for her which becomes her extremely."

strung tricolor banners from all the buildings. (The local revolutionary color scheme was blue, yellow, and red.) In cities all across southern Italy, French-inspired patriots and freethinkers seized the reins of power. Taranto was no exception. Its local liberals also declared their city republican and free.

But at the same time, large, angry mobs took to the streets in towns and cities throughout the kingdom, seeking out nobles or rich merchants known to be sympathetic to equality, enlightenment, liberty, or any other "French idea." They hauled "French" libraries into public squares for burning. Sometimes they didn't stop at books but tied the books' readers to stakes to be roasted alive. Such autos-da-fé—literally, "acts of faith"—had not been seen in Europe since the heyday of the Spanish Inquisition. The population was "ignorant, highly superstitious, fanatically loyal to Ferdinand and hostile to the French," wrote a member of the French occupying army. "Had they the opportunity and the means they would not let a single one escape. . . . [We] seem to have forgotten that we are in the land of the Sicilian Vespers."*

In the countryside, too, French troops found themselves engaged in fierce battles against groups of irregular antirevolutionary militias, who did not yet have a name or any real structure. The exiled Ferdinand sponsored this insurgency—an anti-French, anti-democratic amalgam of peasants, aristocrats, priests, and bandits. The man who led it was Cardinal Fabrizio Ruffo, a churchman from a prominent aristocratic Neapolitan family. Ferdinand deputized Ruffo his "vicar-general" and commanded him to do "whatever was necessary" to purge southern Italy of liberal, pro-French ideas.

The cardinal announced that the movement was to be called *L'Esercito della Santa Fede*—the Holy Faith Army—and it was he who designed the flag that symbolized Crown and Church. Under that flag—red and

---

* The reference was to one of the grisliest events in Italian history—the frenzied slaughter of French soldiers in Palermo in March of 1282 by local mobs angered at a supposed slight to a Sicilian woman's honor. The mobs of that time, too, were doing the bidding of conservative forces who wanted to keep French influence out. Tall, blond Franco-Vikings of the north, the Normans, had first reached Sicily in the eleventh century and, by the thirteenth century, under the reign of a half-Norman genius named Frederick II, had brought tolerance and innovation to the island: poetry, science, and rational thought all flowered; there was even peace between Christians and Muslims. But the apocalyptic riots at the start of vespers at sundown on Easter Monday, 1282, ended all this, buried it along with the bodies of Frenchmen hacked to death by angry mobs. The legacy of the Sicilian Vespers turned the crossroads of Europe into one of its backwaters.

white—the Holy Faith troops would battle the nefarious French Revolution's blue-white-and-red-clad armies.

As the *Belle Maltaise* careened toward Tarantine waters, the Holy Faith Army was consolidating its hold over Italy's southernmost terrain. Republican Taranto had fallen. Now "infamous," its tree of liberty was uprooted from the harbor square and burned. The *tricolori* were replaced with Cardinal Ruffo's lily-crucifix standards.

The Holy Faith Army had been massacring liberals, Jews, republicans, and anyone accused of having the remotest tie to anything French. As Dumas and the others stood answering their questions, the ancient port city was still strewn with bodies, though none were visible in the harbor square. The very day the unlucky ship came into port, the Marquis de la Schiava, the Holy Faith's local deputy, was appointed the new governor—"the Lord"—of the Taranto fortress.

The Marquis de la Schiava sent word to Cardinal Ruffo that he had captured two high-ranking French generals who had been shipwrecked, along with a French scientist of international renown. Then the marquis waited for orders from the cardinal about what to do with his captives. But since the Holy Faith Army had the irregular structure and rhythms of an insurgency, it was impossible to get a straight answer. The man they called vicar-general, in addition to supreme general, had previously served as the pope's treasurer before managing King Ferdinand's royal silk works. Though Ruffo was committed to rebuilding Church domination in the kingdom, the army he led attracted, according to one of its own officers, "assassins and robbers driven by the hope of plunder, vendetta and murder." All sorts of people were coming out of the woodwork and claiming they had the authority of the Holy Faith Army or the cardinal.

So it was that—after days of seeing no one but underlings, despite his protests—Dumas suddenly received a visitor who introduced himself as "Crown Prince Francis, son of King Ferdinand of Naples." Dumas tried to tell him about their mistreatment and their need to see the French ambassador, but the prince cut him off. "After he asked about the health of Generals Bonaparte and Berthier and the military situation of the Army of Egypt, he left abruptly," Dumas recalled with puzzlement.

As later Italian accounts reveal, this man claiming to be Ferdinand's son was actually a Corsican adventurer named Boccheciampe, who had been going from town to town in the Holy Faith zone, posing as the prince and giving orders. The false Prince Francis had dismissed magistrates, appointed governors, raised taxes, and spent money from the public purse. His managing to do all this without getting caught suggests that he was surely a good deal smarter than the real Prince Francis, who was known to be as cowardly a dilettante as his father. It also suggests the chaos that prevailed in the kingdom at the time.

The scoundrel may not have been the real crown prince, but it was he who occasioned the first direct communication Dumas received from Cardinal Ruffo.

One day not long after the impostor's visit, the guards gave Dumas a letter from the cardinal. "He invited us, General Manscourt and me, to write to the Generals in Chief of the French Armies of Naples and Italy to exchange ourselves for Monsieur Boccheciampe, prisoner at Ancona, adding that the King of Naples [Ruffo's master] had more concern for the case of Monsieur Boccheciampe alone than for all of the other generals in his employ who were prisoners of war in France."

It seems that "Prince Francis," just after his visit to Dumas's cell, had made his way north and to the other side of the peninsula at the head of a bunch of Holy Faith troops, his intention being to fight and plunder his way up the coast. But he was then taken prisoner by the French, hence the possibility of the trade. (Despite his rogue behavior in Taranto, Boccheciampe had recently won the province of Apulia back for King Ferdinand from the French-allied republicans in a successful conspiracy with three other outlaw Corsicans, who also posed as royals.)

"I consequently addressed the necessary letters to the cardinal," Dumas recorded, and his hopes rose that this peculiar prisoner exchange would free him. But then word came that the French had actually killed Boccheciampe, not taken him prisoner, and Cardinal Ruffo lost interest in using Dumas and Manscourt as bargaining chips.

Instead of liberation Dumas received an order declaring that, nearly seven weeks after they were first taken into custody, he and Manscourt were now official prisoners of war of the Holy Faith Army. The order applied only to them; the other passengers from the *Belle Maltaise* were to be held separately.

Confirming this description of events in Dumas's report, I found an order dated May 4, 1799, that authorized "the departure of all French and Genoan prisoners, with the exception of the two generals, who shall remain in Taranto, under custody of a good guard." The document stated that all the other prisoners were to be released after signing an oath that "they vow for two years not to take up arms against His Majesty, the King of Naples, God Bless Him, [or] against his allies, in omnibus." Before being freed, however, they were first to be "relieved of every weapon . . . even small knives," and the authorities also ordered the confiscation "of their money, if they possess any, excepting a small sum for use while traveling, and of jewelry or other items of value." The confiscated jewels, watches, gold and silver coins, cups, knives, silk shawls, bits of fabric, and so forth were all then duly inventoried—the list running on for pages in detail only a pawnbroker or insurance adjuster could appreciate, but overall showing the seizure of the *Belle Maltaise* to have been quite a boon for the Holy Faith Army. The inventory concluded by reporting that "all the silver and golden coins were put inside a striped box . . . made stronger with a cord and sealed with Spanish wax."

A subsequent order explicitly authorized the release of "Deodato Dolomieu," identified as a "member of almost all the European Academies and Professor of Natural History in Paris." Sadly, Dolomieu's fate was neither to be set free nor to stay imprisoned with Dumas and Manscourt in Taranto. His arrival there had been discovered by some Sicilian Knights of Malta, bitter at Dolomieu's role in persuading them to surrender their fortress island to Napoleon. Despite the fact that he had not intended to betray the Knights, they blamed him for collaborating in Napoleon's double-dealing. An international "republic of letters" mobilized on Dolomieu's behalf. Pleas for the scientist's release came from every nation in Europe including Great Britain. A letter from famed British explorer and botanist Joseph Banks to the British consul in Naples evokes the ferment: "You have no idea how much sensation his confinement has made in the Literary world here, and how anxious men of Science feel in all parts of Europe for his Liberation." From Egypt Conté and two other savants wrote a letter on behalf of the Institute pleading for Dolomieu's release: "When Citizen Dolomieu signed on, by order of his government, to the expedition, he thought of it as the occasion for a literary voyage. He never could have imagined the invasion of Malta."

But none of this could keep the Knights of Malta from exacting their revenge. Dolomieu was transferred from Taranto's fortress to a dungeon in Messina, Sicily, where he was cruelly kept in solitary confinement for nearly two years. During his imprisonment, using a pen of whittled wood dipped in ink crafted from lamp-smoke, he passed the time writing a treatise on geology in the margins and between the lines of the few books his jailers allowed him. He published it as *Mineralogical Philosophy* after his release, and it is remembered in the annals of science as a landmark work of geology. Dolomieu died a few months after its publication.

General Dumas's imprisonment in the fortress of Taranto would, of course, be used by his son as the basis for the experiences of his falsely imprisoned hero Edmond Dantès in *The Count of Monte Cristo*. Like Dumas, Dantès would disembark from a ship expecting to get on with his life only to find himself trapped, a pawn of others' machinations and schemes that had nothing to do with him, in a medieval fortress-prison with no chance of a trial and no way to communicate his fate to the outside world. But the travails of Dolomieu in the Messina dungeon would be equally crucial to the novel: Dolomieu would become the Abbé Faria, the genius-of-all-trades who tunnels into Edmond's cell by mistake and befriends him. The Abbé teaches Edmond the secrets of science, philosophy, religion, and fencing, and gives him the map to the treasure that will be his fortune.

Like Dolomieu, Faria keeps his spirits up by composing his academic masterpiece in charcoal on found objects. "When you visit my cell, my young friend," Faria tells Edmond, "I will show you an entire work, the fruits of the thoughts and reflections of my whole life . . . I little [imagined] at the time that they would be arranged in order within the walls of the Château d'If." He writes part of his treatise on one of his shirts, and for a pencil uses a piece of wood covered with soot that has been "dissolved with a portion of the wine brought to me every Sunday; and I assure you a better ink cannot be desired. For very important notes, for which closer attention is required, I have pricked one of my fingers, and written the facts claiming notice in blood."

＞－＜

IN the archives of the city of Taranto, I found a document dated May 8, 1799, specifying that Dumas and Manscourt would be locked in the Taranto fortress until such time as they could be turned over "to His Eminence Cardinal D. Fabrizio Ruffo, servant of His Majesty Ferdinand IV, may God bless Him always."

The order remanding Dumas and Manscourt to indefinite detention without trial was penned in the typical, elaborate eighteenth-century latticework of blue ink swirls and dips and dots. But following the trail of General Dumas had by then definitively cured me of seeing any romantic associations between fine quill penmanship and a sense of humanity.

The order went on for seven pages, outlining the directive from the "Commander of the Fifth and Sixth divisions of the Christian troops of the Kingdom of Naples"—the Holy Faith Army—that the two French generals be handed over to the "Illustrious Knight, Sir Giambattista Teroni, Military Commander of the Royal Fortress." The document was witnessed by a medieval-sounding litany of local nobles, but there were also non-noble witnesses, like a local real-estate attorney.

All these people confirmed that, as of May 13, the prisoners were in good condition, but since there was nowhere else in Taranto they could be safely put, they would be "kept in the fortress tower . . . well guarded, together with one of their servants, also French, who has been vouchsafed to serve them." (Even the most malicious jailer, especially if he worked for the forces of Church and Crown, did not think to deprive a gentleman of his lackey.)

So, in full accordance with all this flowing ink, Dumas was moved into a cell in the fortress, where he slept on straw atop a stone bench. In winter, cold and damp would enter through the one tiny barred window. Dumas and Manscourt were kept apart, but they were allowed to meet for certain periods each day under supervision. "We felt the necessity to spend all the money we had left and to sell our belongings to subsidize our insufficient provisions," Dumas would recall, "as we were forced to supply ourselves with everything" to assure their continued survival during imprisonment.

The doors to Dumas's and Manscourt's cells were often left unlocked during those first weeks, for they led into a heavily guarded interior courtyard from which it was judged impossible to escape. When I inspected the cell where Dumas had likely been kept—the Taranto fortress is currently the property of the Italian navy—the distance from that interior courtyard to the outer walls, with a number of wide parapets and guard towers in between, seemed to confirm this judgment.

The cell was bigger than I expected, and that somehow added to the feeling of doom I had inside it, even when I was visiting with a clutch of cheerful, elegant Italian naval officers dressed in their impeccable whites. It could have been a storeroom—indeed, that's how it was currently being used—but the admiral pointed to the small window in one wall with its heavy, corroded iron grating. "That's how we know it was a prison cell." The window looked out onto the interior courtyard, and the only thing Dumas would have seen from it, aside from more gray stones, were his Holy Faith guards, armed with open bottles of red wine and an assortment of plundered weaponry. The admiral had just shown me a pair of corroded buttons festooned with the symbols of the French Republic, from 1796 or '97. "We found these digging in one of the adjoining cells . . . perhaps from Dumas?"

The prisoners were allowed to have wine themselves, if they could pay for it, as well as whatever spirits their guards happened upon. Their food was irregular, often consisting of no more than biscuits, though once a week they got local fish. Everything depended on the mood of the jailers. The prisoners were sometimes allowed to take baths, in an old metal tub.

They were permitted one constitutional around the courtyard each day, so long as they stayed within a demarcated area of thirty square yards. This "promenade" was crucial to General Dumas, the athlete and outdoorsman, for keeping up some semblance of psychological, if not physical, well-being. But what really kept his mind together was the thought that he would awaken from this nightmare, that the surreal misunderstanding would be cleared up and he would be placed on a fast ship back to Toulon, where he would find a good mount to take him across France to Villers-Cotterêts and his family.

Whenever the jailer brought his food, Dumas demanded to see the governor of the fortress. The Marquis de la Schiava had not yet visited his high-value prisoners. Dumas knew there must be a reason. Perhaps the cardinal had sent word that he and Manscourt were to be kept incommunicado.

Dumas's jailer smiled in what seemed a condescending way—but that may simply have been incredulity at the scope of his prisoner's demands—and said he would make inquiries on Dumas's behalf, through channels, to Ruffo. More than that he could not do. And there would be a certain cost involved, to cover expenses.

General Dumas's son would spend years mulling over his father's predicament in the Taranto fortress—to be imprisoned indefinitely, for unknown

crimes, by men he never met—and reimagining his continual dead-end dia-
logues with his jailer. They expressed the same predicament that would one
day concern Kafka, but these concerns arose eighty years earlier and in a
form one can instantly grasp. In *The Count of Monte Cristo* Edmond entreats
his jailer: "I wish to see the governor."

"I have already told you it was impossible."
"Why so?"
"Because it is not allowed by the rules."
"What is allowed, then?"
"Better fare, if you pay for it, books, and leave to walk about."
"But I wish to see the governor."
"If you bother me by repeating the same thing I will not bring you
any more to eat."
"Well, then," said Edmond, "if you do not, I shall die of famine,
that is all." . . .
As every prisoner is worth sixpence a day to his jailer, he replied in
a more subdued tone:
"What you ask is impossible; but if you are very well behaved you
will be allowed to walk about, and some day you will meet the gover-
nor; and if he chooses to reply, that is his affair."
"But," asked Dantès, "how long shall I have to wait?"
"Ah! A month—six months—a year."
"It is too long a time. I wish to see him at once."
"Ah!" said the jailer, "do not always brood over what is impossible,
or you will be mad in a fortnight."

✦

IN the wild month of April 1799, though, Cardinal Ruffo hardly had time to
consider the fate of his two high-ranking French prisoners. He was busy coor-
dinating an alliance of his Holy Faith Army with the British, the Russians, and
the Turks. British warships occupied Capri and other islands along the Amalfi
coast and blockaded the Bay of Naples, starving the French-backed Parthenopean Republic of supplies. An Ottoman force landed near Brindisi, the main
southern Italian port on the Adriatic, and joined the Holy Faith forces. It did

not escape Ruffo's detractors that the Catholic generalissimo was relying on the help of Protestant, Eastern Orthodox, and Muslim armies to carry on his crusade. But the menace of French ideas made the age-old disputes among religions seem quaint. At a time when all faced the threat of godless liberty, equality, and fraternity, the Holy Faith Army continued to recruit local toughs and brigands as they went.

On June 13, the Holy Faith Army would enter Naples, where it flung itself into an orgy of atrocities. An army of toughs largely recruited from the surrounding countryside joined in what became a rising of the wretched against the educated—a repeat of the murderous autos-da-fé of January, only this time with a true, "religious" army leading them in the pillage.* Ferdinand did not return to Naples himself until July, and even then, once the royal flotilla reached the bay, the king was too scared to disembark. He waited with his court at sea while the semi-official Holy Faith Terror continued on land. The massacres continued sporadically throughout the summer.

▶━◀

MEANWHILE, in Taranto, Generals Dumas and Manscourt learned of the collapse of the Neapolitan republic in the way prisoners often learn of political events: the rules changed.

"A guard came and told us that, now that the republic was gone and the French were out of the Kingdom, we would no longer be leaving our cells for daily promenades," Dumas recalled. "Then workers came later the same day to bolt our doors shut."

But if they were now well and truly prisoners of war, they should be accorded "provisions worthy of prisoners of war and due our rank," protested General Dumas. They should be allowed exercise. There was nowhere to go in the fortress courtyard, so to deny them their daily constitutional was simply abuse.

---

* The Holy Faith Army had many of the worst aspects of the original crusader armies of the twelfth and thirteenth centuries, among them its habit, wherever it went, of murdering Jews. Its excuse was that Jews had supported the establishment of French-style republics, an accusation that was in the main correct. Wherever the French had established republics, whether in Milan, Naples, or Rome, the lot of Jews improved, so they supported the Revolution. Now, wherever the republics fell, persecution of the Jews started up again with new fervor.

"The guards responded to our demands with derision," Dumas recalled. "I will not retrace here the evil and lewd threats of the cowardly soldiers encouraged by their own leaders which maddened us night and day, but I shall make known to the French government the full extent of the abuse that characterized the royal government of Naples and particularly the villains who represented them in Taranto."

If Dumas had been his old self, he might have overwhelmed one of the guards and attempted escape. The Holy Faith soldiers in the fortress were a well-armed but lackadaisical and unprofessional bunch, and the regular garrison of the fortress was even less formidable. Once manned by Swiss mercenaries, in more recent years the Taranto fortress had been staffed by Neapolitan soldiers recovering from wounds, many of them living in the fortress with their families, giving the place half an air of a veterans' home. Was this a force to hold the man who had beaten back the Austrians at the bridge at Clausen? If Dumas could scale an ice cliff to take an enemy redoubt, could he not outwit his guards and rappel down a fortress wall?

But Dumas was not the same man who had fought his way to glory over the past decade. He had left Egypt because he felt his health deteriorating, and after arriving in Taranto he had been hit with "a strange paralysis" in his face. While he was in quarantine, the Taranto authorities had assigned him a doctor, and he had "begun some treatments for it." The doctor continued to see Dumas in his fortress cell. Then on June 16, at ten o' clock in the morning, "having taken a glass of wine and a biscuit in the bath, according to the doctor's orders," Dumas fell to the floor, doubled over in pain.

"CITIZENESS DUMAS . . . IS WORRIED ABOUT THE FATE OF HER HUSBAND"

BY the summer of 1799, Marie-Louise was frantic. With the slowness of communications and the continuing British seizures of the mails, it was usual for her to go many weeks without hearing from her husband. But she had received Alex's letter dated March 1, explaining that he was leaving Egypt and expressing his fervent hope to follow his letter "very closely" into her arms. It had been three months since he had written those words. Even if his ship had been captured by the English, she would have had word by now. Generals of the Republic of France did not simply disappear from the face of the earth.

She wrote to the Ministry of War to see if there had been news of her husband's ship being captured, and though she received no reply, by the end of July Marie-Louise had somehow gotten an idea—perhaps from Dolomieu's friends, who had received letters from him in June—of her husband's plight: that he had been taken prisoner. She reached out to Alex's colleagues, who did what they could to make inquiries.*

The first letter I found was from General Jean-Baptiste Jourdan, who in 1799, having suffered a humiliating defeat by the Austrians, temporarily retired from the army to political life, where he continued to wield considerable influence. Jourdan had served with Dumas in the Army of the North in 1794, and again in the Army of the Rhine in 1795. On July 25, he wrote to the new minister of war, Jean-Baptiste Bernadotte:

---

* It would not be until September 11, nearly six months after the event, that the *Gazette Nationale du Moniteur* published the following item: "General Dumas has been taken by the Neapolitans"—the only published notice I ever found of Dumas's imprisonment.

Citizeness Dumas, the wife of Citizen General Dumas, is worried about the fate of her husband, who was stationed with Citizen General Bonaparte in Egypt, and whom she has heard was obliged to embark back to France. . . . She has heard trustworthy opinions that he was taken prisoner in the Gulf of Taranto and taken to Messina during the month of Germinal. If you have any certain information of his whereabouts, you would please me greatly by passing it on to me.

Kindly make inquiries.

In addition to the appeal through Jourdan, Marie-Louise herself wrote to various figures at the Ministry of War multiple times, including this letter to Minister Bernadotte, sent three weeks later:

Villers-Cotterêts, 24 Thermidor, Year VII [August 11, 1799]
Of the French Republic, one and indivisible
The Citizeness Dumas

To the General Bernadotte, Minister of War:
I had the honor, Citizen Minister, of writing you on the 4th of this month, but having not received your response, I feared my letter may not have reached you. I plead with you, sacrifice a moment of your time to give me information on what has become of my husband.

On 26 Germinal [April 15], I received from him a letter dated the 11th Ventôse [March 1] in which he announced to me that since his health had deteriorated he was coming back to France to recuperate. He left from Alexandria between the 11th and the 17th of Ventôse [March 7] on the ship called the *Belle Maltaise*. . . . From that time on, I have received no news from him and various reports leave me in no doubt that he has been taken prisoner. Everything seems to indicate that he was taken in the Gulf of Taranto and from there conducted to Messina.

I pray you, citizen minister, tell me what you might have heard. . . . The interest that you take in your brothers in arms gives me confidence in the interest you take in my husband. His gratitude as well as mine will equal the important service I await from you.

Salute and respect,
Wife Dumas

Bernadotte was a republican general like her husband and Marie-Louise had reason to think he would help her. But as minister of war, Bernadotte had other things to worry about.

In the summer of 1799, France, its allies, and its satellites were under siege by a new coalition of powers bent on reversing all the gains of seven years of hard-fought revolutionary war: England, Russia, Austria, Portugal, Turkey, and Naples. After sinking the French fleet the summer before at Aboukir Bay, the British—with the help of the Turks—had pinned down the leading divisions of the French army in the Middle East.

Now, in the heartland of the pan-European republican revolution, France's "sister republics" in Italy were falling like dominoes. The debacle in Naples had been followed by routs in the north, where the Austrians and the Russians, bankrolled by British gold, attacked the French everywhere. The republics that Dumas and his comrades had fought for over a year to create fell in a matter of weeks. The Cisalpine Republic was toppled in April 1799, and at the end of that month, the Austrians occupied Milan. The Italian patriots proved unable to defend themselves and, as often as not, hampered their own defense because they chafed under French occupation, finding it unworthy of their new revolutionary ideals. Bloody massacres of French-friendly patriots took place in Verona and other northern Italian cities, especially in Tuscany, where republican symbols were smashed and the trees of liberty were used to string up *Giacobini*. In Siena the counterrevolutionaries massacred the Jews and, everywhere, they reestablished the Jewish ghettos—whose dismantling they had seen as a key symbol of French liberal perdition. Most often, however, pro-French northern Italy collapsed as a result of Austrian—and now also Russian—invasion. The old powers of Europe were on the march again.

With a significant element of the French military still in the Middle East, it took the Austrians only three weeks to recapture the fortress city that had taken Dumas and his comrades nine months of siege fighting to secure: the French surrendered Mantua on July 28. After the battle the Austrians took the entire French general staff in the region hostage. It was a total reversal of the glorious campaign of 1797. Dumas's former commander and comrade General Joubert was appointed general-in-chief of the French Army of Italy, but he was killed at his first engagement, the Battle of Novi, on August 15. The Republic of Rome fell on September 30.

The nation that had so recently spread its revolution to all the corners of Europe stood, once again, on the verge of invasion and defeat. It was hardly surprising, then, that General Bernadotte, at the helm of the French War Ministry, could not offer much help to Marie-Louise. He replied, in the last week of August, that the ministry could regrettably provide no "satisfying information on the situation of General Dumas," but that "if I receive any word of him, rest assured I will notify you as soon as I can."

➤—◄

FAILING to get help from the army, Marie-Louise began a letter-writing campaign to influential members of the government. On October 1, she wrote to Paul Barras, the chief political Director and Napoleon's old patron, beseeching him to take an interest in her husband's case. But Barras, who had no time for anything that did not line his pockets, was disinclined to help. He did not much care about republican generals or their fate. Earlier that year he had been engaged in betraying the Republic—helping agents of Louis XVIII, the murdered king's brother, in a conspiracy to get Louis on the throne, help for which Barras was offered twelve million francs.

With the war going badly, the government lost the support of even the corrupt men who ran it. France was again on the verge of economic and social collapse, as factions took to the streets in all parts of the country. Small vagrant armies pillaged and looted in the countryside. Financial mismanagement and military disasters had left Paris unable to sustain law and order, not to mention necessities like hospitals and schools. The men in power were looking for a way out. And in early October, a way out arrived.

When General Bonaparte landed back in France, on October 9, the conqueror of Egypt was just the strongman the government needed. Though Napoleon had left bloody hell behind him, the most recent news that had reached France was of his victory against the Turks at the Battle of Aboukir ten weeks before. Despite its short distance from France, Egypt was on another continent—made more distant by the British naval blockade—and there were few sources of reliable news from there that were not controlled by Napoleon himself. When his ship arrived, the standard quarantine was set up to ensure that neither Napoleon nor his staff were infected with plague, which was known to be devastating the troops who had stayed behind. But the quarantine could not restrain the exuberant crowds who rushed onto his ship crying, "Better the plague than the Austrians!"

Napoleon made a triumphant trip from his port of landing to Paris, where Bishop Talleyrand, always choreographing the show behind the show, arranged meetings between Napoleon and members of the Directory. Meanwhile, Napoleon's younger brother, Lucien Bonaparte, had managed to get himself elected to the Council of Five Hundred—and was even made its president. The maneuver required Lucien to lie about his age—he was only twenty-four, when the official minimum age was thirty—but this paled in comparison with his larger deviousness: he was getting himself elected president of the country's main legislative body and at the same time he was about to help his big brother stage a coup d'état to eliminate it.

The details of the conspiracy were worked out over after-dinner drinks at Lucien Bonaparte's house on November 1. The philosopher Volney, who had done so much to inspire the Egyptian expedition, also appeared as a co-conspirator, as did Napoleon's banker, Collot, who put up the money.

➤◄

MARIE-LOUISE continued writing to everyone she could think of to beg for help in finding her husband. At last, on October 29, she received the first confirmation that Alex was still alive, in a letter from a top government figure:

> I received, Citizeness, your two letters in which you describe your concern for your husband's fate. Believe me when I say I very much share this concern. We have left no stone unturned to discover where he is detained, but we do not [yet] know for sure; however, all reports lead us to believe that he is in Naples or in Sicily. You can rest assured he is alive—none of the information we received about him leaves us in any doubt of this. You can also believe that we will use the most suitable means to assuage your concern that he be exchanged. I pray you to rest assured that I will take the greatest care to inform you as soon as I have more news.
>
>   Salute and fraternity,
>   Moulin

Marie-Louise was lucky to get this news, as Moulin (and the rest of the government) would be deposed eleven days later.

That same week she received further details, from the minister of the navy and the colonies, who told her that he had corresponded about General Dumas with the French consul general in Genoa, capital of the recently created Republic of Liguria.* The consul had confirmed that her husband had been "taken prisoner of war by the Neapolitans," and the minister was opening up channels with Spain in order to get Dumas further news from his family. The minister promised "to call on the Spanish government to free your husband." (The reason for pressing Spain rather than the Kingdom of Naples directly was that the Kingdom of Naples had no diplomatic relations with France at this point.) "I hope, Citizeness, that this step will meet with some success," the minister concluded. But events later that week would distract everyone from all such business.

On November 9, 1799, Police Minister Joseph Fouché's men posted a proclamation from Napoleon on walls throughout Paris: "Under the present special circumstances, the Council of Five Hundred needs the unanimous support and trust of all patriots. Rally round it, that is the way to place the republic on a foundation of civil liberty, domestic happiness, victory, and peace." The members of the Five Hundred were woken up early the next morning, at their homes, and told that a plot was under way against the Republic and that they needed to assemble immediately in a special session; they were warned not to meet in Paris but to take immediate measures to move out of the city to a safe place. This place was the old Palace of Saint-Cloud, six miles outside the capital, where the members could be better "protected."

On the cold, gray Sunday of November 10, at dawn, Napoleon ordered five thousand troops to surround the Palace of Saint-Cloud Orangerie, where the Five Hundred had gathered. At first, things did not go smoothly. When Napoleon tried making an appearance in the Orangerie, the tricked legislators—all clad in their official uniforms of red togas, worn over their regular clothes, and tricolor scarves—began shouting.

---

*After the reversals of the past months, the Ligurian Republic, a tiny strip along the coast, was the sole outpost of republican government left in Italy. Hence, it was the only place left in Italy that *had* a French consul.

"Down with the dictator!" Napoleon, who had little experience of civilian politics and lost his cool, shouted back: "You are sitting on a volcano!" He found himself booed, showered with curses, and even spat on. "Down with the dictator! Down with the tyrant!" Someone grabbed Napoleon's collar and shook him. The Council members called for a motion to "outlaw" General Bonaparte, which could have been tantamount to a death sentence.

The day was saved for Napoleon by Lucien, the underage president of the Five Hundred. Seeing his fellow deputies turn violently against his brother, he turned the accusations of usurping democracy back on them: "There is no liberty left in here," he cried, taking off the red toga he wore over his suit and placing it on the podium. "Your President, in a sign of public mourning, is abandoning the symbols of the popular magistracy." With that, Lucien walked out of the hall and into the courtyard, along with his brother, where they both mounted horses. From horseback, Lucien delivered a speech to the troops in which he announced that "audacious brigands, who are doubtless inspired by the fatal genius of the English government, have risen in rebellion against the Council." He called on the troops, in the name of his brother, to liberate the Council from these brigands and to expel them from the chamber— "so that, protected against daggers by bayonets, we might be able to deliberate on the fate of the Republic."

Napoleon attempted to clarify things for the soldiers in case his younger brother's speech had been too subtle: "If anyone resists, kill, kill, kill! Follow me, I am the god of battles!" At this point Lucien supposedly told his brother, sotto voce, that he should hold his tongue because he was in Paris, not Egypt. "You're not talking to your Mamelukes!" And then he performed his most flamboyant and effective gesture of the coup, grabbing Napoleon's sword from its scabbard and pointing it at his brother's chest. "I swear that I will stab my own brother in the heart if he ever attempts anything against the liberty of Frenchmen!" At this point, General Murat, who in Egypt had griped about Napoleon's despotism with his comrade General Dumas, now did what needed to be done to inspire the cavalry to subvert the democratic order. He reared his horse and waved his saber and shouted *"Vive le général! Vive le président!"* and then he pointed at the doors of the Orangerie and shouted "Charge!" The invasion of the hall by armed cavalry made an impression on France's legislators, who ran to the windows and began jumping out to escape.*

That night a group of allied deputies stayed up late with the plotters, working by candlelight, taking votes and drafting papers, to make it all legal. By 3 a.m. it was finished. France had a new government, with Napoleon appointed first consul at the head of a ruling body of three consuls. Naturally, the other two would do his bidding. "Consul" was an evocation of Rome, and everyone could see that, as in Rome, one Caesar had emerged supreme.

The fate of everything and everyone in Europe would soon hang on the whim of this dictator in a tricolor sash. The decade of French republicanism and democracy—the age of seemingly infinite emancipation, with all its expansive horrors and hopes—was over.

→←

SIX days after the coup, Marie-Louise received a tortuously bureaucratic letter from her husband's old comrade Murat, now a rising star in the new order:

At the General Headquarters in Paris, on 25 Brumaire, Year VIII [November 16, 1799] of the French Republic, Cavalry Division

Joachim Murat, General of Division

To the Citizeness Dumas—Villers-Cotterêts
Madame, to address the concerns contained in the letter that you did me the honor of sending me on the 15th of this month, I had Citizen Beaumont, my aide-de-camp, look into the information in which you were interested. It shows that according to the report issued by the Offices of the Ministry of Foreign Affairs, on 15 Fructidor [September 1], Citizen Berthelin, ambassador in Rome, wrote to Citizen Belleville, Consul General in Genoa, and gave him the responsibility

---

* Among the officers leading the cavalry into the hall would likely have been the French army's second-highest-ranking man of color after General Dumas: the Cuban-born former slave Joseph "Hercules" Dominguez, who had served Napoleon in Italy and Egypt.

of informing the ministers of Foreign Affairs and of the Navy that Generals Dumas and Manscourt were held prisoner in Taranto, having been held by Cardinal Ruffo in exchange for various Neapolitan demands. Citizen Belleville fulfilled his intentions, and the Ministry of Foreign Affairs, thinking that your husband had been released, had not thought it necessary to take care of. Informed by me to the contrary, he is about to speak to the ministry of Spain and to the general-in-chief leading the Army of Italy so that they may call for his release. I am delighted, Madam, that this opportunity provides me with the advantage of assuring you that I am entirely devoted to you.

Your fellow citizen

J. Murat

A few years later Napoleon would crown Murat the king of Naples, enthroning him along with his wife, Napoleon's younger sister Caroline. Together, they would establish a hedonistic Napoleonic court in the very place that had caused his old friend Dumas so much misery.

THE DUNGEON

DUMAS lay doubled up on the damp stones, the sounds of the sea and the guards' shouting on the towers coming in through the high window. The wooden doors to the courtyard were not locked, but they were heavy, and he was in too much pain and too weak to reach them or to cry out. His servant eventually discovered him lying there in darkness, half delirious with pain and lying in a puddle of vomit. His white military breeches were soiled and a sheen of sweat covered his skin. The servant ran to find General Manscourt, who was soon at Dumas's side. Manscourt then went to the governor of the fortress and begged him to bring a doctor urgently, saying he feared for Dumas's life.

While they waited for the doctor, Manscourt and the servant struggled to help Dumas. On his whispered instructions, the servant gave him some milk from a little goat that Dumas had brought with him from Egypt. At first he seemed to tolerate it fairly well, but he soon doubled over in even fiercer pain.

When he recovered enough to sit up, the servant fed Dumas spoonfuls of olive oil mixed with lemon juice and gave him "over forty enemas in three hours," both widely used remedies for parasitic worms in the eighteenth century that Dumas would later credit with saving his life.*

All the while, they waited for the doctor who had supposedly been summoned. Hours passed. The governor eventually informed them "with

---

*Enemas are one of the most common remedies in history, going back to ancient Egypt. In the seventeenth century Louis XIV, who was known to have received thousands of them, made the procedure an everyday ritual of civilized hygiene. Enema syringes featured prominently in Molière's comedies, and by the eve of the nineteenth century "every household had an enema stool by the fireside, where it was used with complete openness by everyone in turn."

indifference" that the doctor was in the countryside and would not be back for some time.

The doctor finally arrived, accompanied by an entourage of Holy Faith officials and escorted by twelve armed soldiers. General Manscourt "could not help but declare his indignation" and demanded that everyone leave the room. Some of the soldiers did leave, and the physician approached. Dumas recognized the man who had been treating him over the past week for the paralysis in his cheeks.

"Upon seeing me the doctor became as pale as death," Dumas recalled. He noticed a look of embarrassment on the man's face, as if he hadn't expected to be confronting this particular patient alive again. Dumas then became convinced that the doctor "was the instrument of the crime, if not the author."

The doctor told Dumas to remain lying down and to drink icy cold water, and hastily left. The servant prepared a glass, but "the little that I took of the iced drink made me feel like I would die if I went on, so I abandoned it to take up my previous treatments once again." More lemon juice, olive oil, and enemas. The doctor returned some time later and prescribed a series of regimens that included blistering and "ear injections that [for a time] caused complete deafness" (again, standard practices of the era, though medical research had already shown by the 1770s that ear injections caused deafness).

His medical treatment over the following two weeks, Dumas would reflect, "left me in no doubt that they intended to poison me to death." General Manscourt, too, experienced a sudden and frightening ailment—in his case in the form of rapidly escalating violent headaches that "reached the point of attacking his brain," as General Dumas later put it—and "he could be brought out of that state only by means of a quick bloodletting and a great number of enemas and drinks that I made him myself before our own eyes" (a precaution to make sure they would not be poisoned).

＞—＜

DUMAS had no doubt the doctor was trying to kill them both by every means at his disposal, except the obvious one of slitting their throats. But it is not so easy to determine whether the doctor's "perverse regimens" should be attributed to evil intentions or simply standard medical practice of the time. After all, Dumas attributed his own salvation to the "forty enemas in three hours." Though the scientific revolution of the eighteenth century had created great interest in the natural sciences and in medicine, this had not yet translated into an understanding of disease. (Some doctors even argued that the very qualities of the Enlightenment itself—urbanity, refined manners, too much reading and introspection—caused disease.) Instead an individual's constitutional idiosyncrasies were minutely scrutinized, so a doctor could develop a highly personalized cure to treat the patient more than the disease. It was the ultimate in "personal attention" from a primary care provider—though not perhaps with the benefits we now assume come from that relationship. Molière's observation from the previous century still applied: "Nearly all men die of their remedies and not of their illnesses."

Two of the doctors who visited Dumas believed that his symptoms—the loss of hearing and vision, the paralysis in his face, the excruciating stomach pain—were signs of melancholia (i.e., depression). Reading this diagnosis in their reports, I thought, "How modern!" But in fact there was a well-established belief in the eighteenth century that depression was the cause of everything from infections to heart disease and cancer.

Although the scientific revolution of the seventeenth century had officially repudiated it, the age-old theory of humors still formed the basis of medical common sense in the late eighteenth century. In the humoral paradigm, there was a continuum between health and illness on which each individual found him- or herself at any given time. At the bottom of every person's condition lay the balance among his or her humors—mysterious bodily substances that determined well-being: too much of one or too little of another caused either disease or the "putrefaction" of the entire organism. Many treatments of the age—sweating, purging, bleeding, emesis—were designed around this basic premise.

Aside from his declining physical condition, Dumas found what he thought was more evidence that his doctor was trying to do him in: it came to light one afternoon when he was taking a bath and the physician visited him for a chat while he sat naked in the tub. The doctor said he wanted to speak to General Dumas while they had absolute privacy, "to tell me that he was sure that we were going to have everything stolen, like our compatriots [e.g., Dolomieu before his departure for Messina], and he wanted us to entrust him with our most valuable remaining things to be returned to us on our departure. I noted from my bath that this man was not avoiding being seen or heard by an artilleryman named Samarrou." The doctor made no real effort at secrecy, Dumas wrote, "despite his air of trying to establish conspiracy between us." (Dumas's description of his captivity feels almost hallucinatory at this point, and it is unclear what he thought the conspiracy was about, except keeping him in a state of weakness and dependency that he was determined to avoid.)

Though he did not pinpoint any sort of poison in his own food or medicine, Dumas believed he'd found the source of Manscourt's brain malady one day when he examined his snuffbox: someone appeared to have mixed a kind of metallic powder into the snuff which was "so corrosive that it had eaten several holes in the box."

The final event that made Dumas suspect the doctor was, ironically, that a few days later the doctor himself suddenly dropped dead. From this Dumas concluded that the doctor had been poisoned by the "very same authors of my poisoning" and that it had been "without doubt a precaution to avoid it going public."

Dumas's persistent fretting over his failing health and the treatment he received—he devotes dozens of pages in his report to the tragicomedy of the long gaps between doctors' visits and the bloody and ineffective "cures" when they did show up—compounded his paranoia that he was being assassinated by degrees by unknown authors for unknown reasons. Adding to his grim mood, the day after the doctor's sudden death Dumas woke to find his goat strangled—an accident, said the guards, though Dumas was certain "the animal was killed in the fear that it could still be useful to me."

—◄

OVER the next two months, whether or not he was being poisoned, the conditions in the damp fortress took a further toll on Dumas's health. He wrote letters to the French government, to the king of Naples, and home to Marie-Louise and his little Louise Alexandrine. The prison governor evidently took the letters, but there is no evidence that they were ever delivered (he mentioned these lost letters in a later missive). Dumas became blind in one eye, deaf in one ear, and continued to suffer from facial paralysis.

Finally Dumas had no choice but to ask for medical attention once again, as hazardous as that must have seemed. But this time he was sent a doctor who spoke French fluently and who told him frankly how harmful his previous treatments had been; he prescribed entirely new ones. Every doctor measured an individual's humoral imbalance differently, after all. This doctor diagnosed Dumas's illness as being caused chiefly by melancholia and prescribed "injections into my ears," a powder blown into his eyes, and half an ounce of cream of tartar, "a regimen that far from relieving me only aggravated the terrible state of my stomach."

But this doctor was very friendly, and "visited me regularly enough for a month and took all opportunities to lead into political conversation by affecting a lot of patriotism and friendship for the French in order to win my trust." The chance to hear news and opinions in his native language was a precious thing for a man in captivity far from home. Along the way, his deafness was alleviated. But suddenly one day the governor ordered that the doctor no longer come because he might inadvertently disclose secrets, and because the jailers could not monitor their conversations since they did not speak French. Dumas suspected a new trick, one in which the doctor had been a willing participant: to make him drop his guard and develop an attachment—then to remove it and further break his will.

The governor later relented, but on two conditions: the doctor must not communicate with Dumas in his native tongue, and the governor himself must be present during examinations. When the doctor arrived, Dumas heard him admonished icily by the governor before the cell door was unbolted: " 'You are going to see your General Dumas. If you say one sole French word you are lost. You see this cell door? It will open and close on you for the last time.' " A French surgeon who accompanied them got the same warning.

"Everyone entered the room and crowded around me," Dumas wrote. "I tried to make eye contact with the surgeon," but he looked away. "I spoke to the doctor, but he remained silent." After a brief discussion in which the French surgeon was both intimidated by the governor's threats and hobbled by his difficulty understanding the Italian language, he

> recommended that I return to my original course of treatment, adding new blistering on the arms and the nape of the neck and behind both cars—this violent regimen, more than all the other pernicious drugs

made up in pills, made such ravages upon me that over the month I followed it I endured perpetual insomnia and an abundant and continuous
loss of sperm, resulting in the total slackening of all parts of my body
and an affliction like that of a man not far from death.*

—•—

AT this point, Dumas received a message from the world outside the dungeon that probably saved his life. The Friends of the French at Taranto—the
local republican patriot underground—"knowing the traumas I'd suffered
secretly passed me two volumes of *The Country Doctor* by Tissot." (In fact,
Tissot never published a book with this title; the book was most likely Tissot's *Health Advice for the Common People*, published in two volumes, with
eleven editions between 1761 and 1792.)

Just as it is hard to overstate the power of communication from the outside
world on a prisoner, it is hard to convey the power of a volume of Tissot for
a sick man in 1799. Samuel-Auguste Tissot was a lion of eighteenth-century
medicine—the Louis Pasteur of humoral imbalance. Published over a
thirty-year period from the 1750s to the 1780s, Tissot's works were used by
doctors, surgeons, midwives, healers of all sorts, and patients.† In a world in
which a printed book was a valuable object, Dumas was suddenly holding the
full force of contemporary medical knowledge in his hand. Someone on the
outside wanted him to live!

Paging feverishly through his Tissot, Dumas came across something
even more remarkable: the article on poison was marked and underlined. It
was a message, and it confirmed all his suspicions. From then on, Dumas
continued to accept all the pills the doctor gave him, but he only pretended to

---

* The sperm escaping Dumas's body at an "abundant and continuous" rate was a classic symptom of fatal disease in the eighteenth century. In the world of humoral medicine, sperm was much more than what we think it to be today, though it was also that.
Sperm was believed to be a "nervous fluid" that flowed from head to toe.

† Tissot professed that the most surefire way to lose your life force was the obvious one.
His 1758 book on sperm conservation—*Onanism: A Treatise on the Diseases Produced by
Masturbation*—argued that semen loss via masturbation led to disease and death. Tissot's
revelations about masturbation and illness—especially his "proof" that the act caused
blindness—formed mainstream medical opinion on the subject until Kinsey's *Sexual Behavior in the Human Male* overturned him in 1948.

take them. Instead, he put them aside, carefully wrapped, planning to have them analyzed in the future. "I was quite pleased to have some material evidence of the villainy of the agents of the king of Naples," Dumas wrote. He now had a new will to live, to leave the fortress of Taranto alive, hoping the pills would "one day demonstrate to the French government all the darkness of my murderers."

➤—◄

A few nights later another package came from the underground Friends of the French—this one arriving through the window of Dumas's cell on a string that lowered it to the floor. It was a large chunk of chocolate, wrapped in plain paper, along with some kind of medicinal herb. Chocolate was not a mere treat in those days—like sugar, it was one of the wonder drugs in the eighteenth-century arsenal. The herb turned out to be cinchona, the bark of a tropical tree containing quinine, considered to have great healing properties for fevers and nervous conditions.

"I owe a marked improvement," Dumas wrote, "to the cinchona and the chocolate that the humane patriots clandestinely passed me by means of a string and a hook during the night." He added, however, that these "courteous acts" could not prevent his becoming deaf in the left ear, paralyzed in the right cheek, from having his right eye practically lost, and from suffering terrible headaches and permanent buzzing in the ears.

The year 1800 brought new, pragmatic reasons to show leniency toward French prisoners, for by that summer everyone in Taranto—prisoners, guards, Holy Faith Army, and secret republicans alike—must have known something of the great events then going on in the north, where the French had launched a second invasion of Italy. Napoleon had left the government in Paris to personally lead the campaign. As if atoning for the tawdriness of his coup d'état and his assumption of dictatorial powers, the first consul had mounted his horse and led his armies through the Saint Bernard Pass, the scene of one of Dumas's greatest military triumphs, and down again into the Italian plain. (Actually, Napoleon crossed the Alps on a mule, though his propaganda experts carefully disguised the fact.)

The second Italian campaign, capped by a magnificent victory over the

Austrians at Marengo on June 14, utterly reversed the French rout of 1799. By the fall, Italy seemed once again on its way to becoming the laboratory of revolutionary nation-building, the main outpost for "French ideas" beyond France's borders. Once more the Italians were raising all their various tricolor flags and planting trees of liberty. It is impossible to know for sure how much of this news was reaching the prisoners. But Dumas's captors no doubt sensed that the balance of power was shifting beneath their feet and that tricolor flags might soon be the order of the day in Taranto as well.

Dumas learned that he and Manscourt and some other prisoners were to be moved from Taranto to another fortress—at Brindisi, on the Adriatic. He was informed that the move concealed an assassination plot: "only on the day of the transfer did some people come by our window, and from their gestures we understood that we were to be torn from Taranto and killed en route." That night, around 11 p.m., the bolts on his door were drawn and the Marquis de la Schiava (president of the province of Lecce) "burst into our rooms" followed by men armed with swords and daggers. They told the prisoners that they were leaving for Brindisi and that Dumas was to pack his things immediately. The manner of the marquis's entry—in the dead of night, with so many armed men—left Dumas in no doubt about his real intentions. "I expressed my strong disapproval of such an indecent manner to the marquis at the top of my voice," Dumas wrote. "The marquis responded by drawing his sword."

Dumas at that point grabbed his old walking stick, the closest thing to a weapon in the cell, and brandished it against the marquis's sword and all the other steel in the room. He did not think much of his chances for success, but he was prepared to make a stand, no matter how futile. Dumas must have retained something of his old talent for intimidating opponents. Judging from a subsequent written complaint from "the Ministry of State and War" about Dumas's "recklessness" and "threatening behavior" when the guards came to get him, his militant defense was apparently effective. After a brief standoff, the guards retreated from the cell.

At this point Dumas's hallucinatory fury clearly made him suspect only the worst from his captors. But in fact when he and Manscourt were transferred to a fortress in Brindisi, in September 1800—about a day's ride away—far from being killed en route, their situation actually improved dramatically. In this fortress overlooking the Adriatic, Dumas fell into regular conversations with a priest. The man's name was Bonaventura Certezza, and apparently he and Dumas developed a real friendship. The only record that survives is a poignant letter the priest wrote to Dumas after he'd gotten out of prison: "Let it be known to you, my dearest General, that I have always kept and always will keep my feelings [of esteem for you] alive in my soul and [they] obligate me to pay my respect to you forever. In fact, I have left no stone unturned to try and obtain news of you. I know that hearing praise annoys you, but, knowing your warm heart, I dare to speak this way. I wish I could embrace you, damned distance, I speak with my heart on my sleeve." The priest promises not to talk so much if Dumas comes to visit him at his house, where he is always welcome.

There is far more evidence of Dumas's amusing if testy relationship with a prison officer named Giovanni Bianchi, who was a kind of regional commander of all the southern Neapolitan prison fortresses. They corresponded constantly starting in September 1800, even though Bianchi appears to have been based in the Brindisi fortress itself, at least much of the time. (Manscourt was presumably accorded similarly courteous treatment, but he largely drops out of Dumas's account until after they were liberated.) Bianchi's letters, elegantly addressed to "Gentlemen, French Generals, Prisoners in the Fort by the sea," relay the news that Dumas's requests for food, clothing, and basic supplies—an iron cooking pot, for example, which was the subject of a tortuously minute exchange—were now being passed up the chain of command, all the way to King Ferdinand himself. Good news, Bianchi informs him: the king has approved! That a request for a cooking pot could be passed up the chain of command to the king tells one everything one needs to know about the Kingdom of Naples . . . except perhaps for the important detail that, as Bianchi regrets to inform Dumas, it would be "some time" before the king's approval could be acted on "at the local level." Hence, still no cooking pot.

Thus began a picayune exchange of letters in which Bianchi asks the general for things like sketches of his shoes and precise quantities of kindling to be used per day. (This is the first mention that the prisoners were allowed to make fires.) I imagine prisoner and jailer, at opposite corners of this medieval fortress, each at a wooden table—one huge and polished, the other small and rough—dipping his quill into ink and preparing his requests or excuses in equally elaborate swirls.

On October 31, 1800, Bianchi asks Dumas to verify "the number of jackets, shoes, shirts and other items you need, with the corresponding prices. I ask that you send [the list] to me immediately so that it can be verified by the Kingdom's Ministry of Finance." Bianchi arranged for shoemakers and tailors to come to the prison, as well as carpenters, though Dumas had to continue to find things to trade or sell to pay for these services. He also had to pay for food and for wood to burn in his stove.

Gradually, Bianchi began offering to provide basic services to Dumas without receiving payment, and even offering to reimburse Dumas for previous outlays. In a letter dated January 8, 1801, in which Bianchi announces that he has decided to reimburse Dumas "7 ducats and 90 grani" for "the room and board of yourself and your officials," Bianchi asks for a forwarding address to send the payment to: a sign that at this point the jailer knew, at least in principle, that his prisoner's release was imminent.

On January 22, 1801, Bianchi sent an extraordinary letter to Dumas. In it, he explains that the general's attack on the Marquis de la Schiava has caused a scandal in court—that the king himself is outraged enough that he has written a memo about it "by his own Royal hand" to the kingdom's highest-ranking army officer. Bianchi describes King Ferdinand's condemning Dumas's "uncooperative and threatening behavior" in choosing to attack the marquis with a cane. The king has demanded that Dumas and Manscourt be placed in solitary confinement, and has complained that the authorities have been too lenient with the French generals. But what made Bianchi's letter remarkable was that he states all this—and quotes extensively from King Ferdinand's memo—before revealing that he will *ignore* the order to place the generals in solitary. He will go "against the Orders of My King," he says, because he has come to see Dumas and his companion as good men.

Reading this flowery document from the dawn of the nineteenth century, I was reminded of countless World War II movies I saw growing up, where the "good" Luftwaffe commandant decides to behave decently toward his American or British prisoners despite orders from Nazi superiors to mistreat them. Was Bianchi partly motivated by a kind of southern Italian enjoyment of defying authority—of thumbing his nose at his fancy-pants boss from here in his drafty provincial fortress, where he lacked the resources to authorize a batch of kindling without receiving money from divisional headquarters? But why *did* Bianchi feel free to write the whole thing down—to express his defiance of the king in writing? Was it a deliberate act taken in the hope that it would be read—because Bianchi, knowing of the French invasion, assumed that in a matter of weeks he might well have a French superior officer and a French government to report to, rather than a royal highness in Palermo? Reading his letters, I began to suspect that Giovanni Bianchi was not only anticipating the French conquest of his kingdom but positively hoping for it. Perhaps Dumas's jailer was a secret *Giacobino,* who liked the French prisoners because he liked France and the ideals of the Revolution.

▸◂

IN March 1801, Dumas learned of plans to repatriate him and Manscourt by boat via Ancona, a city on the Adriatic coast, north of Rome. But they remained wary. "We understood," Dumas wrote, "that they wanted to deliver us to the English or the Barbary pirates." He asked Bianchi to inform his superiors of the high "imprudence of exposing us on an ocean covered with enemy ships."

Bianchi attempted to reassure Dumas, in a string of letters that had an almost slapstick obsequiousness, closing with phrases like "I'm always at your disposal for your commands" and "I remain always eager to serve you." This made Dumas even more suspicious. There was really nothing for the dear general to worry about, Bianchi replied—the boats sail along the coast and, in case of any untoward event, they would easily find mooring. Now he wanted to take the opportunity to send Dumas, for his approval, some "fabric samples" for his new post-prison uniform—would a nice, medium-weight blue wool "suffice for the needs of your officials?" Bianchi inquires. "Please pray let me know what would be to your liking."

Bianchi wrote his prisoner on the subject of his confiscated property, specifically the general's weapons and equipment that had been taken in the first months of his imprisonment. But Dumas dismissed all these bureaucratic overtures as the machinations of a cowardly enemy, now squirming in fear at the approach of French justice. Bianchi particularly infuriated Dumas when he wrote to apologize that the general's "double-barreled rifle . . . was thrown into the sea. . . . Nevertheless, I shall do my utmost and, should I succeed in finding it, it shall be my pleasure to have it sent to you."

In his relentless campaign of flattery, Giovanni Bianchi always returned to his favorite subject—clothes. He regrets deeply that it has been impossible to procure the sort of hat the general prefers, but he can produce another that is both "safer and more comfortable" for sea travel. He assures Dumas that he will send men to show him the alternate hat style "immediately"—for surely Dumas, after surviving eighteen months of mistreatment and poisoning in a dungeon cell, would not want to go another day worrying about his choice of hat styles. Bianchi "begs" the general to "get some air" and to "do it without fear." In response to Dumas's one serious sartorial query, Bianchi reassured the republican general that of course he should also feel free "to wear the cockade of your nation" within the fortress walls—"the same way," Bianchi adds, "that our people wear our cockade." (Cardinal Ruffo had created a cockade especially for the Holy Faith Army: pure white set in a crucifix.)

At the end of December 1800, with everyone from the Austrian emperor to the pope making peace deals with Napoleon, King Ferdinand of Naples suddenly found himself the lone defender against the resurgent French colossus in Italy. Napoleon sent Dumas's fellow cavalry general, the flamboyant Murat, to lead an army south against Naples. It did not take Ferdinand long to begin negotiating his surrender in the face of the approaching French forces: his subjects did not call him *Il re Gambalesta*—loosely, "King Walkaway"—for nothing.

In February 1801, General Murat took pleasure in informing Ferdinand's emissary that, as part of the terms of surrender, all French prisoners of war held anywhere in the kingdom must be freed immediately. From the letters he had received from Marie-Louise, as well as orders from the minister of war, Murat knew that this last stipulation would deliver his old comrade-in-arms Alex Dumas.

King Ferdinand quickly agreed to this condition, but before Murat could celebrate a successful armistice, Napoleon ordered Murat to renege on those terms. He added a new condition, requiring Ferdinand to accept French occupation of the Gulf of Taranto. Napoleon hoped to use that area as a base from which to launch a new campaign to retake Egypt, then in the midst of falling to the British and the Turks. Ferdinand again quickly agreed, and Murat's army marched right into Naples without firing a shot. If Dumas had only known this news—that his old comrade was riding into the land of his oppressors!

He must have learned it soon enough. By the end of March, Dumas was on a ship bound for the French base at Ancona, wearing a freshly made light wool waistcoat, new shirt, socks and shoes, and a sharp-looking new hat. Still, at thirty-nine, he must also have been barely recognizable. In his first weeks out of prison, Dumas was partially blind and deaf, and weakened by malnourishment; he walked with a limp from yet another of his medical treatments—blood-letting that had severed a tendon. He was determined to heal himself, but he swore never to forget any detail of his captivity or of "the most barbaric oppression under heaven, driven by unremitting hatred for all those who call themselves Frenchmen."

➤—◄

THE French commanding officer at Ancona greeted General Dumas warmly and, since there was no formal policy in place for dealing with POWs, gave his battered fellow officer some money out of his own pocket to buy food and basic supplies. On April 13, Dumas wrote to the government: "I have the honor of informing you that we [Manscourt and I] arrived yesterday in this city, with ninety-four [former] prisoners . . . for the most part blind and maimed." When he arrived in Florence, Dumas would compose his remarkable account of his captivity relating all the misadventures that occurred from the moment he left Egypt on the *Belle Maltaise*, the account his son would later draw on for the iconic scenes of human suffering in *The Count of Monte Cristo*.* In his letter to the government, Alex Dumas limited his reflections to a brief mention of "the treatment we have endured from the government of Naples [that] dishonors them in the eyes of humanity and all nations."

That same day, he also wrote Marie-Louise for the first time as a free man. The letter includes a message for Alexandrine Aimée, "if by luck she is still of this world," that he is "bringing various little things for her from Egypt."

---

* The novelist would also reproduce a version of the account in his memoir, but he would soften many of the details of his father's suffering that appear in the original, which I found in the safe, perhaps because they were too difficult or depressing for him to write about. This book is the first to base its recounting of General Dumas's prison experiences on his original statement, rather than on his son's bowdlerized version of it.

Curiously, even after a near shipwreck and two years in captivity he'd somehow managed to hang on to souvenirs for his daughter from the *Expédition d'Égypte.*

In another letter to Marie-Louise from Florence, written two weeks later, he tells of his joy at having received her letters and one from their now eight-year-old daughter, both of which he "has kissed a thousand times":

> It is with deep gratitude and emotion that I realize with what devotion and care you have overseen her education. Such conduct, conduct so worthy of you, makes you dearer and dearer to me, and I am impatient to give you proof of my feelings.

In none of the letters he writes her on his journey homeward—a journey to revolutionary France, the land of opportunity and fraternity in which he once found success, and which he will find no longer exists—does he choose to tell her the details of his ordeal, because, as he writes, "I don't want to bring pain to your heart that is wounded enough by its long privations. I hope to bring your rare, precious spirit the healing balm of my consolation within the month." He closes:

> Adieu, my beloved, you will now and forever be so dear to my heart because misfortunes cannot but draw tighter the bonds that hold us fast to one another. Embrace for me my child, our dear parents, and also all our friends.
>
> Yours without reserve,
>
> Alex Dumas, General of Division

WAIT AND HOPE

"WHAT dark and bloody secrets the future hides from us," Alexandre Dumas would one day write in his memoir, meditating on his father's fate. "When they are revealed, men may realize that it is by the good providence of God they were kept in ignorance of them until the appointed time."

By the time he returned to France, in June of 1801, the Revolution and the nation Alex Dumas loved had declined almost as precipitously as he had. He must have felt like Rip Van Winkle returning from the hills—only Rip Van Winkle had found a king replaced by a revolution, while Dumas found a revolution replaced by a king, of sorts. And it was the same king he had left Egypt to escape. When Dumas arrived on French shores, Napoleon had had over a year to remake France in his image and to turn the gains of the Revolution to his own purposes.

His first step in remaking France had been to make a government. Everything still had to look democratic, because this was the land of the Revolution, and this king still wore red, white, and blue. The idea of "the consuls"—there were three—created the fiction that executive power was still split at the top, as it had been under the Directory and, before that, under the Convention. (Revolutionary France had never tried a simple president or prime minister.) But clothing themselves in the trappings of democracy, dictators may, like drag queens, tend to overdo it, and Napoleon wanted there to be no doubt that his French Republic was more democratic than any before it. Where the Directory had shared power with two legislative bodies, now there would be no fewer than four: the Senate, the Tribunate, the Legislature, and the Council of State. Of course these many checks and balances made the democratic process as dysfunctional as possible. The tribunes were allowed to discuss laws but not to vote on them. The legislators were allowed to vote on laws but not discuss them. The senators were allowed to appoint members to both of those other bodies but could not themselves vote, except that they could vote to annul laws they judged unconstitutional. The Council of State was stacked with Bonaparte's backers and cronies, and though it was the only body to have some real power, it still functioned, in essence, as his advisory board.

On December 15, 1799, just over a month after the coup, Napoleon and his plotters had published the Constitution of the Year VIII, with the following claim in its preamble: "It is founded on the true principles of representative government, on the sacred rights of property, equality and liberty. The powers which it institutes will be strong and stable, as they must be in order to guarantee the rights of the citizens and the interests of the state. Citizens! The Revolution is made fast to the principles which began it; *it is finished.*"*

At that time, the only people who really knew Napoleon Bonaparte—aside from his mother and siblings, who feared him—were his generals, who held him in differing degrees of fear, awe, contempt, and adulation. Most people outside the army command knew him only as a man who could deliver results. There were civilians who had spent time with Napoleon up close and reported some dark quality that belied all the public adoration. "The terror he inspires is inconceivable," Madame de Staël wrote to her father after spending a weekend with him at the estate of his older brother, Joseph. "One has the impression of an impetuous wind blowing about one's ears when one is near that man."

---

* In another faux-democratic sleight of hand that would set a model for the future, Napoleon submitted his personalized constitution to a plebiscite to receive the stamp of popular approval. With his characteristic impatience, he did not wait for the plebiscite's results to be tallied before declaring the new constitution in force; but he would return frequently to the plebiscite ruse whenever he wanted to justify some fundamental change in France's government or law. Even if it was a rubber stamp, it gave him the best excuse for outrageous policy shifts: the people's will. Napoleon had also learned the value of the press during the Italian and Egyptian campaigns. In December 1799, there were seventy-three independent newspapers and journals publishing in Paris, offering a wide opportunity to broadcast critiques of the government. Within less than a month of proclaiming a constitution to "guarantee the rights of the citizens," he had closed sixty of them. The *Moniteur*, the main newspaper of the Revolution since 1789, was allowed to remain as an official mouthpiece of the government.

—◄

DURING Dumas's journey home, Marie-Louise had written him an unusual love letter about the ordeal in the dungeon and how she would overcome it for them both:

> I promise to avenge myself by proving to you that I know how to love,
> and that I have always loved you. You know the price that I still place
> on the possession of your heart and, because it is with me, you should
> never doubt my happiness.

They were finally reunited in Paris at the apartment of Dumas's old friend General Brune. One can only imagine how changed Marie-Louise found her husband, and how hard she must have worked to conceal her reaction. But their mutual happiness and relief can't be doubted. Soon back at home in Villers-Cotterêts, Dumas basked in the love of his family. Although he didn't regain his former vigor, he was soon able to ride again. He began to look forward to rejoining the service and taking up his career where he had left it when he got aboard the *Belle Maltaise* in Egypt.

But Dumas quickly found that there were other obstacles in his way. First of all, he had an urgent need of money. The family had not had an income while he was a prisoner of war, and when he heard that the French government had worked out a reparations deal with the Kingdom of Naples, he assumed his claim would be high on the list. On April 22, 1801, while Dumas was still in Italy, the French ambassador to Naples told Dumas that he was to "receive the sum of 500,000 francs payable by the Court of Naples, as compensation to French citizens who have lost their belongings." The catch was that the money, so the ambassador said, had gone to Paris, and Dumas would have to request it there from the minister of foreign affairs. Dumas would try to pursue that claim, but never received a single franc.

Not only did he get no reply regarding the reparations money, he found that all his letters and inquiries met with stony silence. For Dumas, the most important ministers were those of the military; unfortunately, the new minister of war was none other than his old nemesis General Berthier, who informed him that the consuls had decreed that officers like Dumas were due only two months of active-duty pay no matter how long they were imprisoned. Dumas protested, in a September 1801 letter to Napoleon:

> I hope . . . that you will not allow the man who shared your work and your dangers to languish like a beggar when it is within your power to give him a testimony of the generosity of the nation for which you are responsible.

As important to Dumas as getting his back pay was getting reinstated in the army and gaining a new command. In February 1802, he wrote to "Citizen Minister Berthier": "I have the honor of reminding you of the promise you made to me when I was in Paris, to employ me at something you were working on at the time. I can say, without blushing, that the misfortunes that have so severely tested me must be powerful motives for the government to put me back into active service."

But in the new climate his appeals went nowhere. In the early 1820s a historian still close to the events observed that Dumas "hardly showed himself at the new court, where his political opinions, and everything about him, down to the color of his skin, was out of favor."

＞－＜

WHEN Napoleon seized power, it had been nearly eight years since republican France granted full rights and citizenship to free men of color in the colonies and five years since France had ended slavery. Since 1794, both the French constitution and the Declaration of the Rights of Man and of the Citizen had applied anywhere in the world where the French flag was flown.* It's worth repeating that the greatest emancipation in history had been initiated by the country possessing perhaps the world's most lucrative slave empire.

---

* Though mandated by the 1794 law for all French territories, slavery had been effectively abolished in only three of them: in French Guyana on the northern edge of South America, on the island of Guadeloupe, and above all on Saint-Domingue, whose massive slave insurrection had precipitated French colonial emancipation to begin with. On many other islands—Martinique, Saint-Lucie, Réunion, Île-de-France, and others—the 1794 emancipation had been blocked, either because those places had been under British occupation, or because slaveholders themselves had successfully repulsed the attempt by the distant government in Paris to impose the new law, as happened in France's Indian Ocean colonies.

There were many things wrong with the French Republic at the time of Napoleon's coup, but there was one thing most modern people would see as marvelously right: it offered basic rights and opportunities to people regardless of the color of their skin. For all their faults, the revolutionary French governmental bodies—the legislatures in Paris with their ever-changing names—admitted black and mixed-race representatives among their members as equals. Although the French still referred to black and mixed-race men in their country as "Americans," the American Congress at that time would rarely admit a black person into its presence except to serve refreshments or sweep the floor.

Much support for Napoleon's coup had come from a coalition of slavers and exiled plantation owners, who calculated that a dictator in tricolor trimmings would mean a better chance for reestablishing slavery than any sort of actual representative government—especially one that included blacks, abolitionists, and assorted revolutionary idealists. Napoleon visited Normandy and was fêted at a banquet by Charles de la Pailleterie's old rivals in the slaving business, Constantin and Stanislas Foäche, who hoped a new era of slave-driven profits was just around the corner.

These businessmen argued that, in a world where its global competitors still practiced slavery, France could not afford to continue with its bizarre policy of emancipation and equal rights. Revolutionary ideas simply cost too much. The exports of Saint-Domingue in the years 1799–1800 were *less than a quarter* of what they had been in 1788–89. Even General Toussaint Louverture—the French Revolution's standard-bearer among Saint-Domingue's blacks and a brilliant leader of men—struggled to get field-workers to go back to the plantations. Thousands of these former slaves had served as soldiers of the Revolution and had no desire to return to hacking cane.

Days after his coup, Napoleon received a proposal for lifting the French ban on the slave trade. It was too early for such bold action, but he did begin repaying his political debt to the pro-slavery lobby, which had lent him important support. He replaced the minister of the navy and colonies, a member of the Society of the Friends of the Blacks, and seeded pro-slavery figures throughout the government. The Constitution of Revolutionary Year VIII that Napoleon proclaimed in December 1799, a month after seizing power, was vague on the race issue but contained an ominous line for all people of color: "The regime of the French colonies is to be determined by special laws."

But Napoleon played a double game. On Christmas Day, 1799, shortly after issuing the new constitution, he made a proclamation to the people of Saint-Domingue: "Remember, brave Negroes, that the French people alone recognize your liberty and your equal rights." Five days later he made a secret decision to begin building a new armada, which would ferry forty thousand French troops across the Atlantic to the Americas. It would ultimately grow even larger than the one he had taken to Egypt. Its goal: the reconquest of France's most profitable colony. Barely a month in power, Napoleon was planning a full-scale military invasion of Saint-Domingue.

There could be no misinterpreting the racial component of such an invasion: Saint-Domingue was not some foreign country. It had a French administration and had still considered itself part of the French Republic throughout the years since emancipation. Moreover, the educated black and mixed-race citizens of Saint-Domingue were devoted to French thought and politics, while the island's white Creoles were quite ready and even eager to go over to the English or the Spanish in exchange for maintaining slavery. (Napoleon wrote to a Martinique planter to express sympathy for the man's decision to defect to the English rather than lose his slaves.) No large invasion of Saint-Domingue would make sense unless it was part of a strategy to turn back the clock and reimpose white rule of the island. But Napoleon had to wait until he had a peace treaty with England, so the fleet would not be intercepted on its way across the Atlantic. For the time being, he would pretend to be a friend to the blacks and a republican defender of their universal human rights.

◆━◆

GENERAL Toussaint Louverture, a skilled diplomat as well as a military tactician, also kept his cards close to his vest. He played the British and Spanish off against the French, as he had for much of the past decade, and cut deals with whoever he thought might increase his own and his island's power. Unlike many other black revolutionaries, he was a pragmatist and a long-term thinker, determined to bring prosperity back to Saint-Domingue and even to reintegrate white plantation owners, if necessary. There was only one red line that could not be crossed: slavery must never return.

General Louverture had two sons who were living in Paris. Isaac

Louverture was studying full-time, while his half brother, Placide, was serving as an aide-de-camp to a French general. At the beginning of 1802 these two distinguished young men of color were still living an existence that, while unheard-of in any other country, was not only possible but was almost normal in France. They were nervous, however, about certain changes in the city, and about rumors of a "formidable expedition" the government was preparing to send to their homeland. They had heard warships were massing at many of France's Atlantic ports—Brest, Lorient, Rochefort, and Toulon.

One day the headmaster of Isaac Louverture's college was surprised by an order to appear before Minister Denis Decrès at the Ministry of the Navy and the Colonies. Knowing that Decrès hated people of color and was opposed to mixed-race education, the headmaster must have feared a diatribe or a fine, or worse. Instead, Minister Decrès "invited" the headmaster to accompany the sons of Toussaint Louverture back with the French armada to Saint-Domingue. Though this might have been interpreted as a deportation order, Minister Decrès played his part well, since the headmaster returned to his college where, as Isaac later remembered in his memoir, he "announced the news to his young scholars, and embraced them, saying with tears in his eyes that the French government was motivated only by peaceful considerations." A few days later he sent the headmaster a letter saying that the first consul himself wished to see the Louverture brothers before their departure. Decrès arrived at the college personally to escort the boys to the Tuileries Palace to meet Napoleon, who gave them a hearty welcome.

"Your father is a great man," said Napoleon, addressing Isaac Louverture:

He has rendered eminent service to France. You will say to him that as the first [consul] of the French people, I promise him protection, glory, and honor. Do not believe that it is the intention of France to carry war into Saint-Domingue. The army sent by France is not destined to combat the troops of the country, but to augment their force. Here is General Leclerc, my brother-in-law, whom I have named captain-general, and who will command this army. Orders have been given that you may be fifteen days in advance at Saint-Domingue, to the end that you may announce the coming of the expedition to your father.

Napoleon also quizzed Isaac on mathematics and acted pleased with his answers. Before their departure Minister Decrès presented both young men with a suit of dazzling armor, manufactured at Versailles, and "a rich and brilliant officer's costume, in the name of the government of France."

The sons soon determined that they were being used against their father—the trip across the Atlantic with Napoleon's brother-in-law General Leclerc and forty thousand French soldiers left little doubt in their minds—and by the time they reached Saint-Domingue they were more or less officially acknowledged to be hostages. Still, once the fighting began, their father would repel the French invasion forces for four months before agreeing, after an even more venal deception on the part of the French command, to come to an informal diplomatic meeting. On the way, Napoleon's soldiers ambushed the black republican hero of Saint-Domingue and sent Toussaint back to France in chains. This man of the tropics was thrown into a freezing cold cell with dripping wet walls and a fire that, on orders from Napoleon, was inadequately fed with wood. "His iron frame, which had withstood the privations and fatigues of ten incredible years, now huddled before the logs measured out by the orders of Bonaparte," wrote C. L. R. James. "The hitherto unsleeping intellect collapsed periodically into long hours of coma. Before the spring he was dying. One April morning he was found dead in his chair."

Toussaint's capture did not stop the resistance. By August, a despairing General Leclerc wrote to Napoleon: "It is not enough to have removed Toussaint. Here there are two thousand leaders to arrest. If I take the weapons the taste for insurrection still dominates. I have captured 20,000 guns but there are at least as many still in the hands of the freedmen."

Napoleon gave Leclerc strict orders that no officers of color over the rank of captain could be left alive in Saint-Domingue—they were all to be either killed, or captured and deported back to France. Rekindling the cruelest traditions of *Ancien Régime* slavery in the sugar islands, French soldiers tortured, raped, and murdered blacks in every gruesome way imaginable. Most of the more than three thousand soldiers of color deported at gunpoint were illegally sold into slavery elsewhere in the Caribbean by corrupt naval commanders.

By 1804, Haitians had succeeded in creating a new nation and identity.

More than forty thousand French soldiers died in the futile operations—half the number sent—and many times that number of blacks and mulattos, both military and civilian, perished. Evoking a particularly chilling image in light of twentieth-century mass murders, some blacks were killed by deliberate asphyxiation using burning sulfur in enclosed spaces aboard French vessels in Port-au-Prince harbor. Black fighters were equally vicious in their treatment of the local white population, but they also welcomed some whites (such as units of Polish soldiers who had arrived with the French but switched sides).

In the summer of 1802 French forces also invaded Guadeloupe, the other French sugar island where the emancipation had applied, and rampaged through the colony, seizing any uniformed blacks they came across and either killing them or throwing them in irons. Cornered at a plantation on the slope of La Soufrière volcano, some three hundred of the island's leading black and mulatto rebels—men and women—chose to take their own lives rather than live to see slavery return. Screaming "Live free or die!" they blew themselves up with their remaining gunpowder. Their leader was Louis Delgrès, a colonel who had served in the Black Legion in 1792 under Dumas's command.

◆—◆

DURING the 1790s, the National Colonial Institute in Paris had taken the revolutionary step of educating black, mixed-race, and white children together. Now Napoleon's government cut the Institute's funding and ended its experiment in color-blind education.

One of its students, Louis-Blaise Lechat, the son of a black French officer from Saint-Domingue, remembered an official school visit in 1801 by the same minister of the navy and colonies who "invited" Isaac and Placide Louverture to return to Saint-Domingue. Lechat described the visit in a letter to Isaac and Placide some years later: "Minister Decrès came to the Institute, assembled all of the Americans [i.e. the blacks] into the courtyard, and gave them a very harsh speech. The government would no longer pay for their education: They had already done too much for the likes of us."

As the school's reputation quickly plummeted, the paying students abandoned it, and by 1802 there were only about two dozen pupils on public scholarship attending: of these, nine were black, six mixed-race, and seven white. At the end of the year, the school abruptly closed its doors. Many students of color were sent to orphanages, while the older ones, though only in their teens, were put into military service as errand boys.

Ten-year-old Ferdinand Christophe, the son of Henri Christophe, one of Saint-Domingue's top black generals—and the future King Henri I of Haiti—had the misfortune to arrive at the Institution's gates in 1802, just as it was being dismantled. Taken by the authorities, he was put into an orphanage called La Pitié ("The Merciful"), and the "small fortune" in jewels and gold that he carried to support his education was stolen. The last anyone saw of him, the young man had been turned into a kind of security guard for the orphanage. A woman in 1814 recalled the following incident, witnessed ten years earlier, to a memoirist:

> [She] saw a young man standing guard at the gate of La Pitié. Because Mlle Marie had told them about Christophe's son, they went over to him, crying out, "Here is the son of Christophe." The young man joyfully said, "Yes it's me." But in the same moment a man who was at the gate of La Pitié gave Christophe two powerful blows that made Christophe drop his rifle and fall over, after which it was necessary for him to retreat inside. It was impossible to catch a glimpse of him from this time forward, but it is known that they sent him to learn the trade of shoemaking, requiring him to take it up. Christophe continually refused, saying that his father had sent him to France to get a fine education, not to be a cobbler.

Ferdinand Christophe continued to refuse to take up the manual trade the government had chosen for him. In 1805 he was found dead at the orphanage. He was twelve years old.

➤━◄

ONE of the institutions Napoleon is best remembered for is the Legion of Honor, the first "order of merit" that really deserved the name. Though it took its cues from the monarchic tradition of knighting individuals as a reward for outstanding service, the Legion was genuinely open to men of all professions and backgrounds. It was proclaimed law on May 19, 1802, and even today it remains indelibly associated with the best legacy of Napoleonic France.

General Dumas's son would later lament that his father died "without even having been made a Chevalier of the Legion of Honor—he who had been the hero of the day at Maulde . . . at Mont Cenis, at the Siege of Mantua, at the bridge of Brixen, at the revolt of Cairo, the man whom Bonaparte had made governor of Treviso and whom he presented to the Directory as the Horatius Cocles of the Tyrol." (Indeed, I would find a letter to General Dumas from Murat indicating that he would "pass on with pleasure" General Dumas's own request to be admitted to the Legion.)

But there was an obvious reason Dumas could not have been admitted, even if Napoleon had not personally detested him. On May 20, 1802, the day after creating the Legion of Honor, Napoleon issued another proclamation, one that revealed his true position on slavery in the French Empire. Colonies where the 1794 abolition hadn't gone into effect—those, like Martinique, which the British had seized during the revolutionary wars and only recently returned to France—were to officially remain in a state of pre-1789 slavery. Though Saint-Domingue and Guadeloupe weren't explicitly affected, the proclamation included a clause stating that for ten years, "in spite of all previous laws," all colonies would be subject to new regulations imposed by the central government. The door to the complete reimposition of slavery had been opened. This infamous clause was followed by a series of now forgotten laws that crushed the rights the Revolution had given to men of color within France.

Two weeks after the slavery decree, Napoleon issued a law banning all officers and soldiers of color who had retired or been discharged from the army from living in Paris and the surrounding area. In July, a new order revived the old royal Police des Noirs laws, except now they forbade "blacks, mulattos, and men of color . . . from entering the continental territory of the Republic under any cause or pretext, unless supplied with special authorization." And this time the racist laws would be enforced, not merely proclaimed. All those in noncompliance would be held until deported. In such circumstances, the Legion of Honor was a pipe dream.

The following year, Napoleon outlawed marriages between people of different skin colors. The minister of justice wrote to all prefects that it was "the intention of the government that no act of marriage between whites and blacks will be accepted" and that it was their duty to enforce the law. When a mulatto servant in Napoleon's own household wished to marry a white man, Josephine had to personally intercede with her husband for an exception to the no-mixed-marriages law.

Dumas had been released from the fortress dungeon only to find his world transformed into one. Surreal degradations now menaced him in his own country, as the government methodically restricted, rolled back, and finally eliminated rights for French citizens of color. Less than a year after arriving back in France, General Dumas would need to request a special dispensation to be allowed to stay in his own house in Villers-Cotterêts—part of the zone forbidden to retired military men of color.

The war hero now had to appeal to his former army comrades to pull strings so he wouldn't be deported.

Once, when Dumas had felt slighted by the army's failure to give him an important combat posting, he had written an angry letter to the minister of war stating that if he really merited such poor treatment, then he would prove to be "no longer worthy of the cause for which I have a dual interest because of the climate that saw my birth." This was as close as Dumas ever came to invoking the deepest origins of his zeal in the service of the French Republic. He did not invoke such things now.

>—<

IN reading through Dumas's letters from these years at the archives in the Château de Vincennes, I came across another folder of letters written at the time, by members of the Black Pioneers—a battalion initially made up of some eight hundred prisoners of war from Saint-Domingue and Guadaloupe who had been deported to France and forced to serve in the same military that had invaded and routed their homeland. The side on which they had fought in the complex island conflicts often made little difference. Napoleon shipped them south to Italy, where for years they were given only hard manual labor to do. In French military parlance, "pioneers" signified companies of infantry troops who often did the army's dirty prep work, building fortifications and digging trenches before the soldiers rushed in.

The Black Pioneers folder was full of letters from demoted black officers.

In the same period when Dumas was asking his comrade generals to help him attain some small measure of what he was due, unbeknownst to him, these officers—of much lower rank—were also writing, begging to resume their commands. They and Dumas were experiencing the same betrayal. Starting in 1802, just as Dumas was being released from prison, Napoleon attempted to impose a return to the pre-revolutionary standard of allowing only white officers to command. The folder also contained an order, signed by Napoleon and Berthier, creating segregated infirmaries so that "colored men who will be treated there will be placed in a separate room, so that they have no communications with the White patients."

Talented men of color were so bereft that even membership in the segregated Black Pioneer companies became fiercely competitive. Looking through the voluminous correspondence in the archives, I read dozens of long and eloquent letters from black soldiers explaining why they should merit a spot in one of the units and how grateful they would be to be so blessed by the generous French state. Often the letters begin, "I find myself stranded in France in a difficult situation. I cannot return to my homeland and am no longer allowed to report to my job."

The roughly one thousand soldiers who served in this battalion were eventually formed into the so-called Royal African Regiment, which greatly distinguished itself in service in 1805 and 1806. But having enjoyed prestige as "Americans" during the Revolution, black and mixed-race soldiers now found themselves denigrated as "Africans." As France rejoined the wider world of slaveholding nations, the elevation of nonwhites to positions of power or respect became a dangerous anachronism. In the armies that General Dumas once led, suddenly the very concept of a black soldier commanding white troops was impossible—a black general of division or general-in-chief of an army, unimaginable.

→—←

ON July 24, 1802, Marie-Louise bore their third and last child. Alex Dumas would spend the last four years of his life inseparably attached to little Alexandre.

But even in the joy of his son's birth, General Dumas was reminded of his new fallen status. In his memoir, his son recalls how "before the Egyptian campaign it had been settled that if my mother bore a son, the godparents of this said son were to be Bonaparte and Josephine. But things had changed greatly since then, and my father had no inclination to remind the first consul of the general-in-chief's promise."

Instead, two days after the birth, Dumas wrote to an old friend, General Brune:

LIBERTY, EQUALITY.
From the Headquarters of Villers-Cotterêts, 7 Thermidor Year X of the French Republic.

ALEXANDRE DUMAS, General of Division,
To his best friend General Brune,
I hasten to announce, my dear Brune, the happy delivery by my wife of a large baby boy who weighs 10½ pounds, and at 18 inches, you see I hope that if this child has no accidents he will not be a pygmy by age 25. This is not all, my friend, you have to prove yourself to me, to pass muster, my friend, by being the godfather, [along] with my daughter. The matter is not urgent, because the child carries himself well, and my daughter will not be here for a month, when she takes her vacation. I need a prompt response from you, my dear Brune, to know what to expect—farewell, my friend, you have no better one than
        Alex Dumas

To this warm note, Brune replied that "a superstition prevents my complying with your request," and he asked Dumas's "indulgence" on his having to offer his "sincerest regrets to [Dumas's daughter Aimée Alexandrine] and to your charming wife."

Dumas couldn't help wondering at his friend's coolness and his refusal to attend. Dumas refused to accept his friend's rejection. He tried for weeks to get him to come to Villers to be Alexandre's godfather. But Brune only made excuses. Finally he agreed to be the godfather, but would not come to the ceremony, and so Claude Labouret, the baby's grandfather, stood in for him.

▸-◂

DUMAS continued to write to Napoleon, offering his services in combat. Dumas's final appeal asked for a chance—despite his impaired health—to fight England: "As soon as the current war started I have had the honor of twice writing you to offer you my services. Please accept that I once again offer you that service now." In another letter he'd written, with a glimmer of his old swagger: "Whatever my sufferings and pains, I will always find enough moral force to fly to the rescue of my country at the first request the government sends me."

The general loved playing with his precocious son, telling him stories of his childhood in Jérémie and pretending there were alligators in the moat of the small castle outside Villers-Cotterêts that the family managed to rent for a time. Though they were outcasts, they were happy together, especially big Alex and little Alexandre, who was described as "a kind of giant" from toddlerhood on, inheriting his father's prodigious strength, size, and constitution. Even if never again restored to full health, Alex Dumas was capable of physical feats that made a lasting impression on his son. In the memoir, Alexandre recalls how he saw his father emerge after saving a servant from drowning: "It was my father's naked form I saw, dripping with water; he smiled an almost unearthly smile, as a man may who has accomplished a godlike act, the saving of another man's life." As he watched, Alexandre was struck by "my father's grand form (which looked as though it might have been made in the same mold as that which formed the statues of Hercules or Antinoüs) compared with [the servant's] poor small limbs."

"I adored my father. Perhaps, at so early an age, the feeling which today I call love was only a naïve astonishment at that Herculean stature and that gigantic strength I'd seen him display on so many occasions; perhaps it was nothing more than a childish pride and admiration for his braided coat, his tricolor cockade, and his great saber that I could barely lift. But, in spite of all that, even today the memory of my father, in every detail of his body, in every feature of his face, is as present to me as if I had lost him yesterday. No matter what the reasons, I love him today with a love as tender, as deep, and as real as if he had watched over my youth and I had had the happiness to go from childhood to manhood leaning on his powerful arm."

"On his side, too, my father adored me," Alexandre wrote. "I have said it, and I don't know how to say it too often, especially if the dead can hear what is said of them; and though at the end of his life the suffering that he bore tormented him to the point where he could no longer stand any noise or movement in his bedroom, he made an exception for me."

In 1805 General Dumas's health took a sharp turn for the worse, and his stomach pains were diagnosed as cancer. He visited a famous doctor in Paris. Afterward, he held a lunch where little Alexandre met Generals Brune and Murat, and Alex asked his old comrades to take care of his family after he was gone. The boy would remember playing with Murat's sword and Brune's hat. At the end of the luncheon, "My father embraced Brune, shook Murat by the hand and left Paris the next day, with death in both his body and his heart."

The novelist also remembered going with his father to pay a visit to Pauline Bonaparte, the most beautiful of Napoleon's sisters and the young widow of General Leclerc. Father and son went to her château, just outside Villers-Cotterêts, and in the memoir there is the following description:

> A woman reclined on a sofa, a young and beautiful woman, very young and very beautiful; so beautiful that even I, a young child, noticed it. . . . She did not rise when my father entered. She extended her hand and raised her head, that was all. My father wanted to sit by her in a chair; she made him sit at her feet, which she placed on his knees, the toes of her slippers toying with the buttons on his coat.
>
> That foot, that hand, that delicious little woman, white and plump, near that mulatto Hercules, still handsome and powerful in spite of all his suffering, made the most charming picture you could hope to see.
>
> I laughed as I looked at them, and the princess called me to her and gave me a tortoiseshell bonbon box, all inlaid with gold.
>
> I was shocked to see her empty out the bonbons that were inside before she gave me the box. My father made an observation to her. She bent toward his ear, said a few hushed words, and the two began to laugh.
>
> As she bent down, the princess's white and pink cheek brushed against my father's brown one, making his skin look darker and hers, more white.

Inside the safe, I found a note inviting "Madame Dumas" to visit "her Imperial Highness the Princess Pauline" at her mansion in Paris. It gave the time, 2 p.m., and the address, but the date was obscured. I thought it was probably from 1807, following General Dumas's death. Perhaps the princess tried to help the widow and her children. But it's impossible to know. From the time of the visit to Pauline, Alexandre Dumas would write, "Soon after, my father grew weaker, went out less often, rarely mounted a horse, stayed more in his room, took me on his knees with greater sadness. Once again, all this has since come back to me in glimmers, like things seen in a flash of lightning on a dark night."

The night of February 26, 1806, the final night of his father's life, remained illuminated in his mind, surely as his mother described it to him:

> "Oh!" he cried, "must a general who at thirty-five was at the head of three armies die at forty in his bed, like a coward? Oh my God! My God! What have I done that you should condemn me so young to leave my wife and children?" . . .
>
> [The next day], at ten at night, feeling that death was approaching, he asked for [his priest]. . . . It was not a confession that the dying man wanted to make. All his life, my father had never done a single bad thing, committed a single action that could be reproached; perhaps some hatred for Berthier and Napoleon remained at the bottom of his heart. . . . But all feelings of hatred were suspended in those hours before his death, which were spent in trying to comfort those he was to leave alone in the world, when he had departed from it.
>
> Once, he asked to see me; then, as they were about to get me from my cousin's, where I had been sent:
>
> "No," he said. "The poor child is sleeping; don't wake him up."

That night, after they'd heard the knock at the door and his cousin had put him to bed again, and before he'd gone back to sleep, the child felt "something like an exhaled breath" pass over his face, and it calmed him. Of that moment, Alexandre Dumas wrote, "It isn't surprising that my father's soul, before rising up to heaven, hovered for a second over his poor child, whom he was leaving so bereft of all hope on this earth."

I found a detailed inventory of General Dumas's household belongings made the day after his death by a notary, apparently with a view to the family's outstanding debts, which are also listed in detail. In the middle of a list that included side tables, armchairs, "one pair of firedogs in glazed brass," and "30 canvas shirts—360 francs," I found the following entry:

one painting in its black wooden frame representing Horatius Cocles, Roman, estimate—10 francs.

Everything changed for Alexandre when his father died. The pension that was owed General Dumas was withheld and the family was plunged into a poverty that would stretch throughout his childhood.

Marie-Louise supported her children by working in a tobacconist's shop. The impoverished boyhood Alexandre Dumas writes of pluckily in his memoir must, in fact, have been a depressing and humiliating time. Despite his brilliance, he missed a basic secondary education, for lack of scholarship funds. He believed that the rejection was due to Napoleon's hatred for his father: "this hatred extended even to me, for in spite of the attempts made on my behalf by my father's old comrades, I could never gain entrance to any military school or civilian college."

Alexandre Dumas would continually meet up with men who wanted to pay their respects to his father. One of the first I found a record of had sent Marie-Louise a note, in September 1807, thanking her for her hospitality when he had come to town to call on the general, not realizing he had died. "What a shock to find only the ashes of our common friend. I left Paris in hope of seeing him. That hope was soon covered in tears and regrets. What subject is more dignified than General Dumas? Who . . . could cherish the beautiful qualities of his soul?" The letter writer, a Monsieur Doumet, reassures Marie-Louise that "his traits and his virtues are reborn in your lovable children. . . . Your son will resemble his father; he already has the sincerity and the kindness as much as his age permits it."

Marie-Louise would spend the next decade petitioning the emperor through every possible channel for the minimum of support to which she and her children were entitled. But the first modern-world bureaucrats proved implacable. She paid calls on whichever of Dumas's colleagues would see her. Her letters in the War Ministry archives are a sad testimony to an individual's persistence in the face of obdurate officials directed from the very top to ignore her claims. She briefly had hope in 1814, when Napoleon was forced into exile on Elba and she could write the new war minister with candor:

> The death of General Dumas left his family without fortune and without any resources or hopes for his widow to receive the pension normally allocated to the widows of generals, and which, by the most unjust exception, has been refused her. . . . The brave General Dumas, whom the fates of combat had spared, perished in misery and grief, without decoration or military compensation, and victim of Bonaparte's implacable hatred and of his own tenderheartedness.
>
>   Widow Dumas
>   Villers-Cotterêts, October 2, 1814

Murat and Brune tried—"Brune zealously, Murat halfheartedly," Dumas's son wrote—to keep their promise to Dumas to try to help his family. "But it was quite useless." When one of Napoleon's generals once tried to bring up the question of General Dumas's family, the emperor is said to have stamped his foot and said, "I forbid you ever to speak to me of that man."

➤➤

MARIE-LOUISE lived till the age of sixty-nine, long enough not only to pass on to Alexandre all her memories of his father but to watch her son achieve international fame and fortune. Ironically, in his novels the writer would capture—perhaps better than any other novelist—the particular mystique Napoleon held for all Frenchmen of the early nineteenth century and, indeed, continues to hold for young readers introduced to him through Dumas novels.

And of course Napoleon is ultimately the man behind Edmond Dantès's suffering and imprisonment; if not for the innocent task he does on the emperor's behalf, Edmond would have married his true love, avoided prison, and lived happily ever after. But then there would have been no story.

"Unhappiness cannot but draw tighter the bonds which hold us fast to one another," General Dumas had written to Marie-Louise as he made his way home. His son has Edmond Dantès express the same sentiment in a letter to his friend at the close of *The Count of Monte Cristo*: "He who has felt the deepest grief is best able to experience supreme happiness. . . . Live then and never forget that until the day when God will deign to reveal the future to man, all human wisdom is contained in these two words—'Wait and hope.'"

Out of the deepest betrayal Alexandre Dumas would weave imagined worlds that resurrected his father's dreams and the fantastical age of glory, honor, idealism, and emancipation he championed.

"You see, Father," he writes in his memoir, as if for himself, "I haven't forgotten any of the memories that you told me to keep. From the time I could think, your memory has lived in me like a sacred lamp, illuminating everything and everyone you ever touched, even though death has taken it away!"

THE FORGOTTEN STATUE

THE first biographical portrait of General Alex Dumas was published in 1797,* in the wake of French victory in northern Italy. It was one of the high moments of the French revolutionary decade, a time when Alex Dumas was being lauded by Napoleon himself, who compared Dumas to a Roman hero driving back the barbarians. The article's breathless description of General Dumas's heroism makes bittersweet reading when one knows what would befall him only two years later. But something else about the article shocked me: its candid description of Dumas's racial identity.

GENERAL ALEXANDRE DUMAS
MAN OF COLOR

4 Germinal, Year V
It is without distinction as to individuals, status, or rank that the history of Republics consecrates the memory of great deeds to posterity. If, in the course of engraving the annals of a great people, its faithful chisel should cover a hero, a man of virtue, with immortal glory, it does not

---

*In the archives of the French National Library, I found the two printed pages in a battered folder of letters and other original documents by and about General Dumas from the 1790s, during the years of his military command. The library's records show that the folder was part of a kind of scrapbook of papers on the Dumas family given to the library sometime between 1946 and 1956; unfortunately, no further information was kept about who made the donation, and there is no way to determine from what book the short biography was torn, though its chronology, which ends abruptly in March 1797, as well as its very distinctive tone—that of the high point of French republican and emancipatory zeal—make it nearly certain that it was published sometime around the summer of that remarkable year, likely while Dumas was serving as the military governor of Treviso.

stop to consider whether he was born in Europe or under the blazing sky of Africa, whether his face is the color of bronze or something closer to ebony. A negro's feats of courage are every bit as deserving of admiration as those of a native of the Old World. Indeed, who has a greater right to public respect than the man of color fighting for freedom after having experienced all the horrors of slavery? To equal the most celebrated warriors he need only keep in mind all the evils he has suffered.

This is the way Alexandre Dumas—citizen of color, but mulatto and mixed, born in Saint-Domingue in 1762—has always acted since the Revolution. This young man, who came to France to fight among the defenders of the Fatherland . . . displayed such intrepid bravery and such consummate intelligence that he soon distinguished himself even in the Army of Italy, and rose to the rank of Commander of the Second Cavalry Division. The General is six foot one or two inches tall, and one of the handsomest men you will ever meet; his interesting physiognomy is accompanied by a gentle and gracious manner. His frizzy hair recalls the curls of the Greeks and Romans.

Covered in glory during the conquest of Italy, Alexandre Dumas followed the immortal Bonaparte into the Tyrol. On 4 Germinal, Year V [March 24, 1797], he went forward to observe enemy movements with about twenty dragoons detached as scouts. Dumas ordered a brigadier general to take up a position behind a ravine, in order to cover Dumas's flank. Seeing how few men stood in their way, the Austrian cavalry charged vigorously; Dumas's escorting troops were defeated before Dumas could reach them. Arriving at the Clausel [*sic*] bridge, in the village before Brixen, without having been able to take the enemy line, [his troops] were all tightly squeezed into a narrow passage. Seeing the danger, General Dumas rushed alone to the bridgehead and held back a squadron of enemy cavalry for several minutes, forcing them to retreat. Surrounded by some twenty Austrians, he killed three and wounded eight; he took only three minor saber wounds. The enemy, shocked and terrified by his courageous resistance, turned on their heels and fled. Redoubling his blows, Dumas cried "Surrender! The French army is right behind me! A republican general never marches behind his soldiers."

The next biographical sketch I found was published eleven years later, in 1808—after Dumas's death and Napoleon's assumption of imperial powers. This capsule biography was from a book simply titled *Military Anecdotes* (compiled by a Parisian publicist named Pierre Nougaret). As I read it I had a strange sense of déjà vu. "Alexandre Dumas, born in Saint-Domingue in 1762, went to France to fight with its defenders," it began.

> He distinguished himself so much in the Army of Italy that he rose to the rank of Commander of the Second Cavalry Division. He followed his immortal general-in-chief (Bonaparte) into the Tirol [*sic*]; on 4 Germinal, Year V (March 25 [*sic*: 24], 1797), he went forward to observe enemy movements with about twenty dragoons detached as scouts. . . . Seeing how few men stood in their way, the Austrian cavalry charged vigorously. Dumas's escorting troops were defeated before Dumas could reach them. Arriving at the Clausel [*sic*] bridge, in the village before Brixen, without having been able to take the enemy line, [his troops] were all tightly squeezed into a narrow passage. Seeing the danger, General Dumas rushed alone to the bridgehead and held back a squadron of enemy cavalry for several minutes, forcing them to retreat. Surrounded by some twenty Austrians, he killed three and wounded eight; he took only three minor saber wounds. The enemy, shocked and terrified by his courageous resistance, turned on their heels and fled, fearing that Dumas had backup. Redoubling his blows, Dumas cried "Surrender! The French army is right behind me!"

I read this little article—scarcely more than a paragraph—many times before I realized what was so familiar: it was the 1797 biography! Except that all references to race, to slavery, and to republican values had been removed. The descriptions of Dumas's military success and the defense of the Clausen Bridge were identical, down to the wording and syntax. But everything that distinguished Dumas as "a man of color fighting for freedom after having experienced all the horrors of slavery," as the original text put it, had been expunged.

—◆—

THERE was once a statue of General Dumas in Paris, done by a sculptor of the late-nineteenth century, Alfred de Moncel, who specialized in such monuments. It was located in the Place Malesherbes, soon to be known popularly as the Place des Trois Dumas, for the statues it featured of the general, his novelist son, and his grandson the playwright. The commission was conceived in the 1890s, in the midst of a wave of patriotic nostalgia in France for the revolutionary wars a century earlier. The funds for erecting a statue of General Dumas didn't come from the state or any military organization. Rather, a small group of devotees of the legacy of his son—who had once tried in vain to get a statue of his father erected—raised the money by subscription. The fund-raising was spearheaded by two of the biggest celebrities in France at the time, the writer Anatole France and the actress Sarah Bernhardt. Bernhardt gave a special theater performance for the cause. It took more than a decade to have the statue created, and then, once it was actually installed in the Place de Malesherbes on the Right Bank in the fall of 1912, bureaucratic ineptitude resulted in its remaining covered, by official order, for the better part of a year.

After more than two years of searching, I discovered what may be the only set of photos of the statue in existence, snapped in 1913 by a municipal statue photographer. Dumas stands in a simple double-breasted greatcoat, chest out, gazing into the distance in the pose of a resolute patriot, grasping his long rifle like a walking stick. Along with five black-and-white prints of the statue from all angles, there was another one of the bronze General Dumas covered in a tattered white shroud, with just the arm and the rifle exposed; in the background is a horse-drawn delivery truck driven by a man with a handlebar mustache. Seen in these silvery images, the statue struck me as actually not bad; it captured a sense of Dumas's heroic candor and can-do attitude. But what intrigued me was the one in the shroud. A clipping of the newspaper *Le Matin*, dated May 28, 1913, provided a hint, under the headline "The Forgotten Statue":

> The poor general! It looks as if they have abandoned him there, rifle in hand, in the middle of the lawn, as if to be through with him once and for all. The two other Dumas, the father [the novelist] and the son [the playwright] have stood on the green for so long already, their images in bronze. But he, the old soldier, the grandfather . . . has been forgotten. This injustice had to be repaired, and since the square is quite spacious

and our generation is hardly miserly when it comes to statues, we put one of the old general up. . . . But it's one thing to erect a statue, and quite another to inaugurate it.

The newspaper explained that the statue had been in place since the previous year with that shroud over it, thanks to the glacial pace of correspondence between a phalanx of bureaucracies—the Prefecture, the Municipal Council, the Interior Ministry, the Undersecretary of State for the Arts, the Administrative Commission for the Arts, the Bureau of Arts and Museums, the Bureau of Architecture, Walkways, and Landscaping—and finally the sculptor, whose annoyance is palpable in his scrawled complaints about the delay. Since the official inauguration seemed to have been postponed indefinitely, on May 27, a group of satirical wags led by a popular cartoonist, Poulbot, held a mock inauguration in which they pulled off "the sordid Moorish cloak serving as its veil." Madame Poulbot recited a poem and "a little girl came to offer, in memory of the general, the homage of all French youth. Needless to say, the large crowd in attendance witnessed this curious inauguration in astonishment."

An anonymous letter to the editor the next day added a little more to the story:

> For months and months, the Place Malesherbes has featured a scarecrow: it is the statue of a certain General Dumas, cloaked in the frock of a monk . . . given such a fine cause, how is it that no minister has been found to inaugurate it? On Tuesday, a merry band of comedians decided to act on their own. . . . This morning, General Dumas was once more dressed like a Capuchin friar.

By early summer 1913, the president of the republic had signed a decree approving the statue, but there is no record of it ever receiving an official inauguration. A landscaping official complained in July that the now tattered shroud was hanging off of the old general in pieces; after that the paper trail ends.

I had to go to such trouble to find traces of the statue because it was destroyed by the Nazis in the winter of 1941–42.* The German occupiers melted

---

* After the war, the writer and director Jean Cocteau wrote a book describing the Nazis's selective destruction of France's statues, with his friend Pierre Jahan, who had taken priceless and disturbing photos of them as the Nazis broke them apart and hauled them away. Jahan did not photograph the destruction of General Dumas's statue.

down hundreds of French statues, paying more attention to the subjects than to the amounts of metal involved: to melt down the likeness of a mixed-race fighter for liberty, equality, and fraternity was an easy decision for them to make.

→—→

IN 2008, I sat with Monsieur Angot, the founder of the Association of the Three Dumas, in his small apartment across the street from the former palace of the Duke d'Orléans—once the scene of "Adam and Eve nights," now a retirement home—watching a video on his TV. It was a documentary featuring a tall, light-skinned black man, dressed in full eighteenth-century military costume, riding on a white horse through Villers-Cotterêts; from the compact cars and DVD shops in the background, it was evidently not meant to be the eighteenth century. The rider makes his way through the modern town to the cemetery, where he ties up his horse and walks to the grave of General Dumas to pay his respects. The visitor, a French writer and political activist originally from Guadeloupe named Claude Ribbe, had arrived with a film crew to tape himself making this ride. Angot had watched some of the filming, and after the camera was shut off, Ribbe had broken out weeping, he said, proving his devotion to General Dumas.

I tracked down Claude Ribbe in Paris. He was lobbying the Sarkozy government to get General Dumas a posthumous Legion of Honor, he explained, and a big new statue in the center of the city. It turned out that Ribbe led one of those microscopic French political associations, and this one lobbied the French government on issues relating to the legacy of slavery in the Caribbean. It appeared to have only a handful of members, but Ribbe kept his opinions circulating in the press and in book-length polemics. On his website, he described himself as a "historian of diversity." He was remarkably active. He showed me stacks of letters to the president and the mayor of Paris, along with books and articles he had published.

"Why did General Dumas not get the Legion of Honor?" he fumed. "Every revolutionary general got one! Why did they not rebuild his statue after the Nazis destroyed it? We have statues on every block here in Paris. Racism, racism, pure racism."

Ribbe's relentless campaign apparently produced results, for the next time I met him, it was with the mayor of Paris, who had endorsed his statue proposal. Then, some time later, I saw a French television clip of him standing with the mayor, both of them raising a little tricolor flag beneath an imposing bronze sculpture of slave shackles, each perhaps fifteen feet tall. In the race politics of twenty-first-century France, the statue of General Dumas had morphed into a symbolic monument to all the victims of French colonial slavery, in the form of these mega-shackles. A military marching band played the "Marseillaise" in Alex Dumas's honor, followed by an Afro-Caribbean drumming group, then by the mayor and the activist, who both made impassioned speeches. Then everyone went home.

There is still no monument in France commemorating the life of General Alexandre Dumas.

⟜ ACKNOWLEDGMENTS ⟝

Tracking down the life story of a man who died more than two hundred years ago was a new experience for me. I met many wonderful people along the road, as I always do, but none of them had known my subject personally. This time I had to rely on old papers—letters, diaries, memoirs, manuscripts, newspaper cuttings, and battlefield reports. That's why now I must first give thanks to the many people who watch over these precious scraps of paper and parchment and who gave their time to help me sift through the thousands of puzzle pieces to put this story together. I want to thank all the archivists and librarians of France for preserving their country's heritage with such exemplary zeal—when you are the center of the Western world for so long, there is a lot of *patrimoine* to preserve—and I want to give a special thanks to the generosity and care of the following people and institutions: first and foremost, the former, current, and future staff at the Musée Alexandre Dumas (Viller-Cotterêts); the Société historique régionale de Villers-Cotterêts; Madame Decubert and Alain Guena at the Archives de l'armée de la terre at the Service historique de la Défense (Chateau de Vincennes); Claudine Boulouque at the Bibliothèque historique de la Ville de Paris; Gilles Henry; Aurelia Rostaing at the Archives nationales; Baron de Méneval and the library staff at the Fondation Napoléon; Catherine Fevrier at the Bibliothèque universitaire de Nantes; Jean Hournon; Alfred Fierro; Brigitte Julien-Leynaud at the Bibliothèque de la Sorbonne; the research staff of the Bibliothèque nationale de France; Michel Albert and Pierre Kerbrat at l'Académie des sciences morales et politiques; Mireille Pastoureau at the Bibliothèque de l'Institut de France; Bibliothèque central du Service de santé des armées; Agnès Plaire at the COARC (Conservation des oeuvres d'art religieuses et civiles); the Bibliothèque du musée de la Préfecture de Police (Paris); Frédérique Desmet at the Archives départementales du Pas-de-Calais; the Archives départementales de l'Aisne; the Archives départementales du Morbihan; the Archives nationales d'outre-mer (Aix-en-Provence); Valérie Hubert at the Archives départementales de Seine Maritime; Carole Pilarz at the Bibliothèque des arts décoratifs; Véronique Nachtergal at the Centre des archives économiques et financières of the Ministère de l'Économie, des Finances et du Commerce extérieur; Alexandra Vaquero Urruty and Sophie Harent at the Musée Bonnat-Helleu of Bayonne; André Azzam at the Institut français d'archéologie orientale (Cairo); the Institut d'Egypte (Cairo); the officers of the Italian Navy at the Castel Sant'Angelo (coastal fortress) at Taranto, and the sea and inland fortresses at Brindisi, Italy; the Biblioteca Nazionale, Napoli; the Archivio di Stato di Taranto; Cécile Bosquier at the Centre de documentation at the Atelier de Restauration et de Conservation des photographies de la Ville de Paris; Jean-Christophe Clamagirand at Roger Viollet; Jessica Almonte at the Image Works; Mimi Awad at the Bibliotheca Alexandrina (Alexandria).

Once again, countless people on various continents sustained the author in his wanderings and helped him on his quest, and I thank everyone for their hospitality, their generosity, their company. First, I must give special thanks to the Dumasians of Villers-Cotterêts, who helped get my hunt off to such an explosive start, and who made it always enjoyable on subsequent visits: Chief Musketeer François Angot, Alain Goldie, Xavier Blutel, Barbara Neavyn, and former Deputy Mayor Fabrice Dufour. A bit outside of Villers-Cotterêts, I owe particular thanks to Erick Noël, who showed me the slavers' mansions in Nantes and Paris; Claude Schopp, maître of all things Dumas; and Ulrike Voswinckel, who introduced me to the wonders of Apulia. Thanks to Andre Aciman, Madame d'Albufera, Charles Ardai, Noga Arikha, Chahira Arnaout, Jojo Boulad, Eliane Bros-Brann, Peter Canby, Jean Charles de Castelbagac, Marion Charobim, Jean Luc Colonna, the Daubeuf family, Carine Delaporte, Patricia Delouard, Amir and Nathalie Farman-Farma, Henry Finder, John Glassie, Betsy Gotbaum, Prince Michel de Grèce, Nigel Hetherington, Todd Jackson, Melik Kaylan (for his obsession with the death of Porthos), Sylvie and Keith King, Ali Korhan, Liz Macklin, Dott. Gino Maddalena, Chah Mafouz, Ada Martella, Maestro Ramon Martinez (of the Martinez Academy of Arms), Meryam Mashak, Amy Matouk, Fabienne Meurrens, David Remnick, Aaron Retica, Beatrice Monti von Rezzori, Claude Ribbe, Admiral Francesco Ricci, Jacqueline Jorcin Roch, Paola Romagnani, Mahmoud Sabit, Henri and Estelle Saint-Bris, Commissaire Julien Sapori (de la police), Sue Shapiro, Dan Simon, Marcello Simonetta, Raymond Stock, Ben Tyner, Bob Weil, Marc Weitzmann, Dorothy Wickenden, and Massimo Zanca. Thanks also to three people whose names I neglected to write down: the Haitian man who showed me how to cut cane, the Dominican farmer who taught me about coffee growing, and the Apulian fencing coach who demonstrated how Dumas likely fought off his attackers in the cell with his cane.

On to the people who helped me bring this story from the world to the page, beginning with those who kept me sane, organized, and alive during the process:

Until she went off to China to become a television host, pop singer, and movie martial artist, the inimitable Aventurina King was the world's best assistant. She lent me a hand with, among other things, document photography, computer programming, archive sifting, arm twisting, and strategizing, not to mention French, Italian, and Arabic translation, dietary advice, and music selection. (I was annoyed to find out she knew nothing about auto repair.) Along the way, she kept accumulating new skills so frequently that I was reminded of a useful truth: you can self-improve your way out of almost anything.

For keeping me from getting lost in the old growth forests of eighteenth- and nineteenth-century French documents, my deep thanks to Lorraine Margherita, a born archivist who turned out to have many other talents up her sleeve, along with unparalleled energy. Lorraine originally helped me by transcribing and translating some of the document backlog I was accumulating; then she revealed her genius at organizing and turned thousands of high-resolution photographs into a vast online archive. But it was only toward the end of my years of traveling, accumulating, researching, and writing—after I thought I'd found all it was possible to find—that Lorraine asked if she could try doing a little research for me and, lo and behold, various treasures that had been eluding me for years—notably the missing photographs of the Dumas statue the Nazis destroyed, certain papers from Dumas's arrival in France, and the priceless third volume of Dr. Desgenettes's Egyptian memoir—materialized. And despite the difference in our time zones, Lorraine was always on the other end of a Skype line when something crucial came up.

After research is said and done, there is the fact-checking. Helping me with eagle-eyed persistence and doggedness to review every line of the manuscript was, first, Alexandra Schwartz, who has since brought her razor-sharp intelligence to the *New York Review of Books* (which is very lucky to have her), and then Paul Sager, another keen intellect and class act. Both Alex and Paul combed over the manuscript and found microscopic—and not so microscopic—errors to correct. Paul also turned out to be an expert proofreader, crack researcher, and a great sounding board for how my assertions might sound to an academic historian.

On the "New York" side of this endeavor, I have been blessed by my association with some of the best people working in publishing. My miraculous agent, Tina Bennett, is a legend for good reason. Tina has been ready to follow General Dumas up the ice cliff face and into the line of fire since the day I first mentioned him to her, and her unwavering faith is a key reason why this book is in your hands. (If Tina had been there when Napoleon and Dumas faced off, the outcome might have been less certain.) A musketeer shout is also due to Svetlana Katz, another loyal supporter of the general, who has shown kind support to me over many years.

I owe a huge debt to my fearless editor, Rick Horgan, who also well knows what it means to wait and hope, but who never stopped believing that, someday, I would bring him the goods. Rick is the king of laconic understatement (except when he sits down to write you one of his incisive twenty-page letters), and all his communications, on paper and in person, make me pleased once again that I chose this crazy profession. It's a rare and wonderful thing to have a "boss" who always means what he says and can always make you smile. Nathan Roberson helps Rick out a lot with wrangling his more troublesome authors; therefore I definitely owe him thanks as well.

Crown is truly a team—a regiment—and while many of the faces around the table have changed since I signed on, this spirit and sense of shared enterprise seems, if anything, to have gotten stronger. Maya Mavjee and Molly Stern weren't here when I started out, but they are two generals who inspire supreme confidence; I am deeply grateful for their support. The other officers in this army are equally stellar. I would cheerfully march alongside Jay Sones, Dyana Messina, Annsley Rosner, and Jill Flaxman any day of the week. I thank Tina Constable for her early support and enthusiasm, though I never got to work with her. Thanks to Linda Kaplan, Courtney Snyder, Karin Schulze, and Rachel Berkowitz for signing up great European publishers for *The Black Count*. Thanks to Sam Weber for his remarkable painting of General Dumas, and to Christopher Brand and Eric White for using it to design such a striking and elegant cover. And thanks to Cindy Berman, she of infinite patience, and Maria Elias, and all the people in production who made the moving parts here—multiple map revisions, anyone?—fit perfectly together.

In the European theater of operations, I thank the remarkable people who are bringing *The Black Count* to the U.K. I was sad to lose Rebecca Carter as my editor when she switched hats to agenting, but it was my great good fortune that her replacement was Michal Shavit from Granta. Meanwhile, while I was still polishing drafts, Tom Drake Lee sent me letters that made me impatient to buy my own book—surely a good sign in a marketing director—and Liz Foley and Fiona Murphy were equally supportive. I also want to say a word about my new French publisher. Given the book's subject, no translated edition could be more important than the French one. This is why I am so happy that General Dumas's French legacy is in the hands of Alice d'Andigné at Flammarion.

I met Alice through my friend Clémence Boulouque, whom I met in turn when I brought *L'orientaliste* to France: getting to know Clémence has been one of the great added bonuses of choosing to devote myself to a French topic these past years. She is unfailingly generous and witty (especially, so I'm told, in old Aramaic).

As she did the last time, the wonderful Basia Grocholski allowed me to pull herself out of her real life to discuss the all-important topic of fonts and title spacing. Chuck Lin and Danielle Cacnio returned with their Zen mastery of the art of website construction.

Particular thanks are due to Melanie Thernstrom—my old friend of epic proportions, and the author herself of a growing pile of fascinating books—who put down her life, and her two adorable twins, to pick up my final manuscript and vastly improve it with her brilliant queries and suggestions. The child of historians, Melanie has never been very interested in history, which made her an unexpectedly ideal reader: though she came to appreciate military tactics more than I ever could have imagined, she posed the most fundamental questions, accepted nothing but the clearest answers, and, crucially, forced me to pull out a saber and slash "the boring parts." I tried. Melanie's husband, Michael Callahan, was also infinitely helpful and welcoming. When I needed a quiet place to work, they invited me stay on for weeks in an unused wing of a 1920s mansion they were renting; I worked round-the-clock, undisturbed, but got bright and witty company whenever I wanted to be disturbed. I literally cannot thank them enough.

This ideal writer's retreat was capped off when Melanie's father, Professor Stephan Thernstrom—who *does* like history—stopped by and generously read my manuscript; I thank Steve for his valuable suggestions, especially about the Thirteen Colonies and the early American republic.

On the home front, my remarkable wife, Julie Just, somehow managed to read and edit my pages with her usual literary clairvoyance and tireless devotion, while at the same time raising our two daughters and pursuing her own demanding career as an editor and agent. Though an expert reader of what we now call "YA literature," she had somehow missed *The Three Musketeers*; I'm glad I could give her a new favorite novel. I'm sure all the nocturnal living that anyone so closely associated with me must bear has taken its toll, but I believe we will one day discover that good coffee and late nights of intellectual stimulation are, in fact, the cure for most modern maladies. At any rate, Julie's ear is still incomparable, her taste impeccable, and her editorial eye essential. I find talking with her about sentences to be one of life's great pleasures, and her reaction to what I write is half the fun of writing it.

As usual, my brother, Pete, who does double duty as my best friend, has been a rock of sanity and support during the years it took me to write this book. My amazing daughters, Lucy and Diana, drove me insane in the best possible way. I thank my well-read mother-in-law, Jean Bower, and the rest of my family for shows of support and kindness for the "writer in the family." I thank my father, James, for bringing me up surrounded by books and for teaching me a respect for knowledge above material things. Finally, I thank my mother, Luce, a child of France in the late 1930s, who was raised there at a time when the Germans were destroying a lot more than statues. In an orphan's home after the war, at age nine, my mom was given a book inside a care package: the 1938 Hachette edition of *Le Comte de Monte-Cristo*. She tore through it late into the night, under the covers, until it was confiscated—and she had to wait six months to find out what happened to Edmond Dantès after he escaped from the Chateau d'If. She eventually brought it with her when she came to the United States, and this old green edition of *Le Comte* still sits on a shelf in my parents' library, along with the other Dumas novels that my mom's adoptive father, my beloved Great Uncle Lolek, gave her in her new home beneath the George Washington Bridge. These modest editions surely have something to do with why I just devoted the better part of the last decade to chasing down this story.

I have written a biography of a French historical figure, based mostly on French sources, but I've written it for a general English-speaking audience. In this sort of situation it is always tricky to decide on rules of spelling and punctuation. I decided to avoid an obsessive scholarly style in favor of an accessible approach that is most common in popular biographies (and least distracting to an American reader) while offering the kind of extensive sourcing that some readers and critics will be looking for in the back matter.

Among the choices affected by this approach include the following points:

I opt to refer to Napoleon as "Napoleon" throughout the narrative, even though the practice among historians (and French speakers) is to refer to him as "General Bonaparte" or "Bonaparte" until about 1799, when he seized political power in France, and then to switch to "Napoleon" around 1802 or even in 1804, when he officially takes the title Emperor Napoleon I. I hope purists will forgive me. (Of course, when I quote from letters by Dumas or other contemporaries, they usually refer to him as "General Bonaparte.")

I don't want to translate names, so Antoine-Alexandre Davy de la Pailleterie keeps his hyphen and his "de"—the common article that is a part of French noble names. But I do give the English equivalents of an aristocrat's title, which is more familiar to most people. Hence, readers will meet "the Count de Maulde," not "*le comte de Maulde*"—but also not "the Count of Maulde." All these are possible, but I have chosen the form that I think best preserves the essence of the French name without littering the text with italics and foreign words.

The French also love to hyphenate place-names, and generally I include the hyphen as a matter of respecting the accuracy of names. So the action of this story will take place in Saint-Domingue and Saint-Germain-en-Laye.

By the same token, when a name—or title—is familiarly translated in English, I will follow that form, even when it creates a slight inconsistency. Hence, you read about "the Count of Monte Cristo" in this book, not "the Count de Monte-Cristo."

NOTES

ABBREVIATIONS

ADA	Archives départementales de l'Aisne (Laon, France)
ADM	Archives départementales du Morbihan (Vannes, France)
ADPC	Archives départementales du Pas-de-Calais (Dainville and Arras, France)
ADSM	Archives départementales de Seine-Maritime (Rouen, France)
AN	Archives nationales (Paris, France)
ANOM	Archives nationales d'outre-mer (Aix-en-Provence, France)
BNF	Bibliothèque nationale de France (Paris, France)
CGH	Collection Gilles Henry (documents privately collected by Gilles Henry)
COARC	Conservation des oeuvres d'art religieuses et civiles (Paris, France)
MAD	Musée Alexandre Dumas (Villers-Cotterêts, France)
MAD Safe	Safe in the Musée Alexandre Dumas*
MM	Alexandre Dumas (*père*), *Mes mémoires*, Vol. 1
SHD	Service historique de la Défense (Vincennes, France)

PROLOGUE, PART 1: FEBRUARY 26, 1806

p. 1: *Alexandre at his uncle's house:* MM, p. 224.

p. 1: *"My cousin called to me":* Ibid., pp. 228–29. This and all other translations are my own, except in cases where I cite English-language publications.

p. 1: *General Dumas dies*: Death certificate of Alexandre Dumas ("Acte de Décès de Monsieur Thomas Alexandre Davy Dumas Delapailleterie [*sic*][,] Général de Division"), February 27, 1806, MAD.

p. 3: *"I was four years old":* Alexandre Dumas (*père*), *Le comte de Monte-Cristo*, Vol. 5, p. 42.

PROLOGUE, PART 2: JANUARY 25, 2007

p. 5: *"I am afraid the situation is most delicate"* (and the entire dialogue that follows this): Deputy Mayor Fabrice Dufour, author interview, January 25, 2007, Villers-Cotterêts.

---

* The documents cited to "MAD Safe" were located in a safe at the Musée Alexandre Dumas (Alexandre Dumas Museum), in Villers-Cotterêts, at the time of my research (as I recount in the second part of the Prologue). Readers can inquire at the museum to locate these documents in their subsequent reorganization.

p. 5:   *"Adam and Eve nights"* and *"after the champagne"*: Ernest Roch, "L'ancien château royal," p. 249, quoting Madame de Tencin and the Duke de Richelieu. (Active as a local historian of Villers-Cotterêts and the region in the years before World War I, Roch was instrumental in helping create the Alexandre Dumas Museum. He had a personal reason: his mother, Louise Boivin, had had an affair with Alexandre Dumas, and it was always believed in town that Ernest himself was the novelist's illegitimate son—hence the grandson of General Dumas.)

p. 8:   *"In addition to being a first-class soldier"*: David Johnson, *The French Cavalry, 1792–1815*, p. 43.

p. 8:   *three duels in one day:* MM, p. 28; Ernest d'Hauterive, *Un soldat de la Révolution*, p. 78; Placide David, "Le général Th. Alexandre Dumas," p. 40.

p. 8:   *captured twelve enemy soldiers:* Report by the National Convention on a letter from Dumas, December 4, 1792, cited in *Le Moniteur*, reprinted in *Réimpression de l'ancien Moniteur*, Vol. 14 (1858), p. 651.

p. 9:   *"Such brilliant conduct"*: Jean-Baptiste Courcelles, "Dumas (Alexandre Davy)," p. 502.

p. 9:   *"My dear Dumas, you make"*: The officer is General Barthélemy Joubert, in the Tyrol. Report by Dermoncourt, cited in MM, p. 118.

p. 9:   *commanding thousands of troops:* For example, Dumas led a division with three thousand men in the Bardonnèche and Cezanne valleys in the campaign to capture Mont Cenis. Dumas to the Committee of Public Safety, May 14, 1794, SHD 3B9.

p. 9:   *general-in-chief:* National Convention to Dumas, December 22, 1793, SHD 7YD91, and National Convention to Dumas, November 22, 1793, MAD.

p. 9:   *four-star general today:* According to an 1898 military dictionary that seems applicable even today, a *général de division* wears three stars, a *général de corps d'armée* four stars, and a *général d'armée* five. Dumas held the equivalent of all these ranks. *Dictionnaire militaire, encyclopédie des sciences militaires* cited in "Les grades," French Ministry of Defense, website: http://www.defense.gouv.fr/terre/bloc-les-essentiels/les-grades.

p. 9:   *spiked boots:* Dumas to Citizen Guériot, March 13, 1794, SHD 3B107; Dumas to the Committee of Public Safety, March 21, 1794, SHD 3B9.

p. 9:   *He captured the enemy's matériel*: Dumas to Committee of Public Safety, May 14, 1794, SHD 3B9.

p. 9:   *Horatius Cocles:* Antoine-Vincent Arnault et al., "Dumas (Alexandre Davy-de-la-Pailleterie)," p. 161; Simon Linstant, *Essai sur les moyens d'extirper les préjugés des blancs contre la couleur des Africains et des sang-mêlés*, p. 78; Edmond Chevrier, *Le Général Joubert d'après sa correspondance*, p. 98; Henri Bourgeois, *Biographies de la Vendée militaire*, pp. 9–10.

p. 9:   *Dumas went as Napoleon's cavalry commander:* Note from the office of commanding officers, January 8, 1800, SHD 7YD91; note from the Ministry of War, November 6, 1848, SHD 7YD91; director of the Avre Union Commission (Amiens) to the minister of war, October 23, 1880, SHD 7YD91.

p. 9:   *"Among the Muslims"*: René-Nicolas Desgenettes, *Souvenirs de la fin du XVIIIe siècle et du commencement du XIXe*, Vol. 3, p. 124. To my knowledge, only two copies of this unpublished volume exist, one in the Bibliothèque de l'Institut de France (Paris), the other in the Bibliothèque centrale du Service des Armées (Val de Grâce).

p. 10:   *at over six feet:* Registry of the Dragoons in the Regiment of the Queen, Dumas entry, June 2, 1786, CGH: "5 pieds 8 pouces." (The modern conversion is 1.85 meters or 6 feet and 1 inch.)

p. 10:   *to pay his passage back to France:* Robert Landru, *À propos d'Alexandre Dumas*, pp. 65–66.

p. 10:   *falling-out with his father:* MM, pp. 21–22.

p. 10:   *he enlisted as a horseman:* Registry of the Dragoons in the Regiment of the Queen, Dumas entry, June 2, 1786, CGH.

p. 10:   *first civil rights movement:* Sue Peabody, *"There Are No Slaves in France": The Political Culture of Race and Slavery in the Ancien Régime*, pp. 5–6.

p. 10:   *"so far inferior":* Dred Scott v. Sandford, 60 U.S. 393 (1857).

p. 11:   *the Black Legion:* Report on the creation of the Free Cavalry Legion of the Americans and the South, September 15, 1792, SHD XK9.

p. 11:   *Dumas promoted to general:* Director of the Avre Union Commission (Amiens) to the minister of war, October 23, 1880, SHD 7YD91.

p. 11:   *"horror of negroes"* and next two quotations: Paul Thiébault, *Mémoires du général baron Thiébault*, Vol. 1, p. 60 and Vol. 2, p. 31.

p. 11:   *offered Jews full civil and political rights:* National Assembly decree of September 27, 1791, in *Archives parlementaires de 1787 à 1860*, Vol. 31 (1888), pp. 372–73.

p. 11:   *"was a living emblem":* Chevrier, p. 98.

pp. 11–   *Dumas opposes the bloodshed:* General Dumas, "Rapport sur l'état de la guerre de la
12:      Vendée," October 8, 1794, cited in MM, pp. 41–45.

p. 12:   *"generous republican":* Bourgeois, p. 16.

p. 12:   *"I worshipped my father":* MM, p. 225.

p. 12:   *Marie-Louise Labouret:* (Hereafter "Marie-Louise.") Birth certificate, July 4, 1769, MAD Safe.

p. 12:   *Marie-Louise's father, Claude Labouret:* Marie-Louise's marriage certificate, November 28, 1792, MAD Safe.

p. 12:   *General Alexandre Dumas's children:* Alexandrine Aimée Dumas, b. 1793; Louise Alexandrine Dumas, b. 1796, d. 1797; Alexandre Dumas, b. 1802, d. 1870.

p. 13:   *the standard account of the novel's origin:* Dumas's version is repeated in, for example, David Coward, "Introduction," in Alexandre Dumas (*père*), *The Count of Monte Cristo*, ed. David Coward (Oxford, 2008), pp. ix–xxi; Harry Ashton-Wolfe, *True Stories of Immortal Crimes*, pp. 15–33; Arthur Davidson, *Alexandre Dumas, père: His Life and Works*, pp. 258–61. An exception is Gilles Henry, *Les Dumas: Le secret de Monte Cristo*.

p. 13:   *Dumas wrote in an essay:* Alexandre Dumas (*père*), "État-civil du Comte de Monte-Cristo."

p. 14:   *influence on pop culture and Batman:* See Luc Sante, "Introduction," in Alexandre Dumas (*père*), *The Count of Monte Cristo*, p. xxv.

p. 14:   *"that negro":* Philibert Audebrand, *Alexandre Dumas à la Maison d'Or*, pp. 49–50.

p. 14:   *"Scratch Monsieur Dumas's hide":* Eugène de Mirecourt, *Fabrique de romans*, p. 7.

p. 14:   *One well-known caricature:* "Nouvelle bouillabaisse dramatique par M. Dumas père" (about Dumas's five-act play *Les Gardes Forestiers*), *Le Charivari*, 1858, Collection de la Société des Amis d'Alexandre Dumas.

p. 14:   *"many self-proclaimed Nietzscheans":* Antonio Gramsci, *Prison Notebooks*, trans. Joseph A. Buttigieg, Vol. 3 (2011), p. 382.

p. 16:   *"dedicated to the life":* Brochure, Musée Alexandre Dumas.

p. 16:   *looking into the matter,* and following quotations: Conversations with Deputy Mayor Fabrice Dufour, February and March 2007, Villers-Cotterêts.

p. 17:   *a little castle that General Dumas had rented:* Ernest Roch, "Le Général Alexandre Dumas," p. 105.

p. 17:   *the house where Dumas died:* Ibid., pp. 107–8.

p. 18:   *"What's an adventure":* Conversation with François Angot, March 2007, Villers-Cotterêts.

BOOK ONE
CHAPTER I: THE SUGAR FACTORY

p. 23: *Alexandre Antoine Davy de la Pailleterie's birth:* Baptism certificate, parish of Bielle-ville, October 8, 1714, *Registres paroissiaux*, ADSM.

p. 23: *"without ceremony":* Ibid.

p. 23: *firstborn son:* Document about Antoine's property sales and the Count de Maulde, March 16, 1776, ADPC 10J34c.

p. 23: *an old family:* Alexandre Mazas, *Histoire de l'ordre royal et militaire de Saint-Louis*, Vol. 2, p. 58. Mazas cites a May 8, 1755, letter sent to the minister of the navy, referring to the Davy de la Pailleterie family as "a good noble family . . . [its] origins are also known by an ennobling under Louis XI, nearly 300 years ago."

p. 23: *"I loved war too much":* Voltaire, *Histoire du siècle de Louis XIV*, p. 81.

p. 23: *family's coat of arms:* Testimony about the Davy family, 1770, BNF NAF 24641, refers to "French Armories, Volume I, Part I, pg. 183"; François-Alexandre Aubert de La Chesnaye Des Bois, *Dictionnaire généalogique, héraldique, chronologique et historique*, Vol. 4, p. 546; Gustave Chaix d'Est-Ange, *Dictionnaire des familles françaises anciennes ou notables à la fin du XIXe siècle*, Vol. 15 (1903–29), p. 31; Henri Gourdon de Genouil-lac, *Recueil d'armoiries des maisons nobles de France*, p. 171.

p. 24: *provincial aristocrats . . . their fortune was not enough:* Réginald Hamel, *Dumas—insolite*, p. 19.

p. 24: *claim the title of "marquis":* The Count de Maulde's legal claim mentions "Messire Alexandre Antoine Davy, Chevalier Marquis de la Pailleterie," November 30, 1778, ADPC 10J35. A judgment refers to "Alexandre Davÿ Marquis de la Pailleterie," August 9, 1786, AN Y1787.

p. 24: *limited prospects in Normandy:* Fernand Gaudu, "Les Davy de La Pailleterie, seigneurs de Bielleville-en-Caux."

p. 24: *Charles's birth date:* His baptism certificate, October 13, 1716, ADPC 10J26.

p. 24: *Louis's birth date:* His marriage certificate, June 18, 1753, ADPC 10J26.

p. 24: *sought their fortunes in the army:* Louis is identified as a colonel in the Royal Artillery in Count de Maulde, legal claim, November 30, 1778, ADPC 10J35. Charles is identi-fied as "ancien officier des troupes détachées de la marine à St Domingue" in a legal decision dated October 17, 1761, ADPC 10J35. Antoine joined the Corps Royal de l'Artillerie: Dumas's marriage certificate, November 28, 1792, MAD Safe. See also Robert Landru, *A propos d'Alexandre Dumas, les aïeux, le général, le bailli, premiers amis*, pp. 56–57.

p. 24: *served at the front as a gentleman:* Document discussing the dispute between Alexandre Dumas (then Thomas Rethoré) and his stepmother, November 22, 1786, AN LX465.

p. 24: *the king's dashing, fabulously rich cousin:* Jacques Levron, *Le maréchal de Richelieu: Les trésors des princes de Bourbon Conti*; Jacques Roujon, *Conti: L'ennemi de Louis XIV*; Jonas Boyve, *Annales historiques du comté de Neuchatel et Valangin*; Jonathan R. Dull, *The French Navy and the Seven Years' War*, p. 23.

p. 24: *"perfect example of how not":* Karl von Clausewitz, *On War*, p. 403.

p. 24: *fleeing a royal arrest warrant:* "Epitre XLV," Voltaire, *Oeuvres complètes*, Vol. 2, p. 612.

p. 24: *Voltaire at Philipsburg:* Frank Hall Standish, *The Life of Voltaire*, p. 141.

p. 24: *offering bon mots between bouts:* "A Monsieur *** / Du camp de Philippsbourg, le 3 juil-let 1734," *Oeuvres choisies de Voltaire: Poésies*, pp. 234–35.

p. 25: *duel between Lixen and Richelieu:* Emile Colombey, *Histoire anecdotique du duel*, p. 82; Levron; Jean Fougeroux de Campigneulles, *Histoire des duels anciens et modernes*, Vol. 1, p. 200; Augustin Grisier, *Les armes et le duel*, p. 47; Roger de Beauvoir, *Duels et duellistes*, pp. 21–22, 23; Andrew Steinmetz, *The Romance of Duelling in All Times and Countries*, Vol. 1, p. 221; Louis François Armand du Plessis de Richelieu, *Mémoires historiques et anecdotiques du duc de Richelieu*, Vol. 6, p. 5; MM, p. 17.

p. 25: *torchlit swordfight in the trenches:* Hugh Noel Williams, *The Fascinating Duc de Richelieu*, pp. 124–25.

p. 25: *with Antoine watching:* Colombey, p. 82; Steinmetz, p. 221.

p. 25: *the duke sank his blade:* Louis-François Faur, *Vie privée du Maréchal de Richelieu*, pp. 309–11; Fougeroux de Campigneulles, p. 200; Alexandre Dumas (*père*), "Préface en forme de causerie ou causerie en forme de préface," pp. 46–47; Colombey, p. 82; de Beauvoir, pp. 21–22.

p. 25: *a sort of poetic justice:* Robert Baldick, *The Duel: A History of Duelling*, p. 79; Martine Debaisieux and Gabrielle Verdier, *Violence et fiction jusqu'à la Révolution*, p. 381.

p. 25: *the name Richelieu "appears so often":* MM, p. 16.

p. 25: *Antoine got out of the army:* Count de Maulde, legal claim, November 30, 1778, ADPC 10J35.

p. 26: *Charles settled in Saint-Domingue and Antoine followed:* Ernest d'Hauterive, *Un soldat de la Révolution: Le Général Alexandre Dumas, 1762–1806*, p. 11.

p. 26: *Marie-Anne Tuffé and her family's plantation:* Marriage certificate, February 17, 1738, ADPC 10J26 ("marie anne Tuffé"); legal decision, dispute between Charles de la Pailleterie and M. Petit des Landes, October 17, 1761, ADPC 10J35 ("Marie Anne de Tuffé").

p. 26: *sugar as medicine:* Sidney W. Mintz, *Sweetness and Power*, pp. 96–99.

p. 26: *"two drams of fine sugar-candy":* Quoted in ibid., p. 107.

p. 26: *"like an apothecary without sugar":* Peter Macinnis, *Bittersweet: The Story of Sugar*, p. 18.

p. 26: *Columbus and sugar:* Mintz, p. 32.

p. 27: *Hayti in the native tongue:* Laurent Dubois, *Avengers of the New World*, p. 299.

p. 27: *artisans from the Canaries:* Elizabeth Abbott, *Sugar: A Bittersweet History*, p. 25.

p. 27: *enslaving almost everybody else:* Thomas R. Martin, *Ancient Greece: From Prehistoric to Hellenistic Times*, p. 68.

p. 27: *Greek and Roman slavery:* Thomas S. Burns, *Rome and the Barbarians: 100 B.C.–A.D. 400*, pp. 104–6.

p. 27: *slavery not based on race:* David Brion Davis, *Inhuman Bondage*, pp. 56–58.

p. 27: *nearly all slaves imported into Europe were "slavs":* Ibid., p. 82.

p. 27: *Islam and slavery:* W. G. Clarence-Smith, *Islam and the Abolition of Slavery*. (For a contrasting view of the racial aspect to Muslim slavery, see Robin Blackburn, *The Making of New World Slavery: From the Baroque to the Modern, 1492–1800*, p. 79: "By the tenth century an association between blackness and menial slavery had developed in the Muslim and Arab world: the word '*abd*,' or black, became synonymous with slave.")

p. 27: *Ottomans diverted Europe's supply:* Davis, pp. 82–84.

p. 28: *blacks now came to be considered uniquely destined:* Ibid., pp. 55, 73.

p. 28: *slaves in Madeira:* Hugh Thomas, *The Slave Trade*, p. 70.

p. 28: *bois d'ébène:* Phillipe Haudrère and Françoise Vergès, *De l'Esclave au Citoyen*, p. 10.

p. 28: *two-thirds of France's overseas trade:* Christopher Miller, *The French Atlantic Triangle: Literature and Culture of the Slave Trade*, p. 26.

p. 28: *more sugar than the British West Indian colonies combined:* Laurent Dubois and John Garrigus, *Slave Revolution in the Caribbean, 1789–1804*, p. 11.

p. 29: *most valuable colony in the world:* Robert Louis Stein, *The French Slave Trade in the Eighteenth Century*, p. 23.

p. 29: *one-third of all slaves died:* Dubois and Garrigus, p. 8.

p. 29: *the punishment:* C. L. R. James, *The Black Jacobins: Toussaint l'Ouverture and the San Domingo Revolution*, pp. 252–53.

p. 29: *eighteen hours a day:* Bernard Moitt, *Women and Slavery in the French Antilles, 1635–1848*, p. 39.

p. 29: *le Code noir (the Black Code):* "Le code noir ou Édit du roy, touchant la Discipline des esclaves nègres des Isles de l'Amérique française. Donné à Versailles au mois de mars 1685," in *Le Code noir et autres textes de lois sur l'esclavage*, pp. 11–37.

p. 30: *Charles marrying into money:* Marriage certificate, February 17, 1738, and Count de Maulde, legal claim, November 30, 1778, both ADPC 10J35.

p. 30: *Cap Français:* Stewart R. King, *Blue Coat or Powdered Wig*, pp. 22–23.

p. 30: *Charles gets one half of the plantation:* Marriage certificate, February 17, 1738, ADPC 10J26, and letter to the Count de Maulde mentioning the acquisition of the other half, March 17, 1789, ADPC 10J35.

p. 30: *sugar production:* Mintz, pp. 19–22; Stein, pp. 60–61.

p. 30: *slaves for the brute fieldwork:* Stein, p. 44.

p. 31: *plantations owned by people of color:* John D. Garrigus, *Before Haiti: Race and Citizenship in French Saint-Domingue*, p. 72.

p. 31: *Antoine with his brother in Saint-Domingue:* Count de Maulde, legal claim, November 30, 1778, ADPC 10J35.

p. 31: *Charles buys the second half of his plantation:* M. Tardivy to Marianne de Maulde, June 26, 1773, ADPC 10J26; letter to the Count de Maulde mentioning the acquisition of the other half, March 17, 1789, ADPC 10J35.

p. 31: *the old marquis swore:* Gaudu, p. 46, referring either to a burial certificate in the *Registre paroissial de Bielleville* or to a tax document ("capitation des privilégiés de l'élection de Caudebec"), in ADSM C 2223.

p. 31: *Antoine was cut from a different:* Gilles Henry, *Les Dumas: Le secret de Monte-Cristo*, p. 18; Dominique Fernandez, *Jérémie! Jérémie!*, p. 85.

p. 31: *"A stay in Saint-Domingue":* Michel-René Hilliard d'Auberteuil, *Considérations sur l'état présent de la colonie française de Saint-Domingue*, Vol. 2, p. 24, quoted in Garraway, pp. 219–26.

p. 32: *"given to amusement":* Moitt, p. 99.

p. 32: *"Creole" had a different meaning:* Doris Lorraine Garraway, *The Libertine Colony: Creolization in the Early French Caribbean*, p. 248.

p. 32: *"contribut[ing] to the population":* Alexandre-Stanislas de Wimpffen, *Haïti au XVIIIe siècle*, p. 281 of the 1817 imprint, quoted in Garraway, p. 229.

p. 32: *"to debauch negresses":* "Reglement de M. de Tracy, Lieutenant Général de l'Amérique, touchant les Blasphemateurs et la police des Isles," in Médéric Moreau de Saint-Méry, *Loix et constitution des colonies françaises de l'Amérique sous le vent de 1550 à 1785*, Vol. 1 (1784–90), pp. 117–22, quoted in Garraway, p. 201.

p. 32: *"abuse of intimacy"* and next quotations: De Wimpffen quoted in Garraway, pp. 207–8, 228.

p. 33: *the brothers quarrel:* M. de Chauvinault to the Count de Maulde, June 3, 1776, CGH. (Maulde later maintained that Antoine's disappearance was mysterious and without obvious cause: see his legal request, November 30, 1778, ADPC 10J35.)

p. 33: *parents owe money to Charles:* Receipt, June 29, 1757, ADPC 10J34.

p. 33: *"full of honor":* M. de Chauvinault to the Count de Maulde, June 3, 1776, CGH.

p. 33: *Catin, Antoine's mistress, and two other slaves:* Document about debts and slaves, 1748, CGH; M. de Chauvinault to the Count de Maulde, June 3, 1776 (describes Antoine taking Catin, Rodrigue, and Cupidon with him), CGH.

p. 33: *Antoine absent for nearly thirty years:* Count de Maulde's request at the Parliament, November 30, 1778, ADPC 10J35.

CHAPTER 2: THE BLACK CODE

p. 34: *"Charles Edouard searched all the French possessions":* Count de Maulde, legal claim, November 30, 1778, ADPC 10J35.

p. 34: *Antoine had fled into the jungle:* M. de Chauvinault to the Count de Maulde, June 3, 1776, CGH.

p. 34: marron *communities:* Richard Price, *Maroon Societies: Rebel Slave Communities in the Americas*, 3rd ed., pp. 107–12.

p. 34: marron *derived from* cimarrón: Carolyn F. Fick, *The Making of Haïti: The Saint-Domingue Revolution from Below*, p. 275.

p. 35: *Antoine had left no trace:* Count de Maulde, legal claim, November 30, 1778, ADPC 10J35.

p. 35: *Charles's parents die:* Tax document ("Capitation des privilégiés de l'élection de Caude-bec"), ADSM C 2223, cited by Fernand Gaudu, "Les Davy de La Pailleterie," p. 46.

p. 35: *"it is not known"* and *"had married a wealthy woman":* M. Le Flamang, report, September 26, 1760 ("Capitation des privilégiés de l'élection de Caudebec"), ADSM C 2223 (quoted in Gaudu, p. 60).

p. 35: *Grand Anse ("Great Cove"):* Médéric Moreau de Saint-Méry, *Description topographique, physique, civile, politique et historique de la partie française de l'isle Saint-Domingue*, Vol. 2.

p. 35: *communications went by sea:* Keith Anthony Manuel, *Slavery, Coffee, and Family in a Frontier Society: Jérémie and Its Hinterland, 1780–1789*, p. 10.

p. 35: *second-most-lucrative crop:* Ira Berlin, *Cultivation and Culture: Labor and the Shaping of Slave Life in the Americas*, p. 124.

p. 35: *largest coffee producer:* James E. McClellan III, *Colonialism and Science: Saint Domingue and the Old Regime*, p. 66.

p. 35: *capital to start up a coffee plantation:* Stewart R. King, *Blue Coat or Powdered Wig: Free People of Color in Pre-Revolutionary Saint Domingue*, p. 124.

p. 35: *urpent.* Robert Leslie Ellis, *The Mathematical and Other Writings of R. L. Ellis*, ed. William Walton (1863), p. 389.

p. 36: *settled in the parish of Jérémie:* Manuel, pp. 9–16.

p. 36: *Trou Bonbon:* Ibid.

p. 36: *Highland planters lived off coffee:* Ibid.

p. 36: *animals:* McClellan, pp. 31–33.

p. 36: *feral beasts and buccaneers:* John M. Street, "Feral Animals in Hispaniola."

p. 36: *white immigrants from the lower classes:* King, p. 123.

p. 37: *Antoine in La Guinaudée:* Alex Dumas's marriage contract and certificate mention that his mother died in La Guinaudée in 1772, so we can assume that it was where Antoine had settled. November 28, 1792, MAD Safe.

p. 37: *"Antoine de l'Isle":* M. de Chauvinault to the Count de Maulde, June 3, 1776, CGH (spelled "de Lille"); Count de Maulde, legal claim, November 30, 1778, ADPC 10J35.

p. 37: *"The beginnings of Monsieur Delisle":* M. de Chauvinault to the Count de Maulde, June 3, 1776, CGH.

p. 37: *colonial records contain both assertions:* Agreement between Dumas and his father's widow, Marie Retou, November 22, 1786, AN LX465. Cessette is described as a *négresse*.

p. 37: *"for an exorbitant price":* M. de Chauvinault to the Count de Maulde, June 3, 1776, CGH.

p. 37: *Dumas's birth:* Minister of war to the Executive Directory, November 28, 1795, SHD 7YD91 ("dumas alexandre ne à jeremie en amerique le 25 mars 1762"). This is the first time Dumas's date of birth is mentioned in a document. Dumas's marriage certificate says that he was thirty years and eight months old on November 28, 1792 (abstract of the registry with the certificate of Alexandre Dumas and Marie-Louise's marriage, November 28, 1792, MAD Safe). His certificate of enrollment in the dragoons says he was twenty-four years old in June 1786 (Registry of the Dragoons in the Regiment of the Queen, Dumas entry, June 2, 1786, CGH). The exact date is given in military notes about Dumas's career (November 6, 1848, SHD 7YD91; March 2, 1962, SHD 7YD91; March 19, 1962, SHD 7YD91).

p. 37: *"My father's eyes":* MM, p. 14.

p. 38: *"Free men who have one":* Code noir (1685), article 9, in *Le Code noir et autres textes de lois sur l'esclavage,* pp. 15–16.

p. 38: *"an empire based on libertinage":* Michel-René Hilliard d'Auberteuil, *Considérations sur l'état présent de la colonie française de Saint-Domingue,* Vol. 2 (quoted in Victor-Emmanuel Roberto Wilson, *Le Général Alexandre Dumas: Soldat de la liberté,* p. 29).

p. 38: *rights of people of color:* Jeremy D. Popkin, *You Are All Free: The Haitian Revolution and the Abolition of Slavery,* p. 64; Doris Garraway, *The Libertine Colony: Creolization in the Early French Caribbean,* pp. 205, 235.

p. 39: *"expel all the Jews who":* Code noir (1685), article 1, in *Le Code noir et autres textes de lois sur l'esclavage,* p. 12.

p. 39: *free women of color:* Laurent Dubois and John Garrigus, *Slave Revolution in the Caribbean, 1789–1804,* pp. 13–14; Garraway, pp. 230–35; Moreau de Saint-Méry, Vol. 1, p. 105.

p. 39: *slave women's labor:* Bernard Moitt, *Women and Slavery in the French Antilles, 1635–1848,* pp. xiv, 35–36, 45–46.

p. 39: *"concubinage with slaves":* "Ordonnance des Administrateurs, concernant le concubinage avec les esclaves, du 18 Décembre, 1713," Moreau de Saint-Méry, Vol. 2, p. 406.

p. 40: *manumission taxes:* John D. Garrigus, *Before Haiti: Race and Citizenship in French Saint-Domingue,* p. 197.

p. 40: *no evidence of official marriage:* Dumas's marriage certificate identifies "Marie-Cessette" as Dumas's mother and Antoine as his father but never mentions that they are married: Registry abstract with certificate of Alexandre Dumas and Marie-Louise's marriage, November 28, 1792, MAD Safe.

p. 40: *life in Jérémie:* Manuel, pp. 13, 23, 25.

p. 41: *"a courageous act":* Moreau de Saint-Méry.

p. 41: *defenses of Jérémie:* Ghislaine Rey Charlier and Carrol F. Coates, "Memories of a Freedwoman," p. 342; Moreau de Saint-Méry, Vol. 2, p. 788.

p. 41: *"slave pens":* Manuel, pp. 2–20.

p. 42: *"One isn't admitted":* Moreau de Saint-Méry, quoted in Jean Fouchard, *Le Théâtre à Saint-Domingue,* p. 96.

p. 42: *Saint-Domingue fashion:* Charlier and Coates, p. 343; Fouchard, p. 96; David M. Powers, "The French Musical Theater: Maintaining Control in Caribbean Colonies in the Eighteenth Century," p. 230.

p. 43: *Opera and theater:* Fouchard, pp. 95–96; Powers, p. 230.

p. 43: *Minette and Lise:* Powers, p. 238.

p. 43: *"the barbarity of their origin":* "Mémoire concernant l'établissement d'un spectacle à Saint-Pierre de la Martinique," 1780, AN, quoted in David M. Powers, "The French Musical Theater," p. 232.

p. 43: *In the 1970s sociologists doing research in Haiti:* Marlyn Walton Wilmeth and J. Richard Wilmeth, "Theatrical Elements in Voodoo."

p. 44: *"We expressly forbid":* "Règlement provisoire des Administrateurs, concernant le Luxe des Gens de Couleur" (February 2, 1779), Moreau de Saint-Méry, pp. 855–56.

p. 44: *ban on "white" names:* "Règlement des Administrateurs concernant les Gens de couleur libres" (June 24 and July 16, 1779), Moreau de Saint-Méry, pp. 448–50.

p. 44: *three mixed-race siblings:* M. de Chauvinault to the Count de Maulde, June 3, 1776,

CGH; agreement between Dumas and his father's widow, Marie Retou, November 22, 1786, AN LX465. Cessette's daughters Jeannette and Marie-Rose are mentioned.

p. 45: *"I remember hearing my father"*: MM, pp. 14–15.

p. 45: *Dumas's skills:* Dumas himself says that in his "class" (i.e., social class), writing was not something that would be worked on or easily encouraged: Dumas to the Committee of Public Safety, January 4, 1794, SHD 3B9.

p. 45: *"as one learns in those new countries"*: Ernest d'Hauterive, *Un soldat de la Révolution*, p. 12.

CHAPTER 3: NORMAN CONQUEST

p. 47: *Charles buying his plantation:* Record of property acquisition by Charles de la Pailleterie, March 3, 1755, ADPC 10J26.

p. 47: *Charles's gout:* M. Tardivy to Marie-Anne de Maulde, June 26, 1773, ADPC 10J26; M. Leroux to Marie-Anne de Maulde, July 8, 1773, ADPC 10J26.

p. 47: *Charles's administrators:* M. Monjal and M. Papillon are mentioned in the articles of association for a company in which Charles is an associate, January 16, 1760, ADPC 10J26; see also Charles de la Pailleterie to M. Monjal, June 4, 1761, ADPC 10J26.

p. 47: *Charles leaving Saint-Domingue with his wife and daughter:* As of July 1753, we know that Charles was in Saint-Domingue, where he writes his will (July 3, 1753, ADPC 10J26). In March 1755, Charles was in France (see property acquisition record, ADPC 10J26).

p. 47: *Charles in La Pailleterie mansion in the early 1750s:* Robert Landru, *À propos d'Alexandre Dumas*, p. 35; Gilles Henry, *Les Dumas*, pp. 23–24; Réginald Hamel, *Dumas—insolite*, p. 19.

p. 47: *Charles sending money to his parents:* Receipt for 7,000 livres from Jeanne and Alexandre de la Pailleterie to Charles de la Pailleterie, June 29, 1757, ADPC 10J34.

p. 47: *"hit and bit a witness"*: Henry, pp. 19–20.

p. 48: *"not knowing whether their older brother existed"*: Count de Maulde, legal claim, November 30, 1778, ADPC 10J35.

p. 48: *Charles in La Pailleterie castle:* Charles de la Pailleterie to M. Monjal, June 4, 1761, ADPC, 10J26 (mentions that Charles lived at the Pailleterie castle).

p. 48: *Louis's inheritance:* Count de Maulde, legal claim, November 30, 1778, ADPC 10J35.

p. 48: *Charles's connections at Versailles:* Without his connections, the company he started in 1760 could not have existed. See articles of association, January 16, 1760, ADPC 10J26, and M. Bulande to M. Papillon, March 7, 1760, ADPC 10J26b.

p. 48: *the Marquis de Mirabeau:* Mirabeau provided guarantees when Charles bought a property. See legal decision in the dispute between Charles de la Pailleterie and M. Petit des Landes, October 17, 1761, ADPC 10J35.

p. 48: *Charles's loans:* The Marquis de Mirabeau provided guarantees when Charles bought a property. (Legal decision in dispute between Charles de la Pailleterie and M. Petit des Landes, October 17, 1761, ADPC 10J35.)

p. 48: *havoc on colonial shipping:* Benjamin Rand, *Selections Illustrating Economic History Since the Seven Years' War*, p. 98; Lucien Guillou, *André Vanderheyde, courtier lorientais, et ses opérations (1756–1765)*, pp. 13–38.

p. 48: *demand for slaves during the war:* Edouard Delobette, *Ces Messieurs du Havre: Négociants, commissionnaires et armateurs de 1680 à 1830*, p. 1607.

p. 48: *"white sugar of the highest quality"*: M. Bulande to M. Papillon, March 7, 1760, ADPC 10J26b.

p. 48: *Charles formed a partnership:* Articles of association for a company in which Charles is an associate, January 16, 1760, ADPC 10J26.

p. 49:   *Charles in London:* ADPC, 10J34, dossier A, cited in Delobette, p. 1608.

p. 49:   *Charles in slave trading:* Landru, p. 37; Henry, p. 30; Delobette, p. 1608.

p. 49:   *"pieces of India":* Henry, p. 30.

p. 49:   *Foäche's slave-trading ships:* Réginald Hamel, *Dumas—insolite*, p. 172, cited in Delobette, p. 1370.

p. 49:   *Foäche brothers lending money to the king:* Christiane Maubant, "Le 'traité' de traite de Stanislas Foäche, du Havre."

p. 49:   *Charles's ship:* ADPC 10Jc, Chartrier de la Buissière, 26 c: "Achats de nègres: armement de la Douce Marianne, 1763" and 34 a: "Affaire du navire négrier *la Douce Marianne*, 1763–1764."

p. 49:   *Charles's ship:* the *Douce Marianne:* ADPC 10J26c and 10J34a.

p. 49:   *Douce Marianne to Sierra Leone:* Delobette, pp. 695–96, citing ADPC, 10J34, dossier A.

p. 49:   *"300 captives":* Agreement between Charles and the London banker Pierre Simond, in Delobette, pp. 695–96, citing ADPC 10J34, dossier A.

p. 50:   *mutiny on the ship:* ADPC 10J26 and 10J81 cited in Delobette, p. 590; Landru, pp. 40–42, and Henry, pp. 38–40.

p. 50:   *Charles has more debt:* Delobette, pp. 1201, 1239–40, 1607–8, citing ADM E 2373.

p. 50:   *"demanding, unjust":* Foäche & Cie in Cap Français to Veuve Foäche & Fils in Le Havre, June 25, 1774, ADSM 4055, 1 Mi 664 R-2, quoted by Delobette, p. 1370.

p. 50:   *"His plantations could produce":* Delobette, p. 4783, citing M. Bégouën Demeaux, p. 48.

p. 50:   *wedding of Charles's daughter:* Ga_ette de France, April 18, 1764, p. 128, and May 4, 1764, p. 144.

p. 50:   *Marie-Anne's dowry:* Marriage contract between Marie-Anne de la Pailleterie et Léon de Maulde, April 2, 1800, ADPC 10J35.

p. 50:   *cream of French society:* Landru, p. 46; Henry, p. 37.

p. 51:   *Mirabeau as angry creditor:* Legal decision, dispute between Charles de la Pailleterie and M. Petit des Landes, October 17, 1761, ADPC 10J35.

p. 51:   *Charles's slave trading:* ADPC 10J26c and 10J34a.

p. 51:   *"All your creditors":* Maulde to Charles, in Henry, p. 44.

p. 51:   *Charles back in Saint-Domingue:* M. Leroux to the Count de Maulde, July 8, 1773, ADPC 10J26.

p. 51:   *Charles managing his properties:* Landru, p. 49; Henry, p. 44.

p. 51:   *"houses, stables":* M. Tardivy to Marie-Anne de Maulde, June 26, 1773, ADPC 10J26.

p. 51:   *Charles dies:* Many letters to the Maulde couple, including: M. Cabeuil to the Count de Maulde, July 16, 1773, ADPC 10J26; M. Leroux to the Count de Maulde, July 8, 1773, ADPC 10J26.

p. 51:   *"M. de la Pailleterie just died":* Bégouën Demeaux, p. 48 (quoted by Delobette, p. 4783).

p. 51:   *Louis involved in a scandal:* Henry, p. 47.

p. 51:   *Louis dies:* Fernand Gaudu, "Les Davy de la Pailleterie, seigneurs de Bielleville-en-Caux," p. 48, citing Louis's burial certificate, *Registres paroissiaux*, Saint-Léger de Fécamp, ASM.

p. 51:   *Reading court documents:* Count de Maulde, legal claim, November 30, 1778, ADPC 10J35.

p. 51:   *the Pailleteries' creditors:* Landru, p. 55; Henry, p. 49.

p. 52:   *"possessions are deteriorated":* M. Cabeuil to the Count de Maulde, July 16, 1773, ADPC 10J26.

p. 52:   *Maulde plans to sell the château:* Official document about Mme de Maulde's inheritance from her husband, April 2, 1800, ADPC 10J35.

p. 52:   *December 1775:* The exact date is not known. Count de Maulde, legal claim, November

30, 1778, ADPC 10J35; Abbé Bourgeois to the Count de Maulde, December 11, 1775, CGH (mentions the return of M. de la Pailleterie).

p. 52: *"Antoine Delisle":* M. de Chauvinault to the Count de Maulde, June 3, 1776, CGH; Count de Maulde, legal claim, November 30, 1778, Archives ADPC 10J35.

p. 52: *Antoine at the inn:* Landru, p. 61; Henry, p. 50.

p. 52: *"I am Alexandre Antoine":* Ibid.

p. 52: *Antoine convincing the Abbé:* Henry, pp. 50–51.

p. 53: *"December 11, 1775":* Ibid., p. 51.

p. 53: *Mademoiselle Marie Retou:* Judgment in the dispute between Marie Retou and Thomas Rethoré/Retoré, November 22, 1786, AN LX465.

p. 54: *1776 agreement between Antoine and the Mauldes:* Count de Maulde, legal claim, November 30, 1778, ADPC 10J35.

p. 54: *Chauvinault's findings about Antoine* (including quotations): M. de Chauvinault to the Count de Maulde, June 3, 1776, CGH.

p. 54: *Future legal documents:* Marriage certificate, November 28, 1792, MAD Safe; marriage contract, also November 28, 1792, ADA 304E268.

p. 54: *"wife, to whom he had":* MM, p. 15.

p. 55: *Thomas-Alexandre's arrival:* The Abbé Bourgeois to the Count de Maulde, June 3, 1776, ADPC 10J34d.

p. 55: *"the slave Alexandre":* Landru, p. 65.

p. 55: *Thomas sold in Port-au-Prince:* M. de Chauvinault to the Count de Maulde, June 3, 1776, CGH.

p. 55: *Antoine buys Thomas back:* Ibid.

p. 55: *Abbé Bourgeois about Thomas:* Abbé Bourgeois to the Count de Maulde, June 3, 1776, CGH.

p. 55: *"Monsieur and dear lord":* Ibid.

p. 56: *legal battle:* Count de Maulde, legal claim, November 30, 1778, ADPC 10J35.

p. 56: *Antoine sells his properties:* Document recording Antoine de la Pailleterie's sale of the properties that the Count de Maulde is buying back, ADPC 10J35.

p. 56: *"Never has fortune":* Landru, p. 64.

p. 56: *"Thomas Retoré":* Baptism certificate, Lisieux, September 5, 1777, CGH.

p. 57: *other people in Saint-Domingue with the name Retoré:* Ministère des finances, *État détaillé des liquidations opérées à l'époque du Ier janvier 1829 par la Commission chargée de répartir l'indemnité attribuée aux anciens colons de Saint-Domingue,* Vol. 4 (Paris, 1829), p. 498–99.

p. 57: *Saint-Germain-en-Laye:* François Boulet, *Leçon d'histoire de France,* pp. 95, 110–12.

p. 57: *rue de l'Aigle d'Or:* Marriage contract between Marie Retou and Alexandre Antoine Davy de la Pailleterie, February 13, 1786, CGH.

p. 57: *Davy coat of arms:* Testimony about the Davy family, 1770, BNF NAF 24641; François-Alexandre Aubert de La Chesnaye Des Bois, *Dictionnaire généalogique, héraldique, chronologique et historique,* Vol. 4, p. 546.

p. 57: *La Boëssière academy:* Henry Daressy, ed., *Archives des maîtres-d'armes de Paris* (Paris, 1888), pp. 169–70.

p. 57: *Antoine recognizing his son:* Alexandre's parents are identified in his marriage certificate (abstract of the registry with the certificate of the marriage between Thomas-Alexandre Dumas Davy de la Pailleterie and Marie-Louise Labouret, November 28, 1792, MAD Safe).

p. 57: *Count Thomas-Alexandre Dumas Davy de la Pailleterie:* Gaudu, p. 46; Hauterive, p. 13.

CHAPTER 4: "THERE ARE NO SLAVES IN FRANCE"

p. 58:   *Antoine selling Thomas-Alexandre:* M. de Chauvinault to the Count de Maulde, June 3, 1776, CGH and Sentence dated November 22, 1786; judgment in the dispute between Marie Retou and Thomas Rethoré/Retoré, AN LX465.

p. 58:   *aristocrats' education:* Daniel Roche, *France in the Enlightenment*, p. 651; Olivier Bernier, *Pleasure and Privilege: Daily Life in France, Naples, and America, 1770–1790*, p. 143.

p. 58:   *Dumas's physical abilities:* Ernest d'Hauterive, *Un soldat de la Révolution: Le Général Alexandre Dumas (1762–1806)*, p. 12; Hippolyte Parigot, *Alexandre Dumas Père*, p. 9.

pp. 58–   *Dumas meets Saint-Georges at the academy:* MM, p. 15; Hauterive, p. 13; Paul
59:    Thiébault, *The Memoirs of Baron Thiébault*, trans. Arthur John Butler, Vol. 1 (1896), p. 52.

p. 59:   *his skin was light:* Gabriel Banat, *The Chevalier de Saint-Georges: Virtuoso of the Sword and the Bow*, p. 83.

p. 59:   *Saint-Georges's fight with the Italian:* Ibid., pp. 95–96.

p. 59:   *Saint-Georges was born:* Erick Noël, "Saint-Georges: Un chevalier de sang mêlé dans la société des lumières," pp. 160–63; J.-C. Prod'homme, "Le chevalier de Saint-Georges, escrimeur et musicien," pp. 38–41; La Boëssière (*fils*), *Traité de l'art des armes à l'usage des professeurs et des amateurs*, pp. xv–xvi; Jean Fougeroux de Campigneulles, *Histoire des duels anciens et modernes*, Vol. 1, p. 318; Pierre Bardin, *Joseph de Saint Georges, le Chevalier Noir*, p. 59; Banat, pp. 25, 36–40.

p. 59:   *Saint-Georges's father:* Fougeroux de Campigneulles, p. 318 ("fermier-général"); Prod'homme, pp. 38–41 ("contrôleur général" and planter); Noël, pp. 132–35.

p. 59:   *Saint-Georges's mother:* Fougeroux de Campigneulles, p. 318; Prod'homme, pp. 38–41.

p. 59:   *title of "chevalier":* Erick Noël, *Être noir en France au XVIIIe siecle*, p. 159; Banat, p. 70.

p. 59:   *Marie-Antoinette as patron:* Banat, pp. 150–53, 158.

p. 59:   *"is the most accomplished man in Europe":* Ibid., p. 232.

p. 60:   *letter of protest:* Roger de Beauvoir, *Le Chevalier de Saint-Georges*, p. 405.

p. 60:   *"very rich young man":* Thiébault, *Mémoires du général baron Thiébault*, Vol. 1, p. 193.

p. 60:   *"Man is born free":* Jean-Jacques Rousseau, *Du contrat social, ou principes du droit politique*, p. 4.

p. 60:   *French parlements:* Roland Mousnier, *The Institutions of France under the Absolute Monarchy, 1598–1789: Society and the State*, Vol. 1, p. 256.

p. 61:   *Parlement of Paris: Encyclopédie méthodique: Jurisprudence*, Vol. 6, p. 384; Sue Peabody, *"There Are No Slaves in France": The Political Culture of Race and Slavery in the Ancien Regime*, p. 5.

p. 61:   *jurisdiction of Parlement of Paris:* Peabody, p. 5.

p. 61:   *Somerset decision:* Seymour Drescher, *Abolition: A History of Slavery and Antislavery*, pp. 99–105; Mark S. Weiner, *Black Trials: Citizenship from the Beginnings of Slavery to the End of Caste*, pp. 70–88.

p. 61:   *"The King has been informed":* Peabody, p. 12.

p. 62:   *"not found any ordinance":* Lucien Peytraud, *L'Esclavage aux Antilles françaises avant 1789, d'après des documents inédits des archives coloniales*, Vol. 2, p. 376, quoted in Peabody, p. 13.

p. 62:   *"England was too pure":* Prince Hoare, ed., *Memoirs of Granville Sharp*, p. 77; Weiner, p. 361.

p. 62:   *"Rule, Britannia!":* Helen Kendrich Johnson, *Our Familiar Songs and Those Who Made Them: Three Hundred Standard Songs of the English-Speaking Race* (1909), p. 577.

p. 62:   *"The law takes no notice":* Smith v. Brown and Cooper, 2 Salkeld 666 (1706), in Peabody, p. 5.

p. 62: *1715 Nantes slavery case:* Ibid., pp. 15–16.

p. 62: *Nantes as main transit port for slaves:* Robert Harms, *The Diligent: Worlds of the Slave Trade*, p. 15.

p. 62: *Edict of October 1716:* "Edit du roi, concernant Règlement au Sujet des Esclaves Negres qui seront amenés en France," October 1716, in M. de Boug, *Recueil des édits, déclarations, lettres patentes, arrêts du conseil d'état et du conseil souverain d'Alsace*, Vol. 1 (1657–1725) (1775), pp. 483–84.

p. 63: *"If the masters fail":* Edict of October 1716, Article V.

p. 63: *refused to register the law:* Peabody, p. 22.

p. 63: *"the God of the Christians":* Ibid.

p. 63: *Jean Boucaux case:* Peabody, pp. 24–40; Léo Elisabeth, *La société martiniquaise aux XVIIe et XVIIIe siècles, 1664–1789*, p. 338.

p. 63: *marry only with owners' permission:* Edict of October 1716, Article VII.

p. 63: *"the object of Verdelin's hatred":* Jean Mallet, *Mémoire pour Jean Bocaux*, p. 5.

p. 64: *Gauls and Franks:* Mallet, pp. 2–3.

p. 64: *etymology of franc:* Auguste Scheler, *Dictionnaire d'etymologie française d'après les résultats de la science moderne*, p. 143.

p. 64: *"The custom is such":* Peabody, p. 29.

p. 64: *Dred Scott: Dred Scott v. Sandford*, U.S. 393 (1857).

p. 64: *"French, because he was born":* Peabody, p. 36.

p. 64: *an Anglo-American courtroom:* Since America was a series of colonies, not directly analogous with England or France, it is hard to say what would have happened in England in a similar case. But the British colonies all had anti-miscegenation laws in place. Interracial marriage was outlawed in Maryland in 1661 (Kevin R. Johnson, *Mixed Race America and the Law: A Reader*, p. 11), in Virginia in 1691 (John Van Houten Dippel, *Race to the Frontier: "White Flight" and Westward Expansion*, p. 32), in Massachussetts in 1705 (first colony in New England), in North Carolina in 1741, and so forth. The attitude was not unique to North America. "In 1644 the Antigua Assembly passed a law forbidding 'Carnall Coppullation between Christian and Heathen,' the latter being defined as Negro or Indian," writes Karen Woods Weierman in *One Nation, One Blood*, p. 15.

p. 65: *"whoever sets foot":* Peabody, p. 36.

p. 65: *"the infinite riches":* Ibid., p. 34.

p. 65: *4,200 livres in back pay, plus court costs and damages:* Ibid., p. 36.

p. 65: *"terminate this affair":* Maurepas to M. Le Clerc du Brillet, April 25, 1739, cited in ibid., p. 40.

p. 65: *"the greater part of the negroes":* "Déclaration du Roi, Concernant les Esclaves Nègres des Colonies, qui interprête l'Edit du mois d'Octobre 1716."

p. 65: *"confiscated for the profit of the King":* Peabody, p. 38.

p. 65: *new flood of freedom suits:* Ibid., p. 55.

p. 66: *"Servitude, like a destructive volcano":* Alexandre Ledru-Rollin, *Journal du palais*, Vol. 1 (1840), p. 635.

p. 66: *"The introduction of too many blacks":* Guillaume Poncet de la Grave, quoted by Pierre Boulle, *Race et esclavage dans la France de l'Ancien Régime*, p. 90.

p. 66: *compulsory registration:* Peabody, p. 74.

p. 66: *"disfigured" by mixed blood:* Ibid.

p. 66: *"No one has ever deployed":* La Boëssière (*fils*), quoted in Banat, p. 67.

p. 66: *"La Boëssière's mulatto" incident:* Banat, pp. 68–70.

p. 67: *"a perpetual series of hits":* Ibid., p. 70.

p. 67: *gen d'armes:* Banat, p. 74; Lucien Mouillard, *Les régiments sous Louis XV*; Charles Magnin, *Histoire des marionnettes en Europe: Depuis l'antiquité jusqu'a nos jours*, p. 61.

p. 67:   *1762 ordinance: Ordonnances (de l'amirauté de France) . . . (Des 31 mars et 5 avril 1762)* (Paris, 1762).

p. 67:   *Nanon:* Banat, pp. 40, 45, 72.

p. 67:   *La Boëssière's appearance at the registration tribunal:* Banat, pp. 72–73.

p. 68:   *"multiplies every day":* Peabody, pp. 85–86.

p. 68:   *allowed to retain its colonial outposts in India:* Jaswant Lal Mehta, *Advanced Study in the History of Modern India, 1707–1813,* p. 358.

p. 69:   *"In the end, the race":* Peabody, p. 117.

p. 69:   *Police des Noirs:* "Déclaration du Roi, pour la police des Noirs, donnée à Versailles le 9 août 1777," ANOM, F1B 1 à F1B 4; François-André Isambert, Decrusy, and Alphonse-Honoré Taillandier, *Table du recueil général des anciennes lois françaises, depuis l'an 420 jusqu'à la révolution de 1789,* vol. 29 (1833), p. 251.

p. 69:   *certificate for "colored" subjects:* Peabody, p. 129.

p. 69:   *race laws poorly administered*: Ibid., p. 124.

CHAPTER 5: AMERICANS IN PARIS

p. 71:   *"One of the handsomest men":* Author unknown, "Le général Dumas, homme de couleur," n.d. [1797], BNF NAF 24641.

p. 71:   *"dark—very dark":* Arthur Davidson, *Alexandre Dumas (père): His Life and Works,* p. 4.

p. 71:   *"well built":* MM, p. 15.

p. 71:   *average height*: Paolo Malanima, *Pre-modern European Economy: One Thousand Years,* p. 310.

p. 71:   *Dumas's height:* Registry of the Dragoons in the Regiment of the Queen, Dumas entry, June 2, 1786, CGH.

p. 71:   *Dumas's hands and feet:* MM, p. 15.

p. 72:   *Dumas's youth in Paris:* Ernest d'Hauterive, *Un soldat de la Révolution,* p. 13; Placide David, "Le général Th. Alexandre Dumas," p. 39; Victor-Emmanuel Roberto Wilson, *Le Général Alexandre Dumas: Soldat de la liberté,* p. 57.

p. 72:   *"In the midst of the elegant youth":* MM, p. 15.

p. 72:   *Louis XVI's passion for hunting, clocks, and locks:* Simon Schama, *Citizens: A Chronicle of the French Revolution,* p. 54; François Barrière and Mme Maigné, *The Private Life of Marie Antoinette: Autobiographical Memoirs of Madame Campan,* p. 164.

p. 72:   *After a hunt:* Michael Forsyth, *Buildings for Music,* p. 112.

p. 72:   *Antoine spending money in Paris:* M. Delisson to the Count de Maulde, June 25, 1786, ADPC 10J35.

p. 72:   *men of color as "Americans":* John D. Garrigus, " 'Sons of the Same Father': Gender, Race, and Citizenship in French Saint-Domingue, 1760–1792," p. 152.

p. 73:   *alliance with the American colonies:* Treaty of Amity and Commerce, February 6, 1778, in *The Controversy over Neutral Rights Between the United States and France, 1797–1800,* ed. James Brown Scott and John Chandler Davis, p. 441.

p. 73:   *"electrical ambassador":* Schama, p. 44.

p. 73:   *humiliation in French India:* N. R. Madhava, *Criminal Justice India Series: Pondicherry,* p. 7.

p. 73:   *free blacks at Siege of Savannah:* Michael Lee Lanning, *African Americans in the Revolutionary War,* p. 85.

p. 74:   *two wires hanging to the ground: American Footprints in Paris,* ed. Frances Wilson Huard, p. 104.

p. 74:   *"à la John Paul Jones"* and *sailing-ship hats:* Guillaume Imbert de Boudeaux, *Correspon-*

dance secrète, politique & littéraire, Vol. 8, p. 288; Gabriel d'Èze and A. Marcel, *Histoire de la coiffure des femmes en France*, pp. 166–68.

p. 75: *"France retained glory and ruin"*: Jules Michelet, *Histoire de France au dix-huitième siècle: Louis XV et Louis XVI*, p. 247.

p. 75: *full-length portrait of Louis XVI:* Catalogue, "The Final Sale of the Relics of General Washington," p. 36, item 266.

p. 75: *"the protector of the rights of mankind"*: Benson John Lossing, *Harpers' Popular Cyclopaedia of United States History from the Aboriginal Period to 1876*, Vol. 2, pp. 1490–91.

p. 76: *Le Club de Boston ou des Américains*: *Fortnightly Review*, Vol. 117 (London, 1922), p. 219.

p. 76: *"French affairs are harder"*: Lafayette to Washington, quoted by André Maurois, *A History of France*, p. 270.

p. 76: *French optimism about American slavery:* Edward Seeber, *Anti-Slavery Opinion in France During the Second Half of the Eighteenth Century*, p. 117.

p. 76: *plays about idyllic life in Virginia:* Adam Zamoyski, *Holy Madness: Romantics, Patriots, and Revolutionaries, 1776–1871*, p. 19.

p. 76: *three-hour coach ride:* François Boulet, *Leçon d'histoire de France: Saint-Germain-en-Laye*, p. 109.

p. 76: *candlelit lamps:* Nicholas Papayanis, *Planning Paris Before Haussmann*, p. 44; Louis de Sivry and M. de Rolot, *Précis historique de Saint-Germain-en-Laye*, p. 284.

p. 77: *"dazzle, but close to give"*: Louis-Sébastien Mercier, *Panorama of Paris* (1999), p. 132.

p. 77: *lackeys:* Fernand Braudel, *Civilization and Capitalism, 15th–18th Century*, Vol. 3: *The Perspective of the World*, p. 328.

p. 77: *Dumas lost his lackey at sea:* Alexandre Dumas to Marie-Louise, June 18, 1798, MAD.

p. 77: *"long and brown"*: Alexandre Dumas (*père*), *Les trois mousquetaires*, vol. 1, p. 6.

p. 77: *"so stunning [and] appalling"*: Mercier, *Panorama of Paris*, p. 45.

p. 77: *fishwives and peddlers:* Louis-Sebastien Mercier, *Paris*, Vol. 2 (1817), p. 151.

p. 77: *"M. le Marquis wasn't living"*: M. Delisson to the Count de Maulde, June 25, 1786, ADPC 10J35.

p. 78: *"France is to fashion"*: Mrs. John Melville, "Point d'Alençon," *Overland Monthly* 4 (Jan. 1870), p. 64.

p. 78: *"A carriage is the grand object"*: Mercier, *Paris*, Vol. 2, p. 205.

p. 78: *"is necessarily filthy, black"*: Mercier, *Panorama of Paris*, p. 41.

p. 79: *diamonds:* Mercier, *Paris*, Vol. 2, pp. 295–96.

p. 79: *"No, no, this is not me"* and *"back from the dead"*: Letter cited by Robert Landru, *À propos d'Alexandre Dumas*, pp. 66–70.

CHAPTER 6: BLACK COUNT IN THE CITY OF LIGHT

p. 80: *rue Étienne:* Certificate with Dumas's address in Paris, rue Étienne (spelled "Estienne"), undated, BNF NAF 24641.

p. 80: *Paris's remodeling:* Eric Hazan and David Fernbach, *The Invention of Paris: A History in Footsteps*, pp. 14–15; Colin Jones, *Paris: The Biography of a City*, p. 180.

p. 80: *"The Palais Royal was the heart and soul"*: Johannes Willms, *Paris, Capital of Europe: From the Revolution to the Belle Epoque*, p. 5.

p. 80: *palace of Cardinal Richelieu:* Jones, p. 222.

p. 80: *went to the Orléans family:* Henry Sutherland Edwards, *Old and New Paris: Its History, Its People, and Its Places*, Vol. 1, p. 166.

p. 80: *"In a single day"*: Jones, p. 193.

p. 81: *mesmerism:* Robert Darnton, *Mesmerism and the End of the Enlightenment in France*, p. 161.

p. 81:   *Philippe Curtius and Marie Tussaud:* Pamela M. Pileam, *Madame Tussaud and the History of Waxworks*, pp. 17, 23–24.

p. 81:   *Parisian cafés:* W. Scott Haine, *The World of the Paris Café: Sociability Among the French Working Class, 1789–1914*, pp. 209–10; Thomas Okey, *Paris and Its Story*, p. 334; Schama, pp. 135–36.

p. 81:   *Marx and Engels at the Palais Royal:* Karl Baedeker, *Paris and Its Environs*, 6th ed., p. 18.

p. 81:   *"The chairs, which are placed":* Melchior von Grimm and Denis Diderot, *Correspondance littéraire, philosophique et critique*, Vol. 2, pp. 535–37, in Willms, p. 6.

p. 82:   *"brown and mellow" eyes:* MM, p. 23; Hippolyte Parigot, *Alexandre Dumas Père*, p. 9.

p. 82:   *Nicolet's Theater:* F. W. J. Hemmings, *Theatre and State in France: 1760–1905*, pp. 2, 27–40.

p. 82:   *replacing a sick leading man with a monkey:* Ferdinand Hoefer, *Nouvelle biographie générale*, Vol. 37.

p. 83:   *incident at the Nicolet theater:* Thomas-Alexandre Dumas, testimony about the incident, September 15, 1784, BNF NAF 24641. See also Jean-Pierre Titon's testimony, September 15, 1784, BNF NAF 24641. Dumas's testimony provides details about the racial insults that cannot be found in M. Titon's testimony.

p. 83:   *Thomas-Alexandre attending a performance:* Dumas, Nicolet incident testimony.

p. 83:   *"a very beautiful Creole":* MM, p. 18.

p. 83:   *two armed companions:* Or only one? Dumas, in his testimony, mentions only one man with Titon, but Titon says he was with two men.

p. 83:   *"You are quite beautiful":* Dumas, Nicolet incident testimony.

p. 83:   *"I would be pleased":* Ibid.

p. 83:   *M. Titon's position in the West Indies:* Several letters and military notes about him, 1779, ANOM COL E 379bis.

p. 83:   *"like Americans?"* and the following eight quotations: Dumas, Nicolet incident testimony.

p. 86:   *"Oh, I beg your pardon":* MM, p. 18.

p. 87:   *"every smile an insult":* Alexandre Dumas (*père*), *Les trois mousquetaires*, Vol. 1, p. 9.

p. 87:   *declaration by the marshals; Thomas-Alexandre freed:* The marshals' testimony about the incident at the Nicolet theater, September 16, 1784, BNF NAF 24641.

CHAPTER 7: A QUEEN'S DRAGOON

p. 89:   *the marriage:* Marriage contract between Marie Retou and Alexandre Antoine Davy de la Pailleterie, February 13, 1786, CGH.

p. 89:   *"marriage caused a cooling-off":* MM, p. 21.

p. 89:   *money problems with the new stepmother:* Judgment in the dispute between Marie Retou and Thomas Rethoré/Retoré, November 22, 1786, AN LX465. See also Dumas to Marie-Louise, September 15, 1796, MAD Safe.

p. 89:   *"it is very dishonorable":* Horace Walpole to Richard West, in Eliakim Littell and Robert S. Littell, *Littell's Living Age*, Vol. 78, p. 307.

p. 90:   *Thomas-Alexandre enlists:* Registry of the Dragoons in the Regiment of the Queen, Dumas entry, June 2, 1786, CGH.

p. 90:   *"[My father] told him":* MM, pp. 21–22.

p. 91:   *first record of the name:* Registry of the Dragoons in the Regiment of the Queen, Dumas entry, June 2, 1786, CGH.

p. 91:   *"Dumas, Alexandre":* Dumas signed his name "Alexandre," but the military administration kept referring to him as "Thomas Alexandre" (either "Dumas Davy de la Pailleterie" or "Dumas") well into the 1790s.

p. 91: *"Thomas Retoré"*: The name is spelled Rethoré in the transcription of a sentence dated November 22, 1786, AN LX465. It is spelled Rettoré in legal notes about a dispute between Dumas and Castillon, August 9, 1786, AN Y1787.

p. 91: *"son of Antoine and Cecette Dumas"*: Registry of the Dragoons in the Regiment of the Queen, Dumas entry, June 2, 1786, CGH.

p. 91: *"Native of Jemerie"*: Registry of the Dragoons in the Regiment of the Queen, Dumas entry, June 2, 1786, CGH.

p. 91: *"from Jeremie, in America"*: Military certificate, September 9, 1792, SHD 7YD91.

p. 91: *"show proof"*: "Règlement portant que nul ne pourra être proposé à des sous-lieutenances s'il n'a fait preuve de quatre générations de noblesse"—the so-called "Segur ordinance," named after the Count de Segur, the minister who passed it on May 22, 1781.

p. 92: *Antoine died:* Death certificate of Alexandre-Antoine Davy de la Pailleterie in Saint-Germain-en-Laye, June 16, 1786, MAD Safe.

p. 92: *a letter to the Count de Maulde:* M. Delisson to the Count de Maulde, June 25, 1786, ADPC 10J35.

p. 92: *"The death of M. le Marquis"*: Document recording the sale of properties owned by the Count de Maulde, August 12, 1786, ADPC 10J35.

p. 93: *four-century-long connection:* The Manoir de la Pailleterie in Bielleville was built in 1602. Jacques Vauquelin, *Châteaux, manoirs, monuments et sites de la région bolbécaise*, p. 92.

p. 93: *a serious sum:* Document about the sale of properties owned by the Count de Maulde, August 12, 1786, ADPC 10J35.

p. 93: *dragoons:* Commandant Bucquoy, *Dragons et guides d'état-major*; René Chartrand and Eugène Leliepvre, *Louis XV's Army (1): Cavalry and Dragoons*; Erik A. Lund, *War for the Every Day: Generals, Knowledge, and Warfare in Early Modern Europe, 1680–1740*, p. 71.

p. 93: *got their name from carbine muskets:* Auguste Scheler, *Dictionnaire d'étymologie française d'après les resultats de la science moderne* (1888), p. 162.

p. 93: *musketeers:* Richard Mowery Andrews, *Law, Magistracy, and Crime in Old Regime Paris, 1735–1789: The System of Criminal Justice*, Vol. 1, pp. 38–39; André Corvisier and John Childs, eds., *A Dictionary of Military History and the Art of War*, p. 334.

p. 93: *they got poorer horses:* Lund, p. 71.

p. 93: *dragoons battled smugglers:* Joseph Tiré de Cléron, *Abrégé de la vie de Louis Mandrin, chef de contrebandiers en France*, pp. 28–30. Much as anti-drug agents sometimes fall victim to the temptation of trafficking, dragoons were sometimes implicated in salt-smuggling rackets (see Roland Mousnier, *The Institutions of France under the Absolute Monarchy, 1598–1789*, p. 459).

p. 94: *France's so-called iron belt:* Michael Wolfe, *Walled Towns and the Shaping of France*, p. 151.

p. 94: *"The liberty that he had known"* and the next two quotations: MM, pp. 23–24.

p. 95: *weight of a musket:* Encyclopédie Didérot d'Alembert, Vol. 15 (1782), p. 568; *Aide-mémoire à l'usage des officiers d'artillerie de France* (1819), p. 562; Captain Gervais, *À la conquête de l'Europe* (1939), cited in Terry Crowdy, *French Revolutionary Infantryman, 1791–1802* (2003), p. 13.

p. 95: *the dragoons' Norman horses:* Robert Landru, in *À propos d'Alexandre Dumas* (p. 80), mentions that the Queen's Dragoons in Laon used "chevaux normands."

p. 95: *weight of a Norman horse:* "Site officiel du Syndicat national des éleveurs et utilisateurs de chevaux Cob Normand," www.cobnormand.com.

p. 95: *"many feats"*: Arthur Davidson, *Alexandre Dumas (père): His Life and Works*, p. 4.

p. 95: *it seems impossible:* By comparison, the current world record for lifting weights is 580 pounds hoisted by Rezazadeh Hossein, in a clean and jerk lift during the 2004 Athens Summer Olympics. International Weightlifting Federation, http://www.iwf.net.

p. 95: *duels illegal:* Philippe-Antoine Merlin, *Répertoire universel et raisonné de jurisprudence*, Vol. 5 (1827), p. 492; Fougeroux de Campigneulles, *Histoire des duels anciens et modernes*, Vol. 1, p. 310.

p. 95: *gashed twice in the head:* MM, p. 54.

p. 96: *"My father had hardly rejoined":* Ibid., p. 28.

p. 98: *crowds in Grenoble pelted royal troops:* J. A. Félix Fauré, *Les assemblées de Vizille & de Romans en Dauphiné durant l'année 1788*, pp. 102–15.

p. 98: *freakish weather returned:* Charlotte Julia von Leyden Blennerhassett, *Madame de Staël: Her Friends and Her Influence in Politics and Literature*, Vol. 1, p. 273.

p. 99: *French Guards:* Andrews, pp. 38–41, 520.

p. 101: *population of 650,000:* Colin Jones, *Paris: The Biography of a City*, p. 177.

p. 101: *fewer than ten thousand men:* Andrews, p. 38.

p. 101: *"We are Citizens before Soldiers":* Simon Schama, *Citizens: A Chronicle of the French Revolution*, p. 375.

p. 101: *"The ferment at Paris":* Arthur Young, *Travels During the Years 1787, 1788, and 1789 . . .*, Vol. 1, pp. 249–50.

p. 101: *Charleville muskets:* Schama, pp. 388–89.

p. 102: *king met the new Paris municipal government:* Louis Blanc, *Histoire de la Révolution Française*, Vol. 2, pp. 418–22.

p. 102: *dragoons stationed in Laon:* "Régiments de dragons," L'Union Nationale de l'Arme Blindée Cavalerie Chars website, http://unabcc.free.fr/historique/régiments-de-dragons.

p. 103: *Claude Labouret with the National Guard:* Labouret is identified as "Commandant de la Garde, Nationale de Villers-Cotterêts & propriétaire de l'hôtel de l'Ecu" when his daughter marries Dumas. Dumas's and Marie-Louise's marriage certificate, November 28, 1792, MAD Safe.

BOOK TWO

CHAPTER 8: SUMMERS OF REVOLUTION

p. 107: *Great Fear:* David Andress, *The French Revolution and the People*, pp. 68–69, 94, 113–15; Simon Schama, *Citizens: A Chronicle of the French Revolution*, pp. 428–33; Donald M. G. Sutherland, *The French Revolution and Empire*, pp. 65–68.

p. 107: *famine pact:* Andress, p. 205. There were also theories that nobles were behind the alleged brigands (see Sutherland, p. 67; Schama p. 429).

p. 107: *destitution and bread prices:* Sutherland, pp. 46, 50–51.

p. 107: *raised expectations:* François Furet, *Interpreting the French Revolution*, pp. 110–11.

p. 107: *backstory of opportunism:* Sutherland, pp. 46, 65–68; Schama, p. 433.

p. 108: *brigands and village bells:* Lefebvre, *The Great Fear of 1789*, p. 156.

p. 108: *brisk aristocratic tourist trade:* Ernest Roch, "L'ancien château royal" and "Le Général Alexandre Dumas"; André Moreau-Néret, "L'Hostellerye de l'Escu de France," p. 136.

p. 108: *best hunting in France:* Louis-Ferdinand-Alfred Maury, *Les forêts de la Gaule et de l'ancienne France*, p. 165.

p. 108: *brief family embarassment:* Roch, "L'ancien château royal," pp. 306–7.

p. 109: *sent for the dragoons:* Roch, "Le Général Alexandre Dumas," pp. 89–90.

p. 109: *twenty dragoons:* Roch, "La Reine Dragons," pp. 74–76.

p. 109: *One in particular:* Letter from a citizen of Villers-Cotterêts to another from Pierrefonds, cited in Roch, "Le Général Alexandre Dumas," pp. 90–91.

p. 109: *nearly half a head taller:* See physical descriptions in Pierre Nougaret, *Anecdotes mili-*

taires, anciennes & modernes de tous les peuples, Vol. 4, p. 260; Jean-Baptiste Courcelles, "Dumas (Alexandre Davy)," p. 502; René-Nicolas Desgenettes, *Souvenirs de la fin du XVIIIe siècle et du commencement du XIXe*, Vol. 3, p. 124.

p. 109: *"Dear Julie"*: Roch, "Le Général Alexandre Dumas," p. 91.

p. 110: *Hôtel de l'Ecu:* Moreau-Néret, "L'Hostellerye de l'Escu de France," p. 92.

p. 111: *Viscount de Noailles:* "Séance du 4 août 1789," *La Tribune Française* (August 4–13, 1789), p. 47.

p. 111: *to consider abolishing slavery:* "Assemblée Nationale, Séance du 27 Juin 1789," *Journal des débats, des lois du pouvoir legislatif et des actes du gouvernement* (1971), p. 69.

p. 111: *Society of the Friends of the Blacks:* Marcel Dorigny and Bernard Gainot, *La Société des Amis des Noirs, 1788–1799.*

p. 111: *a "moment of patriotic drunkenness":* Marquis de Ferrières, *Correspondance inédite*, p. 114.

p. 111: *"the representatives of the French people":* Declaration of Human and Civic Rights of 1789. The Declaration has become the preamble to the current French Constitution.

p. 111: *Jefferson and the Rights of Man:* William Howard Adams, *The Paris Years of Thomas Jefferson*, pp. 284–85; Harlow G. Unger, *Lafayette*, pp. 233–34.

p. 112: *"Where is that villain?":* James de Chambrier, *Marie-Antoinette, reine de France*, Vol. 1, p. 62.

p. 113: *performance space for the Comédie-Française:* Francis Miltoun, *Royal Palaces and Parks of France*, p. 112.

p. 113: *National Assembly in the Manège:* Armand Brette, *Histoire des édifices où sont siégé les assemblées parlementaires*, pp. 158–68.

p. 113: *"I have always been afraid":* Thomas Jefferson to Thomas Paine, July 11, 1789, in *Memoirs, Correspondence and Private Papers of Thomas Jefferson*, Vol. 2, p. 496.

p. 113: *a delegation of free men of color* and the *"Club Massiac":* Dubois, *Avengers of the New World*, pp. 75–77, 80–85.

p. 113: *"the terror of the colonists":* Florence Gauthier, *L'aristocratie de l'épiderme*, p. 90.

p. 113: *"to lose everything":* *Journal encyclopédique ou universel*, Vol. 8, part 2 (1790), p. 248.

p. 114: parlement *courts were suspended and abolished:* Lynn Avery Hunt, *Revolution and Urban Politics in Provincial France*, p. 130.

p. 114: *"active citizens":* Law of December 22, 1789, "De la formation des assemblées pour l'élection des représentants à l'Assemblée nationale," in Leopold Georges Wickham Legg, ed., *Select Documents Illustrative of the History of the French Revolution*, p. 161. Approximately 4.3 million men, or two-thirds of the adult male population, became citizens in this way (Sutherland, p. 83).

p. 114: *women and Republican citizenship:* David A. Bell, *The Cult of the Nation in France*, p. 127; Susan G. Bell and Karen M. Offen, *Women, the Family, and Freedom: 1750–1880*, pp. 97–109.

p. 114: *Nearly a million positions:* Sutherland, p. 82.

p. 115: *Alexandre and Marie-Louis were engaged:* Claude Labouret to Jean-Denis Leroy, in Roch, "Le Général Alexandre Dumas," p. 92.

p. 115: *Dumas left Villers-Cotterêts:* Roch, "Le Général Alexandre Dumas," p. 92.

p. 116: *Fête de la Fédération:* Henri Gourdon de Genouillac, *Paris à travers les siècles*, p. 175; Henriette Dillon, *Journal d'une femme de cinquante ans*, Vol. 1, pp. 241–43.

p. 116: *"The Nation, the Law, the King":* *Gazette Nationale*, no. 197, July 16, 1790, in *Réimpression de l'ancien Moniteur*, Vol. 5, p. 129.

p. 116: *"King of the French":* Ibid., p. 131.

p. 116: *"Frenchmen, we are free":* *Dictionnaire de la conversation et de la lecture*, Vol. 26, p. 381.

p. 116: *first American flag displayed outside the United States:* Unger, p. 266.

p. 117: *feasting and public balls:* Gourdon, pp. 178–79; Rebecca L. Spang, *The Invention of the Restaurant: Paris and Modern Gastronomic Culture*, pp. 100–103.

p. 117: *Louis's apparent enthusiasm:* Schama, p. 506.

p. 117: *hundreds of thousands of aristocratic émigrés:* Colin Jones, *The Longman Companion to the French Revolution*, p. 199.

p. 118: *"done their business for us as rivals":* Edmund Burke, *The Works of Edmund Burke*, Vol. 1, p. 451.

p. 119: *cover story to explain Louis's flight:* Schama, p. 555.

p. 119: *petition was drafted denouncing Louis:* François-Alphonse Aulard, *La Société des Jacobins: Juillet 1791 à juin 1792*, Vol. 3, p. 20.

p. 120: *royal plot to destroy republicanism:* Andress, p. 191.

p. 120: *Alex Dumas and the Sixth Dragoons also rode:* Dumas to the Committee of Public Safety, January 4, 1794, SHD 3B9.

p. 120: *Champ de Mars Massacre:* Andress; Wickham Legg, pp. 110–14.

CHAPTER 9: "REGENERATION BY BLOOD"

p. 121: *"Remember those crusades":* Patriote françois, no. 857, December 13, 1791, reprinted in Albert Mathiez, *La révolution et les étrangers: Cosmopolitisme et défense nationale*, p. 61.

p. 121: *"the forces necessary":* The Pillnitz Declaration, signed by the Austrian emperor and the king of Prussia on August 27, 1791. Text reprinted in Raymond Williams Postgate, *Revolution from 1789 to 1906*, p. 39.

p. 121: *"It is a cruel thing to think":* Jeanne-Marie Roland to Bancal des Issarts, June 25, 1791, in Charles-Aimé Dauban, *Étude sur Madame Roland et son temps*, p. ci.

p. 122: *"simplicity, goodness, and that dignity":* Eloise Ellery, *Brissot de Warville: A Study in the History of the French Revolution*, p. 72.

p. 122: *Washington demurred:* Ellery, p. 80.

p. 122: *slaves, pitted against the land of liberty:* The rhetoric of slavery could apply to internal enemies as well, e.g., Brissot at the National Assembly on June 1, 1792: "Slaves of the Austrian system, the Montmorins and Lessarts have never been more than puppets whose main string was in Vienna; this same string controlled the committee at Versailles while the people were toppling the Bastille." *Archives parlementaires de 1787 à 1860*, Vol. 44 (May 22–June 8, 1792), p. 445.

p. 123: *"The War Song for the Army of the Rhine":* François Le Roy de Sainte Croix, *Le chant de guerre pour l'armée du Rhin, ou la Marseillaise*, pp. 38–39.

p. 123: *"What do they want, this horde of slaves":* Second verse of the "Marseillaise" as published on September 4, 1792, in the *Courrier de Strasbourg*, in Le Roy de Sainte Croix, p. 15.

p. 123: *"We cannot be at ease":* Robert Roswell Palmer, *The Age of the Democratic Revolutions*, Vol. 2 (1959–64), p. 60.

p. 123: *"It is because I want peace":* Baron Cloots quoted in David A. Bell, *The First Total War*, p. 115. (See Bell's excellent description of Cloots and the international revolutionary warmongers.)

p. 124: *Louis de la Pailleterie military service:* An official document dated 1766 refers to Louis as *"Lieutenant Colonel commandant l'artillerie a Dieppe Chevalier de l'ordre royal est militaire de St Louis,"* ADPC, file 26; Edouard Delobette, *Ces Messieurs du Havre*, p. 1243; Alexandre Mazas, *Histoire de l'ordre royal et militaire de Saint-Louis*, p. 57 (giving Louis's ranks in the *Registre des Officiers supérieurs d'artillerie avant 1789*).

p. 124: *"I lead a gang of thieves":* Count de Saint-Germain to Joseph Pâris du Verney, November 11, 1757, cited in Claude Louis, *Correspondance particulière du comte de Saint-Germain*, p. 1.

p. 124: *nearly a third of central Europe:* Cathal J. Nolan, *The Age of Wars of Religion, 1000–1650* (2006), p. 857.

p. 126: *"Now suppose there arises":* Jacques de Guibert, *Essai général de tactique*, Vol. 2, p. 16.

p. 126: *maps:* William McNeill, *The Pursuit of Power*, pp. 161–62.

p. 127: *strike at the Austrian Netherlands under Biron and Dillon:* Ernest d'Hauterive, *L'armée sous la Révolution, 1789–1794*, pp. 197–98; Edward Baines, *History of the Wars of the French Revolution*, Vol. 1, p. 25; Heinrich von Sybel, *History of the French Revolution*, Vol. 1, pp. 447–50.

p. 127: *recently promoted to corporal:* Executive Council to Dumas, September 2, 1792, SHD 7YD91, and note of the Historical Service, November 6, 1848, SHD Y7D91.

p. 128: *recommended for court martial:* d'Hauterive, p. 198.

p. 128: *the Austrian-Prussian coalition issued another threat:* The Coblentz Declaration, or "Brunswick Manifesto," written by the Duke of Brunswick, a commander in the Prussian army, July 25, 1792, in Adolphe Thiers, *The History of the French Revolution, 1789–1800*, Vol. 1, pp. 296–300.

p. 129: *Dumas at Maulde:* Le Moniteur Universel, reprinted in *Réimpression de l'Ancien Moniteur*, Vol. 13 (1842), p. 434; Antoine-Vincent Arnault et al., "Dumas (Alexandre Davy-de-la-Pailleterie)," p. 160; Ernest Roch, "Le Général Alexandre Dumas," p. 93.

p. 129: *Dumas's charge:* Arnault et al., p. 160.

p. 129: *"Spotting them":* MM, p. 30.

p. 130: *"cut [the enemy riders] off so deftly":* Le Moniteur Universel, August 18, 1792, in *Réimpression de l'ancien Moniteur*, Vol. 13 (1842).

p. 130: *"Citizen Dumas, American":* Dumas, letter about the event in Maulde, *Gazette nationale*, no. 341, December 6, 1792, in *Réimpression de l'ancien Moniteur*, Vol. 13 (1842).

CHAPTER 10: "THE BLACK HEART ALSO BEATS FOR LIBERTY"

p. 131: *Verdun commander committed suicide:* Colonel Nicolas-Joseph Beaurepaire took his own life rather than face the indignity of handing over the fortress to the Prussians. See Arthur Chuquet, *La première invasion Prussienne*, and "The Campaign in France," in *Miscellaneous Travels of J. W. Goethe*, ed. L. Dora Schmitz (1884), p. 93, in which Goethe discusses how, in Beaurepaire's suicide, "a trait of a republican character was presented to us . . . [an] example of the highest patriotic devotion."

p. 131: *"ardently pray":* London Times, Monday, September 10, 1792.

p. 132: *Lafayette was arrested by the Prussians:* Harlow G. Unger, *Lafayette*, p. 290.

p. 132: *"Here and now a new epoch":* Richard Friedenthal and Martha Friedenthal-Haase, *Goethe: His Life and Times*, p. 313.

p. 133: *Edict of Fraternity:* "Décret qui promet secours et fraternité à tous les peuples qui voudront recouvrer leur liberté," November 19, 1792, in *A Collection of Addresses Transmitted by Certain English Clubs and Societies to the National Convention of France*, p. 19.

p. 133: *"free legions":* Bernard Gainot, *Les officiers de couleur dans les armées de la République et de l'Empire, 1792–1815*, pp. 22–33.

p. 133: *their own legions:* Belgian legion and Germanic legion: Gainot, p. 32; English legion: Adam Zamoyski, *Holy Madness*, p. 79.

p. 133: *legion of "Vandals":* Marita Gilli, *Le Cheminement de l'idée européenne dans les idéologies de la paix et de la guerre*, p. 43.

p. 133: *The group was led by Julien Raimond:* Gainot, pp. 33–38.

p. 134: *"Free Legion of Americans":* "Formation du Régiment d'hussards américains et du Midy, d'après le décrêt du 7 septembre," 1792, SHD XK9.

p. 134: *Saint-Georges:* Jean Fougeroux de Campigneulles, *Histoire des duels anciens et modernes*, pp. 300–303; J.C. Prodhomme, "Le chevalier de Saint-Georges, escrimeur et musicien," *Les annales coloniales*, no. 51 (March 1936), pp. 38–41; Gainot, pp. 43, 49; Erick Noël, "Saint-Georges, Un chevalier de sang mêlé dans la Société les Lumières," pp. 131–53; Gabriel Banat, *The Chevalier de Saint-Georges*; Pierre Bardin, *Joseph de Saint George, le Chevalier Noir*, pp. 59–61.

p. 134: *Hussars of Liberty and Equality:* Executive Council document, September 2, 1792, SHD 7YD91.

p. 134: *Dumas's commission with the Hussards of the South:* Ibid.

p. 134: *Dumas joined up with the Americans:* Approval of Dumas's nomination as lieutenant-colonel in the Legion, September 15, 1792, SHD XK9; also see Léon Hennet, *État militaire de France pour l'année 1793*, p. 222.

p. 134: *Dumas's commission with the Black Legion:* Military report dated September 15, 1792, SHD XK9; minister of war to Dumas, October 10, 1792, MAD Safe.

p. 135: *law reaffirming the freedom principle:* Declared by the National Assembly, September 18, 1791, "sanctioned" by the king on October 16. *Collection générale des décrets rendus par l'Assemblée Nationale, Mois de Septembre 1791, deuxième partie*, p. 725.

p. 135: *lobbyists to work the deputies:* Laurent Dubois, *Avengers of the New World*, pp. 85–90.

p. 135: *Julien Raimond:* On Raimond's life and his efforts on behalf of free blacks, see Dubois, pp. 60–83, and John D. Garrigus, *Before Haiti: Race and Citizenship in French Saint-Domingue.*

p. 136: *"new whites":* Garrigus, p. 220.

p. 136: *"that there will be no change":* Abbé Grégoire, *Lettre aux philantropes sur les malheurs, les droits et les réclamations des gens de couleur de Saint-Domingue*, p. 12.

p. 136: *French colonies received word:* Dubois, pp. 80, 98.

p. 137: *ten insurgents killed for every white death:* Jeremy D. Popkin, *A Concise History of the Haitian Revolution*, p. 42.

p. 137: *"The black heart also beats":* Brissot, December 1, 1791, in Claude Wanquet, *La France et la première abolition de l'esclavage, 1794–1802*, p. 27.

p. 137: *full citizenship to freed blacks:* "Décret relatif aux moyens d'apaiser les troubles des colonies," April 4, 1792, in J. B. Duvergier, *Collection complète des lois, décrets, ordonnances, réglements, avis du conseil-d'état*, Vol. 4, pp. 90–91.

p. 138: *"sale, impression, or distribution":* Dubois, p. 103.

p. 138: *"If Nature, inexhaustible":* Gainot, p. 35.

p. 138: *"Sirs, Virtue in Honor":* Ibid.

p. 139: *"The future marriage between citizen":* Marriage contract, November 28, 1792, ADA 304E268.

p. 139: *"Citizen" and "Citizeness":* Gabriel Demante, *Définition légale de la qualité de citoyen*, pp. 25–26.

p. 139: *"will not suffer the title":* Excerpt from the *Patriote François*, printed in *Le Moniteur Universel*, no. 270, September 26, 1792, in *Réimpression de l'ancien Moniteur*, Vol. 14 (1858), p. 39.

p. 140: *The couple were married:* Marriage contract, November 28, 1792, ADA 304E268.

p. 140: *Dumas père's baptism:* Alexandre Dumas to General Brune, July 26, 1802, BNF NAF 24641; baptism certificate, *Registres d'état civil*, Commune de Villers-Cotterêts, ADA.

p. 140: *"Citizen Louis Augustin":* Dumas's and Marie-Louise's marriage certificate, November 28, 1792, MAD Safe.

p. 140: *Espagne rising to Count of the Empire:* Charles Mullié, *Biographie des célébrités militaires des armées de terre et de mer de 1789 à 1850*, Vol. 1, pp. 497–98.

p. 140: *"widow of the late Anoine":* Dumas's and Marie-Louise's marriage certificate, November 28, 1792, MAD Safe.

p. 140: *reconciliation between Dumas and Retou:* Judgment in the dispute between Thomas Rethoré/Retoré and Marie Retou, November 22, 1786, AN LX465.

p. 140: *financial conditions of the marriage*, including quotation: Marriage contract, November 28, 1792, ADA 304E268.

p. 141: *The honeymoon was brief:* The town gave Dumas a certificate verifying that he was a "good citizen," dated December 15, 1792, which suggests he left on that day—or at the very least shortly after (certificate, December 15, 1792, SHD 7YD91). According to Ernest Roch, "Le Général Alexandre Dumas," p. 94, Dumas left seventeen days after his wedding.

p. 141: *first child:* Alexandrine Aimée's birth certificate, September 10, 1793, ADA.

p. 141: *evolution of the Legion:* Jacques de Cauna, *Haïti: L'éternelle révolution* (2009), p. 211; Bardin, p. 153; Banat, p. 380; Gainot, pp. 51–54; and Erick Noël, "Une entreprise originale—La Légion Noire de a Révolution," p. 233.

p. 142: *"As the head of the regiment":* MM, p. 34.

p. 142: *"[Dumas] led his young warriors":* Antoine-Vincent Arnault, "Dumas (Alexandre Davy-de-la-Pailleterie)," pp. 160–61. The [correct] name of the city is "Mouvaux."

p. 143: *Saint-Georges going to Lille:* Ernest d'Hauterive, *Un soldat de la Révolution: Le Général Alexandre Dumas (1762–1806),* pp. 32–33.

p. 143: *Saint-Georges going to Paris:* Erick Noël, "Saint-Georges: Un chevalier de sang mêlé dans la société des Lumières," p. 143.

p. 143: *Saint-Georges accused:* Banat, pp. 380–81 (citing a letter from General Dufrenne, May 2, 1793, SHD, 2Y); Noël, "Saint-Georges. . . ," p. 175.

p. 143: *"As Saint-Georges's books"* and following three quotations: MM, pp. 55–56.

p. 145: *neither a reprimand nor a summons:* d'Hauterive, p. 32; Banat, p. 381.

p. 145: *Alex Dumas promoted to brigadier general:* Provisional Executive Council, letter signed by the minister of war, July 30, 1793, MAD Safe.

CHAPTER 11: "MR. HUMANITY"

p. 146: *Dumas promoted to general of division:* Administrative note from the Ministry of War, November 6, 1848, SHD 7YD91.

p. 147: *civilian "commissioners":* Established by decree on April 9, 1793. See Henri Wallon, *Histoire du tribunal révolutionnaire de Paris,* Vol. 4, p. 95; Gunther Erich Rothenberg, *The Art of Warfare in the Age of Napoleon,* p. 111.

p. 147: *"to encourage the others":* *Biographie universelle et portative des contemporains,* Vol. 4 (1834), p. 464. During 1793–94, 84 generals were executed and 352 fired (David Bell, *The First Total War,* p. 151).

p. 147: *"You no longer have any reason":* "Rapport sur la nécessité de déclarer le gouvernement provisoire de la France révolutionnaire jusqu'à la paix," in Alexis Eymery, *Choix de rapports, opinions et discours prononcés à la Tribune Nationale depuis 1789 jusqu'à ce jour,* pp. 118–30.

p. 147: *"the Organizer of Victory":* On Carnot, see A. Picaud, *Carnot: L'organisateur de la victoire;* and Marcel Reinhard, *Le Grand Carnot.* (For more on Carnot's important contributions to mathematics, see Gert Schubring, *Conflicts Between Generalization, Rigor and Intuition,* Section V, pp. 309–69.)

p. 148: *levée en masse:* Bell, pp. 148–51. (Essentially every other Western power would institute conscription during the Napoleonic wars.)

p. 148: *increased France's troop strength:* Colin Jones, *The Longman Companion to the French Revolution,* p. 147–55, 156; Gregory Freemont-Barnes, *The French Revolutionary Wars,* p. 33.

p. 148: *"The pike is the arm of liberty":* John A. Lynn, "French Opinion and the Military Resurrection of the Pike, 1792–1794," p. 4. Carnot was a vehement propagandist on behalf of pikes; see his July 25, 1792, speech to the Legislative Assembly encouraging the distribution of pikes to all soldiers and citizens (*Archives parlementaires de 1787 à 1860,* Vol. 47, p. 122).

p. 148: *"Pikes began the revolution"*: Etienne Cabet, *Histoire Populaire de la Révolution Française*, Vol. 2, p. 511.

p. 148: *pikes*: On French attitudes about pikes, see Lynn; on pikes as a medieval battlefield weapon, see J. F. Verbruggen, *The Art of Warfare in Western Europe During the Middle Ages*.

p. 148: *"If we have not been either Spartans"*: Bell, p. 139.

p. 149: *"Strike en masse"*: From the "general rules" regarding military operations issued by Carnot and the Committee of Public Safety on February 2, 1794 (*Journal des sciences militaires*, Vol. 13 [1902], p. 354).

p. 149: *many letters signed by Carnot*: The extant letters from Carnot and the Committee of Public Safety can be found in SHD 3B9, SHD 7YD91, and in MAD.

p. 150: *"has given up his profession"*: Oscar Browning, *Napoleon, the First Phase*, p. 178.

p. 150: *"What a fool!"*: Louis Antoine Fauvelet de Bourrienne, *Mémoires de M. de Bourrienne*, p. 51.

p. 150: *Dumas's general politics*: For Dumas's expressions of republicanism, see Dumas to the Municipality of Ferrera, August 19, 1797, SHD V3B118; Dumas to the Directory, September 24, 1797, BNF NAF 24641; and Dumas to Marie-Louise, May 12, 1801, MAD.

p. 150: *Alexandrine Aimée*: Birth certificate, *Registres d'état civil*, Villers-Cotterêts, ADA.

p. 150: *Dumas rode to Villers-Cotterêts*: Claude Labouret, letter to a friend, September 20, 1793, cited in Ernest Roch, "Le Général Alexandre Dubois," p. 95.

p. 150: *Dumas appointed commander-in-chief*: Alex Dumas to Minister of War Bouchotte, September 15, 1793, SHD 7YD91; Minister of War Bouchotte to the Convention, September 9, 1793, published in *Le Moniteur*, September 10, 1793, reprinted in *Réimpression de l'ancien Moniteur* (1840), p. 17.

p. 151: *"This appointment"*: Minister of War Bouchotte to Alex Dumas, September 11, 1793, cited in MM, p. 35.

p. 151: *"The General"*: Claude Labouret, letter to a friend, September 20, 1793, cited in Roch, "Le Général Alexandre Dumas," p. 95.

p. 151: *memo about the Army of the Pyrenees*: Ministry of War to Alex Dumas, September 24, 1794, MAD Safe.

p. 151: *"the most important passes"*: Executive Council, memo to Alex Dumas, September 24, 1794, MAD Safe.

p. 151: *"must maintain"*: Ministry of War to Alex Dumas, September 24, 1794, MAD Safe.

p. 152: *the new commander-in-chief could not enter*: Decree by the People's Representatives for the Army of the Pyrénées, October 22, 1793, in MM, p. 35.

p. 152: *"When the terrible hour"*: MM, p. 40.

p. 153: *command of the Army of the Alps*: National Convention decree, December 22, 1793, SHD 7YD91, and memo published in *Le Moniteur*, December 24, 1793, reprinted in *Réimpression de l'ancien Moniteur*, Vol. 19 (1863); Executive Council decree, December 28, 1793, MAD.

p. 153: *"live up to his reputation"*: Executive Council decree, December 28, 1793, MAD.

p. 153: *"in the midst of the army"*: Pierre Chépy, *Un agent politique à l'armée des Alpes*, p. 246.

p. 153: *fourth commander-in-chief*: Jones, p. 147.

p. 153: *Dumas taking Piston and Espagne along*: Alex Dumas to the minister of war, January 11, 1794, SHD 3B9, and April 4, 1794, SHD 3B10.

p. 153: *both men were happy*: Piston was promoted to brigadier general (2 Vendémiaire, Year II); later he was sent to the Pyrenees (A. Lievyns, *Fastes de la Légion-d'honneur*, Vol. 3, p. 486). Espagne was a lieutenant colonel at the end of 1793; he served in the army of the Western Pyrénées (Charles Mullié, *Biographie des célébrités militaires des armées de terre et de mer de 1789 à 1850*, Vol.1, pp. 497–98).

p. 154: *"My father passed through the village"*: MM, p. 53.

p. 154: *Dermoncourt would stay*: At the end of his military career Dermoncourt was a brigadier general (Mullié, pp. 406–10). He was also rewarded with a Legion of Honor medal in 1813 and the title of baron. (Mullié, pp. 406–10; Tony Broughton, "Generals Who Served in the French Army During the Period 1789–1815.")

p. 155: *"popular" societies:* Michael L. Kennedy, *The Jacobin Clubs in the French Revolution, 1793–1795.*

p. 155: *Dumas passing through Lyon:* Dumas to the minister of war, January 11 and 21, 1794, SHD 3B9.

p. 156: *the People's Representatives warned Dumas:* Dumas to the minister of war, January 21, 1794, SHD, 3B9.

pp. 156–58: *Dumas's response to the denunciation,* including quotations: Dumas to the Committee of Public Safety, January 4, 1794, SHD 3B9.

p. 156: *"My father took no part":* MM, p. 29.

p. 158: *Dumas was allowed to go on:* Ernest d'Hauterive, in *Un soldat de la Révolution* (p. 69), speculates that this was because the "Thermidorian Reaction," a revolt against the Terror's excesses, took place right after Dumas was denounced by the People's Commission (June 24).

p. 158: *Saint-Georges and ten officers arrested:* Gabriel Banat, *The Chevalier de Saint-Georges: Virtuoso of the Sword and the Bow,* p. 401.

p. 158: *"renew[ed] their oath":* Bernard Gainot, *Les officiers de couleur dans les armées de la République et de l'Empire, 1792–1815,* p. 57.

p. 158: *three-man delegation:* Laurent Dubois, *Avengers of the New World,* pp. 168–70. For Dufay's speech to the Convention, see Léon-François Hoffman et al., *Haïti 1804: Lumières et ténèbres,* p. 93.

p. 159: *In fact, slavery had already been abolished:* Dubois, pp. 163, 167.

p. 159: *"Your comrade, a soldier":* Dumas to his "brothers in arms," March 6, 1794, SHD 3B9.

CHAPTER 12: THE BATTLE FOR THE TOP OF THE WORLD

p. 160: *Dumas was supposed to dislodge:* Committee of Public Safety, decree, January 25, 1794, SHD 3B9.

p. 160: *approximately fifty-three thousand men:* Army summary of the situation in the Alps, January 14, 1794, SHD 3B9.

p. 160: *"The enemy he needed to get":* MM, p. 50.

p. 161: *set about to whipping his army into shape:* See, for example, letters from Dumas to the chief of staff, January 27, 1794, SHD 3B107.

p. 161: *elite company of Mont Blanc guides:* Dumas to the chief of staff, February 13, 1794, SHD 3B9.

p. 161: *"Mont-Cenis is currently":* General Dours to Dumas, January 30, 1794, SHD 3B9.

p. 161: *"I cannot procure":* Dumas to the minister of war, January 30, 1794, SHD 3B9.

p. 161: *rifles, cannon, saddles, gunpowder, bandoliers:* Dumas wrote a number of letters to the chief commissary of the artillery about all of these supplies, for example, on March 1 and March 20, 1794, SHD 3B107. See also Dumas to the commissioner general, March 24, 1794, SHD 3B9.

p. 161: *the mountain's best guides:* For example, letters from Dumas to the captain of the guides, March 24 and 25, 1794 (SHD 3B9 and 3B107), among many others.

pp. 161–62: *an elaborate operation:* General Petitguillaume to Adjutant General Sandos, February 4, 1794, SHD 3B107.

p. 162: *long letters on organizing:* For examples, see three letters from Dumas to the chief of staff, January 27, 1794, SHD 3B107; Dumas to Brigadier General Pouget, February 5, 1794, SHD 3B9; Dumas to Commissioner Misson, February 15, 1794, SHD 3B107.

p. 162: *Dumas mastered every detail:* Among dozens of examples, see orders from Dumas,

January 28, 1794, SHD 3B9, and Dumas to the *commissaire ordonnateur,* February 28, 1794, SHD 3B107; also Dumas to the Committee of Public Safety, February 20, 1794, SHD 3B9.

p. 162: *"four thousand iron cleats":* Dumas to Citizen Guériot, March 13, 1794, SHD 3B107.

p. 162: *desertion had been a problem:* Committee of Public Safety, decree, mentioned in Dumas to the chief of staff of the Army of the Alps, May 29, 1794, SHD 3B107.

p. 162: *Dumas received an order:* Minister of war to Dumas, January 27, 1794, SHD 3B9.

p. 162: *"We want the conquest":* Committee of Public Safety to Dumas, January 1794, quoted in Claude Schopp, "Préface générale," in *Joseph Balsamo,* p. viii.

p. 162: *"these parts are very difficult":* Dumas to the minister of war, February 7, 1794, SHD 3B9.

p. 163: *"The snow's massive quantities":* Dumas to the Committee of Public Safety, March 1, 1794, SHD 3B9.

p. 163: *Dumas's alternative suggestion:* Dumas to the minister of war, February 3, 1794, SHD 3B108, and February 7, 1794, SHD 3B9.

p. 163: *"The Republic can count on me":* Dumas to the minister of war, February 3, 1794, SHD 3B108.

p. 163: *"I never imagined":* Minister of war to the Committee of Public Safety, February 7, 1794, SHF 3B9.

p. 163: *"You say that the Republic":* Committee of Public Safety to Dumas, February 8, 1794, SHD 3B9.

p. 164: *Dumas called a council of war:* Decisions of the war council ("arrêté pris en conseil de guerre"), February 26, 1794, SHD 3B9.

p. 164: *"Each general":* Dumas to Generals Basdelaune and Sarret, March 2, 1794, SHD 3B108.

p. 164: *it snowed hard:* Dumas to the Committee of Public Safety, March 1, 1794, SHD 3B9.

p. 164: *a careful letter,* including quotations: Dumas to the minister of war, March 1, 1794, SHD 3B108.

p. 165: *"cannons firing":* Dumas to the Committee of Public Safety, March 1, 1794, SHD 3B9.

p. 165: *"In speaking to the Minister":* Ibid.

p. 166: *Dumas's belief that the émigrés:* Dumas to the Committee of Public Safety, March 14 and March 15, 1794, SHD 3B9; Dumas to General of Division d'Ours, April 19, 1794, SHD 3B108.

p. 166: *the threat of the Jacobin clubs:* Dumas, letter, June 26, 1794, SHD 3B11, and letter from the local Jacobin society to the Committee of Public Safety, June 7, 1794, SHD 7YD91.

p. 166: *the impression they made on all the locals:* Dumas to the minister of war, March 30, 1794, SHD 3B9.

p. 166: *Dumas a diplomat:* Dumas to the minister of war, March 13, 1794, SHD 3B10.

p. 166: *"An enlightened society":* Dumas to the Société de Chambèry, May 8, 1794, quoted in d'Hauterive, p. 49.

p. 167: *Gaston likes Dumas:* Dumas to Sergeant-Major Pelet, March 26, 1794, BNF NAF 24641 (Dumas describes Gaston as his friend).

p. 167: *"The General in Chief and I"* and next quotation: Gaston to the Committee of Public Safety, March 13, 1794, SHD 3B9.

p. 167: *Dumas ordered preparations:* Dumas to squadron chief of the Gendarmerie Grandemaison, March 22, 1794, SHD 3B107.

p. 167: *operation on Mont Cenis:* Except where indicated, the following account of the attack on Mont Cenis, including quotations, relies on Brigadier General Gouvion, report, April 7, 1794, SHD 3B10.

p. 168: *subordinate generals take the field:* Dumas to Generals Basdelaune and Sarret, March 2, 1794, SHD 3B108.

p. 169: *"Two Piedmontese deserters":* Dumas to the Committee of Public Safety, April 16, 1794, SHD 3B108.

p. 169: *"The enemy was not surprised"* and the next two quotations: Representative Gaston to the Committee of Public Safety, April 11, 1794, SHD 3B10.

p. 170: *"the artillery General Buenaparte":* Dumas to an artillery commander, March 30, 1794, SHD 3B107.

p. 170: *"Victory, my dear Piston!":* Dumas to General Piston, April 24, 1794, SHD 3B108.

p. 170: *force of approximately three thousand:* Thomas Mante, *The Naval and Military History of the Wars of England,* Vol. 8, p. 36.

p. 171: *"Dumas, commander in chief"* and *"ascended the mountain":* Mante, pp. 36–37.

p. 171: *"How harmless":* John Scottish Young, *A History of the Commencement, Progress, and Termination of the Late War Between Great Britain and France,* pp. 208–9.

p. 172: *"Torrents of fire":* Dumas to the Committee of Public Safety, May 14, 1794, SHD 3B9.

p. 172: *"fled before the brave":* Ibid.

p. 172: *"We took 900 prisoners":* Dumas to the Committee of Public Safety, May 15, 1794, SHD 3B9.

p. 172: *"from position to position":* Alphonse Rabbe, et al., "Dumas (Alexandre-Davy)," pp. 1469–70.

p. 173: *"At each place"* and next quotation: Commander Rougier to Representative of the People Ysabeau, June 28, 1794, BNF NAF 24641.

p. 173: *"Glory to the conquerors":* Carnot to the People's Representatives, May 22, 1794, quoted in d'Hauterive, pp. 64–65.

CHAPTER 13: THE BOTTOM OF THE REVOLUTION

p. 175: *Dumas received a letter:* Committee of Public Safety to Dumas, June 24, 1794, MAD.

p. 175: *"enemies of the people":* "Loi du 22 prairial an II," in Henri Wallon, *Histoire du tribunal révolutionnaire de Paris,* Vol. 4, pp. 541–45.

p. 175: *"national razor":* Albert Marie Victor Barrère, *Argot and Slang,* p. 389.

p. 175: *"I have received, Citizens".* Dumas to the Commission on the Organization and Movement of the Armies, July 4, 1794 (draft), SHD 3B108.

p. 175: *"I anticipate":* Dumas to the Committee of Public Safety, July 4, 1794, SHD 3B108.

p. 176: *8th of Thermidor:* On the fall of Robespierre, see David P. Jordan, *The Revolutionary Career of Maximilien Robespierre,* pp. 211–25; and Ruth Scurr, *Fatal Purity: Robespierre and the French Revolution,* pp. 347–58.

p. 177: *To his chagrin:* Dumas to the Committee of Public Safety, August 10, 1794, SHD 7YD91.

p. 177: *the Committee decided:* Report of the National Convention's session, published in *Gazette Nationale ou le Moniteur Universel,* August 18, 1794 (the session took place on August 17).

p. 177: *bloody rebellion in the Vendée:* See David Bell, *The First Total War,* pp. 155–85.

p. 177: *"brigand army":* A derogatory term used by the government in Paris to describe the peasants. See, for example, the *Moniteur*'s account of the September 25, 1793, meeting of the Convention. Barrère refers to *"l'armée des brigands"* in the region (*Gazette Nationale au le Moniteur Universel,* no. 271, September 28, 1793, p. 756); and the January 21, 1795, *Moniteur* refers to *"l'armée des brigands de la Vendée"* (*Gazette Nationale au le Moniteur Universel,* no. 119, p. 608).

p. 177: *"Invisible battalions lay in wait":* Victor Hugo, *Quatrevingt-treize,* p. 77.

p. 177: *"exterminating angels of liberty":* Georges Jacques Danton, *Oeuvres de Danton,* edited by Auguste Vermorel (1866), p. 20.

p. 177: *"We burned and broke heads":* Bell, p. 156.

p. 178: *one out of four residents:* Ibid.

p. 178: *"Women and men are tied together":* Thomas Carlyle, *The French Revolution: A History*, Vol. 2, p. 298.

p. 178: *mass drownings:* Alfred Lallié, *Les noyades de Nantes*, pp. 40–41.

p. 179: *Dumas arrived in the Vendée:* Dumas to the chief of staff, September 7, 1794, SHD 3B118.

p. 179: *Dumas was appalled:* Alphonse Rabbe, et al., "Dumas (Alexandre-Davy)," p. 1470.

p. 179: *"The Vendéeans no longer needed":* Jean-Baptiste Courcelles, "DUMAS (Alexandre Davy)," p. 502.

p. 179: *"The chief of staff will":* Dumas to the chief of staff, September 7, 1794, SHD 3B118.

p. 179: *"The officer must provide"* and next two quotations: Dumas to the chief of staff, September 9, 1794, SHD 3B118.

p. 180: *"Any soldier who crosses":* Dumas to the chief of staff, September 11, 1794, SHD 3B118.

p. 180: *he inspected thousands:* Dumas to the chief of staff, September 17, 1794, SHD 3B118.

p. 180: *"I have delayed":* Dumas to the Committee of Public Safety, October 8, 1794, quoted in MM, p. 42.

p. 181: *Dumas transferred out of the Army of the West:* Charles Clerget, *Tableaux des armées françaises pendant les guerres de la Révolution*, p. 41.

p. 181: *"deploying a character of justice":* Le Moniteur Universel, no. 36, reprinted in *Réimpression de l'ancien Moniteur*, Vol. 22 (1847), p. 342.

p. 181: *An 1834 biographical dictionary:* Courcelles.

p. 181: *"Fearless and irreproachable":* Henri Bourgeois, *Biographies de la Vendée militaire*, p. 23.

p. 182: *leave to return home:* Committee of Public Safety, decree, December 7, 1794, SHD 7YD91; Commission for the Organization and Movement of the Armies to Dumas, December 9, 1794, MAD Safe.

p. 182: *exempt peasants from normal draft laws:* Treaty of La Jaunais, February 18, 1795. See Paul-Marie du Breil de Pontbriand, *Un Chouan*, p. 97.

p. 182: *"attached to the topographical bureau":* Napoleon to Joseph Bonaparte, August 20, 1795, in Albert Sorel, *L'Europe et la révolution française*, Vol. 4, p. 385.

p. 183: *with the Army of the Rhine:* Minister of war, note, November 28, 1795, SHD 7YD91.

p. 183: *Jean-Baptiste Kléber:* Hubert N. B. Richardson, *A Dictionary of Napoleon and His Times*, p. 244.

p. 183: *Dumas and Kléber:* Dumas to Jean-Baptiste Kléber, September 15, 1798, BNF NAF 24641.

p. 183: *Dumas crossing the Rhine:* Article in *Le Moniteur*, September 8, 1795, reprinted in *Réimpression de l'ancien Moniteur*, Vol. 26 (1854), p. 65.

p. 183: *"The loss of Frenchmen":* Le Moniteur Universel, no. 9, in *Réimpression de l'ancien Moniteur*, Vol. 26, p. 65.

p. 183: *Marie-Louise pregnant:* Marie-Louise to Dumas, January 17, 1796, cited in Ernest Roch, "Le Général Alexandre Dumas," p. 98.

p. 183: *"My good friend":* Ibid.

p. 184: *hyperinflationary cycle:* See François Crouzet, "Politics and Banking in Revolutionary and Napoleonic France," in *The State, the Financial System, and Economic Modernization*, pp. 20–52.

p. 185: *"whiff of grapeshot":* Thomas Carlyle, *The Works of Thomas Carlyle*, Vol. 4 (1896), p. 320.

p. 185: *black and mixed-race legislators:* Laurent Dubois, *A Colony of Citizens: Revolution and Slave Emancipation in the French Caribbean, 1787–1804*, p. 119; Marcel Dorigny and Bernard Gainot, *La Société des Amis des Noirs, 1788–1799*.

p. 186: *the National Colonial Institute:* Bernard Gainot, *Les officiers de couleur dans les armées de la République et de l'Empire, 1792–1815*, pp. 156–63.

p. 186: *"every year, in each department":* Ibid., p. 159.

CHAPTER 14: THE SIEGE

p. 190: *Dumas arrived in Milan:* Dumas to "General in chief Buonaparte," November 26, 1796, SHF 3B118.

p. 191: *"The Cisalpine Republic was":* Constitution des républiques françaises, cisalpine et ligurienne, 1799, pp. 3–5.

p. 192: *most demoralized of all the French armies:* Robert B. Asprey, *The Rise of Napoleon Bonaparte*, pp. 125–26.

p. 192: *one company had renamed itself "Dauphin":* Ida Tarbell, *A Short Life of Napoleon Bonaparte*, p. 26.

p. 192: *"Soldiers, you are badly fed":* Gustave Molinari, *L'évolution politique et la révolution*, p. 342.

p. 192: *"The art of making war":* Jacques de Guibert, *Essai général de tactique*, Vol. 2, p. 210.

p. 193: *took organized theft to a new level:* on Napoleon's systematic pillage in Italy, see Philip G. Dwyer, *Napoleon: The Path to Power, 1769–1799*, pp. 225–26, 235–38; and Timothy C. W. Blanning, *The French Revolutionary Wars, 1787–1802*, pp. 158–64.

p. 193: *"The watchmakers and jewelers":* Dwyer, p. 226.

p. 193: *Dumas clashing with Napoleon:* Dumas to Generals Miollis and Davin, December 29, 1796, SHD 3B118.

p. 194: *"constantly going to the inns":* Dumas to Chief of Squad Maupeou, March 14, 1797, SHD 3B118.

p. 194: *"unworthy to be called a Frenchman":* Dumas to the commander of the 7th Regiment of Hussars, May 6, 1797, SHD 3B118.

p. 194: *"P.S. You will also warn":* Ibid.

p. 194: *Mr. Humanity bristled:* Dumas to Napoleon, January 2, 1797, SHD 3B118.

p. 194: *"soften the order"* and *"you will appoint":* Dumas to Brigadier General Davin, December 30, 1796, SHD 3B118.

p. 195: *"Where will these women":* Dumas to General Motte, February 25, 1797, SHD 3B118.

p. 195: *letter to "General-in-Chief Bonaparte":* Dumas, January 3, 1797, SHD 3B118.

p. 196: *To Dumas, the Republic's generals:* Dumas to General Victor, January 8 and 9, 1797, SHD V3B118.

p. 196: *"The French Revolution stamped":* MM, p. 124.

p. 196: *The Austrian Empire's main line of defense:* Robert Bowman Bruce, et al., *Fighting Techniques of the Napoleonic Age*, p. 20.

p. 197: *Dumas assigned a division at Mantua:* Letters from Dumas to General Kilmaine and Napoleon, December 17, 1796, SHD 3B118.

p. 197: *Dumas's strategy:* Dumas to General Dallemagne, December 26, 1796, SHD 3B118.

p. 197: *arrested three men:* Dumas to General Kilmaine, SHD 3B118.

p. 198: *son of a Veronese lawyer:* Dumas to General Dufresne, December 25, 1796, SHD 3B118.

p. 198: *Dumas accused him:* Paul Thiébault, *Mémoires du général baron Thiébault*, pp. 30–31.

p. 198: *"Among my father's favorite books":* MM, p. 73.

p. 198: *"then they took him":* Ibid., p. 74.

pp. 198–*"if he did not want"* and *"he abided by my orders":* Dumas to Napoleon, December 99: 25, 1796, BNF NAF 24641.

p. 199: *"his valor and his zeal":* Austrian emperor "François" to "Allvintzy" [Alvinczy], November 13, 1796, MAD.

p. 199: *a reason to attack the Vatican:* On the deterioriating relations between France and the Papal States, see Frederick C. Schneid, *Napoleon's Conquest of Europe: The War of the Third Coalition*, p. 16.

p. 199: *"the dispatch might be in German":* MM, p. 75.

p. 199: *Napoleon sent Dumas congratulations:* Ibid., pp. 79–80.

p. 199: *a favorable note:* Napoleon to the Executive Directory, December 28, 1796, in *Correspondance de Napoléon Ier,* Vol. 4, pp. 202–4.

p. 199: *Dumas's division at San Antonio:* Antoine-Vincent Arnault et al., "Dumas (Alexandre Davy-de-la-Pailleterie)," p. 161.

p. 200: *oddly spaced cannon fire:* Dumas to Brigadier Chief Carvin and to General Davin and circular letter to Generals Miollis and Carvin, December 31, 1796, SHD 3B118.

p. 200: *"Venetian scoundrels":* General of Division Joubert to General Guillaume, December 25, 1796, SHD 3B211.

p. 200: *firing of their weapons:* Dumas to Serurier, January 2, 1797, and to Napoleon, January 3, 1797, SHD 3B118.

p. 200: *barely sleep through the racket:* Dumas to Napoleon, January 3, 1797, SHD 3B118, and several letters to Serurier, December 30 and 31, 1796, and January 2, 1797, SHD 3B118.

p. 200: *dozens of letters Dumas wrote:* These letters are in SHD 3B118.

p. 200: *He requested thousands of soup rations:* Dumas to Serurier, January 6, 1797, SHD 3B118.

p. 200: *"Citizen":* Dumas to Commissary of War Bouquet, December 25, 1796, SHD 3B118.

p. 201: *43,000 crack troops:* On the Battle of Rivoli, see Bruce, pp. 20–27; Dwyer, pp. 268–71.

p. 201: *Serurier's desperate letters:* Berthier's report, January 19, 1797, SHD 3B37; Dumas to Chief of Brigade Carvin, January 13, 1797, SHD 3B118.

p. 201: *Dumas and his men were not moving:* Dumas to General Serurier, January 8, 1797, SHD 3B118.

p. 201: *"I am about to mount my horse":* Dumas to Serurier, January 8, 1797, SHD 3B118.

p. 202: *"Ah! There you are":* MM, pp. 89–90.

p. 203: *Dumas fighting multiple opponents:* Jean-Baptiste Courcelles, "DUMAS (Alexandre Davy)," p. 503.

p. 203: *Dumas's horse killed under him:* General of Division Joubert to Napoleon, March 27, 1797, SHD 3B211.

p. 203: *Dumas's new horse killed:* Statement by the Twentieth Dragoon Regiment, January 18, 1797, MAD.

p. 203: *Dumas's actions in beating:* General of Division Joubert to Napoleon, March 27, 1797, SHD 3B211.

p. 203: *official report of the battle,* including *"in observation at San Antonio":* General Berthier's report, January 19, 1797, SHD 3B37.

p. 204: *"January 18, 1797":* Dumas to Napoleon, January 18, 1797, quoted in MM, p. 96.

p. 204: *I made my way through:* Berthier's report, January 19, 1797, SHD 3B37.

p. 205: *he was to command a subdivision:* General of Division and Chief of Staff Berthier to Dumas, January 17, 1797, BNF NAF 24641.

p. 205: *"On Nivôse 28":* Dumas to Napoleon, January 17, 1797, SHD 3B118.

p. 205: *"We, Commander, officers":* Statement by the Twentieth Dragoon Regiment, January 18, 1797, MAD.

p. 206: *Napoleon's praise:* Napoleon to the Executive Directory, January 18, 1797, cited in *Oeuvres de Napoléon Bonaparte*, Vol. 1, pp. 272–79.

CHAPTER 15: THE BLACK DEVIL

p. 207: *"[Dumas] flies from one city to another":* André Maurel, *Les trois Dumas*, p. 15.

p. 207: *the "Black Devil":* Deputazione toscana di storia patria, *Archivio Storico Italiano*, 5th ser., Vol. 21 (1898), p. 231; Ernest d'Hauterive, *Un soldat de la Révolution: Le Général Alexandre Dumas (1762–1806)*, pp. 138–40.

p. 207: *honorary swords:* Gustav Fiebeger, *The Campaigns of Napoleon Bonaparte of 1796–1797*, pp. 84–85.

p. 208: *"I have no less impatience":* General of Division Joubert to Dumas, December 31, 1796, SHD 3B211.

p. 208: *Dumas in Tyrol:* Antoine-Vincent Arnault et al., "Dumas (Alexandre Davy-de-la-Pailleterie)," p. 161. See also General of Division Joubert to Napoleon, March 20, 1797, SHD V3B118.

p. 208: *Joubert briefed Dumas:* General of Division Joubert to Dumas, January 18, 1797, cited in MM, p. 102.

p. 208: *"great gate" of Italy:* On the history of the Brenner Pass, see F. Baillie-Grohman, "The Brenner Pass and Its Traffic in Old Days."

p. 208: *Dumas led a small force:* Dumas, report to General of Division Joubert, March 27, 1797, MAD Safe.

p. 209: *Over and over again Dumas charged:* See Dumas's correspondence of February 22 and March 5 and 6, 1797, in SHD 3B118 and V3B211, as well as orders from General of Division Joubert to General Dumas, March 20, 1797, SHD 3B211.

p. 209: *"The battle was uncertain":* General of Division Joubert to Napoleon, March 24, 1797, SHD 3B21.

p. 209: *Dumas went on to save General Joubert:* Ibid.

p. 209: *"I charged"* and *"The adjutant general Blondeau":* Dumas, report to General of Division Joubert, March 27, 1797, MAD Safe.

p. 209: *"more like a race":* Dermoncourt's report, cited in MM, p. 108.

p. 209: *"My beloved":* Dumas to his wife, March 3, 1797, BNF NAF 24641.

p. 210: *"To the only one I care about":* Dumas to his wife, March 5, 1797, MAD.

p. 210: *"in a terrible position":* Dumas, report to General of Division Joubert, March 27, 1797, MAD Safe.

p. 211: *"crossed Clausen under enemy fire":* Joubert to the general-in-chief (Napoleon), March 24, 1797, SHD 3B211.

p. 211: *Dumas "did more alone":* Dermoncourt's report quoted in MM, p. 109.

p. 211: *dragoons panicked:* Dumas to Representative Garnot, September 2, 1797, CGH.

p. 211: *Dumas and Dermoncourt found themselves alone:* Or was it Dumas alone? Several accounts of the incident mention Dumas but not Dermoncourt on the bridge, including *Oeuvres de Napoléon Bonaparte*, Vol. 1; Arnault et al., p. 161; and Edmond Chevrier, *Le Général Joubert d'après sa correspondance*, p. 98. However, Dermoncourt's long and colorful description of the incident places him squarely alongside his hero, General Dumas (MM, pp. 109–14).

p. 211: *"lift his saber"* and *"continued to hack at me":* General Dermoncourt's report quoted in MM, p. 113.

p. 211: *horse shot:* Dumas, report to General of Division Joubert, March 27, 1797, MAD Safe.

p. 211: *"The Black Devil is dead!":* General Dermoncourt's report quoted in MM, p. 116.

p. 211: *"I managed to turn toward the general":* Ibid., p. 113.

p. 212: *"I must make a full report," "we have taken fifteen hundred,"* and *"[Dumas] has received":* General of Division Joubert to Napoleon, March 24, 1797, SHD 3B211.

p. 212: *"these victories were necessary":* Dumas to his "best friends," April 1, 1797, MAD Safe.

p. 212: *"General Dumas at the head of the cavalry":* Napoleon, report to the Executive Directory, April 1, 1797, *Correspondance*, Vol. 2, pp. 572–75.

p. 213: *"as the General-in-Chief wants":* Napoleon to Dumas, April 3, 1797, BNF NAF 24641.

p. 213: *"I request that General Dumas":* Napoleon to the Executive Directory, April 5, 1797, cited in *Le Moniteur*, Vol. 28 (1863), p. 666; and in *Correspondance*, Vol. 2, pp. 456–57.

p. 213:   *"Rome was in great hazard"*: Plutarch, *Lives of Illustrious Men*, Vol. 1, p. 163.
p. 213:   *Dumas appointed military governor of Treviso:* General Berthier to Dumas, May 21, 1797, BNF NAF 24641.
p. 214:   *"In this state of revolution"*: Municipality of the Asolo canton, May 29, 1797, MAD.

BOOK THREE
CHAPTER 16: LEADER OF THE EXPEDITION

p. 217:   *"He had no sooner"*: In this sole instance, I am not translating from the French edition of *Mes Memoires* but rather using the translation of E. M. Waller. Alexandre Dumas (*père*), *My Memoirs*, Vol. 1, p. 136.
p. 217:   *after leaving his post:* Clément de la Jonquière, *Expédition d'Égypte*, Vol. 1, p. 225; minister of war to Dumas, probably April 1798, SHD 7YD91. Judging by the fact that the stream of letters to Dumas from Italian municipalities ended on December 29, 1797 (MAD), one can surmise that Dumas left Italy following the treaty of Campo Formio of December 20, 1797. A letter from Dumas to his secretary shows that by April 13, 1798 (MAD), Dumas was in Toulon.
p. 218:   *Dumas now rewrote his will* : Gilles Henry, *Les Dumas: Le secret de Monte-Cristo*, p. 95.
p. 218:   *French armada figures:* La Jonquière, Vol. 1, pp. 513–19, 524–25.
p. 218:   *"The object of this grand voyage"*: Dropmore Papers (Hist. MSS. Comm.), IV, British Library, p. 193, as translated and cited by Christopher Lloyd, *The Nile Campaign*, p. 12.
p. 218:   *Dolomieu's identity:* Charles-Vallin; Alfred Lacroix, ed., *Déodat Dolomieu.*
p. 218:   *the Dolomite Mountains:* Jacques Delille, *Dithyrambe sur l'immortalité de l'âme* (1801), p. 93; Thérèse Charles-Vallin, *Les aventures du chevalier géologue Déodat de Dolomieu*, p. 255.
p. 218:   *"geographical engineers, military engineers, mathematicians"*: Dropmore Papers, p. 193, as quoted by Lloyd, p. 12.
p. 219:   *Rear Admiral Nelson:* Roger Knight, *The Pursuit of Victory*, 231.
p. 219:   *fear of German invasion proved inspirational:* Tom Reiss, "Imagining the Worst: How a Literary Genre Anticipated the Modern World"; I. F. Clarke, *Voices Prophesying War.*
p. 220:   *rumors the French government had planted:* J. Christopher Herold, *Bonaparte in Egypt*, p. 35.
p. 220:   *London's preparations for invasion:* Paul Strathern, Napoleon in Egypt, p. 43.
p. 220:   *Napoleon's serious plans to conquer Britain:* Harold Wheeler and Alexander Broadley, *Napoleon and the Invasion of England*, and Tom Pocock, *The Terror Before Trafalgar.*
p. 220:   *commander of the dragoons and "Chief of Staff of the Cavalry"*: La Jonquière, Vol. 1, pp. 99, 365.
p. 220:   *Alexander the Great's pharaonic dynasty, the Ptolemies:* Karol Myśliwiec, *The Twilight of Ancient Egypt*, pp. 178–79.
p. 220:   *rise of literacy:* Jacques Houdailles and Alain Blum, "L'alphabétisation au XVIIIe et XIXeme siècle."
p. 221:   *"The Nile is as familiar"*: Abbé Le Mascrier, *Description de l'Égypte*, p. iv.
p. 221:   *"to replace the [French] colonies"*: Charles Roux, *Origines de l'Expédition d'Égypte*, p. 40; Herold, p. 12.
p. 221:   *products like indigo:* Carl Ludwig Lokke, *France and the Colonial Question*, p. 97.
p. 221:   *utopian philosopher "Volney"*: Michael Heffernan, "Historical Geographies of the Future," pp. 136–46.
p. 221:   *In Volney's view:* Lokke, pp. 99–100.
p. 221:   *toast of English Romantic poets:* Ann Wroe, *Being Shelley*, pp. 59–60; John Keane, *Tom Paine*, pp. 477–78.

p. 221: *Jefferson translated Volney:* Peter Linebaugh and Marcus Rediker, *Many-Headed Hydra*, p. 410.

p. 223: *Volney and Napoleon in Corsica:* Philip G. Dwyer, *Napoleon: The Path to Power*, p. 61.

p. 223: *Napoleon's early identification with Egypt:* Herold, p. 33.

p. 223: *"I dreamed of many things and I saw":* Napoleon, quoted in Madame le Rémusat, *Mémoires de Madame de Rémusat, 1802–1808*, p. 274.

p. 223: *"Even our officers would take":* Constantin-François Volney, *Oeuvres complètes* (1837), p. 773.

p. 223: *transport to Paris of Venice's artistic treasures:* Alistair Horne, *Age of Napoleon*, p. 88.

p. 223: *Napoleon's thoughts while in Venice:* Claude Desprez, *Desaix*, pp. 46–47.

p. 223: *Arabic printing press:* Robert B. Asprey, *Rise of Napoleon Bonaparte*, p. 252.

p. 224: *meetings with the government in Paris:* Herold, p. 18.

p. 224: *Napoleon's dreams of empire:* Ibid., pp. 15–16.

p. 224: *Tippoo Sahib:* Henry Laurens, *L'Expédition d'Égypte*, pp. 47–48.

p. 224: *Napoleon's message to Tippoo Sahib: Napoleon, A Selection from the Letters and Despatches of the First Napoleon*, p. 245.

p. 224: *Tippoo's rocket fire:* Richard Bayly, *Diary of Colonel Bayly, 12th Regiment, 1796–1830*, p. 84.

p. 224: *"So pestered were we":* Ibid., p. 81.

p. 224: *Congreve rockets:* A. Bowdoin Van Riper, *Rockets and Missles: The Life Story of a Technology*, pp. 14–18.

p. 224: *"Soldiers, the eyes of Europe":* Napoleon, speech, May 10, 1798, in *Correspondance de Napoléon Ier*, Vol. 4, p. 96.

p. 225: *six acres of land:* William Lodewyk Van-Ess, *Life of Napoleon Buonaparte*, p. 307.

p. 225: *"Voilà—the six acres of land":* Dominique Vivant Denon, *Voyage dans le Basse et le Haute Égypte*, pp. 38–39; and René-Nicolas Desgenettes, *Souvenirs de la fin du XVIIIe siècle et du commencement du XIXe*, Vol. 3, p. 132.

p. 225: *"Where the devil are you off to":* MM, p. 137.

p. 227: *Dumas and Dermoncourt boarded:* Henry, p. 95; Claude Schopp, *Dictionnaire Dumas*, p. 179.

p. 227: *William Tell section of Paris:* Eli Sagan, *Citizens & Cannibals: The French Revolution, the Struggle for Modernity, and the Origins of Ideological Terror*, p. 127.

p. 227: *largest ship of any navy on earth:* Robert Gardiner, *Warships of the Napoleonic Era*, p. 101.

p. 227: *Nelson loses his frigates:* Brian Lavery, *Nelson and the Nile: The Naval War Against Bonaparte, 1798*, pp. 68–74.

p. 227: *twenty miles visible:* Ibid., pp. 126, 140.

p. 227: *Nelson's Dolland telescope:* Hugh Barty-King, *Eyes Right: The Story of Dollond & Aitchison Opticians, 1750–1985*, pp. 79–82.

p. 228: *history of the Knights of Malta:* H. J. A. Sire, *Knights of Malta*.

p. 228: *"Maltese falcon":* Barnaby Rogerson, *The Last Crusaders*, ch. 13.

p. 229: *prostitutes in Malta:* Herold, p. 46.

p. 229: *the Knights of Malta were ruined:* Dennis Castillo, *Maltese Cross*, p. 96.

p. 229: *overtures to ally with France's enemies:* Desmond Gregory, *Malta, Britain, and the European Powers*, p. 51.

p. 229: *four ships at a time:* La Jonquière, Vol. 1, p. 585.

p. 229: *Dolomieu as a young man:* Lacroix, ed., *Déodat Dolomieu*, Vol. 1, pp. xix–xxii.

p. 230: *"Tell the Knights I will grant them"* and next quotation: Déodat de Dolomieu, "Mémoire," published in *Spectateur militaire*, Vol. 2 (1826), p. 52, quoted in La Jonquière, Vol. 1, pp. 612–14; translated in Lloyd, p. 18.

p. 230: *"No one who has seen Malta":* Louis-Antoine Fauvelet de Bourrienne, *Private Memoirs of Napoleon Bonaparte*, Vol. 1 (1831), p. 136.

p. 230: *who had appraised the Vatican:* Napoleon, *Correspondance*, Vol. 4, p. 147.

p. 230: *1,227,129 francs' worth of loot:* William Hardman, *A History of Malta During the French and British Occupations, 1798–1815* (1909), p. 75.

p. 230: *Napoleon's social engineering in Malta:* Napoleon, *Correspondance*, Vol. 4, pp. 143–77.

p. 230: *Napoleonic Code:* Martin Lyons, *Napoleon Bonaparte and the Legacy of the French Revolution*, pp. 94–99.

p. 231: *"the island fortress of Malta":* James Holland, *Fortress Malta*, p. 267.

p. 231: *"one tiny bright flame in the darkness":* Franklin D. Roosevelt, *Public Papers and Addresses of Franklin D. Roosevelt*, Vol. 12 (1950), p. 543.

p. 231: *"more like a deportation"* and following quotations: Dumas to Marie-Louise, June 18, 1798, MAD.

p. 232: *"General Dumas will command the cavalry":* La Jonquière, Vol. 1, p. 365.

p. 232: *By now Admiral Nelson had learned:* Lavery, p. 125.

p. 232: *"I think their object is":* James Harrison, *Life of the Right Honourable Horatio*, pp. 249–50.

p. 233: *Nelson and Napoleon nearly cross paths on June 22:* Lavery, pp. 126–29.

p. 233: *Ragusan neutrality and trade:* Hugh Chisolm, ed., *Encyclopedia Britannica*, 11th ed., Vol. 7 (1910), p. 775.

p. 233: *on June 23, a day after almost bumping into Nelson:* La Jonquière, Vol. 2, p. 16.

p. 234: *Saint Louis:* Jill N. Claster, *Sacred Violence*, pp. 260–62.

p. 235: *Nelson in Alexandria:* Lavery, p. 129.

p. 235: *seamen could not swim:* Steven E. Maffeo, *Most Secret and Confidential*, p. 76.

p. 235: *transported only about 1,200 horses:* La Jonquière, pp. 349, 364–66, 410–12; Napoleon, *Correspondance*, Vol. 4, pp. 188–89, 202–3, 323, Vol. 5, pp. 12–13, 89.

p. 236: *"My lord, the fleet which has just appeared":* Herold, p. 62.

p. 236: *attack on Alexandria:* Ibid., p. 66.

p. 236: *"I want you to be the first":* MM, p. 141.

p. 237: *"Among the Muslims":* Desgenettes, Vol. 3, p. 132.

CHAPTER 17: "THE DELIRIUM OF HIS REPUBLICANISM"

p. 238: *"The French people, may God thoroughly destroy their country":* Pierre Dominique Martin, *Histoire de l'expédition française en Égypte*, Vol. 1, pp. 243–51. Cited by Paul Strathern in *Napoleon in Egypt*, p. 233.

p. 238: *Napoleon, Kléber, and Breuys:* J. Christopher Herold, *Bonaparte in Egypt*, p. 75; Clément de la Jonquière, *L'expédition d'Égypte (1798–1801)*, Vol. 2, pp. 61, 80; Napoleon, *Correspondance de Napoleon Ier*, Vol. 4, pp. 195 and 224–25.

p. 238: *the savants' brutal entry:* Strathern, p. 76; Herold, p. 73.

p. 239: *"I was assailed by packs":* Dominique Vivant Denon, *Voyage dans le Basse et le Haute Égypte pendant les campagnes du Général Bonaparte*, pp. 58–59, translated in Strathern, p. 77.

p. 239: *the savants homeless in Alexandria:* Strathern, pp. 77–78; Herold, p. 73.

p. 239: *the French would unleash storms that are still igniting conflict:* Henry Laurens, *Orientales 1: Autour de l'expédition d'Égypte*.

p. 239: *French throats slit in Alexandria:* Juan Cole, *Napoleon's Egypt: Invading the Middle East*, p. 25.

p. 240: *calculated lunacy was one of Napoleon's favorite tactics:* Frank McLynn, *Napoleon: A Biography*, p. 169.

p. 240: *"Leaving that city behind":* Adjutant-General Boyer, quoted in MM, p. 152.

p. 240: *carrying their saddles:* Napoleon to Louis-Alexandre Berthier, June 16, 1797, *Correspondance*, Vol. 4, p. 203.

p. 241: *"a pile of huts":* Jean-Pierre Doguereau, *Journal de l'expédition d'Égypte*, p. 58.

p. 241: *"remains etched in the minds"*: M. Vertray, *Journal d'un officier de l'armée d'Égypte*, p. 40.

p. 241: *"When someone shouted in distress"*: René-Nicolas Desgenettes, *Souvenirs de la fin du XVIIIe siècle et du commencement du XIXe*, Vol. 3, p. 132.

p. 241: *"seeing two dragoons"*: Napoleon's 1815 spoken recollections transcribed and edited by Emmanuel Las Cases, *Mémorial de Sainte-Hélène*, Vol. 1, p. 189.

p. 241: French revolutionary anthem: Jean Lombard, *Un volontaire de 1792*, pp. 71–81.

p. 241: *"blew his brains out"*: Devernois, *Mémoires du Général Baron Desvernois*, quoted by La Jonquière, Vol. 2, pp. 136–38. Or perhaps Mireur's death was not suicide (see accounts by Savary, Belliard, and Sulkowski, discussed by La Jonquière, Vol. 2, pp. 136–38).

p. 241: *"This kind of warfare was even harder"*: Napoleon, *Correspondance*, Vol. 24, p. 446.

p. 242: *"threw [his] trimmed hat"*: Desgenettes, Vol. 3, pp. 132–33.

p. 242: *"Saint Watermelon"*: Louis Reybaud, *Histoire de l'expédition française en Égypte*, in Xavier-Boniface Saintine, ed., *Histoire scientifique et militaire de l'expédition française en Égypte*, Vol. 3, p. 183; see also Cole, p. 61; Denon, p. 70; Napoleon, *Correspondance*, Vol. 4, p. 253.

p. 242: *invited some of his fellow generals*: Las Cases, p. 221; Reybaud p. 165; Desgenettes, Vol. 3, p. 132; Ernest d'Hauterive, *Un soldat de la Révolution: Le Général Alexandre Dumas (1762–1806)*, ch. 15.

p. 242: *there was talk*: Las Cases, p. 165; Abel Hugo, *France militaire*, p. 247; Desgenettes, Vol. 3, pp. 132–33; Maurel, *Les Trois Dumas*, pp. 29–32; d'Hauterive, ch. 15.

p. 242: *informants somehow heard everything*: Desgenettes, Vol. 3, p. 132; Maurel, pp. 29–32.

p. 242: *"Eating three watermelons"*: MM, pp. 145–46.

p. 243: *Egyptian blindness*: La Jonquière, Vol. 2, p. 533. Called Egyptian ophthalmia, trachoma, or granular conjunctivitis, this illness remains one of the major health problems of Egypt. R. M. Feibel, "John Vetch and the Egyptian Ophthalmia."

p. 243: *helped found ophthalmology*: R. Sigal and H. Hamard, "Larrey and Egyptian Ophthalmia"; M. Wagemans and O. P. van Bijsterveld, "The French Egyptian Campaign and Its Effects on Ophthalmology."

p. 243: *"the Mamelukes are your enemy"*. Napoleon, *Correspondance*, Vol. 4, p. 235.

p. 243: *troops began to ignore the orders against looting*: La Jonquière, Vol. 2, p. 162; Napoleon, *Correspondance*, Vol. 4, pp. 235–36.

p. 243: *"You cannot imagine the fatigue"* and *"harassed during the whole march"*: Dumas to General Kléber, July 27, 1798, quoted in MM, p. 148.

p. 243: *General Berthier himself witnessed*: Cole, p. 60.

p. 244: *the French army soon encountered*; La Jonquière, Vol. 2, p. 154–61.

p. 244: *their decisive battle*: The following account of the "Battle of the Pyramids" is largely drawn from Strathern, ch. 7; Herold, ch. 3; and La Jonquière, Vol. 2, ch. 6.

p. 244: *"The Mamelukes have a great deal of spirit"*: Dumas to General Kléber, July 27, 1798, quoted in MM, p. 148.

p. 244: *the Mameluke sword*: Edwin Simmons, *The United States Marines: A History* (2003), pp. 23–24.

p. 244: *"covered in sparkling armor"*: Desvernois, *Mémoires du Général Baron Desvernois*, p. 118.

p. 244: *Mameluke military training*: Strathern, p. 111.

p. 245: *The "flaming wads"*: Vertray, p. 59, translated in Strathern, p. 122.

p. 246: *pyramids not visible during the battle*: Ibid, p. 128.

p. 246: *"carpets, porcelain, silverware"*: Napoleon, *Correspondance*, Vol. 29, p. 451, translated in Strathern, p. 127.

p. 246: *"the infidels who come to fight"*: Vertray, p. 64, quoted in Herold, p. 65.

p. 246: *"the French soldiers walked the streets"*: Al Jabarti, quoted in Herold, p. 157.

p. 247: *the French organized garbage collection, established hospitals*: Strathern, p. 141.

p. 247: *measuring the Sphinx, exploring the Great Pyramid:* Ibid., pp. 284, 145.

p. 247: *Four thousand copies:* La Jonquière, Vol. 2, p. 102. Though issued in Alexandria on July 3, this text reached Cairo by July 9 (André Raymond, *Egyptiens et français au Caire, 1798–1801*, p. 87).

p. 247: *"that gang of slaves":* Herold, p. 69.

p. 247: *"Tell the people that the French are . . . true friends":* Ibid.

p. 247: *Arabist savants, who had trouble:* Cole, pp. 29–36.

p. 248: *Cairo clergy offered to issue a fatwa:* Ibid., pp. 127–29.

p. 248: *"We have arrived at last":* Dumas to General Kléber, July 27, 1798, quoted in MM, p. 147.

p. 248: *made beer and distilled spirits:* Terry Crowdy and Christa Hook, *French Soldier in Egypt, 1798–1801*, pp. 21–22.

p. 248: *"You have preached sedition":* Las Cases, p. 222.

p. 249: *over six feet tall:* Charles-Vallin, *Les aventures du chevalier géologue Déodat de Dolomieu*, p. 224.

p. 249: *"General, you conduct yourself poorly":* MM, pp. 155–57.

p. 250: *A different recollection:* Desgenettes, Vol. 3, pp. 201–2.

p. 250: *"That he shows a mixture"* and following quotations: Ibid.

p. 251: *"It is a remarkable circumstance":* Christopher Hibbert, *Nelson: A Personal History*, p. 138.

p. 251: *Nelson already despised Napoleon:* Jack Sweetman, *The Great Admirals: Command at Sea, 1587–1945*, p. 212.

p. 251: *On July 28, tracking false rumors:* Except where noted, this account of the Battle of the Nile relies essentially on Brian Lavery, *Nelson and the Nile: The Naval War Against Napoleon, 1798*, pp. 166–99.

p. 252: *Nelson cared little for caution:* Roger Knight, *The Pursuit of Victory*, pp. 238–39, 247, 554.

p. 252: *less about conventional tactics:* Knight, xxxiv; Lavery, p. 180.

p. 253: *"The* Orient *had nearly demolished":* Sir George Elliot, *Memoir of Admiral the Honourable Sir George Elliot*, quoted by Christopher Lloyd, *The Nile Campaign: Nelson and Napoleon in Egypt*, p. 41.

p. 253: *"When the* Orient *went up":* Lieutenant Laval Grandjean, *Journaux sur l'Expédition d'Égypte*, quoted in Crowdy and Hook, p. 17.

p. 254: *exploration of the* Orient's *wreckage:* Angela Schuster, "Napoleon's Lost Fleet," pp. 34–37.

p. 254: *was it ever there?:* Tom Pocock, "Broken Promises, Sunken Treasure, and a Trail of Blood"; Claire Engel, *Les chevaliers de Malte* (1972), p. 285.

p. 254: *the* Guillaume Tell*:* Lavery, p. 297.

CHAPTER 18: DREAMS ON FIRE

p. 255: *"We now have no choice":* Napoleon, *Correspondance de Napoléon Ier*, Vol. 29, pp. 457–58.

p. 255: *they awarded Admiral Nelson:* James Clarke and John MacArthur, *Life of Admiral Lord Nelson*, p. 538.

p. 255: *a new deference for the savants:* Louis-Alexandre Berthier, *Memoir of the Campaigns of General Bonaparte in Egypt and Syria*, pp. 48–49.

p. 255: *Nicolas Conté:* Alain Quérel, *Nicolas-Jacques Conté, 1755–1805*.

p. 256: *loss of balloons in the Battle of the Nile:* Marc de Villiers du Terrage, *Les aérostatiers militaires en Égypte*, pp. 9–10.

p. 256: *"had all the sciences in his head":* Gaspard Monge, quoted by Vagnair, "Le colonel des aérostatiers militaires d'il y a cent ans," p. 294.

p. 256: *Egyptians were curious about the first launch:* de Villiers du Terrage, pp. 9–10.

p. 256: *"The machine was made of paper":* Le Courrier d'Égypte, no. 20, p. 2, quoted by Paul Strathern, *Napoleon in Egypt*, p. 258.

p. 256: *fire on second balloon:* de Villiers du Terrage, p. 13.

p. 256: *"The French were embarrassed":* Abd al-Rahman Jabarti (Al Jabarti), *Al-Jabarti's Chronicle of the First Seven Months of the French Occupation of Egypt*, p. 113.

p. 257: *"progress and the propagation of enlightenment":* Napoleon, *Correspondance*, Vol. 4, p. 383.

p. 257: *Napoleon and the Institute of Egypt:* Ibid., pp. 390–91.

p. 257: *the Institute caught fire:* "L'incendie de l'Institut d'Égypte, 'une catastrophe pour la science,'" *Le Monde*, December 18, 2011.

p. 257: *Description de l'Égypte:* Commission des Arts et Sciences et d'Égypte, *Description de l'Égypte*, 24 vols. (1809–28).

p. 258: *Dumas in the weeks after the disaster:* Napoleon, *Correspondance*, Vol. 4, p. 322.

p. 258: *"Cairo, the 30th Thermidor":* Dumas to Marie-Louise, August 17, 1798, MAD Safe.

p. 258: *Kléber's opinion of Napoleon:* Henry Laurens, "Étude historique," in Jean-Baptiste Kléber, *Kléber en Égypte*, Vol. 1, pp. 86–101.

p. 258: *"the General who costs 10,000 men":* Jean-Baptiste Kléber, *Mémoires politiques et militaires, Vendée, 1793–1794*, p. 16.

p. 258: *"Is he loved?":* Kléber, *Kléber en Égypte*, Vol. 2, p. 545.

p. 259: *"The caravan from Ethiopia arrived in Cairo":* Antoine Bonnefons, *Un soldat d'Italie et d'Égypte*, pp. 19–20.

p. 259: *army's stated mission:* Napoleon, *Correspondance*, Vol. 4, pp. 182–83.

p. 259: *"We have seen how slavery":* Pierre Gaspard Chaumette, "Discours prononcé par le citoyen Chaumette."

p. 259: *French soldiers buying slaves:* Juan Cole, *Napoleon's Egypt*, pp. 177–80.

p. 259: *the procurement of two thousand slaves:* Bernard Gainot, *Les officiers de couleur dans les armées de la République et de l'Empire, 1792–1815*, pp. 148–52.

p. 260: *Napoleon's decree on Mamelukes joining army:* Ronald Pawly and Patrice Courcelle, *Napoleon's Mamelukes*, pp. 12, 16–38.

p. 260: *Dumas discovers treasure:* Louis Reybaud, *Histoire de l'expédition française en Égypte*, in Xavier-Boniface Saintine, ed., *Histoire scientifique et militaire de l'expédition française en Égypte . . .*, Vol. 3, p. 347. Dumas's son quotes the same letter in his memoir, claims it was "reproduced by the newspapers of New York and of Philadelphia," and even remembers how an American diplomat once repeated the quotation to him, word for word (MM, pp. 160–62).

p. 260: *"The leopard cannot change":* Reybaud, p. 347.

p. 261: *Napoleon to Citizen Poussielgue, August 23, 1798:* Napoleon, *Correspondance*, Vol. 4, p. 391.

p. 261: *the Cairo Revolt:* André Raymond, *Égyptiens et français au Caire, 1798–1801*, pp. 131–38.

p. 261: *dispersing the main rebel groups:* Antoine-Vincent Arnault was the first author to mention Dumas's role in stopping the revolt. Antoine-Vincent Arnault et al., "Dumas (Alexandre Davy-de-la-Pailleterie)," pp. 161–62.

p. 261: *"The Angel! The Angel!"* and the next quotation: MM, p. 164.

p. 261: *the Angel of Death from the Koran:* "The angel of death who is given charge of you shall cause you to die, then to your Lord you shall be brought back" (Holy Koran, surah [chapter] no. 32.11).

p. 262: *" 'Bonjour, Hercules,' he said":* MM, p. 165.

p. 262:   The Revolt of Cairo: Darcy Grigsby, *Extremities*, p. 131.

p. 262:   *In another painting of the incident:* Henri Lévy's "Bonaparte à la grande mosquée du Caire" (1890), as seen in Gérard-Georges Lemaire, *L'Univers des orientalistes*, p. 109.

p. 262:   *Napoleon would leave Cairo:* Napoleon to Kléber, August 22, 1799, in Clément de la Jonquière, *L'expédition d'Égypte*, Vol. 5, p. 593.

p. 262:   *"That bugger has left us here":* Louis-Marie Larevellière-Lépaux, *Mémoires*, Vol. 2, p. 348.

p. 262:   *assassination of Kléber:* Raymond, pp. 215–19.

p. 262:   *the assassin's skull:* Laurens, "Étude historique," in Kléber, Vol. 1, p. 86.

p. 262:   *General Dumas got out of Egypt:* Except where noted, this chapter's account of General Dumas's departure from Egypt, including quotations, relies on his official report cited in the first note of chapter 19.

p. 263:   *the Belle Maltaise:* An 1894 study of Louis Cordier, a minerology student who accompanied Dolomieu, describes the ship as a "corvette," a small gunship or cruiser (M. J. Bertrand, "Notice historique sur M. Pierre-Louis-Antoine Cordier, lue dans la séance publique annuelle du 17 décembre 1894," in *Mémoires de l'Académie des sciences de l'Institut de Frances*, Vol. 47 (1904), p. cii). An August 11, 1799 letter from Marie-Louise to Minister of War Bouchotte (SHD 7YD91) identifies it as a felucca—a small craft propelled by oars or lateen sails, this one specifically for transporting mail ("felouque courrière")—but this seems impossible given the number of passengers it carried. Most likely it was a retired military ship.

p. 263:   *"I have decided to return":* Dumas to Marie-Louise, March 1, 1799, BNF NAF 24641.

CHAPTER 19: PRISONER OF THE HOLY FAITH ARMY

p. 264:   *voyage of the Belle Maltaise from Alexandria to Taranto:* Except where noted, this chapter's account of the voyage and imprisonment, including quotations, relies on Dumas's official report to the French government, "Rapport fait au gouvernement français par le général de division Alexandre Dumas, sur sa captivité à Tarente et à Brindisi, ports du Royaume de Naples," May 5, 1801, MAD Safe.

p. 264:   *Dolomieu would later blame Dumas:* Dolomieu to Doctor de Lacépède, June 5, 1799, in Lacroix, ed., *Déodat Dolomieu*, Vol. 2, p. 186.

p. 264:   *based on a later inventory:* Inventory by di Giuseppe (notary), Taranto, April 1, 1799, MAD.

p. 266:   *on the equinox in late-18th-century meteorology:* Joseph Toaldo Vicentin, *Essai météorologique*, trans. Joseph Daquin (1784).

p. 266:   *"it had been a long time since":* Dolomieu to Doctor de Lacépède, June 5, 1799, in Alfred Lacroix, ed., Vol. 2, p. 187.

p. 266:   *ruins of the temple of Poseidon:* Trudy Ring, ed., *International Dictionary of Historic Places*, Vol. 3 (1995), p. 686.

p. 267:   *Kingdom of Naples and French-inspired revolt:* John A. Davis, *Naples and Napoleon*, pp. 78–80.

p. 267:   *News of the event had reached Egypt:* Déodat de Dolomieu, "Le livre de la Captivité," in Lacroix, éd., Vol. 1, p. 28; Clément de la Jonquière, *Expédition d'Égypte*, Vol. 4, pp. 141, 148, 343–44.

p. 267:   *"After a series of extremely violent gales":* Dolomieu, in Lacroix, ed. Vol. 1, p. 28.

p. 267:   *plague epidemic in Alexandria:* La Jonquière, Vol. 4, pp. 20–41.

p. 267:   *a passenger had just become its latest victim:* Louis Cordier (Dolomieu's student) to Louis Ripault (librarian for the Institut d'Égypte), May 1800, in Lacroix, ed., Vol. 2, p. 288.

p. 267:   *"Instead of the tricolor flag":* Dolomieu, in Lacroix, ed., Vol. 1, p. 28.

p. 267:   *the fleur-de-lis superimposed on a cross:* Davis, p. 117.

p. 267: *"We were interrogated, searched, disarmed"*: Dolomieu, in Lacroix, ed., Vol. 1, p. 28.

p. 267: *"If the plague hadn't claimed one of us"*: Louis Cordier to Louis Ripault, May 1800, in Lacroix, ed., Vol. 2, p. 288.

p. 268: *history of the Kingdom of Naples*: Pietro Colletta, *History of the Kingdom of Naples*, Vol. 1.

p. 269: *the tomato in South America and Italy*: Philip Stansley and Steven Naranjo, *Bemisia: Bionomics and Management of a Global Pest* (2010), p. 291; David Gentilcore, *Pomodoro! A History of the Tomato in Italy* (2010).

p. 269: *became a center of Italian Enlightenment*: Girolamo Imbruglia, "Enlightenment in Eighteenth-Century Naples."

p. 269: *one of the high points of the European Grand Tour*: Judith Harris, *Pompeii Awakened*, p. 2.

p. 269: *Maria Carolina and Acton*: Davis, pp. 23–24.

p. 270: *tree of liberty in Rome's Jewish ghetto*: Ray Hutchison and Bruce Haynes, eds., *The Ghetto: Contemporary Global Issues and Controversies* (2012), p. xvi.

p. 270: *"has now after many years"*: Johann Wolfgang von Goethe, *Italian Journey*, p. 208.

p. 270: *Nelson and the Kingdom of Naples*: Davis, p. 78.

p. 270: *"My dear child, dress them"*: Alexandre Dumas (*père*), *Sketches of Naples*, p. 33.

p. 270: *Ferdinand's flight to Sicily*: Colletta, pp. 259–71.

p. 270: *Republican revolution in the Kingdom of Naples*: Christopher Duggan, *Force of Destiny*, pp. 20–21; Davis, pp. 102–6.

p. 271: *Republicanism in Taranto*: G. C. Speziale, *Storia militare di Taranto negli ultimi cinque secoli*, pp. 128–33.

p. 271: *"ignorant, highly superstitious, fanatically loyal"*: Davis, p. 82.

p. 271: *one of the grisliest events*: Steven Runciman, *The Sicilian Vespers*.

p. 271: *insurgency sponsored by Ferdinand and led by Ruffo*: Davis, ch. 6.

p. 271: *"whatever was necessary"*: Hilda Gamlin, *Nelson's Friendships*, Vol. 1, p. 102.

p. 271: *Holy Faith Army in Taranto*: Speziale, p. 134.

p. 272: *the very day the unlucky ship*: Ibid.

p. 272: *Ruffo's background*: Davis, p. 116.

p. 272: *"assassins and robbers driven by the hope of plunder"*: Ibid., p. 117.

p. 273: *a Corsican adventurer named Boccheciampe*: Speziale, p. 136.

p. 273: *Despite his rogue behavior*: Colletta, pp. 316–17 and 323.

p. 274: *order for "the departure of all French and Genoan prisoners"*: Statement by representatives of the people of the city of Taranto, May 4, 1799, AST.

p. 274: *"member of almost all the European Academies"*: Notarized document, May 15, 1799, AST.

p. 274: *Sicilian Knights of Malta blamed Dolomieu*: Dolomieu, in Lacroix, ed., Vol. 1, p. 29.

p. 274: *An international "republic of letters" mobilized*: Lacroix, Vol. 1, pp. xxxix–xli.

p. 274: *"You have no idea how much sensation"*: Joseph Banks to William Hamilton, November 8, 1799, in G. R. Beer, "The Relations Between Fellows of the Royal Society and French Men of Science When France and Britain Were at War," p. 264.

p. 274: *"When Citizen Dolomieu signed on"*: Institut d'Égypte (represented by David Le Roy, Nicolas-Jacques Conté, and Joseph Fourier) to General-in-Chief Jean-Baptiste Kléber in Alfred Lacrois, ed., *Dolomieu en Égypte, 30 Juin 1798–10 Mars 1799 (Manuscrits retrouvée par A. Lacroix)*, p. 136.

p. 275: *Dolomieu's pen and ink*: Déodat de Dolomieu, *Sur la philosophie minéralogique et sur l'espèce minéralogique*, p. 7.

p. 275: *a landmark work of geology*: Dolomieu, *Sur la philosophie minéralogique et sur l'espèce minéralogique*; Charles Gillespie, *Science and Polity in France*, p. 175.

p. 275: *Dolomieu's death*: Rabbe et al., "Dumas (Alexandre-Davy)," pp. 1469–70.

p. 275: *"When you visit my cell"* and following quotation: Alexandre Dumas (*père*), *Le comte de Monte-Cristo*, Vol. 1, pp. 215–17.

p. 276: *"to His Eminence Cardinal D. Fabrizio Ruffo"*: Record and order of the governor of Taranto, May 8, 1799, AST.

p. 276: *he slept on straw:* Admiral Francesco Ricci, present-day commander of the fortress at Taranto, interview, April 10, 2008. (All descriptions of the prison conditions are based on this interview.)

p. 277: *"That's how we know"* and *"We found these digging":* Ibid.

p. 278: *"I wish to see the governor":* Dumas *(père), Le Comte de Monte-Cristo,* Vol. 1, pp. 107–9.

p. 278: *British naval blockade:* Davis, p. 90.

p. 278: *Ottoman force landed near Brindisi:* Nicolo Capponi, *Victory of the West,* p. 323.

p. 279: *Holy Faith Terror continued:* Tommaso Astarita, *Between Salt Water and Holy Water,* pp. 254–56; Davis, pp. 120–21.

p. 279: *Holy Faith Army murdering:* Timothy Parsons, *Rule of Empires,* p. 268.

p. 280: *Once manned by Swiss mercenaries:* Speziale, p. 134.

CHAPTER 20: "CITIZENESS DUMAS . . . IS WORRIED ABOUT THE FATE OF HER HUSBAND"

p. 281: *British seizures of the mails:* Roy Adkins and Lesley Adkins, *The War for All the Oceans,* pp. 45–46.

p. 281: *she had received Alex's letter:* Marie-Louise to Minister of War Bernadotte, August 11, 1799, SHD 7YD91; Marie-Louise to Member of the Directory Paul Barras, received October 1, 1799, MAD.

p. 281: *to follow his letter "very closely":* Dumas to Marie-Louise, March 1, 1799, BNF NAF 24641.

p. 281: *She wrote to the Ministry of War:* Marie-Louise to Minister of War Bernadotte, August 11, 1799, SHD 7YD91.

p. 281: *perhaps from Dolomieu's friends:* Marie-Louise mentions "le c[itoy]en dumanoir savant" in her first surviving letter to Bernadotte and also thinks Dumas has been taken to Messina, where in fact only Dolomieu had been taken; at least two of Dolomieu's letters had reached Paris by then—one received by the Chair of Reptiles and Fish at the Jardin des Plantes (Botanical Garden), and another by the Conseil des Mines (Mines Council) dated June 6; both tell of being taken to Messina. See Alfred Lacroix, ed., *Déodat Dolomieu,* Vol. 2, pp. 185–91.

p. 281: *she reached out to Alex's colleagues:* For example, see General Joachim Murat to Marie-Louise, November 16, 1799, MAD.

p. 281: *"General Dumas has been taken":* Gazette *Nationale du Moniteur,* Vol. 3, September 11, 1799, no. 355.

p. 281: *the first letter I found:* General Representative of the People Jourdan to the minister of war, July 25, 1799, SHD 7YD91.

p. 281: *Jourdan wielded considerable political influence:* René Valentin, *Le maréchal Jourdan, 1762–1833,* pp. 184–207.

p. 281: *Jourdan had served with Dumas:* In the Army of the North in 1794: Paul Marmottan, *Le général Fromentin et l'armée du Nord (1792–1794),* p. 14; at the Rhine in 1795: for Dumas's role with Kléber, see ch. 13; for Jourdan's presence with Kléber at the same time, see Charles Pierre Victor Pajol, *Kléber: Sa vie, sa correspondance,* p. 179.

p. 282: *"Citizeness Dumas, the wife":* General Representative of the People Jourdan to Minister of War Bernadotte, July 25, 1799, SHD 7YD91.

p. 282: *"Villers-Cotterêts, 24 Thermidor":* Marie-Louise to Minister of War Bernadotte, August 11, 1799, SHD 7YD91.

p. 283: *new coalition of powers:* Alexander Rodger, *War of the Second Coalition, 1798–1801.*

p. 283: *Jews massacred in Siena:* Alexander Grab, *Napoleon and the Transformation of Europe,* p. 157. For the collapse of the Italian "sister republics" in the face of the Austro-Russian invasion, also see Susan Nicassio, *Imperial City.*

p. 283: *Austro-Russian victory at Mantua:* Edouard Gachot, *Souvarow en Italie*, chs. 12 and 14.

p. 283: *General Joubert's death:* Edmond Chevrier, *Le Général Joubert: Étude sur sa vie*, p. 217.

p. 283: *Republic of Rome fell on September 30:* Ronald Ridley, *The Eagle and the Spade*, p. 4.

p. 284: *"satisfying information":* Minister of War Bernadotte to Marie-Louise, August 25, 1799, SHD 7YD91.

p. 284: *Marie-Louis wrote to Barras:* Marie-Louise to Member of the Directory Paul Barras, October 1, 1799, MAD.

p. 284: *Barras's intrigue with Louis XVIII:* Jean-Baptiste Capefigue, *L'Europe pendant la Révolution française*, pp. 236–37.

p. 284: *Small vagrant armies pillaged and looted:* Broers, *Napoleon's Other War*, p. 21.

p. 284: *The men in power were looking for a way out:* Brown, *Ending the French Revolution*.

p. 284: *Bonaparte landed in France on October 9:* Napoleon, *Correspondance de Napoléon Ier*, Vol. 5, p. 582.

p. 284: *the most recent news:* Alan Schom, *Napoleon Bonaparte*, p. 203.

p. 285: *"Better the plague than the Austrians!":* Louis Antoine Fauvelet de Bourrienne, *Mémoires de M. de Bourrienne*, Vol. 3, p. 19.

p. 285: *Tallyrand's role in the coup:* Duff Cooper, *Talleyrand*, pp. 111–17.

p. 285: *Lucien Bonaparte's maneuvers in the Council of Five Hundred:* Andrea Campi, *Memoirs of the Political and Private Life of Lucien Bonaparte*, Vol. 1, p. 34.

p. 285: *Volney and Collot, co-conspirators:* Denis Woronoff, *La république bourgeois de Thermidor à Brumaire*, p. 218.

p. 285: *"I received, Citizeness, your two letters":* Member of the Directory Jean-François Moulin to Marie-Louise, October 29, 1799, MAD.

p. 286: *the Ligurian Republic:* Paul Gaffarel, *Bonaparte et les républiques italiennes (1796–1799)*, pp. 92–94; David Nicholls, *Napoleon: A Biographical Companion*, p. 148; Ludovic Sciout, *La République française et la République de Gênes, 1794–1799*, p. 50.

p. 286: *"taken prisoner of war by the Neapolitans":* Minister Bourdon to Marie-Louise, November 4, 1799, MAD Safe.

p. 286: *"to call on the Spanish government to free your husband":* Minister of the Navy and the Colonies Marc-Antoine Bourdon de Vatry to Marie-Louise, November 4, 1799, MAD Safe.

p. 286: *"Under the present special circumstances":* Christian Fischer, ed., *Collection générale et complète de lettres, proclamations . . . de Napoléon*, p. 76.

p. 286: *On the cold, gray Sunday of November 10:* Schom, pp. 217–19; Dwyer, ch. 21.

p. 287: *the day was saved for Napoleon:* Marcello Simonetta and Noga Arikha, *Napoleon and the Rebel*, pp. 3–5. (This is the source for the account, including quotations, that follows, of Lucien's actions in support of his older brother.)

p. 288: *Joseph "Hercules" Dominguez:* Bernard Gainot, *Les officiers de couleur dans les armées de la République et de l'Empire, 1792–1815*, p. 139.

p. 288: *Murat, now a rising star:* Andrew Hilliard Atteridge, *Joachim Murat*, pp. 52–53.

p. 288: *"At the General Headquarters in Paris":* General Joachim Murat to Marie-Louise, November 16, 1799, MAD.

CHAPTER 21: THE DUNGEON

p. 290: *Dumas lay doubled up:* Except where noted, this chapter's account of General Dumas's experience in prison, including quotations, relies on "Rapport fait au gouvernement français par le général de division Alexandre Dumas, sur sa captivité à Tarente et à Brindisi, ports du Royaume de Naples," May 5, 1801, MAD Safe.

p. 290: *Enemas are one of the most common remedies:* Noga Arikha, *Passions and Tempers*; F. A. Gonzalez-Crussi, *A Short History of Medicine*, p. 191; Gretchen Smith, *The*

Performance of Male Nobility in Molière's Comédie-Ballets, pp. 141–66; Heneage Ogilvie, "The Large Bowel and Its Functions," *Proceedings of the Royal Society of Medicine* 44, no. 3 (March 1951), p. 204.

p. 291: *blistering and "ear injections":* Roy Porter, *The Cambridge Illustrated History of Medicine*, p. 125; James Copland, *A Dictionary of Practical Medicine*, p. 164; Louis Vitet, *Médecine vétérinaire*, vol. 2 (1771), p. 710.

p. 292: *this had not yet translated into an understanding of disease:* Arikha, p. 231.

p. 292: *the very qualities of the Enlightenment:* Anne Vila, *Enlightenment and Pathology*, ch. 3.

p. 292: *"Nearly all men die of their remedies":* Molière, *Le malade imaginaire*, p. 130.

p. 292: *belief that depression was the cause of everything:* Arikha, p. 60.

p. 292: *age-old theory of humors:* Ibid., pp. 174–75, 230, 236.

p. 293: *Dumas's lost letters:* Dumas to Marie-Louise, April 13, 1801, MAD.

p. 295: *the sperm escaping:* Samuel Tissot, *L'onanisme*, pp. 59–60, 106; Arikha, p. 82; Raymond Stephanson, *The Yard of Wit: Male Creativity and Sexuality, 1650–1750* (2004), pp. 38–42.

p. 295: *surefire way to lose your life force:* Tissot, *L'onanisme*; Jean Stengers and Anne Van Neck, *Masturbation: The History of a Great Terror*, p. 163.

p. 295: Health Advice for the Common People: Samuel Tissot, *Avis au peuple sur sa santé*, first published in 1761; the eleventh and final edition appeared in 1792. It was translated into English in 1766 as *Advice to the People in General, Regarding Their Health*.

p. 295: *article on poison:* Tissot, *Avis au peuple sur sa santé*, pp. 223–26.

p. 296: *chocolate as medicine in the eighteenth century:* Susan Terrio, *Crafting the Culture and History of French Chocolate*, p. 279.

p. 296: *cinchona:* Jean-Louis Alibert, *Dissertation sur les fièvres pernicieuses ou ataxiques intermittentes*, 2nd ed. (1801).

p. 296: *Napoleon in the Saint Bernard Pass:* Alexander Rodger, *War of the Second Coalition*, p. 175; Napoleon, *Correspondance de Napoléon Ier*, Vol. 6, pp. 274–97.

p. 296: *Napoleon on a mule:* Donna Smith, *The Book of Mules* (2009), p. 3; Englund, *Napoleon*, p. 318.

p. 296: *Victory at Marengo, June 14, 1799:* Rodger, p. 243.

p. 297: *planting trees of liberty:* Nathan Ausubel and David Gross, *Pictorial History of the Jewish People* (1984), p. 198.

p. 297: *a subsequent written complaint:* Giovanni Bianchi (hereafter, "Bianchi") to "the French Generals," January 22, 1801, MAD.

p. 298: *"Let it be known to you":* Bonaventura Certezza to Dumas, August 6 or 17, 1801, MAD.

p. 298: *"Gentlemen, French Generals, Prisoners":* Bianchi to Dumas, December 28, 1800, MAD.

p. 298: *relay the news that Dumas's requests:* For example, Bianchi to Dumas, October 31, 1800, MAD.

p. 298: *a tortuously minute exchange about a cookpot:* Bianchi to Dumas, October 8, 1800, and January 31, 1801, MAD.

p. 298: *picayune exchange of letters:* Bianchi to Dumas, December 31, 1800, and January 6, 1801, MAD.

p. 299: *"the number of jackets, shoes":* Bianchi to Dumas, October 31, 1800, MAD.

p. 299: *"7 ducats and 90 grani":* Bianchi to Dumas, January 8, 1801, MAD.

p. 299: *Bianchi sent an extraordinary letter to Dumas:* Bianchi to Dumas, January 22, 1801, MAD.

p. 300: *"I'm always at your disposal":* Bianchi to Dumas, October 31, 1800, and January 2, March 9, and March 12, 1801, MAD.

p. 300: *"fabric samples":* Bianchi to Dumas, March 6, 1801, MAD.

p. 300: *the subject of his confiscated property:* Bianchi to Dumas, March 7, 1801, MAD.

p. 300: *"double-barreled rifle . . . was thrown":* Bianchi to Dumas, March 9, 1801, MAD.

p. 301: *it has been impossible to procure:* Bianchi to Dumas, March 7, 1801, MAD.

p. 301: *"safer and more comfortable":* Bianchi to Dumas, March 6, 1801, MAD.

p. 301: *"to wear the cockade of your nation":* Bianchi to Dumas, March 13, 1801, MAD.

p. 301: *Cardinal Ruffo had created a cockade:* John A. Davis, *Naples and Napoleon*, p. 117.

p. 301: *Napoleon sends General Murat to lead an army:* Richard Dunn-Pattison, *Napoleon's Marshals*, p. 29.

p. 301: *Il re Gambalesta:* Silvio Maurano, *La Repubblica partenopea*, pp. 49, 53.

p. 301: *Murat acting on orders from the minister of war:* Napoleon, *Correspondance*, Vol. 6, p. 481.

p. 301: *King Ferdinand and General Murat:* Jean Tulard, *Murat*, pp. 102–8.

p. 302: *by the end of March, Dumas was on a ship:* Dumas to Marie-Louise, April 13, 1801, MAD.

p. 302: *"I have the honor of informing you":* Dumas to the government of France, April 13, 1801, MAD.

p. 302: *"if by luck she is still of this world":* Dumas to Marie-Louise, April 13, 1801, MAD.

p. 303: *"has kissed a thousand times":* Dumas to Marie-Louise, April 28, 1801, MAD.

CHAPTER 22: WAIT AND HOPE

p. 304: *"What dark and bloody secrets":* MM, p. 218.

p. 304: *Napoleon's government:* Isser Woloch, *Napoleon and His Collaborators*, ch. 2.

p. 305: *"It is founded on the true principles":* Will Durant and Ariel Durant, *The Age of Napoleon* (1975), p. 166.

p. 305: *Napoleon's suppression of the press:* Woloch, ch. 7.

p. 305: *"The terror he inspires":* Andrea Stuart, *The Rose of Martinique*, p. 303.

p. 306: *"I promise to avenge myself":* Marie-Louise to Dumas, May 27, 1801, MAD.

p. 306: *reunited in Paris:* Dumas to Marie-Louise, June 4, 1801, MAD.

p. 306: *his claim would be high on the list:* Several letters, including Ministry of War to Dumas, December 6, 1802, MAD; and Dumas to Napoleon, October 17, 1803, SHD 7YD91.

p. 306: *"receive the sum of 500,000 francs":* French Consul in Naples Alquier to General Murat, April 22, 1801, in Joachim Murat, *Lettres et documents pour servir à l'histoire de Joachim Murat*, p. 296.

p. 306: *Berthier informed Dumas:* Minister of War Louis-Alexandre Berthier to Dumas, September 16, 1801, BNF NAF 24641.

p. 307: *"I hope":* Dumas to Napoleon, September 29, 1801, cited in Henry, pp. 100–101.

p. 307: *"I have the honor":* Dumas to Minister of War Louis-Alexandre Berthier, February 22, 1802, SHD 7YD91.

p. 307: *"hardly showed himself":* Antoine-Vincent Arnault et al., "Dumas (Alexandre Davy-de-la-Pailleterie)," p. 162.

p. 308: *a coalition of slavers:* Pierre Branda and Thierry Lentz, *Napoléon, l'esclavage, et les colonies*, 52–61; Thomas Pronier, "L'implicite et l'explicite dans la politique de Napoléon," in Yves Benot and Marcel Dorigny, eds., *Le rétablissement de l'esclavage dans les colonies françaises*, pp. 61–66.

p. 308: *a banquet by Charles de la Pailleterie's old rivals:* Maurice Begouen-Demeaux, *Mémorial d'une famille du Havre*, cited by Erik Noël, "La fortune antillaise des Delahaye-Lebouis," p. 667.

p. 308: *exports of Saint-Domingue:* Branda and Lentz, p. 137.

p. 308: *proposal for lifting the French ban:* Ibid, p. 54.

p. 308: *replaced the minister of the navy and colonies and seeded pro-slavery figures:* Ibid, pp. 52–61.

p. 308: *"The regime of the French colonies":* Constitution of the Year VIII, article 91.

p. 309: *a double game:* Wanquet, *La France et la première abolition de l'esclavage*, pp. 521–656;

Branda and Lentz, pp. 47–74; and Yves Benot, *La démence coloniale sous Napoléon*, pp. 15–56.

p. 309:   *"Remember, brave Negroes"*: Napoleon, *Correspondance de Napoléon Ier*, Vol. 6, p. 54.

p. 309:   *he made a secret decision:* Benot, p. 355.

p. 309:   *size of armada:* Laurent Dubois, *Avengers of the New World*, p. 253.

p. 309:   *Napoleon wrote to a Martinique planter:* Philippe R. Girard, *The Slaves Who Defeated Napoleon*, p. 46.

p. 309:   *Toussaint Louverture:* Madison Smartt Bell, *Toussaint Louverture: A Biography*.

pp. 309–   *Isaac and Placide Louverture:* This account of Toussaint Louverture's sons' experi-
10:   ence in Paris, including quotations, is based on Isaac Louverture, "Mémoires d'Isaac Toussaint," in Antoine Marie Thérèse Métral, *Histoire de l'expédition des Français à Saint-Domingue, sous le consulat de Napoléon Bonaparte*, pp. 227–324.

p. 311:   *"His iron frame"*: C. L. R. James, *The Black Jacobins*, p. 365.

p. 311:   *"It is not enough"*: General Leclerc to Minister of the Navy Decrès, August 25, 1802, quoted by Carolyn Fick, "La résistance populaire au corps expéditionnaire du Général Leclerc et au Rétablissement de l'esclavage à Saint-Domingue (1803–1804)," in Benot and Dorigny, eds., p. 139.

p. 311:   *Napoleon gave Leclerc strict orders:* Napoleon's instructions to General Leclerc, quoted by Ibid., p. 130.

p. 311:   *illegally sold into slavery:* Léo Élisabeth, "Déportés des Petites Antilles françaises, 1801–1803," in Benot and Dorigny, eds., pp. 77–83.

p. 311:   *More than forty thousand French soldiers died*: David Geggus, *Haitian Revolutionary Studies*, p. 178.

p. 312:   *killed by deliberate asphyxiation:* Laurent Dubois, *Haiti: The Aftershocks of History*, p. 40.

p. 312:   *welcomed some whites:* Ibid.

p. 312:   *French forces also invaded Guadeloupe:* Laurent Dubois, *A Colony of Citizens: Revolution and Slave Emancipation in the French Caribbean, 1787–1804*, pp. 317–422; Henri Bangou, *La révolution et l'esclavage à la Guadeloupe, 1789–1802*, pp. 118–43.

p. 312:   *La Soufrière and Louis Delgrès:* Dubois, pp. 236, 239, 353–400; Bernard Gainot, *Les officiers de couleur dans les armées de la République et de l'Empire 1792–1815*, p. 88.

p. 312:   *National Colonial Institute:* This account of the closing of the Institute, including quotations, relies on Gainot, pp. 160–63.

p. 313:   *Ferdinand Christophe:* Deborah Jenson, *Beyond the Slave Narrative: Politics, Sex, and Manuscripts in the Haitian Revolution*, pp. 196–205; Gainot, pp. 161–62.

p. 313:   *"[She] saw a young man"*: Jenson, *Beyond the Slave Narrative*, pp. 203–4.

p. 314:   *"without even having been made a Chevalier"*: MM, p. 231.

p. 314:   *"pass on with pleasure"*: Marshal of the Empire Murat to Dumas, August 16, 1804, MAD.

p. 314:   *Napoleon's true position on slavery in the French Empire:* Law of 30 Floréal, Year X (May 20, 1802), in Claude Wanquet, *La France et la première abolition de l'esclavage, 1794–1802*, p. 641; see also Patrick Geggus, *The World of the Haitian Revolution*, p. 194.

p. 314:   *law banning all officers and soldiers of color:* Law of 9 Prairial, Year X (May 29, 1802), in Wanquet, p. 647.

p. 314:   *"blacks, mulattos, and men of color . . . from entering"*: Law of 13 Messidor, Year X (July 2, 1802), in J. B. Duvergier, *Collection complète des lois, décrets, ordonnances, réglements, et avis du conseil-d'état*, Vol. 13, p. 485.

p. 314:   *"the intention of the government that no act of marriage"*: Law of 18 Nivôse, Year XI (January 8, 1803), in Jean-Simon Loiseau, *Dictionnaire des arrêts modernes*, Vol. 2 (1809), p. 449.

p. 315:   *a mulatto servant in Napoleon's own household:* Stuart, p. 396.

p. 315:   *General Dumas would need to request a special dispensation:* Report by M. Duchateau to the minister of war, between May 21 and June 19, 1802, SHD 7YD91.

p. 315: *so he wouldn't be deported:* Napoleon's regime sought to deport people of color out of the French mainland in the summer of 1802: Élisabeth, p. 92.

p. 315: *"no longer worthy of the cause":* Dumas (then commanding the First Division of the Army of the Rhine and Moselle) to War Minister Aubert du Bayet, February 3, 1796, SHD 7YD91.

p. 315: *another folder of letters:* SHD XH3.

p. 315: *Black Pioneers:* John Elting, *Swords Around a Throne*, pp. 274–75; Gainot, pp. 166–83.

p. 316: *asking his comrade generals to help him:* Marshal Joachim Murat to Dumas, August 16 and October 28, 1804, MAD.

p. 316: *"colored men who will be treated":* Consuls of the Republic, decree, December 4, 1802, SHD 1XH3.

p. 316: *dozens of long and eloquent letters:* SHD XH3.

p. 316: *Royal African Regiment:* Gainot, pp. 204–11.

p. 316: *"Africans":* Ibid., pp. 177–78, 228.

p. 316: *birth of the third child·* Alexandre Dumas's birth certificate, July 24, 1802, *Registres d'état civil*, ADA.

p. 317: *"before the Egyptian campaign":* MM, p. 198.

p. 317: *Dumas wrote to an old friend:* Dumas to General Brune, July 26, 1802, BNF NAF 24641.

p. 317: *"a superstition":* Brune to Dumas, July 29, 1802, quoted in MM, pp. 198–99.

p. 317: *Labouret standing in for Brune:* Ibid., p. 198.

p. 318: *"As soon as the current war":* Dumas to Napoleon, October 17, 1803, SHD 7YD91.

p. 318: *"Whatever my sufferings":* Dumas to the minister of war, May 5, 1801, SHD 7YD91.

p. 318: *"It was my father's naked form"* and *"my father's grand form":* MM, p. 202.

p. 318: *"I adored my father"* and *"On his side, too":* MM, pp. 224–25.

p. 319: *cancer diagnosis and visit to doctor in Paris:* Charles Glinel, *Alexandre Dumas et son oeuvre*, p. 23.

p. 319: *"My father embraced Brune":* MM, p. 217.

p. 319: *visit to Pauline Bonaparte* and *"A woman reclined on a sofa":* Ibid., pp. 219–20.

p. 320: *a note inviting "Madame Dumas":* Princess Pauline to "Mme Dumas" (Marie-Louise), date unknown, MAD Safe.

p. 320: *"I remember that my father":* MM, p. 221.

p. 320: *the final night:* Alex Dumas's death act, February 27, 1806, MAD, and M. Deviolaine to his cousin, February 27, 1806, MAD Safe.

p. 320: *" 'Oh!' he cried"* and next three quotations: MM, pp. 222–23, 228, 231.

p. 321: *I found a detailed inventory:* Inventory of Dumas's belongings after his death, August 25, 1806, MAD Safe.

p. 321: *pension that was owed General Dumas:* Dumas to Napoleon, October 17, 1803, SHD 7YD91.

p. 321: *poverty:* In 1801 Dumas mentions "begging": Dumas to Napoleon, September 29, 1801, cited in MM, p. 193.

p. 321: *tobacconist's shop:* Arnault et al., p. 162.

p. 321: *impoverished:* Marie-Louise to Mme Carmin, December 4, 1806, MAD Safe.

p. 321: *"this hatred":* MM, p. 231.

p. 321: *"What a shock":* M. Doumet to Marie-Louise, September 30, 1807, MAD Safe.

p. 321: *Marie-Louise petitioning:* MM, p. 233.

p. 322: *"The death of General Dumas":* Marie-Louise to the minister of war, October 2, 1814, SHD 7YD91.

p. 322: *"Brune zealously"* and *"I forbid":* MM, pp. 231, 233.

p. 323: *"Unhappiness":* Dumas to Marie-Louise, April 28, 1801, MAD.

p. 323: *"He who has felt":* Dumas (père), *Le comte de Monte-Cristo*, Vol. 6, p. 277.

p. 323: *"You see, Father":* MM, p. 217.

EPILOGUE: THE FORGOTTEN STATUE

p. 324: *first biographical portrait:* Author unknown, "Le général Alexandre Dumas, homme de couleur," n.d. [1797], BNF NAF 24641.

p. 326: *"Alexandre Dumas, born in Saint-Domingue":* Pierre Nougaret, *Anecdotes militaires, anciennes & modernes de tous les peuples*, pp. 260–61.

p. 327: *statue of General Dumas in Paris:* Folder entitled "Général Dumas, 1913, Moncel sc[ulpteur], square Malesherbes, 17e arr[ondissement]," COARC. Also several articles: Jules Chancel, "Les Trois Dumas"; Jules Claretie, "Chronique parisienne"; "La statue oubliée: Les humoristes réparent la négligence des gouvernements à l'égard du général Dumas," *Le Matin*, May 28, 1913.

p. 327: *subscription to commission the statue:* E. de la Charlottrie to the Prefect of the Seine, February 17, Undersecretary of State for the Arts to the Prefect of the Seine, February 21, 1912, both in Général Dumas, 1913, Moncel . . ." COARC.

p. 327: *Anatole France and Sarah Bernhardt:* Chancel.

p. 327: *fall of 1912:* Louis Bonnier, Director of Architecture, Walkways, and Landscaping Services, Department of the Seine, to the Director of Arts for the Seine, July 2, 1913, in "Général Dumas, 1913, Moncel. . . ," COARC.

p. 327: *remaining covered:* "La statue oubliée." *Le Matin*, May 28, 1913.

p. 327: *the only set of photos:* Photographic prints in "Général Dumas, 1913, Moncel . . . ," COARC.

p. 327: *"The poor general!":* "La statue oubliée."

p. 328: *a popular cartoonist, Poulbot:* mentioned in ibid., Francisque Poulbot was a cartoonist best known for painting scenes depicting typical French children, so much so that his name became synonymous with such drawings. Michel Doussot, *Petit futé: Paris, Île de France*, 8th ed. (2009), p. 48.

p. 328: *"the sordid Moorish cloak"* and *"a little girl game":* "La statue oubliée."

p. 328: *"For months and months":* "Doléances d'un habitant de la Place Malesherbes," unidentified newspaper clipping, circa May 29, 1913, in Général Dumas, 1913, Moncel . . . ," COARC.

p. 328: *the president of the republic had signed:* Presidential decree, June 17, 1913, officially allowing the the statue to be "erected" (hence, unshrouded), in "Général Dumas, 1913, Moncel . . . ," COARC.

p. 328: *the now tattered shroud was hanging off:* Louis Bonnier, Director of Architecture, Walkways, and Landscaping Services Department of the Seine, to the Director of Arts for the Seine, July 2, 1913, in "Général Dumas, 1913, Moncel . . . ," COARC.

p. 328: *destroyed by the Nazis:* "Hommage aux Noirs," *Le Parisien*, February 28, 2006; "Alexandre Dumas attend sa statue," *Le Parisien*, November 28, 2007.

p. 328: *a book on the destruction of the statues:* Jean Cocteau and Pierre Jahan, *La mort et les statues*.

p. 329: *a posthumous Legion of Honor:* "La Légion d'honneur pour le général Dumas! À Monsieur Nicolas Sarkozy, Président de la République française," website of Claude Ribbe, http://claude-ribbe.com.

p. 330: *sculpture of slave shackles:* "Fers, un hommage au général Dumas" ("Shackles: An Hommage to General Dumas"), sculpture by Driss Sans-Arcidet honoring General Dumas, located in the place du Général Catroux (formally the Place Malesherbes, known unofficially as the Place des Trois Dumas), inaugurated April 4, 2009. See Conseil Municipal de Paris, proceedings, December 15–17, 2008, www.paris.fr.

◆ SELECTED BIBLIOGRAPHY ◆

PRIMARY SOURCES

ARCHIVES

Most of this book is based on unpublished archival sources, including the all-important contents of the blown safe in the Villers-Cotterêts Museum. For a full list, please see the beginning of the Notes.

MEMOIRS, DIARIES, LETTERS, AND OTHER PRIMARY TEXTS

Barrière, François, and Mme Maigné. *The Private Life of Marie Antoinette: Autobiographical Memoirs of Madame Campan, First Lady-in-Waiting to Marie Antoinette, Queen of France and Navarre.* Vol. 2. London, 1883.

Bayly, Richard. *Diary of Colonel Bayly, 12th Regiment, 1796–1830.* London, 1896.

Berthier, Louis-Alexandre. *Memoir of the Campaigns of General Bonaparte in Egypt and Syria.* London, 1805.

Bonaparte, Napoleon. *Correspondance de Napoléon Ier publiée par ordre de l'empereur Napoléon III.* 32 vols. Paris, 1859–70.

———. *A Selection from the Letters and Despatches of the First Napoleon.* Edited by D.A. Bingham. 3 vols. London, 1884.

———. *Collection générale et complète de lettres, proclamations . . . de Napoléon.* Edited by Christian Fischer. Leipzig, 1808.

———. *Mémoires de Napoléon.* Vols. 1 & 2. Edited by Thierry Lentz. Paris: Tallandier, 2010, 2011.

———. *Oeuvres de Napoléon Bonaparte.* Vol. 1. Paris, 1821.

Bonnefons, Antoine. *Un soldat d'Italie et d'Égypte: Journal d'Antoine Bonnefons, 7 novembre 1792–21 février 1801.* Paris, 1903.

Boudeaux, Guillaume Imbert de. *Correspondance secrète, politique & littéraire. . . .* Vol. 8. London, 1787.

Bourrienne, Louis-Antoine Fauvelet de. *Mémoires de M. de Bourrienne, Ministre d'État, sur Napoléon.* 10 vols. Paris, 1830.

Campi, Andrea. *Memoirs of the Political and Private Life of Lucien Bonaparte.* Vol. 1. London, 1818.

Chaumette, Pierre Gaspard. "En réjouissance de l'abolition de l'esclavage" (speech), February 18, 1794. *Notes et Archives 1789–1794* (website, Philippe Royet), http://www.royet.org/nea1789-1794/archives/discours/chaumette_rejouissance_abolition_esclavage_18_02_94.htm.

Chépy, Pierre. *Un agent politique à l'armée des Alpes: Correspondance de Pierre Chépy avec le ministre des affaires étrangères, Mai 1793–Janvier 1794.* Grenoble: F. Allier, 1894.

Chevrier, Edmond, ed. *Le Général Joubert d'après sa correspondance.* Paris, 1884.

Le Code noir et autres textes de lois sur l'esclavage. Paris: Sepia, 2006.

Denon, Dominique Vivant. *Voyage dans le Basse et le Haute Égypte pendant les campagnes du Général Bonaparte.* Vol. 1. Paris, 1802.

Desgenettes, René-Nicolas. *Souvenirs de la fin du XVIIIe siècle et du commencement du XIXe, ou mémoires de R.D.G.* Vol. 3. Paris, 1836. Unfinished manuscript of the third volume of five intended volumes, copies of which are held at the library of the Institut de France (Paris), and at the Bibliothèque Centrale du Service des Armées (Val de Grâce, France).

Desmoulins, Camille. *Oeuvres de Camille Desmoulins.* Vol. 3. Paris, 1866.

Desvernois, Nicholas Philibert, Baron. *Mémoires du Général Baron Desvernois.* Paris, 1898.

Dillon La Tour du Pin Gouvernet, Henriette. *Journal d'une femme de cinquante ans, 1778–1815,* Vol. 1. Edited by Aymar de Liedekerke-Beaufort. Paris: M. Imhaus & R. Chapelot, 1914.

Doguereau, Jean-Pierre. *Journal de l'expédition d'Égypte.* Edited by Clément de La Jonquière. Paris: Perrin, 1904.

Dolomieu, Déodat de. *Sur la philosophie minéralogique et sur l'espèce minéralogique.* Paris, 1801.

Dumas, Alexandre (*père*). *Le Comte de Monte-Cristo,* 6 vols. Paris: Michel Levy Frères, 1861.

———. "État-civil du Comte de Monte-Cristo." In *Causeries,* 115–32 (Paris: Maisonneuve & Larose, 2002 [1854].

———. *Georges.* Vol. 1. Brussels: Imprimerie du politique, 1843.

———. *Histoire de mes bêtes.* Paris, 1867.

———. *Mes mémoires.* 10 vols. Paris, 1881.

———. *My Memoirs.* 6 vols. Translated by E. M. Waller. London: Methuen, 1907.

———. "Préface en forme de causerie ou causerie en forme de préface." In *Les armes et le duel,* by Augustin Edme François Grisier, 13–54. Paris, 1847.

———. *Sketches of Naples.* Philadelphia: Ferrett, 1845.

———. *Les trois mousquetaires.* Paris: Michel Lévy Frères, 1860.

Elliot, Sir George. *Memoir of Admiral the Honourable Sir George Elliot.* London, 1863.

Ferrières, Marquis de. *Correspondance inédite 1789, 1790, 1791.* Paris: Librairie Armand Colin, 1932.

"The Final Sale of the Relics of General Washington" (catalog). Philadelphia: Thomas Birch's Sons, 1891.

Goethe, Johann Wolfgang von. *Italian Journey.* Translated by W. H. Auden and Elizabeth Mayer. London: Penguin, 1985 [1962].

Grégoire, Henry (Abbé). *Lettre aux philanthropes sur les malheurs, les droits et les réclamations des gens de couleur de Saint-Domingue, et des autres îles françoises de l'Amérique.* Paris, 1790.

Guibert Jacques-Antoine de. *Essai général de tactique.* Vol. 2. Paris, 1773.

Hecquet, Philippe. *La médecine, la chirurgie et la pharmacie des pauvres contenent des remèdes faciles à préparer . . . à donner aux empoisonnés et aux asphyxiés.* Paris, 1740.

Henrion de Pansey, Pierre. *Mémoire pour un Nègre qui réclame sa liberté.* Paris, 1770.

Hilliard d'Auberteuil, Michel-René. *Considérations sur l'état présent de la colonie française de Saint-Domingue.* Vol. 2. Paris, 1776.

Hoare, Prince, ed. *Memoirs of Granville Sharp.* London, 1820.

Jabarti, Abd al-Rahman (Al Jabarti). *Al-Jabarti's Chronicle of the First Seven Months of the French Occupation of Egypt.* Translated and edited by Shmuel Moreh. Leiden, Netherlands: Brill, 1975.

Jefferson, Thomas. *Memoirs, Correspondence, and Private Papers of Thomas Jefferson, Late President of the United States.* Vol. 2. Edited by Thomas Jefferson Randolph. London, 1829.

Kléber, Jean-Baptiste. *Kléber en Égypte.* Edited by Henry Laurens. 4 vols. Cairo: Institut français d'archéologie orientale, 1988.

———. *Mémoires politiques et militaires: Vendée, 1793–1794.* Paris: Tallandier, 1989.

Lacroix, Alfred, ed. *Déodat de Dolomieu.* 2 vols. Paris: Perrin, 1921.

————. ed., *Dolomieu en Égypte, 30 Juin 1798-10 Mars 1799 (Manuscrits retrouvée par A. Lacroix)*. Cairo: Institut français d'archéologie orientale, 1922.

Larevellière-Lépaux, Louis-Marie. *Mémoires de Larevellière-Lépaux*. Vol. 2. Paris, 1895.

Larrey, D. J. *Mémoires de chirurgie militaire et campagnes*. 3 vols. Paris, 1812.

Las Cases, Emmanuel. *Mémorial de Sainte-Hélène: Journal de la vie privée et des conversations de l'empereur Napoléon, à Sainte Hélène*. Vol. 1. London, 1823.

Mallet, Jean. *Mémoire pour Jean Bocaux*. Paris, 1738.

Martin, Pierre Dominique. *Histoire de l'expédition française en Égypte*. Vol. 1. Paris, 1815.

Mercier, Louis-Sébastien. *Panorama of Paris: Selections from "Le Tableau de Paris."* Edited by Jeremy Popkin. Translated by Helen Simpson. University Park: Pennsylvania State University Press, 1999.

————. *Paris*. Vol. 2. London, 1817.

Métral, Antoine Marie Thérèse, and Isaac Toussaint Louverture. *Histoire de l'expédition des Français à Saint-Domingue, sous le consulat de Napoléon Bonaparte*. Paris, 1825.

Molière. *Le malade imaginaire*. Edited by Everett Ward Olmsted. Boston: Ginn, 1905.

Moreau de Saint-Méry, Médéric. *Description topographique, physique, civile, politique et historique de la partie française de l'isle Saint-Domingue*. 2 vols. Paris, 1797–98.

Murat, Joachim. *Lettres et documents pour servir à l'histoire de Joachim Murat*. Vol. 1, *Lettres de jeunesse: Campagnes d'Italie et d'Égypte; Corps et armée d'observation du Midi*. Edited by Paul Le Brethon. Paris: Plon, 1908.

Plutarch. *Lives of Illustrious Men*. Vol. 1. Translated by John Dryden. New York, 1880.

Rémusat, Madame de. *Mémoires de Madame de Rémusat, 1802–1808*. Edited by Paul de Rémusat. Paris, 1880.

Richelieu, Louis François Armand du Plessis de. *Mémoires historiques et anecdotiques du duc de Richelieu*. Vol. 6. Paris, 1829.

Rousseau, Jean-Jacques. *Du contrat social, ou Principes du droit politique*. Paris, 1791.

Saint-Germain, Claude Louis, comte de. *Correspondance particulière du comte de Saint-Germain, ministre d'état, avec M. Paris du Verney*. Vol. 1. London and Paris, 1789.

Saint-Just, Antoine Louis Léon de. *Oeuvres de Saint-Just, représentant du peuple à la Convention Nationale*. Paris, 1834.

"La statue oubliée.: Les humoristes réparent la négligence des gouvernements à l'égard du général Dumas." *Le Matin*, May 28, 1913.

Thiébault, Paul. *Mémoires du général baron Thiébault publiés sous les auspices de sa fille, Mlle Claire Thiébault d'après le manuscrit original par Fernand Calmettes*. Vols. 1 and 2. Paris, 1893.

Tissot, Samuel. *Avis au peuple sur sa santé*. 2 vols. Lausanne, 1761.

————. *L'Onanisme: Dissertation sur les maladies produites par la masturbation*. 4th ed. Lausanne, 1770.

Vertray, M. *Journal d'un officier de l'armée d'Égypte*. Paris, 1883.

Volney, Constantin-François. *Voyage en Syrie et en Égypte pendant les années 1783, 1784 et 1785*. Vol. 1. Paris, 1787.

————. *Les ruines ou méditation sur les révolutions des empires*. Paris, 1791.

Voltaire. *Histoire du siècle de Louis XIV*. Paris, 1752.

————. *Oeuvres complètes*. Vol. 2. Paris, 1870.

Young, Arthur. *Travels During the Years 1787, 1788, 1789 . . .* Vol. 1. Dublin, 1793.

SECONDARY SOURCES

BOOKS

Abbott, Elizabeth. *Sugar: A Bittersweet History*. Toronto: Penguin, 2008.

Adams, William Howard. *The Paris Years of Thomas Jefferson*. New Haven: Yale University Press, 2000.

Ader, Jean-Joseph. *Histoire de l'expédition d'Égypte et de Syrie.* 1826.

Adkins, Roy, and Lesley Adkins. *War for All the Oceans: From Nelson at the Nile to Napoleon at Waterloo.* London: Little, Brown, 2006.

Andress, David. *The French Revolution and the People.* London: Hambledon & London, 2004.

Arikha, Noga. *Passions and Tempers: A History of the Humours.* New York: Ecco Press, 2007.

Ashton-Wolfe, Harry. *True Stories of Immortal Crimes.* London: Hurst & Blackett, 1930.

Asprey, Robert B. *The Rise of Napoleon Bonaparte.* New York: Basic Books, 2000.

Astarita, Tommaso. *Between Salt Water and Holy Water: A History of Southern Italy.* New York: Norton, 2005.

Atteridge, Andrew Hilliard. *Joachim Murat: Marshal of France and King of Naples.* New York: Brentano's, 1911.

Audebrand, Philibert. *Alexandre Dumas à la Maison d'or: Souvenirs de la vie littéraire.* Paris, 1888.

Baedeker, Karl. *Paris and Its Environs.* 6th ed. Leipzig, 1878.

Baines, Edward. *History of the Wars of the French Revolution.* Vol. 1. London, 1817.

Bajot, M. *Chronologie ministérielle de trois siècles.* Paris, 1836.

Baldick, Robert. *The Duel: A History of Duelling.* London: Hamlyn, 1970.

Banat, Gabriel. *The Chevalier de Saint-Georges: Virtuoso of the Sword and the Bow.* Hillsdale, NY: Pendragon Press, 2006.

Bangou, Henri. *La révolution et l'esclavage à la Guadeloupe, 1789–1802.* Paris: Messidor, 1989.

Bardin, Pierre. *Joseph de Saint George, le Chevalier Noir.* Paris: Guénégaud, 2006.

Barrère, Albert Marie Victor. *Argot and Slang.* London, 1889.

Barthorp, Michael. *Napoleon's Egyptian Campaigns, 1798–1801.* London: Osprey, 1978.

Barty-King, Hugh. *Eyes Right: The Story of Dollond & Aitchison Opticians, 1750–1985.* London: Quiller Press, 1986.

Beauvoir, Roger de. *Le Chevalier de Saint-George.* Paris, 1856.

———. *Duels et duellistes.* Paris, 1864.

Bégouën Demeaux, M. *Mémorial d'une famille du Havre, Stanislas Foäche.* Paris: Société française d'histoire d'outre-mer, 1982.

Bell, David A. *The Cult of the Nation in France: Inventing Nationalism, 1680–1800.* Cambridge, MA: Harvard University Press, 2003.

———. *The First Total War: Napoleon's Europe and the Birth of Warfare as We Know It.* New York: Houghton Mifflin, 2007.

Bell, Madison Smartt. *Toussaint Louverture: A Biography.* New York: Pantheon, 2007.

Bell, Susan G., and Karen M. Offen. *Women, the Family, and Freedom: 1750–1880.* Vol. 1. Palo Alto: Stanford University Press, 1983.

Benot, Yves. *La démence coloniale sous Napoléon.* Paris: La Découverte, 2006.

Benot, Yves, and Marcel Dorigny, eds. *Le rétablissement de l'esclavage dans les colonies françaises: Rupture et continuité de la politique coloniale française (1800–1830).* Paris: Maisonneuve et Larose, 2003.

Benson, John Lossing. *Harpers' Popular Cyclopaedia of United States History from the Aboriginal Period to 1876.* Vol. 2. New York, 1881.

Berlin, Ira. *Cultivation and Culture: Labor and the Shaping of Slave Life in the Americas.* Charlottesville: University of Virginia Press, 1993.

Bernier, Olivier. *Pleasure and Privilege: Daily Life in France, Naples, and America, 1770–1790.* New York: Doubleday, 1981.

Blackburn, Robin. *The Making of New World Slavery: From the Baroque to the Modern, 1492–1800.* London: Verso, 1997.

Blanc, Louis. *Histoire de la Révolution Française.* Vol. 2. Paris, 1847.

Blanning, Timothy C. W. *The French Revolution: Aristos Versus Bourgeois?* London: Macmillan Press, 1987.

———. *The French Revolutionary Wars: 1787–1802.* New York: Edward Arnold Publishers, 1996.

Boiteau d'Ambly, Paul. *État de la France en 1789*. Paris, 1861.

Bouchard, Charles. *Historique du 28e Régiment de Dragons*. Nancy, France, 1893.

Boucher, François. *American Footprints in Paris*. Translated by Frances Wilson Huard. New York: George H. Doran, 1921.

Boulet, François. *Leçon d'histoire de France: Saint-Germain-en-Laye, des antiquités nationales à une ville internationale*. Paris: Les Presses Franciliennes, 2006.

Boulle, Pierre. *Race et esclavage dans la France de l'Ancien Régime*. Paris: Perrin, 2007.

Bourgeois, Henri. *Biographies de la Vendée militaire: Alexandre Dumas*. Luçon, France: M. Bideaux, 1900.

Boyve, Jonas. *Annales historiques du comté de Neuchatel et Valangin*. Vol. 4. Berne & Neuchatel, 1858.

Branda, Pierre, and Thierry Lentz. *Napoléon, l'esclavage et les colonies*. Paris: Fayard, 2006.

Braudel, Fernand. *Civilization and Capitalism, 15th–18th Century*. Vol. 3, *The Perspective of the World*. Berkeley: University of California Press, 1992.

Brette, Armand. *Histoire des édifices où sont siégé les assemblées parlementaires de la Révolution française et de la première République*. Vol. 1. Paris: Imprimerie Nationale, 1902.

Broers, Michael. *Napoleon's Other War: Bandits, Rebels, and Their Pursuers in the Age of Revolutions*. Oxford: Peter Lang, 2010.

Brown, Howard. *Ending the French Revolution: Violence, Justice, and Repression from the Terror to Napoleon*. Charlottesville: University of Virginia Press, 2008.

Browning, Oscar. *Napoleon, the First Phase: Some Chapters on the Boyhood and Youth of Bonaparte, 1769–1793*. London: John Lane, 1905.

Bruce, Robert B., Iain Dickie, Kevin Kiley, Michael F. Pavkovic, and Frederick C. Schneid. *Fighting Techniques of the Napoleonic Age*. New York: Thomas Dunne, 2008.

Bucquoy (Commandant). *Dragons et guides d'état-major*. Paris: Grancher, 2000.

Burns, Thomas. *Rome and the Barbarians: 100 B.C.–A.D. 400*. Baltimore: Johns Hopkins University Press, 2003.

Cabet, Étienne. *Histoire populaire de la Révolution Française, de 1789 à 1830*. Vol. 2. Paris, 1839.

Capefigue, Jean-Baptiste. *L'Europe pendant la Révolution française*. Paris, 1843.

Capponi, Niccolò. *Victory of the West: The Great Christian-Muslim Clash at the Battle of Lepanto*. Cambridge, MA: Da Capo Press, 2007.

Carlyle, Thomas. *The French Revolution: A History*. Vols. 2 and 3. London: George Bell, 1902.

Castillo, Dennis. *The Maltese Cross: A Strategic History of Malta*. Westport, CT: Praeger Security International, 2006.

Chambrier, James de. *Marie-Antoinette, reine de France*. Vol. 1. Paris, 1868.

Chandler, David. *The Campaigns of Napoleon*. New York: Scribner, 1973.

Chappey, Frédéric. *Les trésors des princes de Bourbon Conti*. Paris: Somogy, 2000.

Charles-Vallin, Thérèse. *Les aventures du chevalier géologue Déodat de Dolomieu*. Grenoble: Presses universitaires de Grenoble, 2003.

Chartrand, René, and Eugène Leliepvre. *Louis XV's Army*. Vol. 1, *Cavalry & Dragoons*. London: Osprey, 1996.

Chassin, Charles-Louis, and Léon Clément Hennet. *Les volontaires nationaux pendant la Révolution*. Vol. 1. Paris, 1899.

Chernow, Ron. *Washington: A Life*. New York: Penguin, 2010.

Chevrier, Edmond. *Le Général Joubert: Étude sur sa vie, fragments de sa correspondance inédite*. Bourg-en-Bresse, France, 1860.

Chuquet, Arthur. *Les guerres de la Révolution: La trahison de Dumouriez*. 2d ed. Paris, 1891.

———. *La première invasion prussienne (11 août–2 septembre 1792)*. Paris, 1886.

Clarence-Smith, William Gervase. *Islam and the Abolition of Slavery*. New York: Oxford University Press, 2006.

Clarke, I. F. *Voices Prophesying War: Future Wars, 1763–3749*. New York: Oxford University Press, 1993.

Clarke, James Stanier, and John MacArthur. *The Life of Admiral Lord Nelson: From His Lordship's Manuscripts.* London, 1810.

Claster, Jill N. *Sacred Violence: The European Crusades to the Middle East, 1095–1396.* Toronto: University of Toronto Press, 2009.

Clausewitz, Karl von. *On War.* Translated by Michael Howard and Peter Paret. Princeton: Princeton University Press, 2008.

Clerget, Charles. *Tableaux des armées françaises pendant les guerres de la Révolution.* Paris: Librairie militaire Chaplot, 1905.

Cocteau, Jean, and Pierre Jahan. *La mort et les statues.* Paris: Editions de L'Amateur, 2008.

Cole, Juan. *Napoleon's Egypt.* New York: Palgrave Macmillan, 2007.

Colletta, Pietro. *History of the Kingdom of Naples.* Vol. 1. Edinburgh, 1858.

Colombey, Émile. *Histoire anecdotique du duel dans tous les temps et dans tous les pays.* Paris, 1861.

Cooper, Duff. *Talleyrand.* New York: Grove Press, 2001 [1932].

Copland, James. *A Dictionary of Practical Medicine.* London, 1858.

Crowdy, Terry, and Christa Hook. *French Soldier in Egypt, 1798–1801: The Army of the Orient.* Oxford: Osprey, 2003.

Dardel, Pierre. *Commerce, industrie, navigation à Rouen et au Havre au XVIIIe siècle.* Rouen, 1966.

Darnton, Robert. *Mesmerism and the End of the Enlightenment in France.* Cambridge, MA: Harvard University Press, 1986.

Dauban, Charles-Aimé. *Étude sur Madame Roland et son temps.* Paris, 1864.

Davidson, Arthur. *Alexandre Dumas, père: His Life and Works.* Philadelphia: Lippincott, 1902.

Davis, David Brion. *Inhuman Bondage: The Rise and Fall of Slavery in the New World.* Oxford: Oxford University Press, 2008.

Davis, John A. *Naples and Napoleon: Southern Italy and the European Revolutions, 1780–1860.* New York: Oxford University Press, 2006.

Debaisieux, Martine, and Gabrielle Verdier. *Violence et fiction jusqu'à la Révolution.* Tübingen, Germany: Narr Verlag Tübingen, 1998.

De Cauna, Jacques. *Haïti: L'éternelle révolution: Histoire d'une décolonisation, 1789–1804.* Monein, France: Éditions PyréMonde, 2009.

Delobette, Édouard. *Ces messieurs du Havre: Negociants, commissionnaires et armateurs de 1680 à 1830.* PhD thesis, Université de Caen, 2005.

Desbrière, Édouard, and Maurice Sautai. *La cavalerie pendant la révolution du 14 juillet 1789 au 26 juin 1794: La Crise.* Paris: Berger-Levrault, 1907.

Desprez, Claude. *Desaix.* Paris, 1884.

D'Èze, Gabriel, and A. Marcel. *Histoire de la coiffure des femmes en France.* Paris, 1886.

Dippel, John Van Houten. *Race to the Frontier: "White Flight" and Westward Expansion.* New York: Algora Publishing, 2005.

Dorigny, Marcel, and Bernard Gainot. *La société des Amis des Noirs, 1788–1799: Contribution à l'histoire de l'abolition et de l'esclavage.* Paris: UNESCO, 1998.

Drescher, Seymour. *Abolition: A History of Slavery and Antislavery.* Cambridge: Cambridge University Press, 2009.

Du Breil de Pontbriand, Paul-Marie. *Un Chouan, le général de Boisguy.* Paris: H. Champion, 1904.

Dubois, Laurent. *Avengers of the New World: The Story of the Haitian Revolution.* Cambridge, MA: Harvard University Press, 2004.

―――. *A Colony of Citizens: Revolution and Slave Emancipation in the French Caribbean, 1787–1804.* Chapel Hill: University of North Carolina Press, 2004.

―――. *Haiti: The Aftershocks of History.* New York: Metropolitan Books, 2012.

―――, and John D. Garrigus. *Slave Revolution in the Caribbean, 1789–1804.* Boston: Bedford/St. Martin's, 2006.

Duggan, Christopher. *The Force of Destiny: A History of Italy Since 1796.* Boston: Houghton Mifflin, 2008.

Dull, Jonathan R. *The French Navy and the Seven Years' War.* Lincoln: University of Nebraska Press, 2005.

Dunn-Pattison, Richard. *Napoleon's Marshals.* Wakefield, UK: EP Publishing, 1977.

Durant, Will, and Ariel Durant. *The Age of Napoleon: A History of European Civilization from 1789 to 1815.* Vol. 11, *The Story of Civilization.* New York: Simon & Schuster, 1980.

Dwyer, Philip G. *Napoleon: The Path to Power, 1769–1799.* New Haven: Yale University Press, 2008.

Edwards, Henry Sutherland. *Old and New Paris: Its History, Its People, and Its Places.* Vol. 1. London, 1893.

Elisabeth, Léo. *La société martiniquaise aux XVIIe et XVIIIe siècles: 1664–1789.* Paris: Karthala, 2003.

Ellery, Eloise. *Brissot de Warville: A Study in the History of the French Revolution.* Boston: Houghton Mifflin, 1915.

Elting, John. *Swords Around a Throne.* Cambridge, MA: Da Capo Press, 1997.

Englund, Steven. *Napoleon: A Political Life.* Cambridge, MA: Harvard University Press, 2005.

Fabry, Gabriel. *Rapports historiques des régiments de l'armée d'Italie pendant la campagne de 1796–1797.* Paris: Librairie militaire R. Chapelot, 1905.

———. *Histoire de la campagne de 1794 en Italie.* Paris: Librairie militaire R. Chapelot, 1905.

Faur, Louis-François. *Vie privée du Maréchal de Richelieu.* Vol. 1. Paris, 1791.

Fernandez, Dominique. *Jérémie! Jérémie!* Paris: Grasset, 2005.

Fick, Carolyn F. *The Making of Haïti: The Saint Domingue Revolution from Below.* Knoxville: University of Tennessee Press, 1990.

Fiebeger, Gustav. *The Campaigns of Napoleon Bonaparte of 1796–1797.* West Point: U.S. Military Academy Printing Office, 1911.

Fierro, Alfred, André Palluel-Guillard, and Jean Tulard. *Histoire et dictionnaire du Consulat et de l'Empire: 1799–1815.* Paris: Robert Laffont, 1995.

Fitzgerald, Percy. *The Life and Adventures of Alexandre Dumas.* London, 1873.

Forsyth, Michael. *Buildings for Music: The Architect, the Musician, and the Listener from the Seventeenth Century to the Present Day.* Cambridge, MA: MIT Press, 1985.

Foucart, Paul, and Jules Finot. *La défense nationale dans le Nord, de 1792 à 1802.* Vol. 1. Lille, 1890–93.

Fouchard, Jean. *Le théâtre à Saint-Domingue.* Port-au-Prince: Imprimerie de l'État, 1955.

Fougeroux de Campigneulles, Jean. *Histoire des duels anciens et modernes.* Vol. 1. Paris, 1835.

France, Anatole. *La vie littéraire.* Paris, 1889.

Freemont-Barnes, Gregory. *The French Revolutionary Wars.* London: Osprey, 2001.

Friedenthal, Richard, and Martha Friedenthal-Haase. *Goethe: His Life and Times.* Piscataway, NJ: Transaction Publishers, 2010.

Furet, François. *Interpreting the French Revolution.* Cambridge: Maison des Sciences de l'Homme and Cambridge University Press, 1981.

Gachot, Edouard. *Souvarow en Italie.* Paris: Perrin, 1903.

Gaffarel, Paul. *Bonaparte et les républiques italiennes, 1796–1799.* Paris, 1895.

Gainot, Bernard. *Les officiers de couleur dans les armées de la République et de l'Empire, 1792–1815.* Paris: Karthala, 1989.

Gallaher, John G. *General Alexandre Dumas: Soldier of the Revolution.* Carbondale: Southern Illinois University Press, 1997.

Gamlin, Hilda. *Nelson's Friendships.* Vol. 1. London, 1899.

Gardiner, Robert. *Warships of the Napoleonic Era.* London: Chatham, 1999.

Garraway, Doris. *The Libertine Colony: Creolization in the Early French Caribbean.* Durham, NC: Duke University Press, 2005.

Garrigus, John D. *Before Haiti: Race and Citizenship in French Saint-Domingue*. New York: Macmillan, 2006.

Gates, Henry Louis, Jr. *Black in Latin America*. New York: New York University Press, 2011.

Gauthier, Florence. *L'aristocratie de l'épiderme. Le combat de la Société des citoyens de couleur, 1789–1791*. Paris: CNRS Éditions, 2007.

Geggus, Patrick, and Norman Fiering. *The World of the Haitian Revolution*. Bloomington: Indiana University Press, 2009.

Gillespie, Charles. *Science and Polity in France: The End of the Old Regime*. Princeton: Princeton University Press, 2004.

Glinel, Charles. *Alexandre Dumas et son oeuvre*. Reims, 1884.

Glissant, Edouard. *Mémoires des esclavages: La fondation d'un centre national pour la mémoire des esclavages et de leurs abolitions*. Paris: Gallimard/La Documentation Française, 2007.

Gonzalez-Crussi, F. *A Short History of Medicine*. New York: Modern Library, 2008.

Gordon-Reed, Annette. *The Hemingses of Monticello: An American Family*. New York: Norton, 2008.

Goujet, Claude-Pierre. *Bibliothèque françoise, ou Histoire de la littérature françoise*. Vol. 9. Paris, 1745.

Gourdon de Genouillac, Henri. *Paris à travers les siècles: Histoire nationale de Paris et des Parisiens, depuis la fondation de Lutèce jusqu'à nos jours*. Vol. 4. Paris, 1879.

———. *Recueil d'armoiries des maisons nobles de France*. Paris, 1860.

Grab, Alexander. *Napoleon and the Transformation of Europe*. Basingstoke, UK: Palgrave, 2003.

Grandjean, Laval (Lieutenant). *Journaux sur l'expédition d'Égypte*. Paris: Teissèdre, 2000.

Gregory, Desmond. *Malta, Britain, and the European Powers, 1793–1815*. Madison, NJ: Fairleigh Dickinson University Press, 1996.

Grigsby, Darcy. *Extremities: Painting Empire in Post-Revolutionary France*. New Haven: Yale University Press, 2002.

Grisier, Augustin. *Les armes et le duel*. Paris, 1847.

Haine, W. Scott. *The World of the Paris Café: Sociability Among the French Working Class, 1789–1914*. Baltimore: Johns Hopkins University Press, 1996.

Hamel, Réginald. *Dumas—insolite*. Montreal: Guérin littéraire, 1988.

Harms, Robert. *The Diligent: Worlds of the Slave Trade*. New York: Basic Books, 2002.

Harris, Judith. *Pompeii Awakened*. London: I. B. Tauris, 2007.

Harrison, James. *Life of the Right Honourable Horatio, Lord Viscount Nelson: Baron Nelson of the Nile*. London, 1806.

Haudrière, Phillipe, and Françoise Vergès. *De l'esclave au citoyen*. Evreux, France: Découvertes Texto/Gallimard, 1998.

d'Hauterive, Ernest. *L'armée sous la Révolution, 1789–1794*. Paris, 1894.

———. *Un soldat de la Révolution: Le Général Alexandre Dumas (1762–1806)*. Paris, 1897.

Haythornthwaite, Philip, and Richard Hook. *Napoleon's Campaigns in Italy*. London: Osprey, 1993.

Hazan, Eric, and David Fernbach. *The Invention of Paris: A History in Footsteps*. London: Verso, 2010.

Hemmings, Frederic William John. *Theatre and State in France: 1760–1905*. Cambridge: Cambridge University Press, 1994.

Hennet, Léon. *État militaire de France pour l'année 1793*. Paris: Société de l'histoire de la Révolution française, 1903.

Henry, Gilles. *Dans les pas des . . . Dumas*. Cully: Centre Regional des Lettres de Basse-Normandie. 2010.

———. *Les Dumas: Le secret de Monte Cristo*. Condé-sur-Noiraud: Corlet, 1982.

Herold, J. Christopher. *Bonaparte in Egypt*. New York: Harper and Row, 1962.

Hibbert, Christopher. *Nelson: A Personal History*. London: Viking, 1994,

Hochschild, Adam. *Bury the Chains: Prophets and Rebels in the Fight to Free an Empire's Slaves*. New York: Houghton Mifflin Harcourt, 2005.

Hoefer, Ferdinand. *Nouvelle biographie générale*. Vol. 37. Paris, 1866.

Hoffman, Léon-François, Frauke Gewecke, and Ulrich Fleischmann. *Haïti 1804: Lumières et tenèbres; Impact et résonances d'une révolution*. Madrid: Iberoamericana Editorial, 2008.

Holland, James. *Fortress Malta*. London: Phoenix Paperbacks, 2004.

Horne, Alistair. *Age of Napoleon*. New York: Modern Library, 2006.

Hugo, Abel. *France militaire: Histoire des armées françaises de terre et de mer de 1792 à 1833*. Vol. 2. Paris, 1835.

Hugo, Victor. *Quatrevingt-treize*. Paris, 1874.

Hunt, Lynn. *Revolution and Urban Politics in Provincial France: Troyes and Reims, 1786–90*. Stanford: Stanford University Press, 1978.

———, ed. *The French Revolution and Human Rights: A Brief Documentary History*. Boston: Bedford/St. Martin's, 1996.

Hurtaut, Pierre. *Dictionnaire historique de la ville de Paris*. Vol. 4. Paris, 1779.

James, C. L. R. *The Black Jacobins: Toussaint l'Ouverture and the San Domingo Revolution*. 2nd ed. New York: Vintage, 1989 [1963].

Jenson, Deborah. *Beyond the Slave Narrative: Politics, Sex, and Manuscripts in the Haitian Revolution*. Liverpool: Liverpool University Press, 2011.

Johnson, David. *The French Cavalry, 1792–1815*. London: Belmont Publishing, 1989.

Johnson, Kevin R. *Mixed Race America and the Law: A Reader*. New York: New York University Press, 2003.

Jones, Colin. *The Longman Companion to the French Revolution*. Longman, 1990.

———. *Paris: The Biography of a City*. New York: Penguin Books, 2006.

Jordan, David P. *The Revolutionary Career of Maximilien Robespierre*. Chicago: University of Chicago Press, 1989.

Keane, John. *Tom Paine: A Political Life*. Boston: Little, Brown, 1995.

Kendrich Johnson, Helen. *Our Familiar Songs and Those Who Made Them: Three Hundred Standard Songs of the English-Speaking Race*. New York: Henry Holt, 1909.

Kennedy, Michael L. *The Jacobin Clubs in the French Revolution, 1793–1795*. New York: Berghahn Books, 2000.

King, Stewart R. *Blue Coat or Powdered Wig: Free People of Color in Pre-Revolutionary Saint-Domingue*. Athens, GA: University of Georgia Press, 2001.

Knight, Roger. *The Pursuit of Victory: The Life and Achievement of Horatio Nelson*. New York: Basic Books, 2005.

La Boëssière (*fils*). *Traité de l'art des armes à l'usage des professeurs et des amateurs*. Paris, 1818.

Lahlou, Raphaël. *Alexandre Dumas ou le don de l'enthousiasme*. Paris: Giovanangeli, 2006.

La Jonquière, Clément de. *L'expédition d'Égypte (1798–1801)*. 2nd ed. 5 vols. Paris, 1899.

Lallié, Alfred. *Les noyades de Nantes*. 2nd ed. Nantes, 1879.

Lal Mehta, Jaswant. *Advanced Study in the History of Modern India, 1707–1813*. New York: Sterling Publishers, 2005.

Landru, Robert. *À propos d'Alexandre Dumas: Les aïeux, le général, le bailli, premiers amis*. Vincennes: R. Landru, 1977.

Lanning, Michael Lee. *African Americans in the Revolutionary War*. New York: Citadel Press, 2005.

Laurens, Henry. *L'Expédition d'Égypte: 1798–1801*. Paris: Colin, 1989.

———. *Orientales 1: Autour de l'Expédition d'Égypte*. Paris: CNRS Editions, 2004.

Lavery, Brian. *Nelson and the Nile: The Naval War Against Bonaparte, 1798*. London: Chatham, 1998.

Ledru-Rollin, Alexandre. *Journal du palais*. Vol. 1. Paris, 1840.

Lefebvre, Georges. *The Great Fear of 1789: Rural Panic in Revolutionary France*. New York: Schocken, 1989.

Lemaire, Gérard-Georges. *L'univers des orientalistes*. Paris: Éditions Place des Victoires, 2000.

Le Mascrier, Jean-Baptiste (Abbé). *Description de l'Égypte*. Paris, 1735.

Lentz, Thierry. *Napoléon: "Mon ambition était grande."* Paris: Gallimard, 1998.

Levron, Jacques. *Un libertin fastueux: Le maréchal de Richelieu*. Paris: Perrin, 1971.

Leyden Blennerhassett, Charlotte Julia von. *Madame de Staël: Her Friends and Her Influence in Politics and Literature*. Vol. 1. London, 1889.

Lievyns, A., Jean-Maurice Verdot, and Pierre Bégat. *Fastes de la Légion-d'honneur. Biographie de tous les décorés*. Vol. 3. Paris, 1844.

Linebaugh, Peter, and Marcus Rediker. *The Many-Headed Hydra: Sailors, Slaves, Commoners, and the Hidden History of the Revolutionary Atlantic*. Boston: Beacon Press, 2000.

Linstant, Simon. *Essai sur les moyens d'extirper les préjugés des blancs contre la couleur des Africains et des sang-mêlés*. Paris, 1841.

Lloyd, Christopher. *The Nile Campaign: Nelson and Napoleon in Egypt*. New York: Barnes and Noble, 1973.

Lombard, Jean. *Un volontaire de 1792: Psychologie révolutionnaire et militaire*. Paris, 1892.

Lund, Erik. *War for the Every Day: Generals, Knowledge, and Warfare in Early Modern Europe, 1680–1740*. Westport, CT: Greenwood Press, 1999.

Lyons, Martyn. *Napoleon Bonaparte and the Legacy of the French Revolution*. New York: St. Martin's Press, 1994.

Macinnis, Peter. *Bittersweet: The Story of Sugar*. Crows Nest, Australia: Allen & Unwin, 2002.

Maffeo, Steven E. *Most Secret and Confidential: Intelligence in the Age of Nelson*. Annapolis, MD: Naval Institute Press, 2006.

Magnin, Charles. *Histoire des marionnettes en Europe: Depuis l'antiquité jusqu'à nos jours*. Paris, 1852.

Malanima, Paolo. *Pre-modern European Economy: One Thousand Years*. Leiden, Netherlands: Brill, 2009.

Mante, Thomas. *The Naval and Military History of the Wars of England*. Vol. 8. London, 1795.

Mantel, Hilary. *A Place of Greater Safety*. New York: Macmillan, 2006.

Manuel, Keith Anthony. *Slavery, Coffee, and Family in a Frontier Society: Jérémie and Its Hinterland, 1780–1789*. PhD thesis, University of Florida, 2005.

Marmottan, Paul. *Le général Fromentin et l'armée du Nord (1792–1794)*. Paris, 1891.

Martin, Thomas R. *Ancient Greece: From Prehistoric to Hellenistic Times*. New Haven, CT: Yale University Press, 2000.

Martone, Eric, ed. *The Black Musketeer: Reevaluating Alexandre Dumas within the Francophone World*. Newcastle upon Tyne, UK: Cambridge Scholars, 2011.

Mathiez, Albert. *La révolution et les étrangers: Cosmopolitisme et défense nationale*. Paris: La Renaissance du Livre, 1918.

Maurano, Silvio. *La Repubblica partenopea*. Milan: Ceschina, 1971.

Maurel, André. *Les trois Dumas*. Paris: Librairie illustrée, 1896.

Maurice, Charles. *Histoire anecdotique du théâtre, de la littérature, et de diverses impressions contemporaines*. Vol. 1. Paris, 1856.

Maurois, André. *A History of France*. London: Methuen, 1964.

———. *The Titans: A Three-Generation Biography of the Dumas*. Translated by Gerard Hopkins. New York: Harper, 1957.

Maury, Louis-Ferdinand-Alfred. *Les forêts de la Gaule et de l'ancienne France*. Paris, 1867.

Mazas, Alexandre, with Théodore Anne. *Histoire de l'ordre royal et militaire de Saint-Louis depuis son institution en 1693 jusqu'en 1830*. Vol. 2. Paris, 1860.

McClellan, James E. *Colonialism and Science: Saint Domingue and the Old Regime*. Chicago: University of Chicago Press, 2010.

McLynn, Frank. *Napoleon: A Biography*. London: Jonathan Cape, 1997.

McNeill, William. *The Pursuit of Power: Technology, Armed Force, and Society Since A.D. 1900*. Chicago: University of Chicago Press, 1982.

Méry, Joseph, and Auguste Barthélemy. *Napoléon en Égypte: Poème en 8 chants*. Paris, 1828.

Michelet, Jules. *Histoire de France au dix-huitième siècle: Louis XV et Louis XVI*. Paris, 1867.

Miller, Christopher. *The French Atlantic Triangle: Literature and Culture of the Slave Trade*. Durham, NC: Duke University Press, 2008.

Miltoun, Francis. *Royal Palaces and Parks of France*. Boston: L. C. Page, 1910.

Mintz, Sidney. *Sweetness and Power: The Place of Sugar in Modern History*. New York: Penguin Books, 1986.

Mirecourt, Eugène de. *Fabrique de romans: Maison Alexandre Dumas et compagnie*. Paris, 1845.

———. *Les contemporains: Alexandre Dumas*. Paris, 1856.

Moitt, Bernard. *Women and Slavery in the French Antilles, 1635–1848*. Bloomington: Indiana University Press, 2001.

Molinari, Gustave. *L'évolution politique et la révolution*. Paris, 1884.

Mortal, Patrick. *Les armuriers de l'état: Du grand siècle à la globalisation, 1665–1989*. Villeneuve d'Ascq: Presses Universitaires Septentrion, 2007.

Mouillard, Lucien. *Les régiments sous Louis XV*. Paris, 1882.

Mousnier, Roland. *The Institutions of France Under the Absolute Monarchy, 1598–1789*. Vol. 1, *Society and the State*. Translated by Brian Pearce. Chicago: University of Chicago Press, 1979.

Mowery Andrews, Richard. *Law, Magistracy, and Crime in Old Regime Paris, 1735–1789*. Vol. 1, *The System of Criminal Justice*. Cambridge: Cambridge University Press, 1994.

Mullié, Charles. *Biographie des célébrités militaires des armées de terre et de mer de 1789 à 1850*. Vol. 1. Paris, 1851.

Myśliwiec, Karol. *The Twilight of Ancient Egypt: First Millennium B.C.E.* Ithaca, NY: Cornell University Press, 2000.

Nicassio, Susan. *Imperial City: Rome Under Napoleon*. Chicago: University of Chicago Press, 2009.

Nicholls, David. *Napoleon: A Biographical Companion*. Santa Barbara: ABC-CLIO, 1999.

Noël, Erick. *Être noir en France au XVIIIème siècle*. Paris: Tallandier, 2006.

Norwich, John Julius. *The Middle Sea: A History of the Mediterranean*. New York: Doubleday, 2006.

Nougaret, Pierre. *Anecdotes militaires, anciennes & modernes de tous les peuples*. Vol. 4. Paris, 1808.

Okey, Thomas. *Paris and Its Story*. New York: Macmillan, 1904.

Pajol, Charles Pierre Victor. *Kléber: Sa vie, sa correspondance*. Paris, 1877.

Papayanis, Nicholas. *Planning Paris Before Haussmann*. Baltimore: Johns Hopkins University Press, 2004.

Parigot, Hippolyte. *Alexandre Dumas Père*. Paris: Hachette, 1902.

Parsons, Timothy. *Rule of Empires: Those Who Build Them, Those Who Endure Them, and Why They Always Fall*. New York: Oxford University Press, 2010.

Pawly, Ronald, and Patrice Courcelle. *Napoleon's Mamelukes*. Oxford: Osprey, 2006.

Peabody, Sue. *"There Are No Slaves in France": The Political Culture of Race and Slavery in the Ancien Regime*. New York: Oxford University Press, 1996.

Peytraud, Lucien. *L'esclavage aux Antilles françaises avant 1789, d'après des documents inédits des archives coloniales*. Vol. 2. Paris, 1897.

Picaud, A. *Carnot: L'organisateur de la victoire, 1753–1825*. Paris, 1888.

Pileam, Pamela M. *Madame Tussaud and the History of Waxworks*. London: Hambledon and London, 2003.

Pocock, Tom. *The Terror Before Trafalgar: Nelson, Napoleon, and the Secret War*. New York: Norton, 2003.

Pommereul, François-René-Jean de. *Campagne du général Buonaparte en Italie pendant les années IVe et Ve de la République française*. Paris, 1797.

Popkin, Jeremy D. *A Concise History of the Haitian Revolution*. Chichester, UK: Wiley, 2012.

──────. *You Are All Free: The Haitian Revolution and the Abolition of Slavery*. Cambridge: Cambridge University Press, 2010.

Porter, Roy. *The Cambridge Illustrated History of Medicine*. Cambridge: Cambridge University Press, 2001.

Postgate, Raymond Williams. *Revolution from 1789 to 1906*. Boston: Houghton Mifflin, 1921.

Price, Richard, ed. *Maroon Societies: Rebel Slave Communities in the Americas*. Baltimore: Johns Hopkins University Press, 1996.

Quérel, Alain. *Nicolas-Jacques Conté (1755–1805). un inventeur de génie: Des crayons à l'expédition d'Égypte en passant par l'aérostation militaire*. Paris: L'Harmattan, 2004.

Raymond, André. *Égyptiens et Français au Caire, 1798–1801*. Cairo: Institut français d'archéologie orientale, 2004.

Reinhard, Marcel. *Le grand Carnot*. Paris: Hachette, 1952.

Reybaud, Louis. *Histoire de l'expédition française en Égypte*. Vol. 3 of *Histoire scientifique et militaire de l'expédition française en Égypte* . . . Edited by Xavier-Boniface Saintine. Paris, 1830–36.

Ribbe, Claude. *Alexandre Dumas, le dragon de la reine*. Paris: Éditions du Rocher, 2002.

──────. *Le diable noir*. Monaco: Alphée, 2008.

Richardson, Hubert N. B. *A Dictionary of Napoleon and His Times*. London: Cassell, 1920.

Ridley, Ronald. *The Eagle and the Spade: Archaeology in Rome During the Napoleonic Era*. New York: Cambridge University Press, 1992.

Ring, Trudy, ed. *International Dictionary of Historic Places*. Vol. 3. Chicago: Fitzroy Dearborn, 1995.

Roche, Daniel. *France in the Enlightenment*. Translated by Arthur Goldhammer. Cambridge, MA: Harvard University Press, 1998.

Rochegude, Felix. *Promenades dans toutes les rues de Paris, Ier arrondissement*. Paris: Hachette, 1910.

Rodger, Alexander. *War of the Second Coalition, 1798–1801: A Strategic Commentary*. Oxford: Clarendon Press, 1964.

Roger, J. A. *World's Great Men of Color*. Vol. 2. New York: Touchstone, 1996.

Rogerson, Barnaby. *The Last Crusaders: The Hundred-Year Battle for the Centre of the World*. London: Little, Brown, 2009.

Rothenberg, Gunther Erich. *The Art of Warfare in the Age of Napoleon*. Bloomington: Indiana University Press, 1978.

Roujon, Jacques. *Conti: L'ennemi de Louis XIV*. Paris: A. Fayard, 1941.

Roux, Charles. *Les origines de l'expédition d'Égypte*. Paris: Plon, 1910.

Le Roy de Sainte Croix, François Noël. *Le chant de guerre pour l'armée du Rhin ou la Marseillaise*. Strasbourg, 1880.

Runciman, Steven. *The Sicilian Vespers: A History of the Mediterranean World in the Later Thirteenth Century*. New York: Cambridge University Press, 1958.

Sagan, Eli. *Citizens & Cannibals: The French Revolution, the Struggle for Modernity, and the Origins of Ideological Terror*. Lanham, MD: Rowman & Littlefield, 2001.

Saint-Just, Victor-Ernest-Marie. *Historique du 5e Régiment de Dragons*. Paris, 1891.

Sala-Molins, Louis. *Le Code Noir, ou le calvaire de Canaan*. Paris: Presses Universitaires de France, 1987.

Schama, Simon. *Citizens: A Chronicle of the French Revolution*. New York: Knopf, 1989.

──────. *Rough Crossings: Britain, the Slaves and the American Revolution*. New York: Ecco Press, 2006.

Scheler, Auguste. *Dictionnaire d'étymologie française d'après les résultats de la science moderne*. Paris, 1862.

Schneid, Frederick C. *Napoleon's Conquest of Europe: The War of the Third Coalition*. Westport, CT: Greenwood Publishing, 2005.

Schom, Alan. *Napoleon Bonaparte.* New York: Harper Collins World, 1998.

Schopp, Claude. *Dictionnaire Dumas.* Paris: CNRS Editions, 2010.

————. *Alexandre Dumas: Le génie de la vie.* Paris: Fayard, 1997.

Schubring, Gert. *Conflicts between Generalization, Rigor and Intuition: Number Concepts Underlying the Development of Analysis in 17th–19th Century France and Germany.* New York: Springer Science, 2005.

Sciout, Ludovic. *La République française et la République de Gênes, 1794–1799.* Brussels, 1889.

Scurr, Ruth. *Fatal Purity: Robespierre and the French Revolution.* New York: Henry Holt, 2006.

Seeber, Edward. *Anti-Slavery Opinion in France During the Second Half of the Eighteenth Century.* New York: Burt Franklin, 1971.

Simonetta, Marcello, and Noga Arikha. *Napoleon and the Rebel: A Story of Brotherhood, Passion, and Power.* New York: Palgrave Macmillan, 2011.

Sire, H. J. A. *The Knights of Malta.* New Haven: Yale University Press, 1994.

Sivry, Louis de, and M. de Rolot. *Précis historique de Saint-Germain-en-Laye.* Saint-Germain-en-Laye, 1848.

Smith, Gretchen. *The Performance of Male Nobility in Molière's Comédie-Ballets: Staging the Courtier.* Burlington, VT: Ashgate, 2004.

Sorel, Albert. *L'Europe et la Révolution française.* Vol. 4, *Les limites naturelles, 1794–1795.* Paris, 1892.

Spang, Rebecca L. *The Invention of the Restaurant: Paris and Modern Gastronomic Culture.* Cambridge, MA: Harvard University Press, 2000.

Speziale, G. C. *Storia militare di Taranto negli ultimi cinque secoli.* Bari, Italy: Gius, Laterz & Figli, 1930.

Standish, Frank Hall. *The Life of Voltaire.* London, 1821.

Stein, Robert Louis. *The French Slave Trade in the Eighteenth Century: An Old Regime Business.* Madison: University of Wisconsin Press, 1979.

Steinmetz, Andrew. *The Romance of Duelling in All Times and Countries.* Vol. 1. London, 1868.

Stengers, Jean, and Anne Van Neck. *Masturbation: The History of a Great Terror.* Translated by Kathryn Hoffman. New York: Palgrave, 2001.

Strathern, Paul. *Napoleon in Egypt.* New York: Bantam, 2008.

Stuart, Andrea. *The Rose of Martinique: A Life of Napoleon's Josephine.* New York: Grove Press, 2004.

Sutherland, Donald M. G. *The French Revolution and Empire: The Quest for a Civic Order.* Hoboken, NJ: Wiley-Blackwell, 2003.

Sweetman, Jack. *The Great Admirals: Command at Sea, 1587–1945.* Annapolis, MD: Naval Institute Press, 1997.

Sybel, Heinrich von. *History of the French Revolution.* Vol. 1. Translated by Walter C. Perry. London, 1867.

Tarbell, Ida. *A Short Life of Napoleon Bonaparte.* New York, 1895.

Terrio, Susan. *Crafting the Culture and History of French Chocolate.* Berkeley: University of California Press, 2000.

Thibaudeau, Antoine-Claire. *Histoire générale de Napoléon Bonaparte, de sa vie privée et publique, de sa carrière politique et militaire, de son gouvernement et de son administration.* Vol. 6. Paris, 1828.

Thiers, Adolphe. *Histoire du Consulat et de l'Empire.* Vol. 1. Brussels, 1845.

————. *The History of the French Revolution, 1789–1800.* Vol. 1. Tranlated by Frederick Shoberl. Philadelphia, 1894.

Thomas, Hugh. *The Slave Trade: The Story of the Atlantic Slave Trade, 1440–1870.* New York: Simon & Schuster, 1999.

Thomas, Jean-Pierre. *Le guide des effigies de Paris.* Paris: L'Harmattan, 2002.

Tiré de Cléron, Joseph. *Abrégé de la vie de Louis Mandrin, chef de contrebandiers en France.* Paris: Alia, 1991.

Tulard, Jean. *Murat.* Paris: Fayard, 1999.

Unger, Harlow G. *Lafayette.* New York: Wiley, 2002.

Valentin, René. *Le maréchal Jourdan, 1762–1833.* Limoges: Charles-Lavauzelle, 1956.

Van-Ess, William Lodewyk. *Life of Napoleon Buonaparte.* Vol. 2. London, 1809.

Van Riper, Bowdoin A. *Rockets and Missiles: The Life Story of a Technology.* Baltimore: Johns Hopkins University Press, 2007.

Vauquelin, Jacques. *Châteaux, manoirs, monuments et sites de la région bolbécaise.* Yvetot, France: Imprimerie Nouvelle, 1977.

Verbruggen, J. F. *The Art of Warfare in Western Europe During the Middle Ages.* Woodbridge, UK: Boydell Press, 2002.

Vila, Anne. *Enlightenment and Pathology: Sensibility in the Literature and Medicine of Eighteenth-Century France.* Baltimore: Johns Hopkins University Press, 1998.

Villiers du Terrage, Marc de. *Les aérostatiers militaires en Égypte: Campagne de Bonaparte, 1798–1801.* Paris: G. Camproger, 1901.

Wallon, Henri. *Histoire du tribunal révolutionnaire de Paris avec le Journal de ses actes.* Vol. 1. Paris, 1880.

Wanquet, Claude. *La France et la première abolition de l'esclavage, 1794–1802.* Paris: Kathala, 1998.

Weiner, Mark S. *Black Trials: Citizenship from the Beginnings of Slavery to the End of Caste.* New York: Knopf, 2004.

Wheeler, Harold, and Alexander Broadley. *Napoleon and the Invasion of England: The Story of the Great Terror, 1797–1805.* New York: John Lane, 1908.

Williams, Hugh Noel. *The Fascinating Duc de Richelieu.* London: Methuen, 1910.

Willms, Johannes. *Paris, Capital of Europe: From the Revolution to the Belle Epoque.* Translated by Eveline Kanes. New York: Holmes and Meier, 1997.

Wilson, Victor Emmanuel Roberto. *Le Général Alexandre Dumas: Soldat de la liberté.* Quebec: Quisqueya-Québec, 1977.

Wimpffen, Alexandre-Stanislas de. *Haïti au XVIIIe siècle.* Paris: Karthala, 1993.

Winik, Jay. *The Great Upheaval: America and the Birth of the Modern World, 1788–1800.* New York: HarperCollins, 2008.

Wolfe, Michael. *Walled Towns and the Shaping of France: From the Medieval to the Early Modern Era.* New York: Palgrave Macmillan, 2009.

Woloch, Isser. *Napoleon and His Collaborators: The Making of a Dictatorship.* New York: Norton, 2001.

Woods Weierman, Karen. *One Nation, One Blood: Interracial Marriage in American Fiction, Scandal, and Law, 1820–1870.* Amherst, MA: University of Massachusetts Press, 2005.

Woronoff, Denis. *La république bourgeoise de Thermidor à Brumaire, 1794–1799.* Paris: Seuil, 2004.

Wroe, Ann. *Being Shelley: The Poet's Search for Himself.* New York: Pantheon, 2007.

Young. John. *A History of the Commencement, Progress, and Termination of the Late War Between Great Britain and France . . .* Vol. 1. Edinburgh, 1802.

Zamoyski, Adam. *Holy Madness: Romantics, Patriots and Revolutionaries, 1776–1871.* London: Weidenfeld & Nicolson, 1999.

ARTICLES IN DICTIONARIES, NEWSPAPERS, JOURNALS, WEBSITES, AND EDITED VOLUMES

"Alexandre Dumas." *Hogg's Instructor* 3 (July–December 1854): 35–48.

"Alexandre Dumas attend la statue." *Le Parisien,* November 28, 2007.

"Alexandre Dumas Dead." *New York Times*, November 28, 1895.

Arnault, Antoine-Vincent, Antoine Jay, Etienne de Jouy, and Jacques Marquet de Norvins. "Dumas (Alexandre Davy-de-la-Pailleterie)." In *Biographie nouvelle des contemporains*, 160–62. Vol. 6. Paris, 1822.

"Autobiography of Alexandre Dumas." *Littell's Living Age* 35 (October–December 1852): 587–91.

Baillie-Grohman, F. "The Brenner Pass and Its Traffic in Old Days." *Contemporary Review*, no. 613 (January 1917): 375–84.

Broughton, Tony. "Generals Who Served in the French Army During the Period 1789–1815." Napoleon Series website, http://www.napoleon-series.org/research/c_french generals.

Champion, Jean-Marcel. "30 Floréal Year X: The Restoration of Slavery by Bonaparte." In *The Abolitions of Slavery: From Léger Félicité Sonthonax to Victor Schoelcher: 1793, 1794, 1848*, edited by Marcel Dorigny, 229–36. New York: Berghahn Books, 2003.

Chancel, Jules. "Les Trois Dumas." *L'Abeille de la Nouvelle-Orléans*, no. 126 (November 12, 1899).

Courcelles, Jean-Baptiste. "DUMAS (Alexandre Davy)." In *Dictionnaire historique et biographique des généraux français, depuis le onzième siècle jusqu'en 1823*. Vol. 9, pp. 501–3. Paris, 1821–23.

Crouzet, François. "Politics and Banking in Revolutionary and Napoleonic France." In *The State, the Financial System, and Economic Modernization*, edited by Richard Sylla, Richard Tilly, and Gabriel Tortella, 20–52. Cambridge: Cambridge University Press, 1999.

David, Placide. "Le général Th. Alexandre Dumas." In *Sur les rives du passé: Choses de Saint-Domingue*, 37–53. Montreal: Leméac, 1972.

De Beer, G. R. "The Relations Between Fellows of the Royal Society and French Men of Science When France and Britain Were at War." *Notes and Records of the Royal Society of London* 9, no. 2. (May 1952): 244–99.

Debien, Gabriel. "Gens de couleur libres et colons de Saint-Domingue devant la Constituante: 1789–mars 1790." *Revue d'histoire de l'Amérique française* 4, no. 2 (1950): 211–32.

Dumas, Alexandre (*fils*). "Préface." In *Journal d'un comédien, 1870–1894*, by Frédéric Fèbvre. Vol. 2. Paris, 1896.

Élisabeth, Léo. "Déportés des Petites Antilles francaises, 1801–1803." In *Le rétablissement de l'esclavage dans les colonies françaises, 1802: Rupture et continuité de la politique coloniale française* (1800–1830). Edited by Yves Benot and Marcel Dorigny, 69–94. Paris: Maisonneuve et Larose, 2003.

Feibel, R. M. "John Vetch and the Egyptian Ophthalmia." *Survey of Ophthalmology* 28, no. 2 (September–October 1983): 128–34.

"France." *London Times*, September 10, 1792.

Garrigus, John D. " 'Sons of the Same Father': Gender, Race, and Citizenship in French Saint-Domingue, 1760–1792." In *Visions and Revisions of Eighteenth-Century France*, edited by Christine Adams, Jack R. Censer, and Lisa Jane Graham, 137–53. University Park: Pennsylvania State University Press, 1997.

Gaudu, Fernand. "Les Davy de La Pailleterie, seigneurs de Bielleville-en-Caux." *Revue des Sociétés Savantes de Haute-Normandie*, no. 65 (1972): 39–62.

Harten, Stuart. "Rediscovering Ancient Egypt." In *Napoleon in Egypt*, edited by Irene Bierman, 33–46. Reading, UK: Ithaca Press, 2003.

Heffernan, Michael. "Historical Geographies of the Future: Three Perspectives from France, 1750–1825." In *Geography and Enlightenment*, edited by David N. Livingstone and Charles W. J. Withers, 125–64. Chicago: University of Chicago Press, 1999.

Hoffman, Léon-François. "Dumas et les Noirs." In *Georges*, by Alexandre Dumas. Paris: Folio-Gallimard, 1974.

"Hommage aux Noirs." *Le Parisien*. February 28, 2006.

Houdailles, Jacques, and Alain Blum. "L'alphabétisation au XVIIIe et XIXeme siècle." *Population* 40, no. 6 (1985): 944–51.

Imbruglia, Girolamo. "Enlightenment in Eighteenth-Century Naples." In *Naples in the Eighteenth Century: The Birth and Death of a Nation-State*, edited by Girolamo Imbruglia, 70–94. Cambridge: Cambridge University Press, 2000.

"L'incendie de l'Institut d'Égypte, une catastrophe pour la science." *Le Monde*, December 18, 2011.

Kurhan, Ali. "Les révoltes du Caire pendant l'occupation française présentées et commentées par Jean-Joseph Marcel et Alexandre Dumas." In *Dissent and Protest in Egyptian Society During the Ottoman Era*, edited by Nasser Ibrahim. Cairo: Egyptian Society for Historical Studies, 2004.

Laurens, Henry. "Étude historique." In *Kléber en Égypte*, edited by Henry Laurens. Vol 1. Cairo: Institut français d'archéologie orientale, 1988.

Le Bas, Philippe. "Dumas (Alexandre Davy de la Pailleterie)." In *Dictionnaire encyclopédique de la France*. Vol. 6, 773–74. Paris, 1842.

Lentz, Thierry. "La politique consulaire aux Antilles." In *Napoléon Bonaparte: Correspondance générale*. Vol. 3, 1223–36. Paris: Fayard, 2006.

Lynn, John A. "French Opinion and the Military Resurrection of the Pike, 1792–1794." *Military Affairs* 41, no. 1 (February 1977): 1–7.

Maubant, Christiane. "Les Féray, des Négriers Protestants aux Barons d'Empire" (Part 1). *Cahiers Havrais de Recherche Historique*, no. 54 (1995): 91–122.

———. "Le 'traité' de traite de Stanislas Foäche, du Havre." *Historia thématique*, no. 80 (November–December 2002): 12–37.

Maurel, André. "The Three Dumas." *Scribner's Magazine* 19, no. 5 (May 1896): 658–59.

———. "The Dumas Lineage." *Atlantic Monthly* 77, no. 454 (January 1896): 138–44.

Moreau-Néret, André. "L'Hostellerye de l'Escu de France." *Mémoires* (Fédération des sociétés d'histoire et d'archéologie de l'Aisne), 20 (1974): 130–38.

Noël, Erick. "Une carrière contrariée: Alexandre Dumas, homme de couleur et général révolutionnaire." *Françaises*, no. 5 (March 1998): 58–88.

———. "Une entreprise originale: La Légion Noire de la Révolution." *Bulletin de la Société Archéologique et Historique de Nantes et de Loire-Atlantique*, no. 135 (2000): 227–45.

———. "Saint-Georges: Un chevalier de sang mêlé dans la société des Lumières." *Bulletin du Centre d'Histoire des Espaces Atlantiques*, nouvelle série no. 8 (1998): 131–53.

"Nouvelle bouillabaisse dramatique par M. Dumas père . . ." *Le Charivari*, 1858, Collection de la Société des Amis d'Alexandre Dumas. *Actualités*, no. 510 (1858).

Parks Brown, Valerie. "Napoleon and General Dumas." *Journal of Negro History* 61, no. 2 (April 1976): 188–99.

Pocock, Tom. "Broken Promises, Sunken Treasure, and a Trail of Blood." *Evening Standard* (London), July 1, 1999, p. 22.

Powers, David M. "The French Musical Theater: Maintaining Control in Caribbean Colonies in the Eighteenth Century." *Black Music Research Journal* 18, nos. 1/2 (Spring/Autumn, 1998): 229–40.

Prod'homme, J.-C. "Le Chevalier de Saint-Georges, escrimeur et musicien." *Les Annales Coloniales*, no. 51 (March 1936): 38–41.

Pronier, Thomas. "L'implicite et l'explicite dans la politique de Napoléon." In *Le rétablissement de l'esclavage dans les colonies françaises, 1802: Rupture et continuité de la politique coloniale française* (1800–1830). Edited by Yves Benot and Marcel Dorigny, 51–67. Paris: Maisonneuve et Larose, 2003.

Rabbe, Alphonse, Claude-Augustin-Charles Vieilh de Boisjoslin, and Francois-Georges Binet de Boisgiroult, Baron de Sainte-Preuve. "Dumas (Alexandre-Davy)." In *Biographie universelle et portative des contemporains*, 1469–70. Vol. 2. Paris, 1834.

Reiss, Tom. "Imagining the Worst: How a Literary Genre Anticipated the Modern World." *The New Yorker* (November 28, 2005): 106–14.

Rey Charlier, Ghislaine, and Carrol F. Coates. "Memories of a Freedwoman," *Callaloo* 15, no. 2 (Spring, 1992): 342–46.

Ribbe, Claude. "Nicolas Sarkozy, avant de fouler le sol d'Haïti, doit avoir rendu justice au général Alexandre Dumas!" *Le Monde*, February 16, 2010.

Roch, Ernest. "L'ancien château royal." *Bulletin de la Société Historique de Villers-Cotterêts* 5 (1909): 45–346.

———. "Le Général Alexandre Dumas." *Bulletin de la Société Historique de Villers-Cotterêts* 2 (1906): 87 109.

———. "L'Hostellerye de l'Escu de France." *Bulletin de la Société Historique de Villers-Cotterêts* 2 (1906): 32–35, 71–73.

———. "La Reine Dragons." *Bulletin de la Société Historique de Villers-Cotterêts* 3 (1907): 74–76.

Romand, Hippolyte. "Poètes et romanciers modernes de la France; IX: Alexandre Dumas." *Revue des deux mondes* 1, 3rd ser. (January 15, 1834): 129–63.

Ruiz, Alain. "Allemands, français, ou 'nouveaux-francs,' et autres: La région germanique de 1792–93, une unité européene pour la guerre de libération des peuples." In *Le cheminement de l'idée européenne dans les idéologies de la paix et de la guerre*. Edited by Marita Gilli, 37–50. Paris: Diffusion Les Belles Lettres, 1991.

Sante, Luc. "Introduction." In *The Count of Monte Cristo*, by Alexandre Dumas (*père*). New York: Barnes & Noble Classics, 2004.

Schopp, Claude. "Préface générale." In *Joseph Balsamo*, by Alexandre Dumas (*père*), i–xcv. Paris: Robert Laffont, 1990.

Schuster, Angela. "Napoleon's Lost Fleet." *Archaeology* 52, no. 5 (1999): 34–37.

Sigal, R., and H. Hamard. "Larrey and Egyptian Ophthalmia." *Journal français d'ophtalmologie* 9, no. 11 (1986): 757–60.

Street, John M. "Feral Animals in Hispaniola." *Geographical Review* 52, no. 3 (July 1962).

Trench-Bonett, Dorothy. "Introduction." In *Charles VII at the Homes of His Great Vassals*, by Alexandre Dumas (*père*), 1–18. Translated by Dorothy Trench-Bonett. Chicago: Noble Press, 1991.

Vagnair, Rudolphe. "Le colonel des aérostatiers militaires d'il y a cent ans." *La curiosité historique et militaire* 5 (1901–2): 293–94.

Vapereau, Gustave. "DUMAS (Alexandre)." In *Dictionnaire universel des contemporains contenant toutes les personnes notables de la France et des pays étrangers*, 575. Paris, 1858.

Wagemans, M., and O. P. van Bijsterveld. "The French Egyptian Campaign and Its Effects on Ophthalmology." *Documenta ophthalmologica* 68, nos. 1–2 (January-February 1988): 135–44.

Wilmeth, Marlyn Walton, and J. Richard Wilmeth. "Theatrical Elements in Voodoo: The Case for Diffusion." *Journal for the Scientific Study of Religion* 16, no. 1 (March 1977): 27–37.

◂ INDEX ▸